Contemporary Canadian Social Issues

SECOND EDITION

Carmen Niessen and Rebecca Bromwich

2008
Emond Montgomery Publications Limited
Toronto, Canada

Emond Montgomery Publications Limited
60 Shaftesbury Avenue
Toronto ON M4T 1A3
http://www.emp.ca

Printed in Canada.

We acknowledge the financial support of the Government of Canada through the Book Publishing Industry Development Program (BPIDP) for our publishing activities.

Acquisitions and developmental editor: Tammy Scherer
Editorial assistant: Nick Raymond
Marketing manager: Christine Davidson
Copy editor: Jamie Bush
Proofreader: Sarah Gleadow
Production editors: Jim Lyons and Cindy Fujimoto, WordsWorth Communications
Indexer: Paula Pike, WordsWorth Communications
Text designer: Tara Wells, WordsWorth Communications
Cover designer: John Vegter

Library and Archives Canada Cataloguing in Publication

Niessen, Carmen, 1953-
Contemporary Canadian social issues / Carmen Niessen, Rebecca Bromwich.—2nd ed.

Includes bibliographical references and index.
ISBN 978-1-55239-229-4

1. Social problems—Canada—Textbooks. 2. Canada—Social conditions—1991- —Textbooks. I. Bromwich, Rebecca II. Title.

HM585.N44 2008 361.10971 C2008-901433-2

For David and Skye, Fleur, and Caitlyn
— Carmen Niessen

For Matt and Myrina
— Rebecca Bromwich

Table of Contents

Preface

This book builds upon a 1999 work by one of the co-authors, Carmen Niessen, entitled *Contemporary Canadian Social Issues.* Responding to feedback and suggestions from students, police officers, legal practitioners, and professors, we have supplemented the previous work's analysis, rooted in sociological theory, with an enhanced grounding in practical concerns for police officers in Canada. Our new co-author, Rebecca Bromwich, brings legal and practical expertise to the sociological basis of Ms. Niessen's earlier work. These changes enhance the practical relevance of this work to students' careers. The text continues to offer instruction on how to identify a social problem, and it continues to demonstrate ways of looking at social problems through the various sociological perspectives. What has been added is new material concerning those Canadian social problems that are most likely to affect students in their lives as Canadians and as police officers.

In this new and restructured edition, the analytical models and templates of the original text continue to guide the analyses of current social issues, but we have updated the original social issue topics and added many new ones. All should hold great appeal for Canadian students today.

As in the original text, we use sociology's theoretical paradigms as tools of analysis. In addition to the structural functionalist, social conflict, and symbolic interactionist paradigms, feminist and social constructionist paradigms have been included.

Wherever there are social problems, people make formal and informal attempts to respond to them. Seldom are there easy answers or immediate resolutions to social issues. The analysis of social issues entails tracking the responses of various actors, be they government, police, community groups, or individuals. It is important for students to understand how crucial are government and police responses to these problems. Ultimately, our goal in writing this book is to teach students how to use a professional, sensitive, and appropriate approach to issues that they will encounter in their future careers.

Students often find learning about social problems to be difficult, even depressing. Sociological analysis can give students insight into how to address issues and what steps can be taken to resolve them. In other words, students need to understand not just the magnitude and complexity of social problems in Canada but also the potential each individual has to respond to them. Our ultimate goal in this book is to instill in students a sense of empowerment. We encourage students to apply a critical perspective in assessing institutional, policing, policy, and community responses to social problems, and also to be cognizant of the positive roles they themselves can play in addressing these problems. To that end, each of this text's discussions of a social problem concludes with suggestions about the potential for individual involvement in rectifying it.

CHAPTER 1

Introduction

CHAPTER OBJECTIVES

After completing this chapter, you will be able to:

- Understand and define what sociologists mean by a "social problem," and identify four criteria that define an issue as a social one.
- Understand the history and origins of the sociological study of social problems, and identify the five evolutionary phases of a social issue.
- Identify and determine the life cycle of a social issue by considering sample facts and a sample analysis.
- Understand the role of sociology in determining the difference between opinion and fact.
- Recognize the dominant perspectives, or paradigms, of sociology: structural functionalism, social conflict, symbolic interactionism, social constructionism, and feminism.

DEFINING SOCIAL PROBLEMS

In any domain, we call something an "issue" when it becomes unacceptable or disagreeable. A social issue, or social problem, is no different. A social issue is anything that a community, society, or group of people *defines* as unacceptable or *problematic.*

Social issues arise from events and changes in society, but these events and changes do not constitute social issues until they are *defined* as problematic. Take, for example, the tsunami that affected hundreds of thousands of people in the South Pacific on December 26, 2004. An estimated 230,000 people died (Aglionby, 2005); entire cities and regions were devastated. The tsunami was not, strictly speaking, a social issue because of the enormity of the tragedy; the tsunami became a social issue when people criticized how it was dealt with and expressed concerns that better warning systems should have been in place, that better emergency response measures should have been taken, and that there were discriminatory factors determining who received aid and who did not. People realize that a natural disaster such as a tsunami cannot be prevented, but the social preparation for such an event and the poor care for its victims can be criticized. These are the conditions in which an issue becomes a social issue.

If the event itself is not the social issue, then it follows that there are criteria for identifying an issue as a social one. There is also a life cycle for each social issue, from its first being defined as problematic to its being resolved. Your first task is to learn the four criteria by which a social issue is identified. The method we outline below is by no means the only way of identifying a social issue; it is offered as one possible means of identification.

In this book, we have of course not been able to address all social problems, but we have sought to look at some significant ones. These include

- alcohol and drug addiction;
- prostitution and the sex industry in Canada;
- gender issues, including gender inequality, same-sex relationships, and transgender issues;
- family problems;
- economic inequalities and poverty;
- urban and rural issues; and
- globalization and its consequences.

Four Criteria That Define an Issue as a Social Issue

1. A social issue cannot be an event that is experienced by one person alone, however tragic that event may be. A social issue is one that involves a public response. For example, anyone who travels is at risk of being involved in a traffic collision. A traffic accident is not a social issue until, for example, a number of people voice their opinion that too many collisions are happening on a certain stretch of road and that the collision rates are unacceptable. Another way of looking at this is that an individual personal misfortune can become a social issue once it becomes part of a *trend* of events that people find unacceptable and protest against. The accidents on Highway 69 in Ontario between Sudbury and Parry Sound show how individual misfortune, by becoming part of a trend deemed unacceptable by the public, can become a social issue.

   The second point implicit in this first criterion is that, for a social issue to exist, there must be a number of people who *together* are voicing their dissatisfaction over some perceived problem. In the above example, there is a citizens' group that is lobbying the government to make Highway 69 a four-lane highway.

2. A social issue is not created when an event occurs; it is created when a group of people protests the unacceptability of some event. In other words, a social issue is defined; it is a social creation. If you have studied sociology previously, you will know already that any definition of reality is the product of a specific social context. In other words, a social problem is a creation that emerges from a specific social context. Context includes the culture within which the issue is being confronted, and the time or era in which it is identified.

The second criterion a social issue must meet is that the public voices defining it as a problem are part of a specific context. To simplify your research studies of social issues, we are going to arbitrarily stipulate that a social issue must be modern and that it must be Canadian. Therefore, any topic that you choose to study in connection with this text should be one that Canadians are confronting today.

3. Once a group of people identifies something as unacceptable, they must have some vision of what is acceptable or what changes need to be implemented in order to resolve what is unacceptable. For example, on the subject of Highway 69, citizens have voiced their dissatisfaction with the hazards and consequent loss of life on the highway. What they are striving to achieve are changes that will make the highway safer. Specifically, they want to make Highway 69 a four-lane highway from Parry Sound to Sudbury. This is the goal or vision of those voicing dissatisfaction. Thus, the third criterion a social issue must meet is that the voices defining it as a problem have a specific vision or goal they are attempting to achieve.
4. The final criterion a social issue must meet is that the goals or vision of the people defining it as a problem must be achievable. There must be identifiable means or processes of resolving the issue. In the case of Highway 69, citizens' groups have launched a very loud media campaign, lobbying the Ontario government to include road construction in its political agenda, and they have introduced a signage campaign right on the highway. In other words, this fourth criterion concerns whether there are means—technological, financial, and political—of achieving the vision of the people who are defining the social issue.

Note: If, in your investigation of contemporary social issues in Canada, you can perceive all four of these criteria being met, then you know that you have identified not just an issue but a *social* issue. *An account of an event, of "what happened and why," is not the definition of a social issue.*

ORIGIN OF SOCIAL ISSUES

There are two ideas implicit in our choice of criteria for identifying an issue as a social issue. The first idea is that issues arise from change. Social change is prompted by social diversification, by technological innovations, by demographic changes, and by social and cultural events. The second idea is that social issues have a life cycle. The next set of criteria concern the life cycle of a social issue.

The Five Evolutionary Phases of a Social Issue

A social issue begins with its definition. When a group of people identifies a social event as unacceptable, a social issue is created. Once the social issue is defined, then actions must be taken to bring the issue to wider public attention. Eventually, if there is enough action on the part of the persons voicing concern, the issue is politicized and efforts are made to resolve it. Whether the resolution is successful depends on whether the public deems it acceptable. We see, then, that a social issue evolves from a voiced concern to something politically addressed and in some way resolved. Many issues cycle through definition and political action numerous times before they are finally resolved.

1. The first stage in the evolution of a social issue is the voicing of concern. From your research of a social issue, you should be able to identify those groups and organizations that are protesting an event or a response to an event. Protests often arise from a group's experience of disadvantages, from perceived challenges to fundamental values, or from the sudden destruction—owing to some event—of a conventional pattern of behaviour. Those first to voice concern over an event are usually those personally involved in it—that is, those first to feel its ill effects.

   Let's return to the example of Highway 69. Beginning in the late 1990s, citizens of Sudbury and of the regions between Sudbury and Gravenhurst, where Highway 400 ends, petitioned the government to widen the highway. They deemed the death toll on the highway unacceptable, and they believed that a four-lane highway would resolve the issue. In 2002, in the wake of a particularly horrendous traffic collision in which one family lost three lives, a petition of 20,000 names was sent to the member of Parliament for the area, Rick Bartolucci (Ontario Hansard, November 2002).

2. Once a protest is launched, the first step is to gain public support for the vision of change. In the first phase, the protesting group tries to persuade the public that an event or situation is unacceptable. There are many ways of attracting public attention. One way is to stage media events. Boycotts, hunger strikes, and demonstrations are some of the more dramatic kinds of media events. Other ways of attracting attention are the publishing of statistics, the distribution of leaflets, or the creation of symbols—white ribbons, for example. There is a link in the "For Further Research" section at the end of the chapter that will take you to a transcript of the Highway 69 petition. The petition reveals the issue itself and the means adopted by the families launching the protest.

3. As the public grows more aware of an issue, people begin to express their opinions about it and to consider its relevance to them. The people who see no relevance in the issue tend to ignore it; others reject the claims of the protesting voices, while still others assert their support for the voices that are calling for social change. The level of public support an issue enjoys is a measure of how well established it is. As noted above, some citizens—the public voices—banded together to protest the condition of Highway 69. By 2002, the larger public was onside and willing to sign a petition. Those who first identified the problem of Highway 69 successfully used the media to inform the public about the rate and seriousness of the accidents on the highway and to argue that a four-lane

highway was an acceptable solution. Another example of an issue gaining publicity in this way is the anti-smoking campaign of the past few decades. Smoking first emerged as a social issue relating to health in the 1970s. At this point, the majority of the public was dismissive of the minority who were looking for a ban on smoking in public areas. Today, anti-tobacco sentiments appear to be entrenched, and those demanding smokers' rights are clearly in the minority.

4. Issues that attract daily news commentary and stimulate social action are issues that have become politicized. A social issue at this point in its life cycle has become well established. It is usually being addressed in a public way with new policies, laws, or social programs. The plans for the expansion of Highway 69 reveal how the actions of protesting citizens have come to fruition. Since construction on the highway is well under way, protests regarding the highway have all but disappeared (Highway 69 Route Planning Study, n.d.). On the other hand, actions that are implemented to resolve an issue can generate new controversies. For example, in an attempt to address the issue of discrimination against gays and lesbians, Canada has recently established national laws granting same-sex marriage. The proposed changes to the laws and the debate over Canada's constitution with regard to the issue of same-sex marriage have occasioned a great deal of political turmoil.
5. The final stage in the life cycle of a social issue is its resolution or its launch into a new cycle. If the solutions implemented achieve the protestors' vision and satisfy the public, then the issue fades from public concern. Note again the example of Highway 69. But it seems that the resolution of issues is rarely achieved after one cycle. Policies or laws that are implemented to meet the concerns or dissatisfactions of some people are rarely satisfactory to all. Some groups may be greatly disturbed by the changes. In the case of same-sex marriages, for example, the granting of marriage rights to homosexuals has been seen by some as immoral and indecent, and the next cycle of this social issue may be driven by those who are offended by the new definitions of marriage. The gay and lesbian community, on the other hand, would see the issue of discrimination as resolved, and their role in the new cycle of the issue would be as defenders of the newly implemented laws.

We have now reviewed the four criteria that define an issue as a social issue and the five steps in the life cycle of a social issue. These criteria and steps should be referred to any time you are considering whether to view a problem or social event as a social issue. Doing so will help ensure that you are not simply venting your opinion on an issue, and it will help ensure that an issue is a social issue and not simply a documented event.

NINE GUIDE QUESTIONS: IDENTIFICATION AND LIFE CYCLE OF A SOCIAL ISSUE

To make it easier to apply the nine criteria by which social issues and their life cycle are identified, we may reword the criteria as questions, which we will call "the nine guide questions." These nine questions may not all apply to the particular issue being studied, but they are a good starting point for analysis.

Q1. Is the issue problematic to many people, and are there many people voicing their concerns or claiming that the issue is unacceptable?

Q2. Is the issue specific to a particular social context—that is, modern Canadian society?

Q3. Do the people voicing their concerns have a vision of the way things should be—that is, a goal?

Q4. Are there means to improve the situation and to achieve the vision?

Q5. Who and what organizations are calling for public attention?

Q6. What public interest in the issue has there been? What media coverage or promotion has there been?

Q7. How has society aligned itself around the issue? What kinds of demands have been made, and what organizations and coalitions have been formed?

Q8. What policies have been initiated or proposed?

Q9. What impact have these initiatives or proposals had on the resolution or intensifying of the issue?

Sample Facts and Analysis

In this text, you will be given the task of looking at certain recent social events as social issues. The task requires answering the nine guide questions, and then summarizing these answers in one description. The following example shows how this can be done. First is a statement similar to what you might hear or read in a news report. Next is an assessment of the issue as a social issue.

Statement

1. The East Coast cod fish stocks are at an all-time low. Scientists predict that the cod cannot recover.

Adoption of a social issue view

At first, this appears to be an issue concerning the natural environment. But then we start to realize the economic implications of the failure of the East Coast fishing industries. At this point we recognize that human behaviour—legislation against the seal hunt, for example, and superior technology in the fish harvest—has triggered a change, and the public reactions to this change are what have created a social issue out of the environmental change:

Q1 and Q5: This issue has been publicly defined as an issue. The fisheries, the government, and the citizens who depend on the fisheries have all voiced their concerns and opinions about cod harvesting.

Q6, Q3, and Q4: The public has aligned itself by choosing sides in the controversy. Environmentalists call for a moratorium on all cod fishing, while those dependent on the fishery object to any measures that will drastically curtail the harvest. The methods used to manage the fishing industry for generations are no longer effective. Resolution of the problem is believed to lie in better understanding of cod and in better regulation of fishing activities.

Q2: This issue is an ongoing one for Canada and especially for those on the East Coast. Fishing has been a Canadian livelihood for many generations both in Aboriginal and non-Aboriginal communities. Loss of the fishery is viewed as a serious threat to the well-being of these communities.

Q8: To date, bans on fishing in certain regions, drastic restrictions in the number of cod permitted to be harvested, and restrictions on international fishing have been implemented. The government has also introduced compensation measures for those who have experienced a loss in their livelihood.

Q9: The issue remains controversial. Environmentalists continue to express concern that the fishery cannot be restored. The fishery has vehemently rejected many of the restrictions on the grounds that they are being unfairly implemented. Others complain that cultural activities based on the cod industry are unfairly outlawed.

THE ROLE OF SOCIOLOGY

Sociology is a science-based discipline that is devoted to the study and exploration of human social life. Theories and theoretical perspectives guide sociological analysis. Appropriate adoption of these will ensure that your research and research reports on contemporary social issues in Canada are free of biases, opinion, and undocumented hearsay. The following is an exercise that is designed to help you discern the difference between editorial opinion and research documents.

Activity to Demonstrate the Insufficiency of Opinion

TRUTH OR OPINION?

Each of us relies on the learning or "informal expertise" that we gain from personal experiences and from shared opinions. We use this informal expertise to make personal choices and decisions. However, informal expertise does not have enough *breadth* or *objectivity* to be a *reliable explanation* of social events and trends. For a rigorous explanation we must turn to sociology, a discipline that studies social life. Informal expertise is not an acceptable basis for a sociological explanation of why social trends exist, and it is not an acceptable basis from which to predict the outcome of social events. Furthermore, informal expertise is often used to justify personal beliefs. *Personal beliefs backed only by informal expertise are unacceptable as sociological explanations of events or as judgments about people.*

The following table compares the communication differences between informal expertise and social science.

Characteristic of communication	**Citizen**	**Social scientist**
Goal of communication	◆ to persuade ◆ to vent ◆ to convey a personal perspective or "wisdom"	◆ to accurately inform ◆ to understand ◆ to explain
Source of information	◆ personal experience ◆ personal observation ◆ hearsay/common sense	◆ researched information ◆ unbiased logic ◆ scientific observation
Method of communication	◆ use of interpersonal power: authority, charisma, intimidation ◆ use of emotion ◆ use of selective evidence ◆ use of faulty logic	◆ emotional detachment ◆ reliance on scientific rigour ◆ use of correct logic ◆ use of documented information ◆ use of precise vocabulary ◆ use of theoretical models
Outcome of communication	◆ expanded wisdom ◆ affirmation of "common sense" ◆ confirmation of biases ◆ spread of stereotypes and prejudice	◆ expanded knowledge ◆ more accurate account of knowledge and history ◆ better decisions
Presentation of communication	◆ use of emotive power words ◆ attack on person rather than issue ◆ use of cynicism and sarcasm ◆ use of name-calling	◆ presentation of research that backs claims ◆ focus on issue, not person ◆ unbiased language ◆ use of logical argument

Practise Determining the Difference Between Opinion and Social Science

1. Work in groups of two or three.
2. Find and copy an editorial that you have clipped from your local newspaper or from a news journal.

3. Use the following checklist to identify components that make the editorial unsuitable as social science.
4. Find a second article that is not an editorial, and that you think is suitable for social science research.

Conduct the same analysis as you did for the editorial and compare your results.

Characteristic of communication	**Citizen**	**Check (page/line)**		**Social scientist**	**Check (page/line)**	
Goal of communication	◆ to persuade ◆ to vent ◆ to convey a personal perspective or "wisdom"			◆ to accurately inform ◆ to understand ◆ to explain		
Source of information	◆ personal experience ◆ personal observation ◆ hearsay/common sense			◆ researched information ◆ unbiased logic ◆ scientific observation		
Method of communication	◆ use of interpersonal power: authority, charisma, intimidation ◆ use of emotion ◆ use of selective evidence ◆ use of faulty logic			◆ emotional detachment ◆ reliance on scientific rigour ◆ use of correct logic ◆ use of documented information ◆ use of precise vocabulary ◆ use of theoretical models		
Outcome of communication	◆ expanded wisdom ◆ affirmation of "common sense" ◆ confirmation of biases ◆ spread of stereotypes and prejudice			◆ expanded knowledge ◆ more true account of knowledge and history ◆ better decisions		
Presentation of communication	◆ use of emotive power words ◆ attack on person rather than issue ◆ use of cynicism and sarcasm ◆ use of name-calling			◆ presentation of research that backs claims ◆ focus on issue not person ◆ unbiased language ◆ use of logical argument		

State your conclusions about each article. Is it acceptable as sociological evidence? Why or why not?

Summary of Opinion Distinguished from Fact

The following statements are opinions. Opinions very often use *slang expressions* and *generalizations*. Also, the word "should" is usually an indicator of opinion. Rewrite the following statements so that they reflect fact and documented evidence. Eliminate slang, emotive language, the word "should," and unfounded claims.

1. Mad cow disease spreads because food-producing corporations are too greedy to have respect for public safety. The government should ban all imports of foreign beef.

2. Look out! Teens are bad news. The majority are dishonest and disruptive. Every teen from 14 to 16 years of age should attend boot camp.

THE DOMINANT PERSPECTIVES OF SOCIOLOGY

The three dominant theoretical perspectives of sociology are the structural functionalist paradigm, the social conflict paradigm, and the symbolic interactionist paradigm. "Perspective," despite its simple meaning of *point of view*, has profound implications. Perspective guides your investigation and your understanding of a social issue and at the same time obscures other points of view. *The theoretical perspective that you adopt in any analysis will determine both the questions that you ask and the conclusions that you draw.*

The **theoretical perspectives**, or **paradigms**, of sociology are defined as being either macro or micro in focus. A **macro perspective** takes in the broad social trends and features in a society. To help you to remember this, consider a view of Toronto from the top of the CN Tower. From that perspective, you would be able to discern the major regions of Toronto (commercial, residential, and industrial), the overall physical layout (of ravines and lakeshore), and you would be able to see the major traffic arteries. A macro view of society is similar: you see the overall features, but you *do not* see the individual people. In short, macro means *see no people.* A **micro perspective**, on the other hand, is a close-up view of the components of society. You are off the tower and standing in the street. From a street perspective, you see the people, what they are wearing and doing. In other words, instead of being focused on the broader social forces, such as a drop in employment rates, you would be focused on the social interactive patterns—that is, people's social behaviour in response to being unemployed. A micro perspective means *see the people.*

The three major **theoretical paradigms** of sociology are the macro perspectives—that is, the structural functionalist and the social conflict paradigms; and the major micro perspective—the symbolic interactionist paradigm. In addition, this text will adopt the feminist and social constructionist perspectives. The feminist perspective can be either macro or micro, and the social constructionist point of view is a subset of the symbolic interactionist one.

The following is a brief summary of each perspective.

Structural Functionalist Paradigm

A **structural functionalist** perspective reveals society as an *integrated system of parts* (social structures), each with *specialized functions.* A structural functionalist approach asks what a certain *social structure* does for Canadian society *as a whole.*

MANIFEST FUNCTIONS

Manifest functions are the *expected ways that a social structure (pattern) serves the whole society.* They are *expected* because they function in a way that *supports* the foundational values of a society.

DYSFUNCTIONS

Dysfunctions are *unexpected problems that may originate within the whole social system or may come from outside.* Dysfunctions are seen, in the structural functionalist perspective, as the *consequences of unexpected (and often sudden) change.*

A structural functionalist analysis is effective for identifying the changes and social trends that prompt social issues (dysfunctions).

One criticism of the structural functionalist paradigm is that it takes such a negative view of social change. For example, Aboriginal peoples throughout the world have criticized structural functionalist analysis of their societies, by 19th- and early 20th-century anthropologists and sociologists, for denying the existence and impact of their histories and thereby demeaning them.

Social Conflict Paradigm

The **social conflict** perspective makes *society appear as an arena of conflict and inequality among competing groups and organizations.* From this perspective, *society is in constant change because the power differences among the groups and the subsequent impacts of these differences continually cause the groups to be rearranged relative to each other.* A theorist who adopts a social conflict point of view would be interested in which groups are competing and which are likely to "win" given their strength relative to opposing interest groups.

A social conflict theorist would look at the advantageous resources that each competing group controls. Such resources may include

- money,
- political influence,
- strong leadership initiatives,
- strong lobby groups,
- strong public support.

An assessment of how these resources are distributed would enable the social conflict theorist to predict the future of social events.

The chief criticism of the social conflict paradigm is that it fails to consider or recognize any stable, cohesive elements of society. For example, even when a family unit functions well, is entered into voluntarily by spouses, and involves affection and genuine rapport between its members, a social conflict perspective on that spousal relationship will tend to view it as coercively obtained and inevitably hierarchical in favour of one (usually the male) partner and detrimental to the interests of the other (usually female) partner. In other words, this cohesive family unit does not easily accord with a social conflict analysis and its assumption of inequality based on gender.

Symbolic Interactionist Paradigm

The **symbolic interactionist** perspective is *a micro paradigm that focuses on the creation of society and reality through everyday social interaction.* A theorist using this point of view is likely to study the *symbolic meaning of social events and of the social actors' perspectives and experiences of an issue. It is a focus on the subjective meanings attached to events.*

The symbolic interactionist perspective lends itself to a qualitative and interpretive analysis of social behaviour, and for this reason it is sometimes criticized as being insufficiently scientific. Another criticism is that its micro nature fails to take into account broad social forces that influence social interaction. For example, analyzing a family's response to the main breadwinner's being unemployed fails to address the social causes of unemployment.

Social Constructionist Paradigm

A **social constructionist** perspective *looks at reality as a social construction or product of social interaction.* In this respect it resembles symbolic interactionism. However, a social constructionist point of view also *emphasizes the social and cultural patterns underlying concepts, like gender, that are assumed to be wholly natural or innate.* A social constructionist would approach the debate about what is innately masculine by examining the social processes that encourage feminine and masculine differences. The fact that women and men are different is not socially constructed, but the meaning or significance of their difference is a constructed reality. In other words, each social interaction reinforces and recreates the significance of the meaning of gender and thereby recreates the distinctiveness of being a man or woman.

Feminist Paradigm

Feminism is both a socio-political movement and a theoretical orientation. As a social movement, it has many branches or perspectives, but the goal of gender equality is what unites all feminist approaches. As a theoretical approach, it challenges the longstanding academic neglect of women's contributions to society and of topics pertinent to women. It is a theoretical approach that can adopt both a macro and micro orientation. Exposing the social patterns of gender inequality would be the primary goal of a feminist theorist. For example, a study of how the absence of women in government has shaped Canada would be a uniquely feminist topic, one that the other theoretical perspectives would likely ignore.

Any social issue can be analyzed from any or all of the theoretical perspectives. Because of the distinct orientation that each paradigm provides, many facets of an issue can be discovered if all perspectives are applied to it. But a single theoretical perspective can also yield valuable information about an issue. In this text, we sometimes apply various theoretical perspectives to a single, multi-faceted issue; sometimes we adopt a more contained approach. For example, the issue of poverty, which is discussed in chapter 7, has many themes. To conduct the broadest possible analysis, we have applied a structural functionalist perspective to the feminization of poverty, a social conflict perspective to the relationship between race and poverty, and a symbolic interactionist perspective to youth homelessness. In chapter 8 we have approached things somewhat differently, applying three theoretical perspectives to the single topic of urban sprawl.

Activity to Practise Differentiating the Theoretical Perspectives of Sociology

STRUCTURAL FUNCTIONALIST PARADIGM

The following exercise asks you to adopt a structural functionalist view of society. Seen from a structural functionalist perspective, society is an "organic system"—a system of parts each of which is needed for the healthy functioning of the whole system. The organic system with which you are most intimately familiar is the human body. The purpose of the following is not to expose how much (or little) you know about biology and anatomy, but to help you see society as an organic system.

1. Draw the outline of a human body in the centre of a landscape piece of paper. A stick figure is enough. Add some main organs: brain, heart, reproductive organs. (A curly line can be a brain; a valentine shape can be the heart; and a circle can be the reproductive organs.) Under the feet, label your body "human" (in other words, a whole organic structure).
2. On the left side of the drawing create two columns. Make the heading of the column that is closest to the drawing "structures of human body." In the column under this heading, label each of the organs that you drew on the body: brain, heart, and reproductive organs.
3. Make the heading of the other column "functions of structures." Here, beside each label in your first column, list the primary functions of the organ—that is, its role in the health and survival of the whole body. For example, the brain thinks, coordinates, learns, and remembers.
4. Now, with an arrow or circle, show where a heart attack would occur.
5. Explain what functions of the heart would be disrupted by a (non-fatal) heart attack. Remember, you are not a medical practitioner, so don't worry about absolute precision. What in general stops working when a person is ill with heart dysfunction?
6. Now explain how the body's other structures would be disrupted by a heart attack.
7. Draw conclusions about the relationship of the structures to each other and to the whole system.

____

____

____

____

____

____

____

____

____

____

You now have a diagram of an organic system. You have shown how a system is dependent on the specialized functioning of each part and you have revealed that the whole system is integrated through the interdependence of the parts within the whole. You have learned that no part can substitute for another part and that problems or dysfunctions in one part create instability and dysfunction through the entire system. The next exercise will help you apply what you have learned about systems to the study of society. The summary that you wrote in answer to question 7 describes the *perspective* adopted by the *structural functionalist paradigm*. Answering the following questions will help demonstrate this perspective's relevance to the study of society.

1. Now you are going to look at your diagram of the human body as if it were a diagram of society seen from a structural functionalist perspective. Bracket the "human" label below the body and re-label it "society." Create two columns on the right side of the body. At the top of the column closest to the body, put the heading "structures of society." Identify the other column as "functions." In the first column, label the system parts or "organs" as different **social institutions**: government, economy, and family, for example. Refer to any introductory sociology text for examples of social institutions.

2. In the outside column, beside each of the social institutions, list the specialized, expected functions of each institution. The function of government, for example, is to provide leadership, to provide and coordinate social services, and to ensure social order. The function of the economy is to provide and distribute goods and services and to provide employment. The family functions to provide new members of society through procreation and the socialization of children. Note that these functions are *manifest functions* and that each supports the entire social system. Additional social institutions include education, religion, law and justice, and health and medicine.

3. Identify any bonus or unexpected functions associated with the social structures you have listed. Label these as **latent functions**. A bonus or latent function is an unexpected benefit of social actions within any social institution.

4. Using the analogy of the heart attack, identify which social institution on your diagram would *initially* be most affected by the following trend:

   > Recently there has been a great flow of Canadian manufacturing jobs to third world countries. At the same time, many of the industrial jobs that remain in Canada have been assumed by robots and machines.

5. Describe which functions would be negatively affected or fail, both initially and over time, as a result of this altered economy. Identify these failures as **(latent) dysfunctions**.

6. Describe what you have learned about change assessed from the perspective of the structural functionalist paradigm.

____

____

____

____

____

____

____

____

____

____

SOCIAL CONFLICT PERSPECTIVE

Even though a social conflict perspective is macro, its view of society is distinct from a structural functionalist view. You are now going to create a picture of society that conforms to a social conflict view. According to this view, society comprises a number of groups and organizations that are competing over the same limited pool of resources. The gains of one social group are at the expense of all others. Resources gained by one group increase its power, enabling it to gain dominance over other groups in society. Changes in society correspond to the gains and losses of resources by its various competing groups.

1. Identify two sports teams that compete with each other.
2. Create two lists. Head one list with the name of one team and the second list with the name of the opposing team. For each team, list the assets that give it an advantage over the other. Assets might include, for example, money, skills development, star players, and coaching excellence. Try to make each team's list distinct from the other.
3. Compare each team's assets, and make a prediction about which team will win the next match.
4. Create a pie diagram. The pie represents a limited pool of resources. You are going to divide the pie into two pieces. Each piece represents the resources controlled by one team. How the pie is divided represents which team has the greatest share of assets, and indicates which team is dominant. The dominant team should have the greatest share of the pie. Colour coding each team will make this readily apparent. Beside the dominant team's portion of the pie, list the assets that provide for its dominance. Beside the losing team's portion, list the assets that will enable it to pose a challenge to the other team's continued dominance. The relative size of the portions of pie should represent how closely matched the two teams are. An assessment of the assets on each team should enable you to predict the outcomes of future competitions.
5. Now identify any events external to the list of assets that could alter the outcome that you have predicted. For example, if a star player on one team had to retire because of injury, this could alter the outcome. Estimate how likely such events are to occur. Such evaluation should enable you to identify how solid the winning team's hold on dominance is.
6. Draw conclusions about the relationship between power and winning. This is a social conflict perspective.

____

____

____

____

____

____

Now that you have looked at the teams from a social conflict point of view, you have been able to predict the likely outcome of any competitions (matches) between the teams. You can now apply the same thinking to an assessment of competitions within society. The topic that will be adopted for this exercise is crime. Street crime supports more criminals and grabs more media attention than white-collar crime does. White-collar crime can be very damaging, but it has a much lower incarceration rate and conviction rate than does street crime. Without a social conflict perspective, one could interpret such trends as meaning simply that poor people are more criminally minded and less civilized, law-abiding, and moral than successful people are. A social conflict perspective will reveal a different story.

1. Research any introductory sociology textbook for a detailed description of white-collar crime and street crime.
2. Identify white-collar criminals as one group and street criminals as the other group.
3. List the resources available to each type of criminal group. Consider the resources available to commit crime, to evade capture, and to repel social prejudice. Include social networks, technology, availability of information, and money as resources.
4. Create a pie chart of the inequality between the two groups. Identify which criminal group has the greatest power, and label the pie appropriately. (Consider the means to evade arrest or to avoid prison as evidence of power differences.)
5. Identify which type of crime tends to cause the greatest damage to society.
6. Explain why the criminal with the fewest resources to commit crime is the most condemned. Answer from a social conflict perspective.

7. Suggest reasons that disadvantaged groups appear to be the most criminal (to have, for example, the highest incarceration rate).

8. Explain the relationship between **social stigma** and **social power**.

9. Explain the term **social change** in the social conflict perspective.

SYMBOLIC INTERACTIONIST PERSPECTIVE

Read the following article by Patricia Pearson, which first appeared in *Maclean's* magazine.

> The other day, I checked myself into rehab. What a strangely casual announcement that is in our culture. Celebrities and politicians seem to pop into rehab so frequently and nonchalantly that it's as if they're swanning off to spas. Anyone for detox?
>
> Yet in my case, the news veritably shocked friends and relations, because I wasn't trying to wrest myself free of cocaine or painkillers or booze. I just wanted to quit smoking. I wanted to quit, and I knew perfectly well that I couldn't do it unless I was in a structured residential treatment program away from my kids, my day-to-day stressors, and the temptation of cigarettes themselves, lurking in every corner store. I knew this because I have tried and failed to quit before. The withdrawal symptoms—tension, tearfulness, insomnia, cravings—knocked me off course and redirected me back to my vice.
>
> This time, I figured, I needed seclusion, counselling, yoga, massage, peer support, stress management, nicotine replacement therapy (NRT)—the whole nine yards.
>
> "All that?" an amazed friend inquired, "just to stop smoking?" Of course, the key word there is "just," as in the exhortation I've heard countless times in the past 22 years to "Just quit, then" or, "Just give up that filthy habit." Just cut it out, already. Just say no.
>
> As obsessed as we are in this country with the perils of smoking, we seem to have a devilish time grasping the realities of tobacco use, such as the fact that withdrawing from an addictive drug is a more complicated matter than giving up sweets, or taking up tennis. Health Canada mandates that cigarette packages display horrifying messages for smokers to read each time they reach for a butt. You're familiar with these messages, such as "smoking can kill you" and "smoking causes impotence." Well, one of the messages is that "nicotine is more addictive than heroin." Under the circumstances, "just quitting" doesn't work all that well.
>
> Less than 10 percent of the people who quit smoking on New Year's Day will remain smoke-free by next New Year's Eve. Of those who do succeed, most will relapse and then quit again, on average, six times before they manage to go a whole year without taking a puff. This doesn't include smokers who are so intimidated by the prospect of withdrawal that they never quit at all.
>
> So, why is it so shocking that a smoker would need to go into rehab, and why are residential treatment programs for nicotine so scarce that it took me weeks of intensive Web surfing to locate one? I finally found two week-long programs in the US. If more exist out there, all I can say is that they are harder to locate than the Loch Ness monster.
>
> It is also, I might add, much harder to find NRT products—designed to keep smokers off cigarettes—than to find ciggies themselves. At a drug store in Ottawa recently, I had to wait 20 minutes behind three people getting their prescriptions so I could request nicotine gum from behind the pharmacist's counter. With my nerves frayed by withdrawal, I was on the verge of hysterics by the time I reached the front of the line.
>
> A couple of years ago, the Ontario Medical Association urged Health Canada to allow freer access to nicotine gum, patches and the like, pointing out the absurdity of restricting these products more tightly than tobacco. The nicotine inhaler has been approved by Health Canada and will soon be available, but the nicotine lozenge and nasal spray, both used in Europe and the US, are not sold here.

The implication is that ingesting pure nicotine is somehow more dangerous than smoking it, which is flat-out wrong. Nicotine itself doesn't cause any of the diseases associated with smoking. Beyond being addictive, it's considered quite benign. The delivery system, not the drug, is lethal, and if we can be weaned off that and switched to nasal spray, say, or the patch, or a combination of NRTs, then Health Canada should be shouting out that message loud and clear.

According to the 2002 instalment of the Canadian Tobacco Use Monitoring Survey, the most widely held belief among failed quitters, in Canada's population of 5.4 million smokers, is that they need "more willpower" to rid themselves of cigarettes. I find that answer to be terribly sad and poignant, because it suggests that smokers have taken to heart the message in our society that smoking is fundamentally a moral issue, that it has nothing to do with the medical picture of addiction and everything to do with individual failings of character.

When I go to a movie theatre and find myself watching a tragic, heart-wrenching public service ad about a waitress in Ottawa who is dying of lung cancer because of smokers like me, I would also like to see an optimistic announcement along the lines of, "Hallelujah, smokers, guess what? Good news! We have perfected new methods of nicotine delivery that don't make you sick, and don't sicken you with guilt and shame!"

NRTs need to be available wherever cigarettes are sold, and people should be able to use them for as long as necessary. In my rehab program, at the St. Helena Center for Health in California, we were urged to stay with our nicotine replacement products for at least a year to lower the risk of relapse.

Unfortunately, I have already had to give up one of the most effective treatments I was prescribed, the nasal spray, because I can't find it in Canada. I also had to stop taking Zyban, because it isn't covered by the Ontario Health Insurance Plan. But hey, I still have my gum, and the patch, and some willpower. Baby, I've come a long way. (Pearson, 2004, p. 30)

1. Highlight all of the terms in the article that represent or symbolize smoking and smokers.
2. Identify the paragraph that describes the social definition of smokers.
3. Explain the relationship between the social definition of smoking and smokers, on the one hand, and the current availability of help and support for smokers in Canada.

____
____
____
____
____
____
____
____
____
____

4. Draw conclusions about the origin of social issues as explained in the symbolic interactionist paradigm.

CONCLUSION

This chapter has attempted to show you how sociologists look at issues in the world and, in particular, at issues in the *social world.* The exercises should have emphasized the following points for you.

Each theoretical perspective is based on a specific view of the nature of society. Every theoretical perspective has its advocates, but our purpose is not to recommend one perspective over others. No sociological perspective has a monopoly on the truth.

This chapter has provided questions that will help you take an analytical approach to the study of social issues. The next chapter will explain how to adopt the theoretical perspectives as tools of analysis. Each approach is guided by a distinct set of questions. Necessarily, different questions lead to different answers. What we are looking for has an important impact upon what we find.

KEY TERMS

dysfunctions in the structural functionalist paradigm, the negative consequences of change or of social actions; dysfunctions occur as breakdowns within social institutions or as the impaired integration of social institutions

feminist a paradigm and a social movement aimed at achieving equality for women; in sociology, feminism has brought forth research topics of pertinence to women, and it has corrected male-centred research assumptions and conclusions

(latent) dysfunctions within the paradigm of structural functionalism, this is another term for *dysfunctions*; see above

latent functions the structural functionalist term for the unexpected benefits of social actions; they enhance the functioning of society

macro perspective a theoretical perspective (for example, structural functionalist or social conflict) that ignores the everyday details of social interaction and instead focuses on the social forces outside the sphere of individual influence

manifest functions in the structural functionalist paradigm, the positive consequences expected of a social institution

micro perspective a theoretical perspective (for example, the symbolic interactionist paradigm) that focuses on everyday social interactions as the processes that produce society, culture, gender identity, and identity of self

paradigm a model that is based on theory and that guides thinking and research; in sociology, models are of society, and can be macro or micro in focus

social change alteration to established patterns at both the micro and macro levels; at micro levels, social change would entail alteration to norms and values; at a macro level, social change would entail changes to prevailing ideologies

social conflict a macro theoretical paradigm with origins in Karl Marx's theories; a view of society as comprised of competing groups, the more powerful of which exploit those with fewer assets

social constructionist a micro theoretical paradigm within the symbolic interactionist perspective; outlines that reality is a creation of society, and that it has no universal or inherent properties

social institutions the structural functionalist term for social structures; the assemblages of norms, values, beliefs, statuses, roles, and organizations that collectively answer a society's basic needs (for example, education and family are social institutions)

social power the ability to impose one's will or interests on another; the ability to dominate

social stigma a negatively valued marker or characteristic that makes a stigmatized person or group a target for prejudice and discrimination

structural functionalist a macro theoretical paradigm that views society as an organic system of integrated social structures; each structure has specialized functions that maintain the whole society

symbolic interactionist a micro paradigm that describes society as an ongoing product of everyday social interactions, which employ language (that is, symbols)

theoretical paradigm a model of society that has been constructed from sociological theories; used to guide thinking and research about society and social issues

theoretical perspective a term used interchangeably with *theoretical paradigm*

FOR FURTHER RESEARCH

Sociology—Web Reference
http://www.webref.org/sociology.

Wikipedia—Sociology
http://en.wikipedia.org/wiki/Sociology.

WWW Virtual Library—Sociology
http://socserv.mcmaster.ca/w3virtsoclib.

For a review of the history of the Highway 69 lobby and for a copy of the petition for change, go to the following websites:
http://hansardindex.ontla.on.ca/hansardECAT/37-3/L058A-5.htm.
http://www.mto.gov.on.ca/english/traveller/highway69.
http://www.69ea559to522.ca/background.html.

REFERENCES

Aglionby, J. (2005, December 27). Thousands gather on beaches to mourn the day the wave came. *The Guardian.* http://www.guardian.co.uk/print/0,,5363073-115399,00.html.

Highway 69 Route Planning Study. (n.d.). North of Nobel to highway 522: Background. http://www.69ea559to522.ca/background.html.

Pearson, P. (2004, January 26). How I prevailed vs. ciggies: Why does Canada make it hard to get the stuff that helps you butt out? *Maclean's, 117,* p. 30. http://www.macleans.ca/columnists/article.jsp?content=20040126_73943_73943.

CHAPTER 2
The Analytical Method

CHAPTER OBJECTIVES

After completing this chapter, you will be able to:

- Outline the steps of the analytical method.
- Apply the analytical method to the assessment of a social issue.
- Adopt each of sociology's theoretical perspectives as an analytical tool.
- Draw conclusions about a social issue based on analyses undertaken from each of the theoretical perspectives.

THE ANALYTICAL METHOD

In this text, each analysis of social issues follows the **analytical method**. This means that you begin by verifying that an issue is a social issue. Then you determine the stage at which it has arrived in its life cycle. From there, questions about how the issue is likely to unfold or why it exists are answered through a theoretical analysis of the real events giving rise to the issue. Such a theoretical analysis requires the theoretical paradigms of sociology.

The steps of the analytical method are as follows:

1. Gathering information and evidence regarding a social issue;
2. Establishing a topic focus and research statement;
3. Determining a social issue orientation;
4. Determining what stage the issue has reached in its life cycle;
5. Adopting theoretical paradigms as analytical tools;
6. Drawing conclusions about the cause of a social issue and about its future course;
7. Creating a research references sheet.

In this chapter, you will become acquainted with the analytical method and its templates. From time to time, tobacco use in Canada will be cited as an example of a social issue, but not until chapter 3 of this text will you actually apply the analytical method to this issue.

Gathering Information and Evidence

Where is the best place to conduct research into social issues? Contemporary social issues, as you have seen, are publicly viewed as problems, and the people most agitated by a particular problem are usually trying hard to engage public interest and action to resolve the issue. For this reason, current news media would be the most valuable research resource. Such media appear on the Internet, in newspapers, on TV, and on radio. News stories cover the latest events, and most documentaries include analysis by those most concerned about an issue—its major activists and stakeholders. Reviewing the media coverage of an issue will not only provide you with topic ideas, it will illuminate the chronology and impact of events, and it will identify the major players and their notions of how to resolve the issue. Please refer to chapter 1 for a review of the distinctions between truth and opinion. Individual perspectives and judgments, if accepted as credible sources, should be well reasoned and should include valid background information.

All research needs to be guided by a focus more specific than a topic name. A topic name is something like *substance abuse* or *poverty*. A more specific focus is developed through a research statement that becomes, with further research, progressively more narrow and specific. A social issue statement must convey a sense of objective truth, not of opinion. Social issues are at the root of many personal or individual problems, but a statement identifying an issue as social *cannot* reflect personal experience or evaluation.

The following describes the desirable features of a topic statement. Note that a topic statement may consist of more than one sentence.

A topic statement

- *must* identify social factors, not, for example, biological, medical, or natural features. For instance, an earthquake is not a social factor or social issue, but it may trigger a social issue of catastrophic magnitude;
- *should* identify a problem, but *shouldn't* offer solutions because these usually reflect personal opinions and biases;
- *should* indicate controversy and negative impacts;
- *should* indicate cause and effect;
- *should* reflect that the issue being considered represents a negative trend, *not* just an isolated incident;
- *should* include specifics, not vague generalities, and *should* indicate that there is documented evidence available;
- *should* be written in the third person and *must not* have any reference to personal connections or relationships.

A topic statement should *not*

- offer solutions because these usually reflect personal opinion and biases,
- offer judgments or opinions about what is appropriate or correct,
- have any reference to personal connections or relationships.

An example of a topic name would be something general such as *substance abuse.* A topic statement would identify a specific theme within the named topic. For example, within the social issue of substance abuse is the issue of tobacco use in Canada. An initial topic statement for the more specific issue of tobacco use in Canada might be as follows:

> Tobacco use is the greatest cause of preventable illness and death in Canada. The health and financial costs of tobacco use are unacceptable to the majority of Canadians, and it is this growing majority that is strenuously promoting a ban on smoking in Canada.

The more articles and sources you research, the more accurate will be your picture of the social issue. Too few resources will make reporting and understanding your findings very difficult. Furthermore, a small research base will not provide the credibility that more extensive research would.

Establishing a Topic Focus and Research Statement

Once you have gathered current information about the issue, you are ready to refine your topic statement. Your refined topic statement must possess the features described above and it must identify a more specific theme within the general topic. Specific references to the populations involved and to established events will help. In fact, a summary of the answers to the guide questions used to identify a social issue will serve as a topic statement (see chapter 1 to review the guide questions). The following, which is adopted in chapter 3, is an example of an expanded topic statement:

> Tobacco use in Canada is waning in popularity, but it is the greatest cause of preventable illness and death in Canada. The health and financial costs of tobacco use are unacceptable to the majority of Canadians, and it is this growing majority that is strenuously promoting a ban on smoking in Canada. Committed smokers continue to resist, but as long as smoking-related deaths continue to rise, their arguments are largely overwhelmed.

Determining a Social Issue Orientation

Once you have established a research focus, your next step, following the analytical method, is to establish that your issue is a social issue. A more correct way of stating this, perhaps, is to say that you need to ensure that you are viewing the issue, or topic, from a social issue standpoint. While health and biology, for instance, are important considerations in the general issue of tobacco use, they should not be the focus of tobacco use considered as a social issue. A social issue is what is *defined* as problematic; it is not the event itself. To ensure that you maintain a social issue focus in selecting and researching your topic, use the first four guide questions. For your convenience, the guide questions are repeated below:

Q1. Is the issue problematic to many people, and are there many people voicing their concerns or claiming that the issue is unacceptable?

Q2. Is the issue specific to a particular social context—that is, modern Canadian culture?

Q3. Do the people voicing their concerns have a vision of the way things should be—that is, a goal?

Q4. Are there means to improve the situation and to achieve the vision?

Determining the Stage in the Life Cycle of a Social Issue

The next step in the analytical method is to determine how developed a social issue is. If an issue has only recently been deemed unacceptable by a small number of people, the public at large will care little about it and there will be no formal initiatives aimed at resolving it. If, on the other hand, the issue has been actively debated for many years, there will be extensive public engagement and numerous formal initiatives toward resolution. The remaining five guide questions, repeated here from chapter 1, will help you research a social issue, and the answers will serve as the foundation of a social issue report:

Q5. Who and what organizations are calling for public attention?

Q6. What public interest in the issue has there been? What media coverage or promotion has there been?

Q7. How has society aligned itself around the issue? What kinds of demands have been made, and what organizations and coalitions have been formed?

Q8. What policies have been initiated or proposed?

Q9. What impact have these initiatives or proposals had on the resolution or intensifying of the issue?

Adopting Theoretical Paradigms as Analytical Tools

The application of the nine guide questions will help you *identify* whether a social issue exists. The next step in the analytical method is to apply theory in an effort to *understand* the issues you have researched. Using sociology's theoretical paradigms as tools of analysis can help explain why social issues exist, who is most affected by them, and what outcome is most likely. The theoretical paradigms used as tools of analysis in this text are the structural functionalist paradigm, the social conflict paradigm, the symbolic interactionist paradigm, the social constructionist paradigm, and the feminist paradigm.

In general, it is helpful to remember that theoretical paradigms are models of society. In other words, they do not actually exist; they are abstracted patterns. They are helpful precisely because they project models of an ideal society. If you compare real society to a theoretical ideal society, the discrepancies between the model and the reality will teach you what is *wrong* in real society. Just as a surgeon repairs an injured elbow by restoring it to match a model or ideal of an elbow, a social analyst can learn to understand the nature of social problems by comparing the real society to an ideal one. Note that the word *ideal*, as used here, is not meant to connote perfection or utopia. Ideal means a theoretical or imagined model. Theoretical models of society are not flights of fancy, either. They are based on sound research.

As a model, a theoretical paradigm has limits. We have already identified the limits of the macro and micro perspectives. Similarly, if we see society as a system (the functionalist perspective that views all change as disruptive), then we are prevented from seeing the conflict perspective (that social changes can be beneficial).

To help you efficiently employ the theoretical paradigms as analytical tools, we provide you with a set of questions for each model. The questions will help accustom your thinking to the parameters of the given perspective.

A STRUCTURAL FUNCTIONALIST ANALYSIS

The structural functionalist perspective, a macro perspective, views society as a system. In other words, society is seen as a collection, or assemblage, of social structures, each of which has specific and distinct functions that serve the whole system. Because society, according to this perspective, is like an organic system, any change that disrupts the integration and functioning of the social structures is considered a negative change, or dysfunction. For this reason, the paradigm has been criticized for its inherent conservativism.

Criticisms aside, this perspective is useful for pinpointing the origins of changes that do disrupt or upset society, and it is helpful in planning to correct the deficiencies brought on by change. The structural functionalist paradigm as a tool of analysis takes into account the following template of questions.

1. What social institutions or structures are primarily involved in the issue?
2. What are the manifest functions of these social institutions or structures when society is operating as expected?
3. What social events or trends are interrupting specific functions or the integration of the functions?

A SOCIAL CONFLICT ANALYSIS

Like the structural functionalist perspective, the social conflict perspective is a macro perspective, which means that social patterns of personal or particular interaction are ignored in favour of a broader focus. Social conflict analysis assesses the competition among groups and organizations. With a social conflict analysis, one can map the power dynamics among competing groups. By this means, an analyst can understand an issue as the outcome of power differences in society and thereby make predictions about the future of the issue.

There are three questions that will help guide a social conflict orientation. In general, you want to identify the major stakeholders that are involved and then to assess their relative power with respect to the resources that each group controls.

1. Who benefits in this issue? Who is exploited? What are the dominant groups?
2. What resources or bases of power do the dominant groups have at their disposal to preserve their dominance?
3. What is the social definition of the issue? What values are in conflict?

A SYMBOLIC INTERACTIONIST ANALYSIS

By definition, the symbolic interactionist perspective demands a focus on the interactive patterns among people. Social patterns of behaviour reveal prevailing social values and beliefs. Social actions also invite social responses, so that a social issue can be understood as the outcome of interpersonal behaviours. If certain lifestyles or appearances are stigmatized, for example, then those with the stigma may become rebellious or withdrawn, and certain behaviours can be explained as a response to stigma. The resolution of issues, in this instance, would therefore involve education that diminishes the stigmas.

The following guide questions are designed to help you stay in a micro perspective. They also differ from the questions of the macro perspectives in that their answers will be more interpretive and descriptive. The overall goal of a symbolic interactionist perspective is to *describe* a reality and then to *interpret* its various social effects.

1. What does the issue mean to the individuals involved in it? How is this meaning expressed? What labels, myths, stereotypes, and language do individuals use to refer to the issue and to the other individuals involved in the issue?

2. What is the source of these meanings? What is the social context in which these meanings are expressed? How are these meanings enforced or resisted?

3. What are the consequences of this activity? How does the activity affect the individuals involved? How does it affect society's perception of an issue, and how does it affect how an individual participates in the issue?

A SOCIAL CONSTRUCTIONIST ANALYSIS

A social constructionist perspective is a theoretical theme within the symbolic interactionist perspective. It differs from the symbolic interactionist perspective in its focus on dominant cultural patterns that create assumptions about seemingly natural or innate features of our reality. In chapter 1, we cited assumptions about gender—the notion that femininity and masculinity pervade every aspect of behaviour—as one possible focus of a social constructivist perspective. Behaviour that is outside of the social expectations of femininity and masculinity is seen as *unnatural.* However, purposeful rejection of such behaviours results in the modification of social beliefs and values about gender. For a historical example, one can look back to the suffragette movement, which challenged all of the assumptions then current about femininity. Today, many women are rejecting the conventional obligation to shave their legs and to wear makeup and are thereby socially constructing a new meaning of femininity.

The guide questions for a symbolic interactionist analysis can be adopted for a social constructionist analysis. Question 2, for example, asks about the source of the issue's meanings. The answer, from a social constructionist point of view, would centre on the prevailing cultural values and beliefs surrounding an issue rather than on the beliefs and values of one of the groups involved.

A FEMINIST ANALYSIS

As already noted, a feminist analysis can be both micro and macro. Whether a macro or micro analysis is adopted depends on the particular goals being sought within the general context of a search for gender equality. Topics chosen according to a feminist perspective tend to be pertinent to women and, quite often, ignored by the other perspectives and by a majority of theorists who fail to acknowledge the benefits of feminist inquiry. A feminist analysis would also vigilantly avoid **androcentricity**, **gender blindness**, and a gender **double standard** in its treatment of a given topic. For a feminist micro perspective, the questions guiding the symbolic interaction analysis are pertinent, but they need to be guided, in this new context, by the assumption that social patterns work against gender equality. Most pertinent to a macro feminist analysis is a social conflict orientation, which enables you to look at feminist issues as the outcome of competition between gendered traditions and feminist initiatives.

Drawing Conclusions: Determining Why and Making Predictions

Remember the adage, *Begin with the end in mind.* The conclusion of a social issue research paper should offer an improved understanding of the origins, nature, and consequences of social change—in other words, it should meet the basic goals of a social issue paper. A sociological approach to a social issue presumes that change, be it technological, political, environmental, or social, affects society's functioning and the well-being of its members. The analytical method proceeds on the assumption that documenting social change and its impacts will enlarge our understanding of why an issue occurs, why a change has been problematic, and what outcomes are likely; and that such a task can be accomplished through use of the theoretical paradigms.

For example, a structural functionalist analysis explains how change creates faults in a social system, and we use this perspective to study dysfunction, disruption, decay, or deterioration in a social system. An appropriate conclusion for this kind of analysis would include an outline of what could be done to repair the social system. Analyzing the issue from a social conflict perspective answers different questions; it explores an issue in terms of what social groups have most power to affect an issue and what direction the issue will be taken by interest groups. The two perspectives could be used together: the structural functionalist analysis would explain what has failed and needs restoration; the social conflict perspective would help determine the likelihood of such restoration.

The micro paradigms of symbolic interactionism and social constructionism enable a researcher to understand the impacts of everyday social behaviour on the development of an issue. For example, a group living under the burden of a stigma will react to social events and to discrimination differently than will a group unaffected by a stigma.

Finally, the perspective involved in a feminist analysis—whether macro or micro—enables a researcher to draw conclusions about social issues in the context of prevailing gender inequality.

Generally speaking, a conclusion should state research findings in terms of the research goals established at the outset. It should reiterate the dynamics of the issue and project its likely future course. In short, a conclusion should be consistent with what has been reported in the paper.

Creating a Research References Sheet

Any research report, social science or otherwise, must supply a comprehensive list of references. Every college and university provides guidance about what formats are appropriate to use. In most institutions, sociology papers are typically required to adopt the **APA citation style**. Failure to document research sources is treated as academic dishonesty—more specifically, as **plagiarism**. Plagiarism is forbidden and faces increasingly serious sanctions. (Incidentally, the issue of plagiarism could be viewed as an emerging social issue. The information technologies have made plagiarism rampant. Access is vast and traditional methods of detection are inadequate.)

CONCLUSION

The analytical method is a template that directs the research of a social issue and can be applied to any one that you deem worthy of study. The theoretical perspectives are the main ones of sociology. Adopted as they are here, as part of the analytical method, they can be used to gain insights not available from a simple accounting of the facts of an issue.

The analytical method gives you the means to assess, from a sociological standpoint, any news item or social events that you encounter. In the following chapters, this text considers a number of social issues currently facing Canada. You can use these examples to hone your analytical skills, and they may give you ideas about other current social issues that you might want to examine. Needless to say, the passage of time will bring new issues to light as it will bring resolution to current issues. But the analytical method itself, because it is a template, is relatively timeless.

KEY TERMS

analytical method a method or system of steps that provides a structure for the investigation and analysis of contemporary social issues

androcentricity the condition of being male-centred or male-dominated in research and perspective; for example, adopting topics or perspectives that have relevance only to men and that underrepresent women

APA citation style American Psychological Association style; a method of documenting research resources in social science papers

double standard adoption of expectations or benchmarks that differ for men and women; amounts to bias or unfairness

gender blindness having the assumption that gender differences do not exist

plagiarism using information (intellectual property) without acknowledging its source or author

FOR FURTHER RESEARCH

An interesting article that describes the current lack of awareness about and respect for the importance of original work: Chapman, D. (2002–2007). *Using the Internet: The art of plagiarism.* TechTrax MouseTrax Computing Solutions. http://pubs.logicalexpressions.com/Pub0009/LPMArticle.asp?ID=686.

A very quick guide to the APA style of citing references: Delaney, R. (2007). *APA citation style.* Long Island University. C.W. Post Campus. http://www.liu.edu/CWIS/CWP/library/workshop/citapa.htm.

CHAPTER 3

Substance Use and Abuse

CHAPTER OBJECTIVES

After completing this chapter, you will be able to:

Understand significant dimensions of substance use and abuse

- Discuss cultural and social understandings of substance use.
- Understand basic facts about the use and abuse of specific substances, including alcohol, drugs (both illegal and legal), tobacco, and food additives (such as sugars and fats).
- Understand social issues relating to substance abuse, including problems related to family, career, financial standing, criminal activity, accidents and injury, and health.

Understand and apply different sociological perspectives to substance use and abuse

- Structural functionalist
- Social conflict
- Symbolic interactionist

Identify and critique responses to social problems related to substance use and abuse

- Government and policy
- Law and policing
- Community
- Individual involvement

DIMENSIONS

Substance use involves ingesting certain materials, known as drugs, that are **psychoactive**, affecting the user's central nervous system and brain function so as to change his or her mood, consciousness, perceptions, and behaviour. A **drug** is any biological substance, naturally occurring or synthetic, that is taken not primarily for dietary needs but to produce some other bodily effect. Traditionally, with the exception of beer, wine, and narcotic mushrooms, foods have not been defined as drugs, but this has changed as **obesity** has become recognized in North America as a growing epidemic.

These substances are sometimes used *recreationally*, which means that a person deliberately alters his or her consciousness by using the drug. Many of these substances, especially depressants and stimulants, are dangerous to use recreationally; they produce chemical dependencies and can be habit forming. Even where users are not physically dependent upon the substance, they may develop a psychological or social need to continue using it. In many instances, the user becomes dependent upon the drug, starts to *abuse* it, and ceases to be able to function without it.

Canadians are not all affected by substance abuse in the same way. Aboriginal peoples have disproportionately high rates of substance abuse, particularly where alcohol is concerned, as compared with non-Aboriginals. For Native Canadians, this translates into a high level of alcohol- and drug-related illness, violence, injury, and other social problems (First Nations and Inuit Health Committee, 2006; Riley, 1998). In comparison with women, men suffer a disproportionate number of substance-abuse-related fatalities. However, drug use may be even more dangerous for women than for men. Drug use affects women differently than it does men. Females tend to be more physiologically responsive to the psychoactive effects of drugs. Researchers have found that women tend to proceed more rapidly from recreational drug use to drug abuse and addiction than men do. Women may be at greater risk of ill health stemming from drug use, since they are more prone to drug-related stroke and brain damage (Leshner, 1998). Women tend also to use different drugs than men use. In general, women tend to abuse prescription drugs more than men do, while men are more likely to use illegal drugs. Men are more likely to be involved in the illegal drug trade than women are; women are more likely to abuse medications, and in consequence their drug abuse may go unnoticed for long periods of time.

Negative repercussions of drug abuse will be discussed in more detail below, in the section entitled "Addictions."

CULTURAL UNDERSTANDINGS OF SUBSTANCE USE

Psychoactive substances have been used by human beings for millennia, in virtually all known societies. Archaeological evidence indicates that psychoactive substances were used as early as 10,000 years before the present (Merlin, n.d.). Many cultures, including the Aboriginal peoples of Canada, have incorporated psychoactive substances, often found in plants, into their understandings of the sacred and used them in rituals and ceremonies. Perhaps the most prominent such substance is tobacco, which is still considered sacred by many Canadian Aboriginal peoples and continues to be used in traditional ceremonies, rituals, and prayers as it has been for thousands of years (First Nations and Inuit Health Committee, 2006). Another such substance is *peyote*, a kind of cactus, widely used throughout North America by Aboriginal peoples in the 19th century (Schultes & Raffauf, 1992). Psychoactive substances have often been used in the context of religious ritual. Drugs used in this way are known as **entheogens**. A culture that uses these drugs believes they can give the user access to mystical, inspirational, or spiritual enlightenment. Seen in this way, drugs are not a recreational device but a chemical catalyst to religious experience. According to this view, the visions or other perceptual changes experienced through substance use are not so much hallucinations as journeys into a different dimension of reality.

In the 1960s, the use of hallucinogenic drugs was adopted by a broad segment of North America's youth culture. This group, diverse in many ways, was widely known as the *counterculture* in that it was rebelling against the views and values of the cultural mainstream. Adapting, albeit in a secular spirit, the Aboriginal conception of drugs as entheogens, the counterculture saw drugs as "mind-expanding" and used them to explore the world in a new light.

Today, thinkers in Canada as elsewhere are divided about the value and appropriate use of psychoactive drugs. Debates continue to rage about the morality, legality, and risks associated with using such drugs.

In Canada today, some mind-altering substances are quite socially acceptable and are sold expressly for recreational use—caffeine, for example, which is found in chocolate and coffee; and alcohol. The public acceptance level of other substances has changed markedly over the past few decades. Cigarettes and other forms of tobacco, once widely acceptable, are now prohibited by law in most public buildings and cannot be advertised or sold in many places. Other substances continue to have a low degree of mainstream social acceptance, such as cocaine. Still other mind-altering substances are accepted in the North American cultural mainstream not primarily for recreational purposes but rather for their medicinal properties. Physicians prescribe narcotics to control pain; certain stimulants are used to treat conditions like *narcolepsy* (which causes the sufferer to fall asleep uncontrollably in unpredictable situations).

The line between recreational substance use and **drug abuse** is a fine one. Some term all illegal drug use to be abuse, while others define abuse to include only excessive or uncontrolled use of psychotropic substances. Where one draws the line in this regard depends greatly on one's social context. Different subcultures and communities in Canada today have different notions of what constitutes drug abuse.

Many consider colleges and universities to be a social context where widespread substance use is "normal." Students are especially renowned for consuming large amounts of alcohol. For example, a 2003 study conducted at the University of Lethbridge, in Alberta, indicated that 90 percent of students use alcohol, 44 percent consume in excess of six drinks "on a typical day when drinking," and 76 percent drink alcohol at least one to two days per week (University of Lethbridge, 2005). Engaging in *binge drinking*—that is, drinking to the point of gross intoxication—is socially acceptable in most college and university peer groups and is regarded by many as a rite of passage or developmental stage.

Young celebrities sometimes engage in highly publicized substance use. Their social context appears to be a world where the use of cocaine, ecstasy, and other drugs is socially normalized. In 2007, popular young actress Lindsay Lohan entered a rehabilitation program after allegedly abusing cocaine and ecstasy. The previous year, supermodel Kate Moss briefly lost major modelling contracts when a video was released depicting her snorting cocaine. Many other celebrities have, over the years, done stints in rehabilitation for drug problems, including such stars as film icon Elizabeth Taylor and leading men Ben Affleck and Charlie Sheen.

Conversely, in some contemporary religious communities, such as the Church of Latter Day Saints (often known as the Mormon church), alcohol use is considered immoral and is not socially tolerated. For Mormons, even caffeine is seen as undesirable, and it is not socially acceptable to drink coffee.

TYPES OF SUBSTANCES USED

There is a tremendously wide range of substances that can be used to alter brain function. The following substances are commonly used and abused in North America:

- caffeine,
- alcohol,
- tobacco,
- cannabis,
- medications,
- "hard" drugs,
- sugars and fats.

Most of these substances can be taken in a variety of ways: inhaled as vapours; taken orally, as solids (pills) or liquids; injected into either muscles or veins; administered rectally and absorbed through the colon. Persons who are addicted to drugs can be remarkably creative in their methods of ingestion.

Caffeine

Caffeine is a stimulant found in the beans and leaves of the coffee plant and in several other plant species. Most of the caffeine consumed by humans comes from coffee beans. Caffeine is found in tea, coffee, and chocolate, as well as in many soft drinks. Recent figures indicate that over 90 percent of North American adults consume caffeine every day (Lovett, 2005), making caffeine the Western world's most popular psychoactive substance. This may be because it is legal and not subject to regulation in most of the world.

The primary desired effect of caffeine is an energy boost, which can temporarily increase a person's capacity for physical and mental work. As a result, consumption of caffeine, especially coffee, is generally tolerated and encouraged—it is even provided to employees in most Canadian workplaces. Caffeine does not eliminate the user's need for sleep but it does temporarily reduce a person's sensation of fatigue. Caffeine can also be used as a medication, as in the case of infants born prematurely who have breathing difficulties, and can be useful in making pain relievers more effective for treatment of migraine headaches.

Users develop a tolerance to caffeine over time, which means that they have to take higher doses to achieve the desired effect. Because many North American adults consume so much caffeine each day, it is likely that many of them are *tolerant* to caffeine's effects.

Although it is legal and unregulated, caffeine use is not without risk. Furthermore, users of caffeine develop withdrawal symptoms when they miss their regular dosage. They may feel fatigue, stomach aches, irritability, and an inability to concentrate—though these withdrawal symptoms will last no more than five days. Users who consume large quantities of caffeine over long periods of time can also suffer from nervousness, irritability, insomnia, muscle twitching, headaches, increased heart rate, blurred vision, and even heart disease. Pregnant women's bodies have more difficulty absorbing caffeine than do other adults' bodies. Infants and young children also have difficulty absorbing caffeine.

Alcohol

Alcohol is a term generally used for beverages that contain *ethanol*, a grain-based liquid formed by the fermentation of sugars. There are many uses for alcohol. It can be used to fuel vehicles; used as a solvent in perfumes, drugs, and vegetable flavourings; and used, as it has been historically, as a medication. Alcohol has also been used recreationally, for psychotropic purposes, since ancient times.

Alcohol is most commonly consumed in the form of beverages such as liquor, wine, and beer. Consuming small amounts of alcohol for recreational purposes is highly socially acceptable in most mainstream Canadian social circles. According to the 2004 Canadian Addictions Survey, almost 80 percent of Canadians are currently drinkers, with most of them consuming only small amounts, infrequently (Canadian Centre on Substance Abuse [CCSA], 2004). Some studies have shown that infrequent use of small amounts of certain types of alcohol, particularly red wine, may even have beneficial health effects, particularly to a person's heart function (CBS News, 1991).

However, alcohol is a poison. Consumption of significant amounts of it results in a state of intoxication that impairs the user's judgment and physical functions. Such intoxication can lead to reckless and dangerous behaviour, as well as to physical problems such as nausea and a headache the following day. Frequent or chronic consumption of alcohol can lead to addiction, and to health issues such as liver disease, acute respiratory failure, or even death. Consumption of alcohol by pregnant women can lead to their children being born with fetal alcohol syndrome or fetal alcohol spectrum disorder, which entails a wide range of ill effects including brain damage, poor emotional development, memory and attention deficits, and physical deformities. Fetal alcohol syndrome is considered to be the leading cause of mental handicap in the Western world (Abel & Sokel, 1987).

Alcoholism, or addiction to alcohol, can result from frequent consumption of large amounts of the drug. The substance is highly addictive. People who become addicted to alcohol are always considered to have the addiction. If not actively drinking, they are considered to be in *remission* or *recovery*, but still alcoholic. The likelihood of becoming addicted to alcohol varies among people; some can use alcohol in large amounts without becoming addicted while others quite quickly become dependent upon it. Psychological and physical conditions, such as an individual's genetic makeup and their social conditions, can affect their relative likelihood of becoming addicted to alcohol—that is, *alcoholic.* Alcoholism is related to a variety of social problems, which are discussed in more detail below. These include family problems, exposure to violence and disease, trouble with the law, and even untimely death.

Tobacco

Tobacco is a stimulant derived from the leaves of certain nightshade plants that grow in the Americas. There are several ways in which tobacco can be ingested. Most often, it is smoked after being dried and rolled into a cigarette, cigar, or pipe. It can also be chewed or taken up the nose, as is done with *snuff*; there is a range of smokeless tobacco products. Tobacco contains the chemical nicotine, which is one of the most addictive substances in existence. It acts similarly to heroin and cocaine, affecting the same pleasure areas of the brain. Recent research suggests that even a brief exposure to nicotine can be addictive.

There are many serious health risks associated with tobacco use, including early death. The World Health Organization in 2002 estimated that, in developed countries, 9 percent of female deaths and 26 percent of male deaths could be attributed to smoking (World Health Organization, 2002). Long-term smoking has been linked to high risks of cancer and stroke, and to serious respiratory, cardiovascular, and circulatory problems. It is not just the smokers themselves whose health is damaged by smoking. Others are also at risk. Smoking during pregnancy can harm developing fetuses and can even result in miscarriage. Children and adult non-smokers can suffer asthma and other conditions, even cancer, as a result of second-hand smoke.

As public awareness has grown about the health risks of smoking tobacco, smoking has been progressively limited; it has gradually moved from being quite socially acceptable in Canada to being socially undesirable. Over the past several decades, hospitals, workplaces, restaurants, and now most public spaces, have become "smoke-free." According to the Canadian Tobacco Use Monitoring Survey for 2004, 83 percent of smokers were not permitted by their own families to smoke inside their homes. The prospect of a physician smoking at the nursing station after a stressful operation, once quite commonplace, is hard to imagine today.

Fewer Canadians smoke today than in the past. In the 1980s, tobacco use was quite common in Canada, with about 35 percent of adults reporting that they smoked. Today, about 22 percent of men over age 15 smoke and 17 percent of women in that age range do. The most prevalent use of tobacco is by young people aged 15–24 (Health Canada, 2004). Even so, rates of smoking by teen girls and boys are now lower than at any time since smoking rates began to be monitored in 1965.

Cannabis

Marijuana and hashish are derived from the plant *cannabis sativa* and have psychoactive properties. These drugs are illegal but are sometimes called "soft" drugs. The plant is Asian in origin and has been used by humans for various purposes for thousands of years (Rudgley, 1999). Cannabis has been used medically to treat migraines, epilepsy, and bipolar disorder, as well as multiple sclerosis. Since 2003, when the Ontario Court of Appeal set out new rules for access to medical marijuana, it has become easier for Canadians to obtain such cannabis legally. Cannabis plants are also used to make *hemp*, a naturally strong fibre that can be used in textile manufacture. When cannabis is used for its psychotropic properties, it is generally smoked in a variety of forms, with such implements as pipes, *bongs*, or cigarettes, called *joints*. It can also be eaten.

There is some debate about the effects of marijuana on a user. Proponents of the drug's legalization often downplay its potential to be addictive, while officials—particularly US officials—involved in seeking to reduce public use of marijuana stress that its ill effects can be significant, and they characterize it as a "gateway drug" that leads to the use of "harder" drugs. It is difficult, because of the current illegality of cannabis use and because it tends to be used in conjunction with alcohol and tobacco, to determine the precise impact of this drug on a person's health. Unlike tobacco, cannabis has not yet been shown to cause lung cancer and it is thus far unclear to what extent cannabis use by a pregnant woman can contribute to birth defects and other issues regarding her fetus (Dreher, Nugent & Hudgins, 1994). There does appear to be a link between marijuana use and impairments to memory function, and there is some research linking early marijuana use to schizophrenia (Arseneault et al., 2002). Also, while there is a lack of clear evidence that marijuana is physically addictive, it can certainly cause psychological addiction, and this is often related to loss of motivation and to apathy in the user.

Where the social acceptability of tobacco use has decreased over the past few decades, social acceptance of marijuana use has increased. In 2004, 35 percent of Canadians reported having tried marijuana. Fourteen percent of survey respondents reported using marijuana daily, a percentage similar to that of tobacco smokers (Health Canada, 2004). However, while the use of such psychoactive drugs as caffeine, tobacco, and alcohol is legal, marijuana use, though quite common in Canada, remains illegal.

Medications

Certain drugs, known as medications or *pharmaceuticals*, are known to reduce symptoms of, and even cure, illnesses and medical conditions. Sometimes, medications can be used to prevent conditions that have not yet arisen. Legal regulation has divided such medications into two varieties, prescription and *over-the-counter (OTC)*. Note that the medications covered by this distinction tend to vary by country and legal context.

People can become dependent upon or abuse medications as they can any other drug. This is not surprising, given that the active ingredients in some medications are the same as those in certain illegal drugs.

PRESCRIPTION DRUGS

These are medications that can only be dispensed by professionals—generally by a pharmacist—on the written instruction, or *prescription*, of a physician. These medications, also called *behind-the-counter (BTC) drugs*, are generally considered dangerous enough not to be made available to the public for consumption without very stringent restrictions.

Many substances that are otherwise illegal, such as narcotics, are legal when distributed by prescription. There is a wide variety of prescription drugs; they have many different effects and can become dangerous when used in combination with other drugs. There are many prescription drugs to which people can become addicted. Often, they will then abuse them, and start obtaining them illegally. Medications that are commonly abused include opioids (painkillers, like oxycodone), sedatives (like Valium), stimulants (like Ritalin), mood stabilizers (like lithium), and antidepressants (like Prozac). Recent estimates are that nearly 5 million Canadians use or abuse prescription painkillers, sleeping pills, tranquilizers, anti-depressants, and stimulants (Riley, 1998).

OVER-THE-COUNTER DRUGS

Physicians and pharmacists consider these medications safe enough for people to take without specific prescription or instructions about amount and frequency. If taken inappropriately, in large doses or in combination with alcohol and other drugs, these substances—cold remedies, for example—can sometimes produce intoxication, euphoria, and hallucinations. Other OTC drugs that are often abused are diet pills, which are stimulants and can produce psychotropic effects.

"Hard" Drugs

We will include in a single group the large number of illegal drugs other than cannabis. Sometimes called "hard drugs," these include cocaine and its derivatives, including crack, LSD, and heroin.

Cocaine and its derivatives, including crack, which is an impure "freebase" form of the drug, are made from the coca plant found primarily in South and Central America. Cocaine is used medically, as an anaesthetic, in certain surgeries. It is also used recreationally, as a stimulant. Users most often smoke the drug or snort it up their noses, allowing it to coat the mucous membranes of their sinuses, although coca leaves can also be chewed or eaten. Cocaine produces in the user conditions of hyperactivity, nervousness, restlessness, and euphoria. With frequent usage or high doses, the user can experience hallucinations, itching, paranoid delusions, and irregular heart rhythm (tachycardia) that can ultimately lead to fatal heart issues, especially heart attacks. Withdrawal symptoms can include hunger, pain, sleep disturbances, and a runny nose.

LSD, also known as "acid," is a synthetic hallucinogenic drug that gives users visual and auditory hallucinations and changes their perceptions, emotional states, and consciousness. High doses of hallucinogenic drugs taken over time have been linked to many mental illnesses, including schizophrenia and Alzheimer's. Also, some effects of the drug can persist over time; years after they have ceased to consume the drug, users can have *flashbacks* that alter their perception.

Heroin is a semi-synthetic opioid made originally from poppies, most commonly from Afghanistan. It is most often injected or smoked. It is used medically as a painkiller and is also used illegally for recreational purposes. Heroin causes euphoria in the user and is highly addictive. Once a person becomes dependent upon heroin, he or she often becomes tolerant to it and, though no longer experiencing euphoria through its use, will experience intense and extremely painful withdrawal symptoms if the drug is not taken regularly. Heroin can cause respiratory arrest, coma, seizure, and death. Large doses of heroin are fatal. Pregnant women who take heroin may miscarry or may give birth to children who have mental or physical problems and who are themselves addicted to the drug.

Illegal drugs proliferated in Canada beginning around the 1960s and have become common across the country. Currently, illicit drugs can be found in all urban and rural areas of the country and, contrary to popular belief, there are often greater drug problems in rural areas than in the city (Jennisson, 1992). The drugs, very different from each other with respect to their particular physiological effects, are similar in that they are prohibited criminally in Canada, are not generally socially acceptable, and can have significant long-term consequences for the user.

Illegal drug use tends to be more common among young people than among older adults, although, with the exception of cannabis use, it remains relatively uncommon. Less than 10 percent of Canadians in any age group have ever tried these "hard" drugs (Health Canada, n.d.).

Sugars and Fats

As mentioned, a distinction has traditionally been drawn between food consumption and psychoactive drug use and abuse. More recently, this distinction has been blurred. Canada, like the United States and most other Western nations, is experiencing an epidemic of **obesity**, or excessive body weight, which is more and more being seen as a serious social and public health issue.

In many societies, physical plumpness has been sought after as an ideal, associated with fertility and physical health, as well as wealth. More recently, obesity has become widely regarded as unattractive and undesirable. This social distaste for obesity is related to the proliferation of negative body image issues, particularly among young women and girls. It is also related to a rise in eating disorders, such as *anorexia nervosa*, which causes a person to starve him- or herself, and *bulimia*, whose sufferers binge eat and then deliberately vomit. These eating disorders can be fatal. So can obesity itself. Obesity is associated with several health issues, including cardiovascular disease, type 2 diabetes, high blood pressure, and high cholesterol, as well as depression, joint injury, pain, and even early death.

Obesity has many causes, but it is primarily caused by inactivity and overeating, particularly of *junk food*—food that contains high levels of salt, sugar, and fat while lacking proteins, vitamins, and fibre. Junk food ingredients possess many of the properties of psychoactive drugs: they act upon the body in such a way as to produce a brief "high," and can lead some people to *compulsively* overeat—that is, to find it tremendously difficult to stop consuming excess fats and sugars. Increasingly, overeating is being understood as an addiction. New research shows that an obese person's desire for food acts on the brain in the same manner as a drug user's need for narcotics and other substances (CBS News, 2006). There is a 12-step program for compulsive overeaters called *Overeaters Anonymous*, and there are many other support programs to help people lose weight. Canada's Heart and Stroke Foundation proclaimed in 2004 that "fat is the new tobacco," which reflects a growing understanding of overeating as an addiction. There can be little doubt that, in the coming years, public health advocacy will produce a broader public acceptance that fatty, sugary, and salty foods are psychoactive substances (Paradis, 2004).

ADDICTIONS

Addictions are perhaps the most obvious and certainly the most direct harm caused by substance use. **Drug addiction** is the situation or condition in which a person takes a drug by compulsion, despite the potential harm to him- or herself and to others by doing so, and in the face of his or her own desire to stop doing so. There are two aspects to this compulsion, both physical and psychological.

Physically, once a person uses a substance habitually for a certain period of time (the time will vary depending upon the drug and the user), his or her body adapts to a point where he or she does not feel normal without it and its absence triggers physical symptoms of *withdrawal* in the user. Such symptoms are usually the opposite of the effects sought and produced by taking the drug. Most drugs that people abuse produce *euphoria*, and withdrawal from them can result in depression, anxiety, and intense cravings for the drug. Withdrawal by an addict from certain drugs, even alcohol, can result in seizures, *delirium tremens*, and even death.

Psychologically, once a person becomes accustomed to using a substance, he or she can become emotionally dependent upon its effects. The user feels compelled to continue using the drug in order to feel normal.

It is often very difficult for users to recover from drug addiction. The different approaches to recovery vary according to the duration of the addiction and the type of drug being used, and to the particular needs of the individual user. Sometimes psychological therapy is used, sometimes a combination of individual and group counselling. Even acupuncture is sometimes used. The best-known recovery programs are "12-step" programs, including Narcotics Anonymous and, especially, Alcoholics Anonymous. These programs, some of which have a religious orientation, are geared to helping addicts help themselves by taking responsibility for their own recoveries, admitting they have problems, and working in groups to acknowledge their successes, challenges, and failures in dealing with their addictions. There are also non-religious organizations that deal with addictions, such as Secular Organizations for Sobriety (http://www.secularsobriety.org) and others. There also exist residential treatment programs.

SOCIAL ISSUES

Psychoactive drug use affects users in ways both indirectly and directly related to the drug use itself. In addition to the direct harms discussed above, there are many collateral, or indirect, harms related to substance abuse. Many of the indirect effects of drug abuse are related to, and often the cause of, social problems. Drug use affects not just the users themselves but those close to them and, ultimately, Canadian society as a whole. A 1996 study estimated that drug abuse costs Canada at least $18.45 billion annually, a figure representing 2.7 percent of our GDP (gross domestic product) at that time (CCSA, 1996). This monetary figure cannot of course reflect the intangible costs of substance abuse, including pain, suffering, death, and bereavement, or the years irretrievably lost to abusers and their family members. What this figure does reflect is health-care costs arising from drug-related death and illness; research, education, and law enforcement costs; and welfare costs.

Family, Career, and Financial Problems

Drug use can make it difficult for a person to maintain a normal career and family life. People with alcohol dependencies or drug addictions must work like everyone else. Drug use can affect work performance; an employee will not be as productive and may compromise the safety of him- or herself and of others if he or she is impaired or otherwise affected by a psychotropic substance while on the job. Research shows that about 25 percent of accidents at work involve intoxicated people injuring themselves and others. A drug addict's compulsive need to obtain more of the addictive substance interferes with life in a workplace. People who are addicted to drugs often have difficulty attending work regularly, and alcoholism and other addictions are correlated with frequent worker absenteeism. Drug users tend to be absent from work two to three times more often than other employees (Safework: Programme on Safety and Health at Work and the Environment, 2000).

Financial problems often result from drug abuse. A drug user may spend all of his or her available money on alcohol or drugs, which are expensive. Drug addiction often leads to a downward spiral in which a user loses his or her job and is relegated to poverty. Such poverty affects not just the user but all of his or her dependants, and, because the user can become dependent upon social assistance for financial support, it ultimately affects all Canadian taxpayers.

Substance abuse interferes with the user's ability to forge positive relationships within and outside his or her family. One family member's drug addiction often has negative consequences for the entire family group. Drug use is correlated with family violence and disruptions in child rearing. There are several ways in which drug use is related to violence in the home. Men who abuse their partners have often used alcohol or other drugs before committing an assault, and they may abuse drugs and alcohol after the assault to diminish their feelings of guilt and shame. Adults who were abused as children may abuse substances as a mechanism to cope with memories they are not able to deal with emotionally. Women living with an abusive partner may turn to alcohol or other substances, especially sedatives and sleeping pills, to deal with the fear, anxiety, and pain they face in the abusive relationship.

Parents who are dependent upon or addicted to drugs often abuse and neglect their children. As a result, child welfare authorities often have to intervene to take the children of substance abusers into state care. Regardless of whether such an intervention occurs, children of parents addicted to drugs or alcohol will often leave home young. A large proportion of street youth come from homes where drug abuse and violence are problems (Public Health Agency of Canada, 1993). Early homelessness in turn puts these children at great risk of victimization by violence, prostitution, and substance addiction of their own.

Criminalization

Different psychoactive substances or drugs are treated differently by the law in Canada. Because many psychoactive substances are illegal, people involved in even recreational substance use can be subjected to criminal consequences. This legal treatment often reflects no more than a tradition of illegality surrounding a substance, and is not necessarily rational or intuitive. For example, marijuana continues to be illegal in Canada while tobacco use remains legal in the face of a growing lobby of scientists and social advocates. Scientists have provided increasingly sound evidence that tobacco is lethal to its users as well as to those in the users' proximity, who can die from *second-hand smoke.* In any case, whatever the reader's standpoint regarding whether tobacco and marijuana use *should* be illegal, it remains the case that marijuana currently is illegal. Charges for drug use are an entry point into criminalization for many people who do not otherwise engage in criminal activity. Consequences of a criminal record can include barriers to travel, difficulties in obtaining employment, and social stigmatization even after legal penalties are paid. All of these consequences can prevent a person charged with a drug-related offence from resuming a "normal" life. People not directly involved in drug use themselves may lose loved ones, who are important income sources for their families, to criminalization and incarceration. And, of course, all members of society have to pay for the costs of the justice system.

There are strong connections between addictions, substance abuse, and the sex trade. Dependence upon illicit, and usually expensive, substances can be a factor propelling individuals into sex work. Encouragement and fostering of sex workers' substance addictions by pimps or procurers is a key way for these individuals to exert and maintain control over prostitutes. Involvement in the sex trade can become a serious collateral effect of substance abuse. This trade and its consequences for sex workers is discussed in chapter 4.

Illegal Drug Trade

Related to the criminalization of many drugs is the international black market in substances, known as the **illegal drug trade**. Drugs for Canadian consumption are produced here at home and all over the world, in places as remote and disparate as Colombia, Afghanistan, and eastern Europe. Illegal drugs are brought secretly across international borders by various means. Massive profits are made on this trade every year despite the efforts of law enforcement agencies. A United Nations survey conducted in the 1990s indicated that the annual dollar value of the international drug trade runs into the billions and is second only to the annual dollar value of the arms trade (Library of Parliament, 2003). Highly organized crime syndicates have developed around the international trade in illegal drugs. There is also a significant trade in the illegal sale and *trafficking* of legal drugs, such as *opioids* (which have similar effects to heroin), as well as in the illegal sale of *bootleg* alcohol and cigarettes. Violence, imprisonment, and social unrest around the world are part of the collateral damage caused by this illicit international industry.

Motor Vehicle Accidents

Another way in which people who use psychoactive substances can be criminalized and also face regulatory penalties is by operating motor vehicles, such as cars and boats, while under the influence of a psychoactive substance. They can face fines, driving prohibitions, and even jail time for the impaired operation of motor vehicles. A recent statistic, from 2002, showed that police laid 81,000 charges in relation to impaired driving in Canada that year, which translates into a high cost for policing (Statistics Canada, 2003).

Of course, the rationale for laws against the impaired operation of motor vehicles has to do with the activity's enormous cost in human life. A conservative 1992 estimate, for example, was that 1,021 Canadian men and 456 women died that year in motor vehicle accidents caused by impaired driving. More recent figures from MADD (Mothers Against Drunk Driving) indicate that 4 people die and about 190 are injured daily as a direct result of impaired driving (n.d.). Most of these people are young. These figures do not include the many more people who, while not impaired themselves, were injured in such accidents, or whose lives were affected by the injury or death of a loved one in an accident caused by impaired driving. In other words, the most significant collateral damage of impaired driving is less the legal penalties suffered by the guilty individuals than the physical harm suffered by the individuals themselves, by their passengers, and by innocent bystanders.

Accidental Death and Injury

In addition to the physical harm caused by the impaired operation of motor vehicles, substance use also contributes to all kinds of injuries and accidental deaths. There is a strong positive correlation between high rates of per capita alcohol consumption and high rates of accidental death and injury (Skog, 2003). Alcohol abuse contributes to general recklessness and fighting among young males as well as to the involvement of young females in unwanted or unplanned sexual relations, which in turn can lead to the spread of sexually transmitted diseases.

Health Problems

As well as causing health problems through accidents and other incidents, substance abuse can cause health problems more directly, as previously discussed in some detail in the profiles of the particular substances. Most if not all drugs can lead directly to ill health if abused. For example, the negative health effects of tobacco and alcohol have been widely publicized in recent years. A 1992 estimate showed that, in that year, alcoholic liver cirrhosis resulted in 960 deaths and 908 alcohol-related suicides. The same year, an estimated 208,095 Canadians were hospitalized and 33,498 died from lung cancer, pulmonary disease, heart disease, and other health problems caused by tobacco use. An estimated 732 people, mostly men, died as a result of illicit drug use the same year (CCSA, 1996). The numbers in Health Canada's more recent estimates are still higher: 45, 214 drug- and alcohol-related deaths per year (Health Canada, 1999). All of these hospital admissions and deaths, in addition to their human price, cost Canadian taxpayers money.

Drug use can also lead to disease more indirectly. One of the major routes by which the AIDS virus is spread is the needles shared by intravenous drug users—heroin or cocaine users. Drug use and addiction can also weaken a user's immunity, making him or her more vulnerable to opportunistic infections.

ANALYSIS

SOCIAL ISSUES OF SUBSTANCE ABUSE

Implicit in the topic of substance abuse is that there is no settled definition of what substances and what uses constitute it. How a substance is used, who uses it, and when it is used are defined by the norms of the users and not by the nature of the substance itself. Many argue that alcohol is far more harmful than marijuana, but alcohol is publicly recognized as an acceptable substance when controlled. Its abuse is socially defined as an individual weakness. Marijuana, on the other hand, is associated with a fringe element of society, and its use (except for medical reasons) is socially defined as wrong.

Given the very social nature of substance abuse, it would be helpful to take the abuse of tobacco and the issue of obesity as two examples of the social and political nature of substance abuse.

To begin, we will look at tobacco use in Canada. A first step would be to form a topic research statement.

Topic Focus and Research Statement

Once you have gathered current information about the issue, you are ready to compose your topic statement. Your topic statement must adhere to the characteristics already introduced, but it must also narrow your topic to a more specific theme. Inclusion of specific references to populations involved and to events that have occurred will help. The following is an expanded topic statement. (Use the list of characteristics needed for topic statements as a checklist, and see if you can identify those characteristics in the following topic statement.)

> Tobacco use in Canada is waning in popularity, but remains the greatest cause of preventable illness and death in Canada. The health and financial costs of tobacco use are unacceptable to the majority of Canadians, and it is this growing majority who are strenuously promoting a ban on smoking in Canada. Committed smokers continue to resist, but as long as the deaths associated with smoking have continued to rise, their arguments have been largely overwhelmed.

Note that smoking itself is *not* the social issue, *nor* is the number of deaths. You could say that these have *triggered* the issue. But *the issue is a social issue because of the social actions undertaken by those who find tobacco use unacceptable.* This should become clear in the answers to the nine guide questions. It is also an essential distinction in focus. Your goal is to understand what a social issue is; it is not simply to research the various events and the medical, biological, or statistical facts that have prompted the social issue.

A sample outline of answers to the nine guide questions is provided for you here.

The Nine Guide Questions

SOCIAL ISSUE STATUS

Q1. Is the issue problematic to many people, and are there many people voicing their concerns or claiming that the issue is unacceptable?

Yes. Smoking is a leading cause of illness and premature death in Canada, and it places a heavy financial burden on Canadians. (*Trigger* of social issue.) A growing number of Canadians are promoting a smoking ban in Canada. (*Numerous voices* identifying that smoking is not acceptable.)

Q2. Is the issue specific to a particular social context—that is, modern Canadian society?

Yes. Currently, Canadians from every region in the country are advocating the elimination of smoking in all public places. Many municipalities, such as Ottawa and Sault Ste. Marie in Ontario, and Victoria in British Columbia, have passed bylaws that prohibit smoking in all public areas. (Reference to specific and *current* events and actions in *Canada.*) Many more municipalities are about to follow suit.

Q3. Do the people voicing their concerns have a vision of the way things should be—that is, a goal?

Yes. Tobacco is the leading cause of preventable illness and death in the world. Organizations like the Ontario Tobacco-free Network are aggressively working to raise public awareness of the health risks associated with tobacco use and to promote the implementation of smoke-free bylaws (Waddell, 2004). Their aim is for Canada to be 100 percent smoke-free. (*Goals and objectives* established by organizations and groups advocating change; that is, the *goals of the "voices."*)

Q4. Are there the means to improve the situation and to achieve the vision?

Yes. The health risks associated with tobacco use are known. *Government initiatives* through tax legislation and other laws; *municipal actions* such as the banning of smoking in all public places; and *strenuous education* and *intervention* efforts on the part of organizations like the Canadian Medical Association—these are all effective means of achieving the goal of a smoke-free Canada. (Reference to specific actions and proposed actions currently being implemented to resolve the problem of tobacco use.)

Note that these questions and answers serve only to confirm that tobacco use in Canada is a current social issue. The trigger for the issue has been the public's growing awareness of the health hazards associated with smoking. The growth of groups and organizations that are voicing the opinion that smoking is unacceptable indicates that a social issue has emerged.

SOCIAL ISSUE EVOLUTION

The remainder of the nine guide questions help determine how developed a social issue is. A social issue is in an emergent stage when the groups attracting attention to it are a small minority and its public profile is almost non-existent. Once the public starts to choose sides regarding an issue, and once legislation or formal changes to resolve it have been put into place, then an issue has become established. As noted in chapter 1, a social issue may cycle through definition and policy implementation many times before it is finally resolved.

Q5. Who and what groups and organizations are calling for public attention?

> There are numerous groups and organizations calling for attention to the health risks associated with smoking and many others that are striving to make Canada smoke-free. Among these organizations are government-sponsored health organizations such as the Red Cross, the Lung Association, and the Canadian Medical Association. Others include social activist groups such as the Ontario Tobacco-free Network.

Q6. What public interest in the issue has there been? What media coverage or promotion has there been?

> The tobacco issue has generated public debate for years. Arguments asserting the damaging effects of tobacco have been countered by claims that any actions to restrict smoking would hinder civil liberties. Smoking has, with the help of the media, taken on many powerful symbolic meanings such as independence, sexiness, and rebellion. Most recently, public concern has been focused on the damage that second-hand smoke can inflict on non-smokers and children.

Q7. How has society aligned itself around the issue? What kinds of demands have been made, and what organizations and coalitions have been formed?

> In the 1970s, non-smokers felt obliged to defer to smokers, and smokers had majority rights. Now the balance has swung in favour of the non-smoking public. More and more municipalities are voting to be entirely smoke-free. Smokers across Canada have accepted the requirement that they must smoke outside public buildings and workplaces. The last refuge for smokers has been bars and restaurants, and it is in this business sector that resistance to anti-smoking measures has mainly surfaced, from business owners who fear that alienating the smoking public will create revenue losses. However, the fact is that business in these traditional smoking havens has in many cases remained steady or even increased despite the smoking bans.

Q8. What policies have been initiated or proposed?

> The most notable recent policies have been municipal bylaws that make smoking illegal in any public gathering place. Municipalities across Canada and across the world are following suit.

Q9. What impact have these initiatives or proposals had on the resolution or intensifying of the issue?

So far, despite fears about the laws' effects, most municipalities have accepted the change without resistance.

CONCLUSION: WHERE IN ITS EVOLUTION IS THE ISSUE OF "TOBACCO USE IN CANADA"?

From the answers to the last of the nine guide questions, we can now determine whether the social issue of tobacco use in Canada is emerging or established. In view of the public involvement and of the duration of the controversy, you could argue that the issue has become well established. The resolution of the issue—that is, the realized vision of Canada as smoke-free and thus free of health hazards caused by tobacco use—seems near at hand. The next cycle in the issue of tobacco use in Canada may focus on the production and distribution of tobacco products, or it could focus on the rights of smokers to be employed in non-smoking workplaces or on the rights of smokers to benefit from publicly funded medical treatments.

PRACTISE USING THE NINE GUIDE QUESTIONS

Before moving on to a theoretical analysis of the issue of tobacco use in Canada, you have an opportunity to apply the template of the nine guide questions to an assessment of obesity in Canada as a social issue. The following is a summary of information about obesity. Margin notes identifying what guide questions to apply are included as your guide. As you know by now, the first four questions help establish whether an issue is a *social* issue. The remaining five help determine how established the issue is.

OBESITY IN CANADA

What Is the Problem?

answers to the nine guide questions

On average, Canadians are getting fatter. In fact, North Americans are the fattest people on the planet, Canadians being a close second to Americans. Statistics Canada shows that 46 percent of Canadians are overweight, and another 15 percent are medically obese (Ko, 2002).

Being overweight or obese is a problem because obesity is believed to put Canadians at risk of sudden death, heart disease, colon cancer, and other medical conditions such as type 2 diabetes. Furthermore, Health Canada reports reveal that obesity and inactivity cost the country $3.1 billion annually and lead to the deaths of 21,000 Canadians each year (Ko, 2002). Some people have medical conditions that make it difficult for them to lose weight, but most Canadians have developed unhealthy habits of overeating and inactivity. Fast food and lack of exercise are the main reasons that Canadians are gaining weight and declining in health.

trigger

Who Is Complaining?

answers to questions 1 and 5

In April 2002, the World Health Organization (WHO) began warning that physical inactivity and sedentary lifestyles cause 2 million deaths per year. The problem is huge, according to the WHO, because it now ranks among the ten leading causes of death and disability (Wharry, 2002). In response, Health Canada has launched programs and studies to address the problem.

answers to questions 5, 6, and 7

In 2002, the federal health minister, Anne McLellan, announced that she was initiating programs that would focus on childhood obesity. The Canadian Medical Association (CMA), amid reports that the obesity rate in Canada has more than doubled since 1981, was also urging action (Wharry, 2002).

answer to question 8

In addition, medical theorists and mental health workers across Canada are reporting on the connection between stress and illness among employees and a sedentary lifestyle. From a financial point of view, the ultimate outcome of this sedentary trend is not only increased rates of disease and disability, but reduced economic productivity. The Heart and Stroke Foundation and the Canadian Mental Health Association have both documented the high dollar cost of the health and disability caused by stress. For this reason, major corporations, including the Fortune 500 companies of Canada, are taking notice and initiating changes (Robin, 2003).

answers to questions 1, 5, and 8

Where Did This Problem Originate?

Over the past 100 years, Canadians have been doing less and less physical labour in their daily employment. The modern workplace requires of its employees long hours of stress and inactivity. In 1993, Dofasco Steel, based in Hamilton, Ontario, did a health audit of its workforce. The study showed that those workers who smoked and were overweight had an increased risk of accidents and missed an average of 106 work hours annually—double that of their non-smoking, normal-weighted co-workers (Robin, 2003).

answer to question 8

Perhaps a greater cause for alarm is that children today, compared with the past, spend more time watching TV, playing electronic games, and, in short, being inactive. In the past 15 years, obesity rates among children have swelled: 50 percent among children aged 6 to 11, and 40 percent among children aged 12 to 17. In Ontario alone, obesity rates among children have tripled over one generation. The American Psychiatric Association (APA) has advised that reducing TV time would have a significant and beneficial impact on childhood weight problems. Studies show that children who watch four or more hours of TV each day have the highest rates of obesity (Ko, 2002). Not only are kids inactive when they watch TV, but they are bombarded with food ads. Children today see an average of 40,000 food ads per year as compared to the 20,000 that children of the 1970s saw (USA Today, 2004, February 25).

answers to questions 3, 4, and 8

What Changes Can Be Made?

Eat less and exercise more is the refrain of most doctors and health professionals. Be active and eat better are the other admonishments. Others, including Dr. David Butler Jones, chief medical officer of the Canadian Public Health Association in 2002, recommend that Canadians create an environment where the healthiest choices are the easiest choices. At the moment, healthy choices are twice the cost of easy choices like fries and gravy and pop (Ko, 2002). Despite the North American guilt about fat, the consumption of fat has not decreased (Ko, 2002).

answers to questions 8 and 9

Others encourage Canadians to become more active. Compared to Europeans, Canadians walk less than 20 percent of the distances that Europeans on average walk. Only 19 percent of high-school students are active for 20 minutes or more per day (Ko, 2002).

What Changes Are Being Made?

A number of corporate and public measures indicate that a wellness revolution is emerging. Some Canadian corporations, such as BC Hydro and Dofasco Steel, are leading other corporations in acknowledging the link between business success and the health of employees. Such corporations are instituting wellness, diet, and fitness programs. However, as sociologist Graham Lowe of the Graham Lowe Group emphasizes, no investment in wellness programs will help if the corporate culture does not actively support wellness (Robin, 2003).

answers to questions 8 and 9

In response to public demands and competition pressure, numerous fast food chains are promoting healthy menu changes. Recently, McDonald's has followed Wendy's lead by offering "entre salads," and it has altered the composition of its chicken McNuggets to pure white meat (Horovitz, 2004). Subway has recently introduced Atkins-friendly sandwiches (USA Today, 2004, February 9), and Burger King is going bunless (MacArthur, 2004). Any survey of grocery shelves will show the prevalence of diet-conscious options. The recent low-carb trend has prompted a noticeable slump in bread sales (Coxe, 2004).

How Do Canadians React to These Initiatives?

Canadians appear to have wakened to the health risks associated with being overweight. But despite the many diet options, Canadians continue to grow fatter and less healthy owing to sedentary lifestyles, stress, and overabundant food. Canadians flock to fad diets and are conscious about low fat or low carbs, but have not yet adopted effective lifestyle choices. Most Canadians don't know how to put nutritional knowledge into practice, and most are confused by the conflicting claims about what are healthy foods (Gorman, 2003). Despite the immense focus on food, nutrition, and body image, Canadian efforts to be healthy have failed.

answer to question 9

Is Obesity in Canada a Social Issue?

Q1. Is the issue problematic to many people, and are there many people voicing their concerns or claiming that the issue is unacceptable?

____

____

____

____

____

Q2. Is the issue specific to a particular social context—that is, modern Canadian society?

Q3. Do the people voicing their concerns have a vision of the way things should be—that is, a goal?

Q4. Are there means to improve the situation and to achieve the vision?

Where in Its Evolution Is the Issue of Obesity in Canada?

Q5. Who and what organizations are calling for public attention?

Q6. What public interest in the issue has there been? What media coverage or promotion has there been?

Q7. How has society aligned itself around the issue? What kinds of demands have been made, and what organizations and coalitions have been formed?

Q8. What policies have been initiated or proposed?

Q9. What impact have these initiatives or proposals had on the resolution or intensifying of the issue? (Note that this final question often leads back to another cycle through questions 5 to 9: there are groups or organizations that oppose the formal policy changes that have been implemented in response to a social issue, and the new opposing "voices" thus initiate another social issue that can be tracked by questions 5 through 9.)

Draw conclusions, and form a topic sentence for obesity in Canada as a social issue.

THEORETICAL ANALYSES OF SOCIAL ISSUES

Once you have identified a social issue, and once you know whether it is established or emerging, your next task is to try to understand the "whys" of the issue. What social events have given rise it? What impacts is the issue having? What is the likely future of the issue? What is the history of the issue? You can address all of these questions by using the theoretical perspectives of sociology: structural functionalist, social conflict, symbolic interactionist, social constructionist, and feminist. In this chapter, you will be given templates of the structural functionalist, social conflict, and symbolic interactionist perspectives. The templates for the social conflict and symbolic interactionist can be adapted for the social constructionist and feminist paradigms. You will be introduced to these adaptations in later chapters.

A Structural Functionalist Analysis

The structural functionalist perspective, which is a macro perspective, focuses on the functions of society's institutions and structures. According to this paradigm, all social institutions are integrated with all others through their specialized functions. Any change or disruption to the integration of the functions or to the nature of the functions themselves is considered dysfunctional. For this reason, any analysis that adopts the structural functionalist perspective is especially suitable to discovering what in society has changed and what, in consequence, has been disrupted in such a way as to create a social issue. Remember, theoretical perspectives are ideal models, and a social analyst's task is to apply the model to the reality of actual social events. Adopting the structural functionalist perspective means comparing the model of a functioning, stable society with a social reality that is suffering from disruptions caused by social change. Therefore, from a structural functionalist perspective, a social issue can be understood as a *deviation* from the *expected* functioning of society.

In summary, the structural functionalist perspective is useful for determining what in society is stable and contributes to the viability of its people. It is effective for pinpointing the origin and location of a social issue (that is, the disruption of what was once stable and functioning).

QUESTIONS THAT GUIDE A STRUCTURAL FUNCTIONALIST ANALYSIS: TOBACCO USE IN CANADA

There are three questions that will help you assume a structural functionalist perspective. For the issue of tobacco use in Canada, you can accept that the triggers for it have been the reports of smoking's damaging effects on health and the public costs associated with these effects. Your task, as an analyst, is to determine how tobacco use in Canada has impaired the normal or stable functioning of society.

1. What **social institutions** or **structures** are primarily involved in the issue?

   Given the historical importance of the tobacco industry in Canadian society, the structure that is primarily involved in the issue of tobacco use is the **economy**. The institutions of the **family** and of **education** are also involved, but in secondary roles.

Now that you have identified the social institutions most crucially involved, you need to describe their "normal" functioning—that is, how they function when society is stable and integrated. In other words, you need to identify the **manifest functions** of these institutions. Stated in terms of **real** as opposed to **ideal society**, you need to sketch the ideal model of society (manifest functions) so that you can compare it with the real society, with all its social events and disruptions.

2. What are the manifest functions of these social institutions or structures when society is operating as expected?

   Refer to any introductory sociology text for descriptions of social institutions and their manifest functions. Note that the manifest functions of any social institution are its specialized contributions to the whole society's functioning. It is important to repeat that manifest functions contribute beneficially to the survival of society as a whole by supporting its stability and integration. In other words, the manifest functions *are not* the characteristics of a social issue. Rather, *they are the specialized consequences of the social institutions when these institutions are functioning as they should. A social issue is the disruption of these functions.*

   A common set of values underlies the social institutions of Canada. Among these is our belief in democratic rights and freedom and in independence of decision or choice. The general acceptance of these values permits the profit incentive and the free market to prevail in our economic structures. It also means that within the institutions of education and media, we are free to choose and we are free to influence others' choices. Exercise of these freedoms is evident in socialization patterns that begin in the family and in educational institutions. The social institutions of law and justice protect these freedoms. In other words, the prevailing social values are upheld by all institutions in a society, which are thus woven together in a condition of social cohesiveness and interdependency.

The final step in a structural functionalist analysis is to compare real society with the ideal and thus determine what has been changed or disrupted. This step enables you to pinpoint the origin and location of a social issue.

3. What social events or trends are interrupting specific functions or the integration of the functions?

   The manifest functions of the economy are the production and distribution of goods and services, and the employment of an available workforce. According to Statistics Canada (Health Canada, 2004), in 2003 the tobacco products industry contributed $1.1 billion to the economy, and although this represents a 4.8 percent drop in its contribution to Canada's GDP since 1997, the tobacco products industry is still an important part of Canada's economy in terms of the number of jobs it provides and the revenues that it generates.

   However, the consumption of the product generates far greater costs to society than it does revenues. Because the costs to society of tobacco use outweigh its economic benefits, there is an *inherent dysfunction created by the production and distribution of tobacco products.* In other words, there is a dysfunction in the economy that has triggered dysfunction throughout associated social institutions. For example, according to the Canadian Reference Centre as reported in the *Toronto Star* in 2004, 21 percent of Canadians over the age of 15 smoke, and $11.3 billion is the annual cost of treating tobacco-related illness in Ontario. The annual cost in terms of lost productivity is $2.6 billion (Waddell, 2004). In other words, the economic costs of tobacco use far outweigh the economic benefits.

Why is it that, given these figures, there is relatively little voiced concern about the tremendous toll on society from tobacco use? Perhaps the reason is that those who profit (most obviously, tobacco companies) are well known and easily identifiable as a powerful lobby group and voice. On the other hand, those who pay (most obviously, those with lung cancer and heart disease) are not readily identifiable or vocal as social activists. Put another way, the benefits of tobacco use tend to be direct and quantifiable, and the costs tend to be indirect and, therefore, invisible. Clearly this reveals a fault in the functioning of the economy, and this fault has become evident in the burdens (dysfunctions) being borne by the social institutions of government and health care. The specific nature of these burdens/**dysfunctions** has been outlined previously.

There are three important points to make here. The first is that all of the challenges and faults that have been described are *described in terms of the manifest functions that have failed.* The second is that the dysfunction, though originating in the economy, is experienced in other social institutions such as health care and the family. The final point is that a macro perspective has been maintained; at no time does the description of the dysfunction include an account of individual behaviours or individual experiences of the social issue.

A beneficial exercise would be to review the dysfunctions of each social institution so as to specify the manifest function that has failed.

SUMMARY CONCLUSION

A summary conclusion of your structural functionalist analysis should be a few brief statements describing what structures have broken down owing to the failure of certain manifest functions. Any estimations of what can be done to solve the issue would take the form of identifying what is required to bring the social system back to **equilibrium**.

QUESTIONS THAT GUIDE A STRUCTURAL FUNCTIONALIST ANALYSIS: OBESITY IN CANADA

Before moving to a social conflict analysis of smoking, you can now apply your newly acquired skills to creating a structural functionalist analysis of the issue of obesity in Canada. Use the following guide questions to accomplish this, and then write a summary conclusion of your findings.

1. What social institutions or structures are primarily involved in the issue?

   Hint: Name three at least. Begin by identifying a social difficulty created by the growth in obesity rates in Canada. Then name the institution within which the problem is first experienced or acknowledged.

2. What are the manifest functions of these social institutions or structures when society is operating as expected?

   Hint: Manifest functions are part of the model, so they do not change. You can refer to any introductory sociology text to obtain a list of manifest functions for any social institution.

3. What social events or trends are interrupting specific functions or the integration of the functions?

   Hint: This is where you refer to your research about what is currently happening with respect to the rates and trends of obesity in Canada. Compare these real events and social actions to the ideal (what is expected within each social institution). Then you will have identified the location and origin of the social issue of obesity. A final hint is to keep your analysis in the macro perspective: identify social institutions and manifest functions and dysfunctions; do not mention individuals in your analysis. In other words, when you identify a social action that is exerting negative consequences, describe its negative impact in terms of the *social functions* that are impaired or cannot operate.

SUMMARY CONCLUSION

____

____

____

____

____

____

____

____

____

____

Social Conflict Analysis

The social conflict perspective is a macro perspective, so it, too, ignores individuals and their behaviours. This perspective focuses on the competing groups, organizations, and associations that make up society. From this perspective, society is viewed as a dynamic network of organizations with competing interests and objectives. Their competition for a share of a common pool of resources results in shifts in power among the groups. Each group that realizes a gain does so at the expense of the other groups.

Conflict analysis is useful for understanding the history of a social issue, for identifying the dominant groups and their resources or bases of power, and for predicting the future course of an issue.

QUESTIONS THAT GUIDE A SOCIAL CONFLICT ANALYSIS: TOBACCO USE IN CANADA

There are three questions that will help you adopt a social conflict orientation toward a social issue. Each theoretical perspective is an ideal model, and each is used as a benchmark against which to compare real social events. The three questions that guide a social conflict perspective enable you to identify the ideal and then to compare it with the real events.

1. Who benefits in this issue? Who is exploited? What are the dominant groups?

   In order to answer this question, your perspective needs to expand beyond the specific altercations and conflicts that constitute the social issue. For example, simply to ask who benefits from smoking achieves nothing. Instead, pose this question in such a way as to explore how the tobacco industry has become so powerful that smoking, despite its health risks, has become as prevalent as it is. (Remember that 20 percent of Canadians still smoke, and that the tobacco industry remains a significant contributor to the Canadian economy.)

   To find the groups and organizations involved in an issue, you would need to research current journal articles and documentaries. You would already have these if you had identified that an issue was a social issue and if you had determined where it was in its evolution. Each time you encountered mention of a group or organization, you would have added it to a list.

In the case of tobacco use in Canada, you would include organizations such as the Canadian Cancer Society and the Tobacco-free Network. In deciding where to assign a group, ask yourself the following question: "Is this group benefiting or losing?" Or you can ask the following: "What values and interests does this group support or benefit from and therefore on which side is it located?" Choose names for the opposing sides, and finalize their classifications. Note that groups may appear on the same side by virtue of their efforts to achieve common or complementary goals even though in reality they are not allied. A list of major stakeholders and their designations follows.

Tobacco industry	Anti-smoking organizations
Philip Morris Tobacco	Canadian Cancer Society
R.J. Reynolds International	Canadian Medical Association
	Tobacco-free Network
	World Health Organization

Note that the list that appears here is not exhaustive, but it serves as an example.

Now that you have identified the groups that are critically involved, a review of the history of their involvement will reveal their **resources of power**. Resources of power include any assets controlled by a group that bring it advantage, and any events that have given it an advantage. This historical review should be guided by the second guide question for a social conflict analysis.

2. What resources or bases of power do the dominant groups have at their disposal to preserve their dominance?

   Note that this question presupposes that dominance is not static; it also implies the following question: "What resources do the inferior groups have that might threaten, or are threatening, the position of the dominant **stakeholders**?"

   A first step would be to review the history of the tobacco issue. As you read about events in the history of the issue, identify the major stakeholders and the resources that support them. For example, perhaps the most significant blow to the tobacco industries' power has been the success of many citizens groups, backed by health organizations like the CMA, in having municipalities enact laws that prohibit smoking in public areas such as bars, restaurants, bingo halls, and shops.

Once you have determined what resources and events benefit what side, you can make predictions about future changes. In other words, you can make predictions about the course of the social issue with respect to the stakeholders' relative power. Remember, a prediction is not like supporting your favourite team; it is an educated estimate concerning shifts in power and what influences will shape the issue's future. But before any such conclusions are drawn, the third of the three social conflict guide questions should be addressed.

3. What is the social definition of the issue? What values are in conflict?

   As suggested earlier, discerning where a stakeholder group stands in a controversy is difficult unless you understand the stakeholder's fundamental values. (Perhaps this question can serve in both positions one and three.) This question also helps you maintain a macro view of the social issue you are considering. For example, the case of two persons having a fist fight in a parking lot is not representative of a social issue. Simply identifying what prompted their altercation is not sufficient to identify a social issue. However, if their fight was an example of *racist harassment of one group by another*, then the fist fight would represent a social issue. From a social conflict perspective, the focus is the group values setting one party against the other, not the particular individuals involved.

   As indicated by the titles designated for each side, the conflicting values in the issue of tobacco use in Canada are profit and freedom of choice on the one hand, and, on the other hand, health and freedom from noxious substances. These conflicting cultural values figure prominently in the public support given to each side of the issue.

PREDICTION BASED ON A SOCIAL CONFLICT ANALYSIS

It is logical to conclude that the power of the tobacco products industry is being eroded by the growing and sustained anti-smoking sentiments of the Canadian public. However, the tobacco industry's power remains great; therefore, despite the ban on smoking in many municipalities across Canada (and the world), it is unlikely that smoking will be outlawed or eliminated in the very near future.

SOCIAL CONFLICT ANALYSIS OF OBESITY

Before moving to a symbolic interactionist analysis of smoking, you can now apply your newly acquired skills to a social conflict analysis of obesity in Canada. Use the following guide questions to accomplish this, and then write a summary conclusion of your findings.

1. Who benefits in this issue? Who is exploited? What are the dominant groups?

   Hint: Remember to expand your perspective. No one benefits from being fat, and no group is on a mission to make people fat, but what in our industry and lifestyle marketing has created the unprecedented numbers of overweight people? How does the success and power of one sector create the issue?

   ____

   ____

   ____

   ____

   ____

2. What resources or bases of power do the dominant groups have at their disposal to preserve their dominance?

   Hint: Once you have determined the answer to question 1, you can start to list the resources available to each side. Note that your resource list does not have to be equally balanced between the sides. However, your research needs to be as thorough as possible to ensure the accuracy of your evaluation of relative power.

3. What is the social definition of the issue? What values are in conflict?

   This question can be considered while you are doing question 1. It aims to identify the essential values that separate the two sides. As you research various social issues, you will find that groups that support the same side often do not have an actual alliance. It is their common support of certain values and goals that creates the appearance of an alliance.

SUMMARY CONCLUSION

In the space below, write a brief paragraph that outlines the social issue from a social conflict perspective. Be sure to include a prediction of what is in store with regard to obesity in Canada.

A Symbolic Interactionist Analysis

As you have already learned, a symbolic interactionist perspective is a micro perspective, and a social issue examined from this point of view will have an origin distinctly different from that identified by either of the macro paradigms. According to a micro perspective, social issues arise out of how particular people are treated. The theories of G.H. Mead outline the development of perception, belief, and self-perception as products of social interaction. (George Herbert Mead, 1863–1931, was a sociologist who was significant for his development of the symbolic interactionist perspective, and particularly for his theories on the development of self as a social product.) According to the symbolic interactionist perspective, a social issue is a component of social reality that is constructed by the social actors who are involved. As with the other paradigms, there are guide questions that will assist you to maintain a micro perspective.

QUESTIONS TO GUIDE A SYMBOLIC INTERACTIONIST ANALYSIS

The goal of a symbolic interactionist analysis is to describe the "realities" or social contexts of a social issue. The following questions will help you explore the socially constructed realities surrounding an issue. The first question is as follows:

1. What does the issue mean to the individuals involved in it? How is this meaning expressed? What labels, myths, stereotypes, and language do individuals use to refer to the issue and to the other individuals involved in it?

   The meaning of social events and behaviours is often clarified by the advertising media. As you are watching TV or browsing through a popular magazine, focus your attention on articles about smoking. Keep track of the portrayals of smoking and smokers. Then consider what **stereotypes**, **myths**, and **labels** are involved in these portrayals, and whether language is used in a connotative way, to suggest certain meanings.

A symbolic interactionist perspective emphasizes that meaning is not something separate from the circumstances in which it is used or created, so the second guide question asks about the social contexts of the meanings and the issue.

2. What is the source of these meanings? What is the social context in which these meanings are expressed? How are these meanings enforced or resisted?

   The term **context**, as used here, refers to the social circumstances, situation, or background in which the social interactions take place. You will remember from your studies of introductory sociology that social interaction is cued not only by the interpretation of others' meanings, but by the circumstances in which the social actors find themselves. For example, a person who smokes in the presence of children is labelled very negatively by the public whereas a person who smokes outdoors, away from children, is seen as foolish but otherwise socially acceptable. In this example, the two contextual factors determining what smoking behaviour is acceptable are whether children are present and whether the activity occurs in an enclosed space, with non-smokers present. In other words, the social actors' *situation* cues not only what behaviours are appropriate, but also what their actions mean.

The last guide question reflects a main premise of the symbolic interactionist perspective, which is that an activity's social meaning has a powerful influence on whether and how individuals engage in it. The third guide question is as follows:

3. What are the consequences of this activity? How does it affect the individuals involved? How, as an issue, is the activity perceived by society, and how does this perception affect how individuals participate in it?

   The article "How I Prevailed vs. Ciggies," by Patricia Pearson (2004), is an excellent summary of the various interpretations of the meaning of smoking. From this article, you will learn that smokers' commitment to quitting and the resources available to them in this effort are shaped by the negative social definition now given to smokers and smoking.

SUMMARY CONCLUSION

Tobacco use is an excellent example of how the social meaning of an activity can prevail over more logical or scientific meanings. A smoker's desire to quit, the means to quit, and the obstacles to quitting can all be directly attributed to the social meaning of smoking and smokers.

A SYMBOLIC INTERACTIONIST ANALYSIS: OBESITY IN CANADA

You are now ready to apply your newly acquired skills to creating a symbolic interactionist analysis of obesity in Canada. Use the following guide questions to accomplish this, and then write a summary conclusion of your findings.

1. What does the issue mean to the individuals involved in it? How is this meaning expressed? What labels, myths, stereotypes, and language do individuals use to refer to the issue and to other individuals involved in it?

   Hint: Remember that the symbolic interactionist perspective is micro, and that the overall goal is to describe the socially defined reality of the social issue—that is, how it is experienced and how the experiences influence its direction. For this first question, you should be looking for information about what the fatness **stigma** actually is, what the stereotypes about fat people are, and what the current ideals of body image are.

   ____

   ____

   ____

   ____

   ____

2. What is the source of these meanings? What is the social context in which these meanings are expressed? How are these meanings enforced or resisted?

   Hint: You will find that the daily media explore and exploit the stigma of being fat. What are some of the circumstances in which fat people are discriminated against? How are the current stereotypes, myths, and symbols used to **marginalize** heavy people?

3. What are the consequences of this activity? How does it affect the individuals involved? How, as an issue, is the activity perceived by society, and how does this perception affect how individuals participate in it?

   Hint: The marginalization of overweight people affects them in what way? How is this type of interaction counterproductive to a resolution of the issue? What other factors ensure that obesity rates will continue to grow in Canada?

SUMMARY CONCLUSION

Review of the Conclusions Reached by Each Analytical Perspective

Now that you have analyzed a social issue from each of the theoretical perspectives, you will have noticed that each perspective refers to a different set of questions and leads to different conclusions. Comparing the various conclusions will give you the most complete picture of an issue's origin, of its impact on society and on individuals, and of its future. You have an opportunity to do this now.

STRUCTURAL FUNCTIONALIST PERSPECTIVE

The macro focus of the structural functionalist perspective perceives society as a stable, integrated system of structures. A social issue, therefore, is the disruption or destabilizing of the system owing to the failure of one or more of its structures.

In the space below, outline the origins of the issue of obesity in Canada—that is, what is dysfunctional and what the impact has been. Then describe how, through resolution of the issue, a renewed equilibrium and systemic stability can be achieved.

SOCIAL CONFLICT PERSPECTIVE

The social conflict perspective is also a macro perspective, but it views society as a dynamic arena of inequality. Seen from this standpoint, a social issue is caused by this inequality in society.

In the space below, outline the areas in which the power and domination of the food and lifestyle industries have contributed to the obesity issue in Canada, and then predict what the issue's future is likely to be.

SYMBOLIC INTERACTIONIST PERSPECTIVE

The micro focus of the symbolic interactionist perspective is on the nature of social interaction. In other words, a social issue is a product of how people are treated by each other.

In the space below, explain how the social meanings surrounding obesity contribute to its growing seriousness as a problem in Canada.

You'll notice that neither the feminist nor the social constructionist paradigms have been adopted in the analyses of substance abuse and obesity. These perspectives would enlarge even further our comprehension of the Canadian issues under consideration. But our analyses are reasonably thorough without them. This text does not apply all of the paradigms to every issue. Rather than seeing this as an inadequacy, you should see it as an opportunity to apply the unused paradigms yourself.

A feminist analysis, if adopted in the macro perspective, usually follows the template of the social conflict paradigm. The guiding questions might be directed, for example, at whether and how substance abuse apprehension and treatment initiatives are modelled on men's experience of substance abuse and thus overlook the needs of women. If it were to follow instead the micro perspective of symbolic interactionism, a feminist analysis might explore how the patterns and meaning of substance abuse vary between the genders.

A social constructionist analysis is also missing from this chapter. Social constructionism, as you have learned, is a branch of symbolic interactionism. It is an analytical framework that allows a researcher to explore the socio-cultural meanings of social events. The questions that guide a symbolic interactionist analysis are useful for a social constructionist analysis. In the case of substance abuse, the cultural meaning of abuse and of dependence could be researched. Also, the current trend toward the medicalization of deviance (substance abuse and obesity in particular) is a fascinating issue that could be explored from a social constructionist perspective.

RESPONSES

GOVERNMENT AND POLICY

The United States allows the sale of caffeine, alcohol, and cigarettes in corner stores with very little regulation, but its response to the international drug trade is vocal and aggressive. It declared a "war on drugs" in 1972. The US focuses the majority of its anti-drug funds on criminal law enforcement and only 30 percent on treatment and rehabilitation for addicts (Library of Parliament, 2003).

Canada's treatment of drugs under the law is less aggressive than that of the US and not so focused on criminal penalties. Canada makes significant efforts to regulate tobacco and alcohol sales, and to support public health efforts toward rehabilitation and prevention. Even so, our primary public policy strategy in dealing with drug use is criminalization. Canada's first response to drug use was **prohibition**, a system of legal regulation whereby alcohol and drugs were made illegal and it was made a criminal offence to produce, import, possess, or distribute an illegal substance. All Canadian provinces prohibited alcohol by law during World War I. Alcohol is now legal if strictly regulated, but criminal prohibitions against drug use remain the primary strategy employed by most Western nations, including Canada, to combat the costs of substance abuse. In the *Controlled Drugs and Substances Act*, illicit drugs are listed and penalties for their possession and trafficking are set out.

Critics worry that the policy of prohibiting drugs simply fills prisons, empowers the black market to produce ever more potent, addictive, and harmful drug varieties, and enriches the illegal drug trade, when what is needed is a policy that addresses drug-related crime, disease, and death from a public health and educational perspective. This criticism has in recent years, as previously discussed, found support in Canada where marijuana is concerned, although the drug remains illegal to this day.

LAW AND POLICING

Policing responses to substance abuse are closely tied to public policy. Where the policy strongly emphasizes criminal prohibition and reduction in supplies, as is generally the case in the United States, the role of the police is primarily to interrupt and attempt to eradicate international and local drug trafficking. Canadian police have recently had significant success in breaking up drug trafficking rings and disrupting the supply of illicit drugs. In 2004, for example, the Ontario Provincial Police raided massive indoor marijuana grow operations near Barrie, seizing tens of thousands of plants and making dozens of arrests.

However, where public policy is inclined less toward criminal prohibition than toward addressing addictions and reducing the demand for illicit drugs, the police role becomes more complex than simple law enforcement. Some officers and forces take a role in therapeutic initiatives about drug prevention and rehabilitation for addicts. Public education programs for students and others are undertaken by Canadian police, including the RCMP, to prevent drug addiction and thereby reduce the demand for, and social costs of, drugs.

Substance abuse is a factor in most calls made to the police. Domestic violence, as we have said, is frequently related to drug abuse, and domestic disputes give rise to the majority of calls to police. Prostitution is closely tied to the illegal drug trade, and drug abuse is a key to the control of sex workers by pimps. Situations faced by police that seem at first unrelated to drugs often turn out to be, in effect, policing responses to substance abuse.

COMMUNITY

The legalization of marijuana and the decreased legality of smoking are useful counter-examples, showing how public involvement and advocacy can affect the legality, regulation, and social acceptability of psychoactive substances.

Community activism has changed attitudes and done much to change the law respecting cannabis derivatives. Marijuana was first made illegal in Canada in 1923. Eighty years later, between 2000 and 2006, court actions in Ontario as well as two bills proposed by Liberal justice ministers seemed to suggest that Canada was on the verge of *decriminalizing* marijuana use. The current Conservative government has not pursued these decriminalizing initiatives, but the issue remains hotly debated. The legalization or decriminalization of marijuana is currently supported by most Canadian political parties, and this situation has come about through the grassroots activism of community members.

Conversely, public activism has played a very important role in tightening the regulation of tobacco sale and use—especially as regards where tobacco can be smoked. There were virtually no limits on public smoking until the 1980s, when people could smoke in airplanes, theatres, buses, and hospitals (to name just a few venues). All Canadian provinces now have legislation restricting smoking in workplaces, restaurants, and, in some cases, all public spaces. There are now large, pictorial warnings on cigarette packages advising of the dangers of smoking. Primarily responsible for these changes are citizens who joined together to form anti-smoking advocacy groups, such as Physicians for a Smoke-Free Canada.

Citizens' groups have also played an important role in tightening up Canada's prohibitions against the impaired operation of motor vehicles. For example, Mothers Against Drunk Driving (MADD), a group spanning the United States and Canada, has helped popularize the use of "designated drivers," and has successfully lobbied for laws decreasing the legal blood alcohol limits for drivers.

Such advocacy has likely played a significant role in reducing tobacco smoking and impaired driving in Canada.

INDIVIDUAL INVOLVEMENT

Substance abuse is a problem of staggering proportions, with many complex dimensions. But students should not be daunted by the scope of the problem. While it is not possible for one person alone to solve the social problems related to drug use, there is a tremendous amount that individuals can contribute. For example, students could

- volunteer or work with an addiction recovery program in their communities,
- volunteer to assist police with public education initiatives to prevent drug abuse,
- become involved in advocacy against smoking or against impaired driving,
- volunteer with a women's shelter to help victims of violence against women,
- volunteer with a community service agency reaching out to male perpetrators of domestic violence,
- volunteer with child welfare programs in their communities,
- acknowledge and look seriously at their own levels of psychotropic substance consumption and take measures to limit or discontinue it.

CONCLUSION

Substance abuse and its related issues are immense, in terms of the health, economic, political, and social costs involved. More than most social issues, substance abuse demonstrates the role of society in the creation, definition, and resolution of a social issue. For this reason, it is an issue to which the analytical method can be instructively applied. For example, the history of alcohol use in North America shows the diverse ways in which alcohol use has been "socially constructed." When Europeans were first settling this continent, alcoholic beverages were accepted at all types of social events. Early in the last century, the social view of alcohol dramatically changed and all alcohol was prohibited. In the next phase, alcohol became a rigidly controlled substance, and it remains so today, although it now has a universally endorsed popularity. Keep in mind that throughout these changes in the perception and usage of alcohol, the physiological effects of ingesting it have not changed. Only the meaning of alcohol use (and abuse) has changed.

KEY TERMS

context the circumstances or background within which social actions occur; the context not only shapes social events (macro) and behaviour patterns (micro), it cues them as well

drug materials, either naturally occurring or synthetic that, when ingested by various means, are psychoactive

drug abuse use of psychotropic substances that is out of the user's control and may constitute a physical or psychological dependency

drug addiction the situation or condition in which a person takes a drug by compulsion, despite the potential harm to him- or herself and to others, and despite, in many cases, a desire to stop doing so

dysfunctions in the structural functionalist paradigm, the negative consequences of change or of social actions; dysfunctions occur as breakdowns within social institutions or as the impaired integration of social institutions

economy in the structural functionalist paradigm, the economy is a social institution; its manifest functions are the production and distribution of goods and services and the employment of a workforce

education in the structural functionalist paradigm, education is a social institution; its manifest functions are the teaching and training of society's members (so they can move into the economy and become productive members of society), developing knowledge, and reinforcing fundamental social values

entheogen psychoactive substance used in the context of religious ritual

equilibrium in the structural functionalist paradigm, the state achieved when all social institutions are functioning as expected and society is stable

family in the structural functionalist paradigm, family is a primary social institution; its manifest functions are procreation (generating members of society), socialization, and the instilling of fundamental cultural values

illegal drug trade the international black market in illegal psychotropic substances

labels a word or phrase that is used to identify a person or group of persons; usually used by the powerful in society to marginalize or stigmatize less powerful or less valued social groups

manifest functions in the structural functionalist paradigm, the positive consequences expected of a social institution

marginalize create social barriers that prevent persons and groups from full participation in society (for example, racial minorities may be marginalized by mainstream society)

myths stereotypes and false beliefs that enable some members of society to marginalize or stigmatize others

obesity great excess of body weight

prohibition a system of legal regulation that made alcohol and drugs illegal and made it a criminal offence to produce, import, possess, or distribute an illegal substance

psychoactive affecting the user's central nervous system and changing brain function in ways that change the user's mood, consciousness, perceptions, and behaviour

real and ideal society culture and social structure as it actually exists (real society) as opposed to culture and social structure as they are believed to exist according to theoretical paradigms or models of reality (ideal society)

resources of power in the social conflict paradigm, resources of power are assets that give one side in an issue advantage over another side

social institutions the structural functionalist term for social structures; the assemblages of norms, values, beliefs, statuses, roles, and organizations that collectively answer a society's basic needs (for example, education and family are social institutions)

social stigma a negatively valued marker or characteristic that makes a stigmatized person or group a target for prejudice and discrimination

stakeholders in the social conflict paradigm, stakeholders are groups and organizations that have a critical interest or investment in an issue (and are in competition with each other)

stereotypes generalizations and "stories," usually negative, about a person or group; often used to justify the marginalization of or discrimination against minorities

structures in the structural functionalist paradigm, this term is used interchangeably with "social institution"

substance use ingesting by various means certain materials known as drugs

FOR FURTHER RESEARCH

Censorship in the Media
http://www.media-awareness.ca/english/resources/educational/handouts/tobacco_advertising/censorship_in_media.cfm.

How Tobacco Advertising Works
http://www.smoke-free.ca/pdf_1/adbrochure-howadswork.pdf.

Media Awareness Network
http://www.media-awareness.ca.

Mothers Against Drunk Driving Canada
http://www.madd.ca.

Physicians for a Smoke-Free Canada
http://www.smoke-free.ca.

REFERENCES

Abel, E.L., & Sokel, R.J. (1987). Incidence of fetal alcohol syndrome and economic impact of FAS-related anomalies: Drug alcohol syndrome and economic impact of FAS-related anomalies. *Drug and Alcohol Dependency, 19*(1), 51-70.

Arseneault, L., Cannon, M., Poulton, R., Murray, R., Caspi, A., & Moffitt, T.E. (2002). Cannabis use in adolescence and risk for adult psychosis: Longitudinal prospective study. *British Medical Journal, 325*, 1212-1213. http://www.bmj.com/cgi/reprint/325/7374/1212.pdf.

Canadian Centre on Substance Abuse [CCSA]. (1996). The costs of substance abuse in Canada. http://www.ccsa.ca/NR/rdonlyres/A6B92C8C-4EFB-42DD-8AE2-566B602C2B61/0/ccsa0062771996.pdf.

Canadian Centre on Substance Abuse [CCSA]. (2004). A national survey of Canadians' use of alcohol and other drugs: Prevalence of use and related harms. Canadian Addictions Survey [CAS]. http://www.ccsa.ca/NR/rdonlyres/B2C820A2-C987-4F08-8605-2BE999FE4DFC/0/ccsa0048042004.pdf.

Canadian Industry Statistics: gross domestic product (GDP). (n.d.). Tobacco manufacturing (NAICS 3122). http://www.strategis.ic.gc.ca.

Canadian Medical Association. (2003). Tobacco control (Update 2001 to Tobacco and Health). Ottawa. http://www.cma.ca.

CBS News. (1991, November 17). The French paradox. *60 Minutes.*

CBS News. (2006, October 3). The overeating addiction. http://www.cbsnews.com/stories/2006/10/02/health/webmd/main2057123.shtml.

Chauhan, Tara, S. (2003, November 11). Diabetes' rising toll. *CMAJ: Canadian Medical Association Journal, 169*(10). Retrieved March 13, 2004, from Ebscohost: Canadian MAS FullTEXT Elite database.

Controlled Drugs and Substances Act, S.C. 1996, c. 19.

Coxe, D. (2004, February 2). Sex is out, carbs are in. *Maclean's, 117*(5). Retrieved March 13, 2004, from Ebscohost: Canadian MAS FullTEXT Elite database.

Dreher, M.C., Nugent, K., & Hudgins, R. (1994). Prenatal marijuana exposure and neonatal outcomes in Jamaica: An ethnographic study. *Pediatrics, 93*(3), 254-260.

First Nations and Inuit Health Committee, Canadian Paediatric Society [CPS]. (2006). Use and misuse of tobacco among Aboriginal peoples—Update 2006. *Paediatrics & Child Health, 11*(10), 681-685. http://www.cps.ca/english/statements/II/FNIH06-01.htm.

Gilmore, J. (2002, December). Report on smoking in Canada 1985 to 2001. Statistics Canada, Health Statistics Division. http://www.statcan.ca/english/research/82F0077XIE/82F0077XIE2001001.pdf.

Gorman, C. (2003, October 27). How to eat smarter. *Time Canada, 162*(17). Retrieved March 13, 2004, from Ebscohost: Canadian MAS FullTEXT Elite database.

Grace, K.M. (2002, December 2). Now the right hates fat too. *Newsmagazine (National edition), 29*(23). Retrieved March 13, 2004, from Ebscohost: Canadian MAS FullTEXT Elite database.

Hammock, D. (2004, February). Finally … fast food that's actually good for you. *Good Housekeeping, 238*(2). Retrieved March 13, 2004, from Ebscohost: Canadian MAS FullTEXT Elite database.

Health Canada. (1999, January). Deaths in Canada due to smoking. http://www.hc-sc.gc.ca/ahc-asc/media/nr-cp/1999/1999_07bk6_e.html.

Health Canada. (2004). Canadian tobacco use monitoring survey (CTUMS). http://www.hc-sc.gc.ca/hl-vs/tobac-tabac/research-recherche/stat/ctums-esutc/2004/index_e.html. (Version current at November 8, 2006).

Health Canada. (n.d.). Horizons one—Older Canadians' alcohol and other drug use. http://www.hc-sc.gc.ca/ahc-asc/pubs/drugs-drogues/horizons1/illdrugs-illdrogues_e.html.

Horovitz, B. (2004, March 4). By year's end, regular size will have to do. *USA Today*. Retrieved March 13, 2004, from Ebscohost: Canadian MAS FullTEXT Elite database.

Jennisson, T. (1992). Health issues in rural Canada. Government of Canada: Depository Services Program. http://dsp-psd.communication.gc.ca/Collection-R/LoPBdP/BP/bp325-e.htm.

Katzmarzyk, P. (2003, December 9). A modest proposal to meet our Kyoto commitments: The answer lies within. *Canadian Medical Association Journal* [CMAJ], *169*(12). Retrieved March 13, 2004, from Ebscohost: Canadian MAS FullTEXT Elite database.

Ko, M. (2002, April 1). A spreading crisis. *Newsmagazine (National edition), 29*(7). Retrieved March 13, 2004, from Ebscohost: Canadian MAS FullTEXT Elite database.

Leshner, A. (1998, November). Gender matters in drug abuse research. *NIDA Notes, 13*(4). http://www.nida.nih.gov/NIDA_Notes/NNVol13N4/DirrepVol13N4.html.

Library of Parliament. (2003). Illegal drugs and drug trafficking. Political and Social Affairs Division. http://www.parl.gc.ca/information/library/PRBpubs/bp435-e.htm.

Lovett, R. (2005, September 24). Coffee: The demon drink? *New Scientist* (2518).

MacArthur, K. (2004, January 12). Fast-feeders ditch buns to lure dieters. *Advertising Age, 75*(5). Retrieved March 15, 2004, from Ebscohost: Academic Search Premier database.

MADD Canada. (n.d.). Victim services. http://www.madd.ca/english/services/index.html.

Merlin, M.D. (n.d.). Archaeological evidence for the tradition of psychoactive plant use in the Old World. *Economic Botany, 57*(3), 295-323.

Murphy, D. (2004, 1). News about fast foods. *Current Health, 1, 27*(6). Retrieved March 15, 2004, from Ebscohost: MAS Ultra School edition database.

Murphy, D. (2004, 2) Good news about fast foods. *Current Health, 2, 30*(6). Retrieved March 15, 2004, from Ebscohost: Academic Search Premier database.

O'Dea, J. (2003, March). Fad weight loss diets. *Nutridate, 14*(1), 1, 4. Retrieved March 30, 2004, from Ebscohost: Canadian Reference Centre database.

Paradis, S. (2004, February 10). Fat is the new tobacco. *Toronto Observer.* http://observer.thecentre.centennialcollege.ca/life/obesity_hrtstroke_021004.htm.

Pearl, N. (2004, January 15). Stranger than fiction: True tales. *Library Journal, 129*(1). Retrieved March 15, 2004, from Ebscohost: Canadian MAS FullTEXT Elite database.

Pearson, P. (2004, January 26). How I prevailed vs. ciggies: Why does Canada make it hard to get the stuff that helps you butt out? *Maclean's*, p. 30. http://www.macleans.ca/columnists/article.jsp?content=20040126_73943_73943.

Public Health Agency of Canada. (1993). Fact sheet on family violence and substance abuse. http://www.phac-aspc.gc.ca/ncfv-cnivf/familyviolence/html/fvsubstance_e.html.

Riley, D. (1998, November). Drugs and drug policy in Canada: A brief review and commentary. Canadian Foundation for Drug Policy [CFDP]. http://www.cfdp.ca/sen1841.htm.

Robin, R. (2003, December 3). Healthy, wealthy, and wise. *Canadian Business, 76*(23). Retrieved March 13, 2004, from Ebscohost: Canadian MAS FullTEXT Elite database.

Rudgley, R. (1999). *The lost civilizations of the stone age.* New York: Touchstone.

Schultes, R.E., & Raffauf, R.F. (1992). *Vine of the soul: Medicine men, their plants and rituals in the Colombian Amazonia.* Oracle, AZ: Synergetic Press.

Safework: Programme on Safety and Health at Work and the Environment. (2000). Drug and alcohol abuse—An important workplace issue. *International Labour.* http://www.ilo.org/public/english/protection/safework/drug/impiss.htm.

Skog, O. (2003, July). Alcohol consumption and fatal accidents in Canada. *Addiction, 98*(7).

Statistics Canada. (2003, November 7). Impaired driving and other traffic offences. *The Daily.* http://www.statcan.ca/Daily/English/031107/d031107b.htm.

Toronto Star. (2004, May 15). *See also* Doctors take lead in war on smoking. *Toronto Star,* May 31, 2005. Database: *Canadian Reference Centre.*

University of Lethbridge. (2005, April 6). 2003-2004 University of Lethbridge student life and alcohol study: Executive summary. http://www.uleth.ca/alcohol/files/ExecutiveSummaryULASLS.pdf.

USA Today. (2004, February 9). Subway sees success with low-carb campaign, sandwiches. Retrieved March 13, 2004, from Ebscohost: Canadian MAS FullTEXT Elite database.

USA Today. (2004, February 12). Shake the salt, add more water. Retrieved March 13, 2004, from Ebscohost: Canadian MAS FullTEXT Elite database.

USA Today. (2004, February 25). Kids bombarded with TV food ads. Retrieved March 13, 2004, from Ebscohost: Canadian MAS FullTEXT Elite database.

Waddell, D.B. (2004, January 23). Hamilton's smoking bylaw is "extremely lax." *Ancaster News,* p. 9.

Walker, R. (2000). Canada's weapons in smoke wars. *Christian Science Monitor, 92*(31), 6.

Wharry, S. (2002, May 28). Overweight, inactive kids worry Health Canada. *Canadian Medical Association Journal* [CMAJ], *166*(11). Retrieved March 13, 2004, from Ebscohost: Canadian MAS FullTEXT Elite database.

World Health Organization. (2002). The world health report 2002—Reducing risks, promoting healthy life. http://www.who.int/whr/2002/en.

CHAPTER 4

Sex Work

CHAPTER OBJECTIVES

After completing this chapter, you will be able to:

Understand significant dimensions of sex work

- Understand the general issues surrounding sex work, and the significant participants involved.
- Identify the national and international dimensions of sex work.
- Understand the legal implications and consequences of sex work in Canada.
- Understand sex work in a transnational context.

Understand and apply different sociological perspectives to sex work

- Structural functionalist
- Social conflict
- Feminist

Identify and critique various responses to sex-work-related social problems, including the responses of

- Government and policy
- Law and policing
- Community
- Individuals

DIMENSIONS

GENERAL ISSUES: NATIONAL AND INTERNATIONAL DIMENSIONS

The **sex trade** is a term used to describe prostitution, which is the exchange of sexual services between people for money or other goods, with little or no emotional involvement. Other terms used to describe this trade are *the game*, *the trap*, and *the oldest profession*. Certain sexual transactions obviously fall within this definition—

for example, the sexual services of a professional streetwalker in return for money from a *john*. Other kinds of sexual transactions are less readily defined this way, though their basic dynamic is similar. Images of sexuality are pervasively used to sell material goods in advertising. Strip clubs abound. There is a proliferation of pornography on video, in magazines, and on the Internet. The sex trade invariably involves a one-sided relationship. Certain individuals supply sexual services while others—namely, clients or customers—supply the demand. Parties to the transaction almost never switch these roles.

Women, men, children, and transgendered persons can all become involved in the sex trade. While not all those on the *supply* side of the sex trade (that is, those providing sexual services) are women, the trade does have a gendered aspect. The majority of sex workers are female. Even when these sex workers are men, the clients are rarely women. The sex trade in Canada services a male *demand* (that is, a male population of consumers).

Some people characterize prostitution as a form of work: *sex work*. Sex work occurs in most human societies, and always has. Some radical critics would even argue that *all* sex is transactional and that clear lines cannot really be drawn between prostitution and sexual relations in general. Certain radical feminists have argued that a "respectable" woman's performing sexual and reproductive services in exchange for goods—a diamond ring and other gifts, a home, and a husband's surname—is really no different from a sex worker's earning wages by walking the streets soliciting clients. Conversely, others see prostitution as fundamentally different from other sexual relationships. They contend that prostitution can never be fully consensual and is always a form of rape and that, at the very least, it contributes to a social climate where rape is tolerated. Still others, predominantly those viewing the matter from strongly religious viewpoints, are less concerned with the social consequences of the sex trade than with a perception that it is morally repugnant to buy or sell sexual services.

Those who characterize prostitution as sex work—that is, a freely chosen job—differentiate this work from *sexual slavery*, whereby women or men are coerced into providing sexual services. A book that changed the thinking of many readers about the sex trade during the ideologically revolutionary 1970s was Xaviera Hollander's *The Happy Hooker* (1971). Hollander was an unrepentant high-priced New York prostitute; her book questioned prevailing assumptions that women worked in the sex trade involuntarily, and it affirmed, to the contrary, that such women might even enjoy being there. But sex work is not socially desirable or acceptable in most circles. It is the subject of some debate whether anyone freely chooses sex work, and it is certainly safe to say that few, if any, Canadians hope that their children will choose it as a career. Further, women and men from marginalized groups, particularly women of Aboriginal descent, are disproportionately represented in the Canadian sex trade. This fact implies that economic marginalization has a strong connection with sex work; it calls into question the extent to which these service providers freely selected the work.

There are several groups who actively seek to rectify problems related to the sex trade and particularly to child prostitution. Feminists focus on problems with patriarchy, and with the need to protect the "girl child." Persons who view such matters as child prostitution from religious and otherwise moralistic viewpoints tend to focus on its moral implications, on condemning those who consume sexual services from children, and on rescuing children from prostitution. Some professionals are involved in the treatment of former prostitutes. Therapists and psychologists, for example, help survivors cope with post-traumatic stress disorder through therapy and drug regimens. International development workers tend to look at sex work in relation to poverty—that is, at the economics of supply and demand underlying community development. Children's rights advocates tend to make arguments about empowerment and the rights of children to experience a childhood protected from adult exploitation.

There are many ways of providing services in the sex trade.

Pornographic Actors

Pornographic actors are depicted in explicit images either on video or in still photographs, and are available via telephone ("phone sex") as well. Images of pornographic actors are accessible by television broadcast, on video and DVD, and, increasingly, over the Internet. These sex workers tend not to have direct contact with their customers but are, rather, in the business of exchanging "virtual" favours with the consumer.

Exotic Dancers and Exotic Masseuses/Masseurs

These sex trade workers are based in clubs, bars, or massage parlours. Often, but not always, they will negotiate sexual favours as a sideline to their more public work.

Escorts, Call Girls, and Call Boys

These sex trade workers consist generally of higher-end sex workers—individuals who work by appointment, earn higher fees, and have more choice about their working conditions and the customers they take on. In this level of the sex trade, the services are offered at the customer's place of residence or, more commonly, at his or her hotel, or at the escort's own residence, or in a hotel room rented by the escort. These sex workers often work through *escort agencies*, which offer, in print media and on the Internet, attractive companions for social occasions. Such agencies may claim not to provide sexual services, but very few escorts expect to be hired only for social purposes. This line of sex work can be highly lucrative.

House Girls

These sex trade workers are based in *bawdy houses*, *trick pads*, or *brothels*—all terms for the venues in which prostitutes provide their services on-site. This type of sex work disproportionately engages women and girls brought from poor countries, illegally, into wealthier nations like Canada.

Streetwalkers

At the lower end of the price spectrum, streetwalkers publicly **solicit** customers by approaching them on the street, and they charge by the "trick" for their services. Sexual services are usually provided in the customer's car, in a nearby alley, or in a motel room rented by the hour.

Also operating on the supply side of the sex trade, but not as service providers, are pimps. A **pimp** is a person, usually a man, who lives off the proceeds of prostitutes, offering, in return for a portion of the sex worker's earnings, some protection and other services such as food, shelter, and, often, access to narcotics and other substances to which the sex worker may be addicted. The relationship between pimps and prostitutes is almost always abusive. Much of the violence suffered by sex workers is at the hands of their pimps. Researchers contend that pimps recruit marginalized, homeless, or impoverished young women into sex work. Often, a pimp will initially provide some support to the prostitute and act as her boyfriend before asserting that she owes him a debt and asking her to perform sex acts to repay him. Where the sex trade is less criminalized, pimps' control and abuse of prostitutes typically decreases, since the prostitutes are able to seek protection from more legitimate sources such as the police. Nowhere in Canada is prostitution fully legal, but in places like Vancouver, where local governments' public policies are more protective of prostitutes, the power of pimps is diminished. In some instances, a woman occupies a role similar to a pimp's, in which case she is known as a *madam*.

PORNOGRAPHY

Pornography is a hotly debated dimension of the sex trade. Not everyone would classify it with other sex work, such as prostitution. While pornography and erotica themselves are not new, having existed for millennia in graphic and written form, new media have allowed new genres of pornography to proliferate. With the advent of videocassette recorder and then DVD technology, people in the 1980s and 1990s were able to view films in the privacy of their own homes. With the Internet, pornography has become still more accessible and widespread. It is not always easy to categorize pornography, and increasingly, as technology improves, the lines between pornography and prostitution are becoming blurred. Historically, sexual relations could only be represented in static images—photographs, for example. Films, videos, and DVDs lent more intimacy to these representations, imbuing sexual images with movement and sound. However, there was still a clear line between observer and participant: a consumer of pornography was an observer of sex; a prostitute's client a participant. More recent technological change has blurred this line. Interactive video chat via the Internet allows moment-to-moment communication between consumers of pornography and sex workers. There are even sites that allow for interactive use of cameras. Pornography has begun to resemble prostitution more closely, at least in the virtual world.

Pornography can consist of words or pictures in which a person is represented as a sexual object, to the end of eliciting a sexual response from a paying consumer. Pornography is generally considered to be distinct from *erotica*, which also depicts sexual acts or images and is intended to elicit a sexual response. Erotica, however, is understood to have some degree of artistic merit and to take into account the humanness or personhood of the person depicted. There is a wide range of pornography. *Soft-core* pornography implies sexual activity but does not actually depict genitalia or close-up poses of the sex act. Nude photographs in magazines such as *Playboy* or *Maxim*, where women are depicted for their beauty and their sexual appeal to male readers, are on the borderline between soft-core pornography and erotica. *Hard-core* pornography, at the other extreme, contains graphic depictions of sexual activity. Hard-core pornography graphically depicts sex and tends to violate cultural moral prohibitions or standards, also known as *taboos*, such as sexual relationships between people widely divergent in age or size. While pornography that depicts adults having sex is increasingly common and, relatively speaking, socially accepted, **child pornography**, which exploits minors by depicting them in sexually explicit material, is illegal in Canada and elsewhere. However, child pornography is disturbingly common.

The gendered and racist aspects of the sex trade are problematic. But to most people the truly troubling dimension of the sex trade, as it is practised in Canada and around the world, is the age of many of the prostitutes. Prostitution too often involves the exploitation of children. *Child prostitution* involves the sexual exploitation of a child in return for financial or material profit. This exploitation is usually organized by a third party—for example, a parent, family member, pimp, or teacher. Even where the child him- or herself arranges the transaction, the act of prostitution can of course never be fully consensual when one of the parties is not an adult and is therefore not legally qualified to consent to sexual relations. The term *child pornography* means the visual, audio, or other technological depiction of a child for the sexual gratification of a user, and extends, legally speaking, to the production, distribution, or use of such material. Child prostitution, because it is illegal, takes place behind closed doors, which makes it difficult to monitor and difficult to assess as to its scale and scope. Some estimates put the number of children involved in the sex trade as high as 2,400,000 per year (Ennew et al., 1996)—an alarming statistic when one considers what it says about the number of children affected and about the prevalence of pedophilia.

The sex trade varies across cultures and time periods. In Japan, for example, the institution of the female *geisha* had established by 1800 an elite group of women who, though they sometimes exchanged sexual services for money, more often offered their clients companionship, musical performance, and visual displays of beauty, such as dancing and tea service. To this day, prostitution is understood uniquely in Japan; women who perform *fellatio* for money are not considered prostitutes and are not engaged in illegal activity, while intercourse itself cannot legally be exchanged for money.

Some cite the geisha convention in Japan and other variations on the sex trade as evidence that the trade itself need not be a social problem; it is the collateral dangers faced by prostitutes that are the real issue. Others contend that the institution of geisha, like the legalized prostitution found in Amsterdam, which is discussed below, has its own violent and oppressive aspects.

SEX WORK IN CANADA

Those who seek to legalize sex work in Canada differentiate between the sex trade itself and the collateral harms that sex workers are likely to suffer. As mentioned, sex workers are seen as "second-class citizens" by law enforcement officials and by the public at large in this country. Sex workers are disproportionately involved in the drug trade and much likelier than other women and men to be victims of violence. A disproportionate number of the women entering the sex trade in Canada are from marginalized groups such as Aboriginals, and these women tend also to be poor, young, and lacking in higher education. Once they enter the trade, sex workers are at great risk of contracting sexually transmitted diseases such as AIDS and hepatitis C. Sex workers are also at disproportionate risk of being murdered.

A chilling example of sex workers' being at risk of violent death is Vancouver's "missing women" case. This has turned into the Pickton investigation, which is the largest serial-killer investigation and one of the most complex murder trials ever undertaken by police or tried before Canadian courts. The case began in about 1984, when sex workers began to go missing from Canada's poorest neighbourhood, Vancouver's east side, recognized as the city's "skid row." No pattern was clear in the early disappearances. Large numbers of sex workers were disappearing from Calgary and Edmonton around the same time. Police did not focus on the Vancouver trend until 14 years later, in 1998, when an Aboriginal community group sent to police a list of the names of Aboriginal victims who had disappeared from east Vancouver. Shortly thereafter, the police received a tip from a former employee of a pig farm located on the lower mainland, east of the city of Vancouver. The farm was also the site of wild parties where hundreds of people would sometimes be present and where east-side prostitutes would work as entertainment. The tipster asked police to look into two brothers with the last name Pickton. The farm was searched and the brothers were questioned briefly but released. Robert Pickton was not arrested until 2002. Between his original questioning and his arrest, four years passed. Several women were murdered by him in the intervening years. By the time of his arrest, at least 60 and probably closer to 100 sex workers had been killed by Pickton. Approximately half of these women are known to have been of Aboriginal descent.

Vancouver's missing-women case has become infamous, touted by victims groups, Aboriginal community members, and feminists as an example of police and public indifference about the plight of prostitutes, particularly female Aboriginal ones. The investigation became a mammoth task for police, who had to excavate the pig farm in their search for DNA. Unsavoury evidence emerged that some of the women's remains may have been processed with pork products and sold for human consumption. Families of the victims have called for a public inquiry into police handling of the case. In their defence, police have cited the transient lifestyles of the missing women, the lack of clear dates and times for their disappearances, and the delay caused by the magnitude of the investigation.

Although Pickton was convicted in December 2007 of six counts of second degree murder in relation to the deaths of several of Vancouver's missing women, many questions remain unresolved. He has yet to stand trial in relation to the deaths of scores of women with whom he was alleged to be involved. Disturbingly, questions about the possible involvement of other people in the killings also remain unresolved. Furthermore, the incarceration and trial of Robert Pickton have not stopped or even materially slowed the rate of disappearance and the murders of sex workers in western Canada.

Many feminist and community groups have cited the Pickton case as showing why prostitution needs to be legalized. They contend that if these women had been working legally, they would not have been so vulnerable to a predatory serial killer. Their whereabouts would have been easier to determine and their disappearances less mysterious. Patterns of disappearance would have been more clear. The women would not have been obliged to enter Pickton's modified van to perform sexual services had they had a legally sanctioned workplace. The alleged serial killer would not have had such easy access to so many victims.

Legal Issues

Students are often surprised that prostitution itself is legal in Canada. The sex trade, considered in all its dimensions, has an unusual, quasi-legal status under Canadian law. Certain aspects of it are criminal, while others are not.

At one end of the spectrum, exotic dancers are legally allowed to work in Canada. Moreover, there has long been a federal program, put forward by Citizenship and Immigration Canada, that shortlists exotic dancers for work visas by classifying what they do as a "high needs area." This program was expressly ended in 2004 by then Deputy Prime Minister Anne McLellan, but exotic dancing remains on the list of jobs for which short-term work visas can be granted, and it remains a relatively socially acceptable trade in Canada in which many immigrant women from poorer countries find work (Macklin, 2003).

Under the Canadian *Criminal Code*, certain elements of the sex trade are prohibited while others are not. Child prostitution is entirely illegal in Canada and subject to criminal penalties. It is prohibited in broad terms by s. 163.1 of the *Criminal Code*. According to s. 151, it is a criminal offence for an adult to engage in sexual relations with a person under the age of 14. Section 152 of the Code makes it an offence to invite a minor to sexual touching. Section 171 makes it illegal for a householder to permit sexual activity by a person under the age of 18 while they occupy or have control over the premises. *Criminal Code* amendments of 1997 make it possible for Canadian authorities to prosecute Canadian citizens or permanent residents who sexually abuse children, including abuse through prostitution, while outside Canada. Section 212(2) of the Code makes it illegal to live off the avails of prostitution and s. 212(4) makes it illegal to obtain a person under 18 for sexual services.

Where the sex trade does not involve children, it is subject to criminal penalties but not so stringently prohibited. For example:

- It is *illegal* to keep a *bawdy* house. Section 210 of the *Criminal Code* prohibits maintaining, owning, or being an "inmate" of a common bawdy house, while s. 211 prohibits knowingly transporting or directing a person to a bawdy house.
- It is *illegal* to *solicit* for the purposes of prostitution. Section 212(1) of the *Criminal Code* prohibits procuring, attempting to procure, or soliciting a person to have illicit sexual intercourse with another person; inveigling or enticing a person to a bawdy house for the purpose of prostitution. There is a particular prohibition against such solicitation in a public place. Section 213 of the Code prohibits making offers to provide or purchase sexual services in a public place or in public view.
- It is *illegal* to be involved in the sex trade as a third party, which most often means a pimp. Section 212(1) prohibits living off the avails of a prostitute. Section 212(3) places on an accused who lives with or is "habitually in the company of" a prostitute an evidentiary burden to prove that she or he does not live on the avails of prostitution.

- It is *legal* to engage in the act of prostitution so long as the prohibitions mentioned above are not breached. This means that the exchange of goods, services, or money for sex is legal but that there is, practically speaking, really nowhere in which a person can legally engage in such activity more than once and virtually no practical way to arrange for such activity to occur without breaking the law.

Advertising by escort services in public print is protected as a right of free speech, and independent escorts can discuss in private payment for services.

Although the act of prostitution is legal, written or oral contracts for the provision of sexual services are not enforceable under contract law because they are seen as contrary to public policy.

Although prostitution itself is legal in Canada, critics of the current legal regime argue that our criminal law effectively creates a crime of prostitution; it is not practically possible for prostitutes to carry out their profession because there is really nowhere they are allowed to work.

Legal regulation of the sex trade is inconsistent in whom it punishes. At certain times and in certain jurisdictions, movements have been made to criminalize and stigmatize johns by publicizing their identities. Other laws punish the service providers by criminalizing and incarcerating them.

Many Western democracies in the past few decades have moved away from the criminalization of prostitution. Within Canada, certain jurisdictions have sought to legalize, or at the very least decriminalize, aspects of prostitution within their borders. For example, in 2003 Vancouver's city council passed a bylaw that included certain elements of the sex trade among the businesses allowable under the municipal zoning for the city's central core. Such municipal laws cannot officially be enforced where the businesses in question are subject to criminal prohibitions.

However, Canada tightened its federal anti-prostitution laws in 1986 (Supreme Court of Canada, 1990). Recently, an all-party committee of MPs studied Canada's prostitution laws. After engaging in open hearings across Canada and consulting with academics, social workers, police, and prostitutes, the committee was finalizing its report before the 2006 election was called. It appears that this report will still be delivered, but it is not clear what it will contain. A significant majority of persons making submissions to the committee were in favour of legalization. But Canada's new justice minister, Vic Toews, has publicly stated he doesn't support legalizing brothels or prostitution, citing fears that legalization would bring more organized crime into the sex trade (Davis, 2006).

TRANSNATIONAL CONTEXT

While the focus of this book is social issues in Canada, it would be inappropriate and inaccurate to look at the Canadian situation in a vacuum. In this economically "globalized" world, national boundaries do not delimit the scope of crime or communication about it. Gender and race issues transcend national boundaries, and so does the sex trade. Certain authors have argued that, as capitalism develops internationally, the sex trade is undergoing an "industrial revolution" worldwide that is causing the commodification of human beings in unprecedented numbers (Poulin, 2004).

As people become more mobile through international travel, sex tourism and human trafficking are expanding phenomena that link Canada to international sex slavery. A special 2006 report from the United Nations made clear that human trafficking is a global problem affecting every country in the world (United Nations' Office on Drugs and Crime [UNODC], 2006).

On the more benign side of sex tourism, Amsterdam is openly touted as the "sex capital of Europe" and takes pride in its travel guides (Let's Go Travel Guides, n.d.; Virtual Tourist, n.d.). The Netherlands, also known as Holland, is a western European country where the sex and drug trades are legal, accepted by public policy. Tolerance of these industries is equated with sexual and personal freedom more generally. Amsterdam, Holland's capital, has long been a destination of choice for customers seeking to purchase consequence-free sexual adventure. The red light district of Amsterdam consists of streets filled with brothels, all of which are subject to strict governmental regulation, including standards for safety and cleanliness. Prostitutes submit to regular testing for sexually transmitted diseases. If their "tricks" become violent or behave inappropriately, these sex workers enjoy the full protection of the law. It would be overstating the case to say that sex work in the Netherlands is not stigmatized at all, regarded no differently as a career choice from such professions as law and dentistry. But sex workers in the Netherlands do work in a climate of relative comfort and safety.

The American state of Nevada also legally permits prostitution, in a strictly regulated environment much like that in Amsterdam. It is not just legal gambling and the presence of lavish casinos that attracts corporate and professional conventions to Las Vegas in huge numbers. The flippant adage, "What happens in Vegas, stays in Vegas," can often refer to the participation by male consumers—and, less often, by female ones—in the legalized sex trade.

On the darker side of international sex tourism, affluent men, usually from the first world, are, in growing numbers, consuming sexual services in countries such as Thailand and India where they benefit from anonymity and from the low prices that result from the crippling poverty of the Third World. These customers are able to engage abroad in the sex trade without fear of the legal and reputational reprisals they might suffer at home. Many children are involved in the sex trade in Southeast Asia, particularly Thailand and the Philippines (Ennew et al., 1996). Even adult women who participate in the sex trade in these countries are often not freely engaged in sexual activity but are owned by brothels and forced by their "owners" into sexual slavery, after being purchased at as young an age as 12 or 13. More often than not, these prostitutes never partake in a share of the profits gained from their work. In other words, sex tourism does not usually involve a voluntary exchange of services for money. As one Thai prostitute put it, "The sex trade is ancient. It goes back to the beginnings of human history. I am but one brick in that long, unbroken wall of female exploitation and misery" (Lobaido, 2002).

Clearly, there are racist dimensions to international sex tourism, as well as gender issues. Reports indicate that male customers tend to feel less morally troubled by partaking in the sex trade in third world countries, because they view the women in those places as less worthy of human dignity than those at home. In many destination countries, there is a tradition of submissiveness in women's roles. Where different ethnic groups are represented in a brothel's sex workers, the light-skinned women tend to be more popular (Lobaido, 2002).

An offshoot of sex tourism is human trafficking, the coercive, illicit importing of women and girls from poor nations into wealthier ones where they provide sexual services as slaves in brothels. This international sex trade is a form of modern slavery. Sometimes these women and girls are actually sold by their families; in other instances, they are misled with promises of a better life abroad. Sometimes they are lured by phony advertisements for domestic servants, waitresses, factory workers, and mail-order brides. Still others are kidnapped by gangs (UNODC, 2006).

The international sex trade affects growing numbers of women and girls internationally. Estimates from 2001 indicated that 2 million women and children are sold into the sex trade every year, with 120,000 of those being smuggled into western Europe from central and eastern Europe. The same source indicates that upward of 15,000 women and girls, predominantly Mexican, are smuggled annually into Canada and the United States. Asian women are also smuggled into Canada, and women from the former Soviet Union are smuggled into Israel (CNN, 2001).

Once women and girls have been forced into the sex trade, it is difficult if not impossible for them to leave it. Transplanted to an alien country, sex slaves are entirely under the traffickers' control. They are often physically confined, and traffickers use threats and blackmail to control them. Trafficked women and children are dependent upon their captors for food, clothing, and all other necessities (UNODC, 2006). If they do escape, these women and girls have no legal status, and so risk deportation. If they manage to return to their home communities, there is no easy refuge to be found. In the traditional societies from which most of these women come, they are often unwelcome, seen as tainted and as bringing shame upon their families by returning.

The human trafficking and sex tourism discussed above are crimes found in times of peace. Sexual slavery has often been used as a tool of war. During World War II, the Japanese military forced women from other Asian countries to be "comfort women," and in Bosnia more recently, during the 1990s Balkan conflict, rape was used as a tool of genocidal warfare.

ANALYSIS

SOCIAL ISSUES OF THE SEX TRADE

The foregoing survey of the sex trade demonstrates that there are a number of separate issues embedded in the subject:

- Pornography
- Child pornography
- Internet distribution of sexual material—photos, DVDs, virtual sexual activity
- International trafficking of sex workers (sex slaves)
- Canadian exploitation of sex workers in disadvantaged countries

- Prostitution
  - Overlooked exploitation of women
  - Exploitation of women who are marginalized by race or financial need, or both
  - Exploitation of children
  - Criminalization and marginalization of sex workers
  - Sex work as an element of organized crime

Only the last of these issues—that is, prostitution—will be made the subject of a theoretical analysis.

Identifying a Social Issue

WHAT GROUPS ARE CALLING FOR ATTENTION AND WHAT IS THEIR CONCERN?

The *concern* is that sex workers, namely women, are being exploited by consumers of their services, maligned by the Canadian public, and marginalized by the agencies of law, medicine, and social welfare. *Those lodging the complaints* are groups of activists from academic, medical, and legal organizations, all advocating a change in the treatment and the public perception of sex workers.

WHAT IS THE VISION OR GOAL OF THE VOICES OF CONCERN?

The advocates' *goals* are as follows: a resolution of the issues that coerce women into the sex trade; the protection of children, so they are not at risk of being involved in the sex trade; and the support of sex trade workers' health and well-being.

WHAT ARE THE MEANS OF ACHIEVING THE GOALS?

The *means of achieving the goals* are to change Canadian laws, to make media presentations of the sex trade more realistic, and to improve the support systems for women experiencing violence, suffering from drug addiction, and lacking in marketable skills.

Evolution of the Social Issue of Sex Worker Exploitation

WHAT GROUPS AND ORGANIZATIONS ARE ADVOCATING CHANGE?

A number of feminist groups are questioning the public perception of sex workers as immoral and as distributors of disease and violence. Medical personnel and academics, too, are calling for an end to attitudes that marginalize sex workers and thereby put them in harm's way. Aboriginal groups that fought for the investigation of the missing women of Vancouver have brought public attention to the prejudice and harm faced by sex workers.

WHAT HAS PROMPTED PUBLIC AWARENESS AND CONCERN?

The mass murder of sex workers in the Vancouver area (allegedly by Robert Pickton) is arguably what has sparked public attention to the issue of prostitution and the sex trade. Other factors are the following: fears about the vulnerability of children to Internet predators; media publications concerning violence and drug abuse in urban centres and among the homeless; the perceived escalation of drug abuse; and the proliferation of more lethal forms of street drugs. Public awareness of these trends has brought attention to bear on the sex trade. At the same time, advocates for harm reduction policies are loudly recommending the decriminalization of prostitution.

HOW IS THE PUBLIC ALIGNED?

There is active public debate over the appropriateness of decriminalizing prostitution. So far, the media-generated panic about the links between prostitution, organized crime, illegal migrants, and an underworld of violence and drug abuse has caused the general public to oppose decriminalizing sex work.

WHAT INITIATIVES HAVE BEEN TAKEN AND WHAT POLICIES HAVE BEEN PUT IN PLACE?

Currently, the trial of Robert Pickton is keeping public attention on the issue. The trial is likely to illuminate the failures of the legal and social welfare systems. Research into prostitution has been undertaken, and government proposals for changes to legislation have been advanced.

WHAT IS THE PUBLIC REACTION?

The public appears to be more certain about the immorality of prostitution than about the acceptability of sex work as a legitimate occupation.

ANALYTICAL APPROACHES TO UNDERSTANDING THE SEX TRADE

In this chapter a structural functionalist analysis, while showing how sex work can benefit society, mostly focuses on the numerous and diverse dysfunctions—for example, the spread of disease and the exploitation of vulnerable persons—associated with such work. After that, a social conflict analysis explores the conflict between the agents and the victims of sex work. The fact that these victims are mostly women has determined our selection of the third analytical approach to be used: a micro feminist analysis. The micro feminist analysis reveals that the exploitation of already marginalized women is rooted in cultural patterns.

A Structural Functionalist Analysis

BRIEF REVIEW OF THE STRUCTURAL FUNCTIONALIST PERSPECTIVE

The structural functionalist view of society is a macro perspective that views society as a system of integrated social structures, also known as social institutions, each of which performs a specialized function for the good of society as a whole. According to a structural functionalist view, a social issue is a disruption or dysfunction in the normal organization and functioning of society. As an analytical tool, the structural functionalist paradigm can be used to locate where a dysfunction has originated or to estimate the future impact of an ongoing social change or event.

MANIFEST FUNCTIONS

The sex trade, namely prostitution, has been dubbed "the world's oldest profession." It follows that this trade benefits society in some way. A review of the social functions of deviance is pertinent here. Contained sexual deviance clarifies the boundaries of a society's morality. Practically speaking, it preserves the institution of the family by defining sexual exploration as sport or as socially frowned-upon exotic behaviour—that is, activities that are not part of family sexual relationships. Another social benefit of the sex trade is that it offers economic independence to otherwise unemployed or difficult-to-employ women and men. Sex as a commodity arguably enables a highly mobile population, unencumbered by the demands of family commitment, to maintain an independent lifestyle. Finally, the sex trade also creates jobs for the law enforcement personnel required to control it.

In short, the elimination of sex as a commodity is most likely impossible and would not be altogether beneficial.

DYSFUNCTIONS

Social trends and events are dysfunctional when their overall impact on the functioning of society is negative. Sex work that contradicts values that are dominant in our society, such as gender equality and freedom of choice, is disruptive and therefore dysfunctional. Sex work that exploits the vulnerable in society, such as child prostitution and child pornography, is dysfunctional. Sex work that invites the participation of organized crime (for example, through the international trafficking of sex slaves) is dysfunctional. Sex work that threatens the public with the spread of serious diseases is dysfunctional. Sex work that risks the lives of its workers is also dysfunctional.

A structural functionalist analysis can locate the faults in the social system that have created dysfunctions, and the theoretical conclusions it produces can be assessed in light of current media coverage.

WHAT CAUSES SYSTEM DYSFUNCTION?

The structural functionalist perspective is sometimes charged with having a conservative nature and with implicitly defending the **status quo**. But its conservative orientation enables this perspective to identify the origin of dysfunctions. The structural functionalist view is that change, whether social or technological, disrupts the overall functioning of a social system; shifts in prevailing social values and technological innovations (electronic information systems, for example) have generated disruptions in modern societal function.

RECENT SOCIAL TRENDS

Value Trends

Feminism has prompted public efforts to achieve gender equality. A consequence of feminist interest in women's lives is that the sex trade is being reassessed. No longer is it acceptable to conclude, on the basis of white middle-class values, that all sex trade workers are exploited or the victims of desperate circumstances. We have also seen how equality rights activists have increased the public tolerance for unconventional sexual behaviours such as openly displayed homosexuality or exotic sexual practices. What is more, advertising media, together with newly relaxed cultural attitudes about eroticism and sex, have encouraged a more public display of sexualized behaviours.

Globalization

An increasingly globalized world has involved increasing migration. In turn, migration has increased the public tolerance of social diversity and subcultural differences.

Technological Innovation

In Canada today, there is an increasingly profound reliance on electronically mediated social interaction. The formation of **virtual communities** is common, and many are formed around immoral and deviant behaviour. At the same time, increased mobility nationally and globally has altered the nature of threats from crime and from disease.

Heightened interest in the sex trade and the reassessment of its meaning and negative impacts are a consequence of the changes described above. It is now important to identify some of the threats and dysfunctions created by the sex trade.

EVIDENCE OF DYSFUNCTIONS

Spread of Sexually Transmitted Diseases

Michael Rekart (2005), in the introduction to his report for the British Columbia Centre for Disease Control, stated that sex work and injection drug use are the world's most dangerous activities. Sex workers have an increased risk of sexually transmitted infections (STIs). Protection, in the form of condoms and safer-sex practices, is often inconsistently used (especially with regular partners or non-paying partners), or it lies in the control of the customers or brothel owners. STIs greatly increase the risk of HIV infection, as do certain activities that heighten genital trauma. Child prostitutes, because of their physical immaturity and their lack of social power and protection, are especially vulnerable to STIs. The UN estimates that, worldwide, 1 million children each year enter the sex trade, often sold or led into the industry by their families.

Drug abuse

Substance abuse among sex workers—alcohol abuse primarily but also, very often, injection drug use—creates adverse health effects such as addiction, malnourishment, and infection. Sex workers who use drugs are also more vulnerable to violence and, because they use disease-protection measures inconsistently, to contracting STIs and HIV (Rekart, 2005).

Violence

Sex workers, especially street workers and those who are young or migrant, face the danger of violence. This can include physical, verbal, and sexual violence, such as gang rape, as well as robbery and murder. However, recent research suggests that the media depictions of violence as a typical element of the sex trade are questionable. Most research has shown that the majority of sex buyers are not violent—that is, that most of the violence is perpetrated by a small minority of sex buyers (Benoit & Shaver, 2006). Most members of the public agree that any violence against women and children, regardless of their occupation, is unacceptable.

Criminalization of Sex Workers

As outlined earlier in this chapter, sex work itself is not illegal, but many elements of the trade are. The ambiguity of the law in this regard has resulted in the ongoing criminalization of sex workers (Benoit & Shaver, 2006). Studies suggest that this has led to their involvement in violence, their harassment by police, their reduced access to health and social services, and their loss of social supports and freedoms (Rekart, 2005). And, as the Pickton case suggests, the marginalization of sex workers that results from their criminalization can make them vulnerable to work-related mortality.

ORIGINS OF DYSFUNCTIONS

Now that some of the difficulties and destructive results of the sex trade have been identified, a structural functionalist analysis of it can help us understand the origin of the dysfunctions. Such an analysis can be used, in turn, to support recommended changes to social policy.

Questions That Guide a Structural Functionalist Analysis

WHAT SOCIAL INSTITUTIONS ARE CENTRALLY INVOLVED?

The social issue of prostitution is embedded in the social institutions of the law and of health and medicine, of the economy, the media, and the government.

WHAT ARE THE MANIFEST FUNCTIONS? WHAT ARE THE DYSFUNCTIONS THAT RESULT FROM THE SEX TRADE?

The critical issue is one of access and fair treatment. The *government* serves society by providing social services and by coordinating their provision. Sex workers, because of the popular disapproval of their occupation, appear to be ignored or made vulnerable by government actions.

The social institution of *medicine* is responsible for caring, curing, and preventing disease. But because of the social stigma against prostitution, sex workers have difficulty acquiring medical care and health counselling.

A main function of the *economy* is the provision of jobs. Many sex workers, having been marginalized by earlier life experiences such as drug abuse or violence in the home, legitimately lack the means to be gainfully employed. Research shows that, once these workers assume debt and become part of the underground economy of the sex trade, they typically are unable to escape.

The institution of *law and justice* is primarily responsible for maintaining social order. However, the laws framing the sex trade make for ambiguities that impede their enforcement and render sex workers vulnerable.

The primary function of the *media* is to inform the general public and thereby maintain the cohesiveness of Canadian society. But media coverage of the sex trade has incited a moral panic in the public and made it view sex workers as villains rather than as workers providing a service.

SOCIAL TRENDS RESULTING IN DYSFUNCTIONS

Stigma

Benoit and Shaver's (2006) overview of current research into the sex trade in Canada shows that there has been very little research into the social construction of stigmas against it. This study does note that the stigmatization of sex work has made sex workers as an easy target for discrimination. In other words, because sex workers are devalued in Canadian society, they experience marginalization, victimization, and the other risks already listed.

Both the entertainment media and the news media are powerful socialization agents. The public perception of sex workers as immoral and disease-ridden or as generating violence in society is in large measure the media's doing. This media-induced public fear, which is inconsistent with the reality of the situation, is called **moral panic**.

Trafficking in Sex Workers

Trafficking in humans is illegal and exploitative. It is the fastest growing international business, according to the UN (Rekart, 2005). Migrant workers in the sex trade are the most vulnerable to violence and exploitation because of their isolation and their lack of social supports.

Lack of Economic Opportunities

Financial need and lack of career options drive people into the sex trade. Research also shows that the greater the sex worker's financial needs, the greater the chances of his or her engaging in risky behaviour. Sex workers who are illegal migrants are often bound to their employers with a debt bond that can never be repaid. The greater the debt is, the less the likelihood of the sex worker's ever escaping.

ACTIONS THAT WOULD RESTORE SYSTEM EQUILIBRIUM

Harm Reduction Policies

Initiatives adopted by the Canadian government, backed by health-care agencies and by academic research, are focused on "harm reduction." Currently, a small number of academics are acknowledging that sex workers may approach their occupation with professionalism and may be able to separate their work lives from their personal lives. These academics also note that sex workers can make sensible decisions about how to reduce risks. For this reason, these academics are recommending "harm reduction policies" that will support rather than undermine the sex workers' own constructive adaptations. Harm reduction involves empowering sex workers through education, preventive care, occupational health and safety protections, and decriminalization. Each of these aspects is briefly described in the Rekart article.

Structural Functionalist Analysis Chart — Chart Guidelines			
Social Action	**Social Institution**	**Manifest Function of Social Institution**	**Dysfunction**
◆ *identification based on researched information* ◆ *identifies a specific social action or event*	◆ *names the social institution affected by the social action or within which it occurs*	◆ *identifies the manifest function of the social institution (the purpose it ideally serves)*	◆ *identifies the impeded function or the disrupted integration of functions caused by the social action*

Structural Functionalist Analysis of the Sex Trade			
Social Action	**Social Institution**	**Manifest Function of Social Institution**	**Dysfunction**
Migration of unemployed to urban centres	Economy	Provision of employment	Lack of employment for the unskilled, the young, and the displaced, producing a rise in the numbers of homeless
Abused children and women escaping to streets	Family	Support and nurture of members	Rise in homeless and in street violence
Rising numbers of homeless and street sex-workers increases their visibility	Municipal government	Maintain social services and social order	Public disdain encourages marginalization of sex workers
Media-driven moral panic in the general public over the sex trade	Media	To inform	Sex-trade workers become villains
Laws passed to "cleanse" streets of homeless and sex workers	Law and justice	Law enforcement	Sex workers forced away from secure work areas
"Communication law," law that prevents soliciting for prostitution in a public place, passed	Law and justice	Law enforcement	Sex workers further marginalized
Sex workers have limited access to support agencies	Health and welfare	Prevention and treatment of disease and maintenance of mental health	Rise in crime, addiction, and despair within sex trade
Sex-trade workers' attempts to organize and unionize thwarted by authorities and moralizing activists	Economy	Provision of employment	Marginalization of sex-trade workers Increased incidence of violence toward sex workers
Growing numbers of abused and addicted sex-trade workers	Law and justice Health and welfare	Provide secure employment Maintenance of health	Reinforcement of anti-sex-trade actions

Your Task: A Structural Functionalist Analysis of Harm Reduction Policies

1. Read through Michael Rekart's (2005) article, "Sex-Work Harm Reduction," at http://www.thelancet.com.
2. Create a structural functionalist analysis chart like the one above (refer to the "Chart Guidelines" before beginning).
3. Select a number of the initiatives discussed in the article and place each under the "social action" heading.
4. Work though the chart.

Draw conclusions based on your analysis of how effectively harm reduction initiatives would restore social equilibrium.

A Social Conflict Analysis of the Sex Trade

BRIEF REVIEW OF THE SOCIAL CONFLICT PERSPECTIVE

A social conflict perspective is a macro perspective that views society as a collection of competing groups in an arena of inequality and conflict. Viewed from this perspective, society is constantly changing. Social changes follow shifts in dominance, and social issues arise from the inequality in society. An understanding of what groups and interests are involved in an issue enables a social conflict analyst to sketch a map of the relationships and power differences among stakeholder groups. With this knowledge, the analyst can predict the issue's future course.

ANALYSIS OF THE SEX TRADE

The popular perception is that all prostitutes are victimized and marginalized, that they typically suffer from STIs and from drug addiction, and are vulnerable to violence that often causes death. According to this perception, prostitutes are a powerless, exploited group and are predominantly women from racial and ethnic minorities. A social conflict perspective would lead one to conclude that prostitutes are the losers in a conflict among groups. In other words, their plight is the outcome of social inequalities.

Evidence of Women's Powerlessness in the Exploitation and Victimization of Prostitutes

The majority of prostitutes are and have always been women. In modern society, gender inequality persists. Radical feminists argue that the exchange of women's sexual favours for money perpetuates the belief that women exist for the pleasure of men and that the female gender itself is subordinate to the male gender. According to this perspective, prostitution also promotes the belief that men are incapable of controlling their sexual appetites. This belief underlies the tendency, in legal contexts, to criminalize the prostitute and excuse the client (Bromberg, 1998).

Street prostitutes, often called *sex slaves*, are on the lowest rung of the hierarchy within the sex industry. These prostitutes rely on the sex trade because they have no other options. They are particularly vulnerable to exploitation. They are slaves to their pimps, their addictions, their debt bonds, and their poverty.

Structural Functionalist Analysis of Harm-Reduction Policies for Sex Work

Social Action	Social Institution	Manifest Function of Social Institution	Dysfunction

Prostitutes have no perceived value in mainstream society. They are often referred to as "nuisances" or as equivalent to street litter—city businesses and respectable residents appeal to the government to "clean up" the streets. Mainstream society seeks to make soliciting and brothels illegal and to close massage parlours and hotels where paid-for sex occurs. The more effort thus applied to ridding the streets of prostitutes, the less access prostitutes have to such resources as health care, police protection, and economic support. Prostitutes' efforts to create union-like associations have been squashed by prohibitionist lobbies (Gardner, 2002).

Many prostitutes have personal histories of violence and have chosen a life on the street as their means of escape. Such a life involves a lack of social supports as well as, quite often, the compounding problems of drug addiction and debt, all of which further marginalize street sex workers.

Prevailing Power Relationships

To date, the status quo perspective on prostitution does not distinguish between escort services and street prostitution. Female escorts, it is sometimes argued, perceive themselves as businesswomen who offer a service. They do not match the media image of the down-and-out prostitute. Street prostitutes, on the other hand, do live a life closer to this media image. The conservative view condemning all sex work is dominant in Canada, even among feminists, and the laws reflect this view insofar as they typically criminalize the sex trade and sex workers. Sex workers have not managed to oppose these attitudes in an organized way, and have been unsuccessful in changing them. Because of the powerful stigma attached to sex work and prostitution, prostitutes are increasingly vulnerable in a context of diminishing social supports.

Predicting the Future of the Issue

The stigma against sex workers will likely continue, but the Robert Pickton trial will bring increased public attention to the plight of sex workers and may lend credibility to the critics of the current laws. This may lead to changes in laws and attitudes that will improve the lives of sex workers.

QUESTIONS THAT GUIDE A SOCIAL CONFLICT ANALYSIS

Who Are the Major Stakeholders in the Issue?

There are a number of organizations involved in the issue of the sex trade, some dominant, some subordinate. As we have mentioned, street prostitutes live on the margins of society. They rely on what has been called *survival sex.* Some organizations are working on behalf of such prostitutes. One example is the Prostitution Alternatives Counselling and Education group (PACE), a Vancouver East organization of former prostitutes, prostitutes, and charity workers who are attempting to organize street workers, so they can advocate for better social supports and security. Their goal is to bring honour and respect to sex work. They believe that attitude changes in the public will lead to supports and protection for sex workers (Gardner, 2002).

Feminist organizations champion the equality of women. Some streams of feminism (radical feminism) categorically deny that prostitution can be anything other than exploitation. Radical feminists have been most successful in promoting the prohibition of prostitution. Their efforts align them with the conservative public majority, although the rationale behind their efforts is their own. Other streams of feminism (for example, liberal feminism) emphasize that emancipated women have the right of choice. This branch of feminism promotes the idea that women have the general right to control how they use their bodies, and this gives prostitutes the right to ply the sex trade legally (Bromberg, 1998).

Many prostitutes are from racial and ethnic minorities. For example, the majority of the murdered prostitutes from Vancouver's east side were Aboriginal. For this reason, Aboriginal communities are part of the sex-trade issue.

Social scientists, who have become concerned about the damaging effects of criminalizing prostitutes, have conducted and published numerous studies identifying problems and opportunities. They recommend the decriminalization of prostitution and advocate the institution of "harm-reduction" initiatives (Rekart, 2005).

A small number of law professionals have also been speaking up on behalf of prostitutes, advocating changes in laws and improved security for sex workers, and challenging popular perceptions about prostitution (Lowman, 2004).

Health-care professionals and social workers have also done studies and lobbied for changes that would improve the lives of sex workers.

Despite the diverse interest groups opposed to the general public's conception of prostitution, the dominant view continues to be that prostitution is morally wrong, that it exploits women, and that it is a blight on the urban landscape.

What Are the Resources of Each Stakeholder Group?

For analytical purposes, let us say there are only two sides to the issue, the anti-sex-trade side and the pro-choice side. Our next step would be to identify all of the resources possessed by each side, so that an estimation of their relative power could be made. Such a comparison will help us assess how strongly dominant the anti-sex-trade side is, so that we can estimate the future of the prostitution issue in Canada.

Anti-Sex-Trade Resources

Anti-sex-trade opinions and images appear to dominate *public opinion*. The news and entertainment *media* have promoted the image of prostitutes as seedy, downtrodden, exploited, criminal, and morally reprehensible. Most media consumers, who constitute the public majority, accept these images.

Every Canadian government since the early 1970s—federal, provincial, and municipal—has supported an anti-sex-trade agenda. The numerous *laws* that have been passed to "crack down on" the *nuisance* of prostitution reflect the strength of the *media image* and of the anti-sex-trade position.

Feminist actions, especially those of radical feminists, support prohibition of the sex trade. These activists strenuously promote the ideal of a society free of the sex trade.

Social trends and *fortuitous events* have also boosted the power of the anti-sex-trade lobby. For example, the increase in child pornography and the growing public awareness of sex predators lurking on the Internet are fuelling public outrage toward all facets of the sex trade. Prostitution's association with crime, organized crime, drug trafficking, and human trafficking has also strengthened the public fear and disgust for the sex trade.

Stigma and *stereotypes* are another power resource that dominant groups use to confirm their superiority over the exploited groups. The current language used in references to prostitutes tends to emphasize their immorality or their "garbage" status. This linguistic stigmatizing reinforces established prejudices and thereby justifies discriminatory actions.

Pro-Choice Resources

The rising crime rate and the victimization of prostitutes are *social trends* that have encouraged *public debate* about the sex-trade issue. These trends, along with *academic research* into the impacts of the marginalization and victimization of prostitutes, have prompted new assessments of the sex trade. Legal and medical studies of prostitution also lend great support to the pro-choice and harm-reduction side of the issue.

The *media coverage* of the Robert Pickton trial has done much to generate public debate over whether laws designed to curtail the sex trade are in fact helping anyone and whether they may in fact be a factor in the violent victimization of sex workers. This public reassessment may turn out to be the most potent factor in altering the balance of power between the anti-sex-trade and pro-choice sides.

The well-known success of certain *role models* in the sex-trade industry—the "happy hooker" Xaviera Hollander being one of the first—has brought support to the pro-choice side of the contest. Similarly, the attempts to *organize* and *unionize* sex workers, although not often successful, lend credibility to the pro-choice side of the debate, and create curiosity about it.

A SOCIAL CONFLICT ANALYSIS TOOL: POWER RESOURCES CHART

As there was for the structural functionalist analysis, there is a chart that can be adopted for the social conflict analysis of a social issue. In this case, the chart will enable you to assess the dynamics of power between the two sides in a social issue. It will permit you to evaluate the relative power of the two sides by weighing their respective assets. Please note that, despite the clear-cut appearance of the chart, your evaluation of relative power is still fundamentally subjective. The more complete your research, however, the more realistic your assessment will be.

Column Headings

The chart represents two sides in the issue. In reality, of course, a social issue has many facets, but condensing them all to two sides will help you assess where the power and advantages lie. What you name each side is immaterial, but the name should be consistent with the groups involved in the issue. It is conventional to situate the more powerful or dominant group on the left side of the chart.

Main Columns: Resources of Power

In each of these columns, you list the assets possessed by each side. The lists should be distinct from each other. For example, each side has money assets, but you would identify money as an asset only for the side that derives the greatest advantage from its money assets. The lists do not need to have an equal number of entries. A greater number of items in a list does not necessarily indicate more power. For example, a side with only two assets—for example, legal authority and public support—could dominate a side with more numerous but less powerful assets such as technical superiority, financial backing, and media attention.

Power Resources Chart—Chart Guidelines					
DOMINANT MAJORITY: Name the side that your research shows to be dominant (have the greatest power and resources) in the issue.			**MINORITY: Name the side that your research shows to be disadvantaged (have fewer resources and less power) in the issue.**		
WIN	LOSE	RESOURCES	WIN	LOSE	RESOURCES
✔ item increases power		◆ Record an asset that delivers advantage to **this** side. This information would come from your research. If both sides have the asset, credit it to the side that has the greatest amount of it. Example: money.		✘ item diminishes power of other side	◆ Record an asset that delivers advantage to **this** side. This information would come from your research. If both sides have the asset, credit it to the side that has the greatest amount of it. Example: public sympathy.
		◆ Note that there is one item per box, and the list on each side can have a differing number of entries.			◆ Note that there is one item per box, and the list on each side can have a differing number of entries.

Smaller Columns: Win Columns and Lose Columns

Each side's assets can be measured against the other side's. To measure the relative power of each side, you need to compare *each* item from one column with *each* item from the other column. For example, number each item in the dominant majority column: 1, 2, and 3 (if there are three items). Label each item in the other column with a letter: a, b, c, d, and e. For your comparison of power or advantage, evaluate *item 1* against *item a.* If everything else were equal, which side would get the advantage? Beside the winning item, put a check under the "win" column of the side that gets the advantage, and put a check under the "lose" column of the other side. "Win" means gaining advantage and power, and "lose" means the opposite. Continue by scoring each item in the first column against all the items in the other: for example, item 1 against items a, b, c, d, and e, or to the end of your list in column two. Then go to item 2 in column one, and measure it against each of a, b, c, d, and e. Keep scoring. At the end of the scoring, the wins on the dominant side should balance with the losses on the other side. (If the dominant side had 3 assets listed and the minority side had 5, you should have 30 check marks by the end of your scoring: $3 \times 5 \times 2 = 30$.)

What can be learned from the table? First, a resource item that has a concentration of win checkmarks next to it is a pivotal asset for that side. If this item belongs to the minority side, it may indicate that the minority is gaining in power, and this development may have a significant impact on the resolution of the issue. If your research indicates that the value of one of the most powerful assets on the dominant side is going to change, you would predict a significant development in the issue. For example, if the discriminatory practices upon which the dominant side relied were going to be made illegal, the dominant side's power would be significantly reduced and the balance of power between the two sides would change.

A completed power resources chart follows. What has been learned from the analysis is outlined by the summary that follows the chart.

Which Side Is Dominant, and What Is the Future of the Issue?

The anti-sex-trade side dominates the issue. As long as this side dominates, it appears that prostitutes will continue to be marginalized and vulnerable to violence and death. The rising death toll among prostitutes is encouraging public debate and academic study by medical and legal faculties. The increasing victimization of prostitutes is sparking a feminist debate. All of these debates may encourage a change in

Power Resources Chart for the Sex-Trade Issue					
Dominant Side: Anti-Sex-Trade/Abolition			**Minority Side: Pro-Choice**		
WIN	LOSE	RESOURCE	WIN	LOSE	RESOURCE
♠♠♠♠♠♠		Public opinion condemning all forms of the sex trade	♠	♦♦♦♦♦♦	Media coverage of the Pickton trial
♠♠♠♠♠♠		Media portrayal of the sex trade as degrading to women and as linked to crime and violence	♠	♦♦♦♦♦♦	Public debate about the sex trade
♠♠♠♠♠♠		Laws that prosecute sex workers in an effort to abolish the sex trade	♠	♦♦♦♦♦♦	Academic research that refutes popular perceptions of the sex trade as immoral and dangerous
♠♠♠♠♠	♦	Radical feminist actions promoting abolition of the sex trade	♠	♦♦♦♦♦♦	Advocates in law and health care lobbying to make sex work less dangerous
♠	♦♦♦♦♦	Expansion of pornography on the Internet and vulnerability of children to sex predators		♦♦♦♦♦♦♦	Role models like the "happy hooker," changing the public perception of prostitution
♠♠♠♠♠♠		Stigma assigned to the sex trade	♠♠	♦♦♦♦♦	Sex-worker organizations such as COYOTE actively engage public support and act as prostitute advocates
♠♠♠♠♠♠		Stereotypes about sex-trade workers			
36	6		6	36	

public perception, which would open the way for policy changes such as harm-reduction initiatives. But such a shift is not likely to happen soon. The inequality of the two sides in the issue, reflected in the Power Resources Chart, indicates that change is not likely in the near future.

A Feminist Analysis of the Sex Trade

BRIEF REVIEW OF THE FEMINIST PERSPECTIVE

Feminism is both a social movement and an ideology. As an analytical tool, the feminist perspective brings to every social issue an agenda of achieving equality for women. Within the ideology, there are diverse views about the best means of achieving this. For example, radical feminists such as socialist feminists argue that the only solution to gender inequality is the restructuring of society. Liberal feminists, on the other hand, seek equality for women within the existing social structures.

The feminist perspective can be both macro and micro. At the macro level, conflict among feminist factions or between feminist and anti-feminist organizations can be studied through a template like that used for a social conflict analysis. At the micro level, the focus would be on the meaning of social actions, the language used to describe the various perspectives, and the patterns of gender socialization.

A FEMINIST ANALYSIS OF THE SEX TRADE

So far, theoretical analyses of the sex trade have pointed to the effects of social stigma on the perpetuation of the sex trade *issue*. It would be helpful now to explore the origins of the stigma, the role of language in preserving it, and the stigma's role in perpetuating the marginalization and victimization of prostitutes. Adoption of a feminist micro perspective is suitable for this.

A Radical Feminist View of Prostitution

Because radical feminism is founded on the belief that women's oppression is the most fundamental form of oppression, prostitution *cannot* be a free choice. Rather, prostitutes are victimized and exploited, coerced into behaviours meant to please men. To radical feminists, prostitution can never be a harmless, private business transaction; in their view, it perpetuates the objectification, subordination, and exploitation of women. The radical feminist view tends to attract greater political support because it is consistent with the view of prostitution promoted by the media. According to this view, even women not directly coerced or exploited have been made vulnerable by their life circumstances, and prostitution only compounds their vulnerability to exploitation and harm.

A Liberal Feminist View of Prostitution

In contrast, a liberal feminist stance is focused more on the prostitute's rights of choice, accepting that prostitution can be a business into which a woman freely enters (Bromberg, 1998). This is the stance adopted by prostitutes who profess to have *chosen* the trade; they are engaged in business, *not* survival sex. They present themselves as successful businesswomen who have stable home lives and lucrative businesses (Gardner, 2002; Lowman, 2004).

Symbolic interaction theories emphasize that perception shapes social and personal realities because it directs action. How does the feminist view of prostitution influence Canada's response to prostitution?

A Definition of Stigma

Stigma is a negatively valued marker that distinguishes a group from others. The process of stigmatization is similar to the process of **labelling**. Labelling enhances the social power of those who impose the labels and it marginalizes those who bear them by shunting them behind social barriers or by restricting their opportunities. Stigmas or labels also shape a person's sense of worth and thus affect personal choices.

The Language of Stigma and Labelling

The general public's view of prostitutes is reflected in the language commonly used to refer to them. It is the language of disposal. Politicians and business people often refer to prostitutes as "a blight" on city streets. They call for a "cleanup" that will rid the streets of the sex trade. They characterize prostitutes, together with the homeless, as "street litter" whose presence is offensive and degrading.

The language of radical feminists, on the other hand, promotes the idea of prostitutes' oppression. Words like *victim*, *enslavement*, *degradation*, and *exploitation* are used (Weitzer, 2006).

The language of liberal feminists promotes the idea of choice for prostitutes, so words like *empowerment*, *service*, and *equality* are used. Two prostitute organizations illustrate the divergent views of the radical and the liberal feminists. Women Hurt in Systems of Prostitution Engaged in Revolt (WHISPER) is an organization whose members have been terrorized, traumatized, and beaten as prostitutes. WHISPER acts as an information network that gives radical feminism a forum. It contrasts with a second organization whose members possess political skills and advocacy advantages not known by the members of WHISPER. The second organization is Call Off Your Old Tired Ethics (COYOTE). This group helps sex workers who want to change their occupation, and it resists the blaming of sex workers for the spread of AIDS and STIs. COYOTE also educates workers and the public about safer sex. The general aim of this organization is to effect changes that will benefit all prostitutes (Bromberg, 1998).

There are distinctions in the way prostitutes view their own lives. Sexual slaves are bound by a debt bond and have no choice. Those who engage in survival sex are driven by poverty, drug addiction, and lack of alternative income sources; they also have no choice. The third category is prostitutes who have choice and have opted for prostitution.

The Impact of Stigma on Prostitutes

Perception and language shape action. It follows that the groups whose perceptions and language dominate discussion of an issue will have the most influence in shaping the social policies concerning it. The language of disposal supports the media portrayal of the sex trade as involving the victimization and exploitation of a powerless and vulnerable group. This dominant perception of prostitution drives public demands for eradication of the sex trade. Whether seen as victims or villains, sex workers are criminalized, and controlling them requires directing ever more resources to law enforcement. Criminalization drives the sex trade underground and degrades sex workers. Lowman (2004) has charged that the radical feminist prohibitionist agenda, by ruling out harm-reduction policies, is sacrificing street prostitutes, who are the most vulnerable, to its utopian goal of a society without prostitution; whereas pro-choice feminists argue that the goal of public policy should be to ensure that prostitution is practised only by those who freely choose it.

Radical feminism, with its view that all prostitution involves the oppression and objectification of women, promotes the total abolition of the sex trade. In this goal—if not in its underlying rationale—radical feminism coincides with public efforts to criminalize and punish sex workers.

The liberal feminist voice promotes empowerment and choice and thus encourages support and organization. However, this view is very weak in the face of the public's moral panic. How the prevailing abolitionist impulse has negatively affected public policy is reflected in the murders of Vancouver prostitutes: so long as these women were permitted to work out of bars and clubs, help was near. But once the laws closed the bars, clubs, and brothels, sex workers were forced to work the streets alone. It was then that the murder rate among prostitutes began to climb astronomically (Gardner, 2002, June 15).

Socialization of the Meaning of Prostitution

Feminist scholars have observed that **patriarchal** social structures remain pervasive in modern Western culture, and that, so long as this is the case, women cannot attain gender equality. Although women have made gains, socialization patterns continue to place them second, behind men. Traditional gender roles preserve the patriarchal norms and beliefs, which, it is argued, keep women vulnerable both in society at large and in the realm of prostitution. As noted in chapter 5, gender, as distinguished from sex, is a social construct. As a social construct, it defines a relationship between men and women. It is the traditional relationship, which places men above women, that is at issue.

The media is an important agent of socialization that plays a large role in shaping and perpetuating the public image of the victimized and criminal sex worker. It has encouraged moral panic and a moral crusade. A **moral crusade** involves activism based on an **ideology** that is promoted as reality. Radical feminists who claim that violence and exploitation are intrinsic to prostitution gain a following because of the power of their beliefs and because of their ability to make others believe. Research contradicts their claims, but it is usually suppressed.

The media is a powerful agent of socialization. It has an important role in promoting the moral panic that gives rise to moral crusades; it tends to provide, maintain, and police the definition of deviance that structures public awareness of and attitudes toward social problems (O'Sullivan et al., 1983). In connection with the sex trade, the mass media has done much to reinforce the idea that *all* prostitution exploits women and that selling sex reduces *all* women to sexual objects.

RESPONSES

GOVERNMENT AND POLICY

There is disagreement among Canadians and public policy makers about what in the sex trade is a problem. Some have mobilized around the central notion that pornography and sex work inevitably denigrate or "objectify" women. Certain legal decisions and political responses have followed this sort of reasoning. Feminists in the 1970s, particularly in the United States, promoted the notion that pornography should be stopped and the sex trade eradicated. Prominent American feminists Andrea Dworkin and Catharine MacKinnon are well-known proponents of this view. This was the view articulated by Canadian Supreme Court Justice Antonio Lamer in his judgment in *Re Prostitution* (Supreme Court of Canada, 1990), when he linked prostitution with violence against women and with the inevitable exploitation of sex-trade workers:

> Prostitution, in short, becomes an activity that is degrading to the individual dignity of the prostitute and which is a vehicle for pimps and customers to exploit the disadvantaged position of women in our society. In this regard the impugned section aims at minimizing the public exposure of this degradation especially to young runaways who seek refuge in the streets of major urban centres, and to those who are exposed to prostitution as a result of the location of their homes and schools in areas frequented by prostitutes and who may be initially attracted to the "glamorous" lifestyle as it is described to them by the pimps. (n.p.)

However, more recently, others have criticized as puritanical this negative view of all sex work. Their arguments take pornography as a case in point. They assert that it is important at least to differentiate between different types or genres of pornography and to recognize that not all are equally harmful to women. More recently, so-called "sex-positive feminists" have argued that pornography can sometimes be a form of artistic expression, that it promotes women's control over their bodies, and that it can be enjoyable for female consumers. These feminists feel that anti-pornographic sentiment helps maintain an oppressive sexual regime in which women's sexual gratification is never celebrated. Notable proponents of this position are academics Laura Kipnis and Susie Bright as well as former pornographic actress Nina Hartley.

Many human rights groups in Canada today are organizing around the notion that it would be best to legalize prostitution in order to protect the women and men involved in it. This position is based on the idea that sex work does not inevitably involve the enslavement of women or of people from marginalized groups. These policy advocates suggest that prostitution should be seen as a private service arrangement between consenting adults, that people should have individual autonomy over their bodies, and that members of the world's oldest profession should not be criminalized (British Columbia Civil Liberties Association [BCCLA], 2005). They contend that prostitution should be legalized and regulated and that sex workers should be treated with respect, protected from harm, and encouraged to unionize.

LAW AND POLICING

The most obvious way for police to deal with the sex trade in Canada is to conduct investigations, undercover where necessary, and to arrest those involved in illegal activities. Some have suggested alternative police approaches. Police are always in a difficult position where there is considerable opposition to an existing criminal law regime. In Vancouver, for example, zoning allows certain aspects of the sex trade to be practised that are prohibited by the *bawdy house* provisions of the *Criminal Code*. Police are thus given unclear messages about how to carry out their duty. On the one hand, the city is effectively asking them to turn a blind eye to certain kinds of prostitution. On the other hand, federal legislation demands they make arrests.

COMMUNITY

Investigative complications compound the difficulties police face as they attempt to unravel the webs of crime and vice spun by pimps and others involved in the sex trade. It is difficult to determine who the real "bad guys" are. Should the sex workers be punished for morally reprehensible conduct in selling their bodies? Should they be arrested and charged for their own protection? Should enforcement efforts focus on pimps? Should the real focus be on humiliating and stigmatizing the johns, as a way of diminishing demand for paid sex work? In their day-to-day work police have to answer these difficult questions, with reference to legislation, bylaws, community views, and local protocols.

INDIVIDUAL INVOLVEMENT

The sex trade is a social issue affecting millions of people worldwide, but students who are concerned about some aspect of it—whether it be gender issues, child exploitation, or human trafficking—need not feel utterly helpless.

In order to determine what sorts of individual responses might be appropriate, students should precisely determine their own views on the sex trade. Some potentially useful questions for reflection might be the following:

- Is prostitution rape?
- Is prostitution inevitably a problem in society?
- What does it mean for women in general that men can pay for sex in our society?
- Are there real choices in sex work?
- Should prostitution be legalized?

There are many effective initiatives already underway in response to these problems. Students can, for example, get involved with local or international organizations that are working to end the exploitation of women and children. They can participate in campaigns designed to "deglamorize" the sex trade or to legalize and regulate it.

CONCLUSION

Academic research papers require unbiased, logical argument backed by valid researched information. Because the issues surrounding sex and sexuality are so value laden, the topic of sex work presents some special pitfalls to the student researcher. That is to say, the student may find him- or herself arguing from a moralistic or "personal-values" position. For a research paper on sensitive topics, the theoretical perspectives of sociology and a social issue perspective are the best insurance against the inappropriate inclusion of personal values. Having personal values and morals is important, but in a research paper, they are misplaced. Furthermore, by keeping your personal perspectives separate from your research interests, you will learn more from your research.

In this chapter, the structural functionalist perspective was adopted to show how societal failure has victimized sex workers already marginalized by their life's circumstances. The social conflict perspective delivered insights about evolving trends, about the direction of that evolution, and about the groups that may successfully challenge the marginalization of sex work. Finally, a micro feminist perspective was used to explain how sex-work stigmas are embedded in the language and belief structures of modern society. Implicit in this micro feminist analysis are the symbolic interactionist and social constructionist perspectives.

KEY TERMS

child pornography the depiction of children under the age of 18 in sexually explicit material

ideology an overarching belief system that guides perspectives and social behaviours and trends (for example, feminism or patriarchy)

labelling the process of applying a label or stigma to a person or group; stigmas, or negative labels, can marginalize persons and groups

moral crusade activism based on an ideology that is promoted as a reality; the implications are that there can be no reasoned dissent; often driven by fanaticism and extremism

moral panic the public perception of a profound threat from crime or social disorder, usually a result of inflated, exaggerated media coverage; perceived threats are to fundamental values and morals

patriarchal the term applied to social organizations, social structures, and ideologies that preserve male dominance over women

pimp an individual, usually a man, who lives off the proceeds of sex work by prostitutes

pornography depictions or images of sexual activity, usually visual, that are produced not for their artistic merit but for the sexual stimulation of the consumer

sex trade prostitution, or the exchange of sexual services for money or other material gain, with no emotional involvement

solicit overtly offering or procuring sexual services

status quo established norms and perspectives of a society's dominant majority

virtual communities groups and organizations, established through the Internet, of people with shared interests and ideals; members interact electronically and not face to face

FOR FURTHER RESEARCH

The following website is set up as a tribute to the missing women of Vancouver's east side: http://www.missingpeople.net. It is a dedication to their memory and a place where family members of the missing women can share their thoughts.

The Lancet is an independent journal that now has a Web presence. It is devoted to issues of global medicine. In it you can find articles that explore current health issues. Michael Rekart's article "Sex-Work Harm Reduction" is available in this journal. http://www.thelancet.com.

You may find that the article at the following link helpfully expands this chapter's definition and explanation of moral panic: www.mediaknowall.com/violence/moralpanicnotes.html.

For a useful discussion of how the public perception of sex trafficking has been influenced by various social forces, see R. Weitzer's paper at the following link: http://www.allacademic.com/meta/p103577_index.html.

COYOTE (Call Off Your Old Tired Ethics) is an organization that is part of the sex-workers education network. As such it is a resource for sex workers and an advocacy group. http://www.bayswan.org/COYOTE.html.

For an account of COYOTE and the general effects of sex workers' activism, see Jenness, Valerie. (1990). From sex as sin to sex as work: COYOTE and the reorganization of prostitution as a social problem. *Social Problems, 37*(3), 403-420.

More information on prostitution and the sex trade can be found at the following link: http://www.rapeis.org. This organization is supported by a number of foundations and is in place to provide support, education, and public awareness of what rape is and what it does.

REFERENCES

Benoit, C., & Shaver, F. (2006). Critical issues and directions in sex work research. *Canadian Review of Sociology & Anthropology, 43*(3), 243-264. Retrieved from academic Search Premier database.

British Columbia Civil Liberties Association [BCCLA]. (2005, January). BCCLA updated position on sex work laws. http://www.bccla.org/positions/privateoff/05sex%20work.htm.

Bromberg, S. (1998). Feminist issues in prostitution. First presented to the 1997 International Conference on Prostitution at Cal State University, Northridge. http://www.feministissues.com.

CNN. (2001, March 8). Sex slavery: The growing trade. http://archives.cnn.com/2001/WORLD/europe/03/08/women.trafficking/index.html.

Court TV: Crime Library. (n.d.). Robert Pickton: The Vancouver missing women. http://www.crimelibrary.com/serial_killers/predators/robert_pickton/12.html.

Criminal Code. (1985). RSC 1985, c. C-46, as amended.

Davis, K. (2006, March 3). Hooker laws won't change. *Sun News Canada.*

Ennew, J., Gopal, K., Heeran, J., & Montgomery, H. (1996). Children and prostitution: How can we measure and monitor the commercial sexual exploitation of children? Childwatch International Report. http://www.child-abuse.com/childhouse/childwatch/cwi/projects/indicators/prostitution/intro.html.

Gardner, D. (2002, June 9). Do some women really choose to be prostitutes? Some say it's a matter of choice, but to many feminists it's akin to slavery. *The Ottawa Citizen.* http://www.missingpeople.net/do_some_women_really_choose-june_9,_2002.htm.

Gardner, D. (2002, June 15). Courting death (part 1): The law has hounded hookers out of safe areas and into dark alleys, making them easy prey for murderers. *The Ottawa Citizen.* http://www.missingpeople.net/the_law_has_hounded_hookers-june_15,_2002.htm.

Hollander, X. (1971). *The happy hooker.* New York: Dell.

Let's Go Travel Guides. (n.d.). Discover Amsterdam. http://www.letsgo.com/destinations/europe/amsterdam.

Lobaido, A. (2002, February 3). Sex-slave trade flourishes in Thailand. *Worldnet Daily.* http://www.worldnetdaily.com/news/article.asp?ARTICLE_ID=26296.

Lowman, J. (2004, July 20). Reconvening the federal committee on prostitution law reform. *Canadian Medical Association Journal* [CMAJ], *171*(2), 147-148.

Macklin, A. (2003). Dancing across borders: Exotic dancers, trafficking and Canadian immigration policy. *International Migration Review, 37*(2), 464.

Moral Panic. (n.d.). http://www.mediaknowall.com/violence/moralpanicnotes.html.

O'Sullivan, T., Hartley, J., Saunders, D., & Fiske, J. (1983). *Key concepts in communication.* London & New York: Methuen. Quotation retrieved from http://www.mediaknowall.com/violence/moralpanicnotes.html.

Poulin, R. (2004, February 12). Globalization and the sex trade: Trafficking and the commodification of women and children. *Sisyphe.org.* http://sisyphe.org/article.php3?id_article=965.

Rekart, M. (2005, December 17). Sex-work harm reduction. *The Lancet, 366*(9503), 2123-2134. http://www.thelancet.com.

Supreme Court of Canada. (1990). *Re ss. 193 and 195.1(1)(c) of the Criminal Code (Man.)*, [1990] 1 SCR 1123. Judgments of the Supreme Court of Canada. http://csc.lexum.umontreal.ca/en/1990/1990rcs1-1123/1990rcs1-1123.html.

United Nations' Office on Drugs and Crime [UNODC]. (2006). Human trafficking a global problem, U.N. report says. http://usinfo.state.gov/xarchives/display.html?p=washfile-english&y=2006&m=April&x=20060424185515mbzemog0.2210504.

Virtual Tourist. (n.d.). Red Light District—Amsterdam. http://www.virtualtourist.com/travel/Europe/Netherlands/Provincie_Noord_Holland/Amsterdam-463377/Off_the_Beaten_Path-Amsterdam-Red_Light_District-BR-1.html.

Weitzer, Ronald. (2006, March). Moral crusade against prostitution. *Society, 43*(3), 33-38. New York: Springer.

CHAPTER 5

Gender Inequality

CHAPTER OBJECTIVES

After completing this chapter, you will be able to:

Understand significant dimensions of sex and gender

- Understand various definitions of sex and gender and the assumptions underlying these definitions.
- Appreciate the existence and significance of minority gender identities.
- Understand what is meant by sexual orientation.
- Appreciate relationships between sex, gender, and issues to do with image and identity.
- Understand relationships between sex, gender, and economic inequalities.
- Understand the importance of violence against women as a Canadian social problem.

Understand and apply different sociological perspectives to sex and gender

- Feminist
- Social constructionist
- Structural functionalist
- Social conflict

Identify and critique various responses to sex- and gender-related social problems, including responses from

- Government and policy
- Law and policing
- Community
- Individuals

DIMENSIONS

GENDER AND SEX

In conversation, people often use the words *gender* and *sex* interchangeably to refer to sexual distinctions between males and females. There is a longstanding debate about identification based on gender or sex. Some students of the matter have sought to distinguish between **sex**—that is, a person's biological characteristics in relation to the reproductive process—and **gender**, which is the role a person learns to play as a member of the social category *man* or *woman*.

Gender roles pervade people's lives. The manner in which people speak, their gestures and words, the way they dress and walk, the career expectations people have for them—all of these are strongly influenced if not determined by gender.

There has long been debate about whether gender is more a social construct or a biological fact. Some, known as *essentialists*, see gender as entirely biological in origin, constituting natural, innate differences. Essentialists think that women and men are naturally or essentially drawn to certain patterns of behaviour according to their gender: women to jewellery and men to beer, to use simplistic examples. **Social constructionist** thinkers tend to see gender and sex as completely separate and to treat gender as a social construct not fundamentally linked to biological sex. They contend that the attributes ascribed to a gender are arbitrary constructions. In other words, gender is a socially imposed disguise. As feminist Gerda Lerner (1986) wrote in *The Creation of Patriarchy*, gender is a "costume, a mask, a strait-jacket in which men and women dance their unequal dance."

Twentieth-century anthropologist Margaret Mead (1935), another social constructionist, studied the gender traits of men and women in three small-scale societies and noted that the traits assigned to genders were not consistent cross-culturally. This discovery implied that much of what we consider to be male or female behaviour is arbitrarily assigned and socially constructed. A key purpose of Mead's work was to educate the American public of the 1930s about social constructionism so that they might take a more open-minded, egalitarian—and non-racist—view of humanity in general. Among those on the essentialist side is Phyllis Schlafly, an American conservative famous for having almost single-handedly prevented an "equal rights" amendment for women (ERA) being entered into the US constitution after it had been approved by 30 states. Schlafly has argued that women have a fundamentally different nature from men, which is God-given, and that formal legal equality with men would effectively demote women from their unique and privileged status. In 1977, she wrote as follows:

> The Divine Architect who gave men a superior strength to lift weights also gave women a different kind of superior strength. ... The differences between men and women are also emotional and psychological. Without woman's innate maternal instinct, the human race would have died out centuries ago. ... The overriding psychological need of a woman is to love something alive.

Many people find appealing aspects in both sides of this debate. Margaret Mead's work had and continues to have a strong following. Phyllis Schlafly's writing has resonated with a large number of women and men who feel that social constructionism overlooks certain realities about gender. Many contemporary thinkers, rather than taking a side in this polarized debate, see a combination of both "nature" and "nurture" in sex and gender roles.

Social theorizing about the roots of gender and its relationship to biological sex has changed with the rapid shift of gender roles in contemporary Canadian society. As women and men have deviated from traditional gender stereotypes, it has become clear that at least some gender roles, norms, and expectations are not essentially tied to biological sex. Where most women once remained in the private sphere, working as wives and mothers, they now enter the professions and other areas of paid work traditionally dominated by men, and even take on combat roles in the Canadian military. The death in Kabul, in May 2006, of Captain Nichola Goddard made headlines around the world. This was not only because Goddard was the most senior Canadian officer killed to date in Afghanistan, but because she was the first Canadian woman to die in combat since World War II, as well as the first female soldier to be killed in an active combat role. By the same token, male cosmetic lines, including 50 brands of hair-care products, are now successfully marketed and sold. A new generation of Canadian fathers is taking a far more active role in parenting than did Canadian men in the past. Men as well as women have in growing numbers expressed a desire to balance paid work with time spent parenting their children (Statistics Canada, 1992), which suggests that the desire to nurture—in Phyllis Schlafly's words, to "love something alive"—is not an essentially female trait alone.

Advances in our understanding of human biology have also sophisticated our understanding about the differences between women and men. Biological studies continue to present new evidence that men and women are in fact different in fundamental ways. For example, the mapping of the human genome has revealed that men and women are separated by 78 different genes, a degree of difference greater than previously thought by scientists. Seventy-eight genes amount to 2–3 percent of a human being's total genetic makeup. This statistic is also significant because it means that men and women are more genetically different from each other than the human species as a whole is from chimpanzees (Hotz, 2005). Incidentally, men are genetically slightly closer to the chimps than women are (Starr, 2006).

The traditional theory held by some that men are smarter than women because their brains are bigger has been debunked. Relative to average body size, there is effectively no difference in brain size between men and women. Even if there were, it has been shown that brain size has little correlation with intelligence within the human population. At the same time, recent research has revealed material differences between male and female brain function. In experiments, women tend to do slightly better with respect to language abilities and men with respect to spatial questions. Another focus has been the differing thickness of the corpus callosum in men's and women's brains. This is the part of the brain that connects its two hemispheres. Some studies have suggested that this connection is more comprehensive in women than in men, allowing them to do several tasks at once, or "multitask," as well as to connect emotionally with situations, more effectively than men do (Chudler, n.d.). Neuroscience, though it does not show one gender to be "better" than the other, is thus providing mounting evidence that men and women genuinely do have some essentially different strengths.

As social, scientific, and legal theories have evolved over the past century, most writers can now see a fundamental logical flaw underpinning both social constructionism and essentialism in their pure forms: *equal* does not necessarily mean *the same.* Most contemporary writers do not think that men and women have to be fundamentally the same to be deserving of fair and equal treatment. Social equality should apply regardless of what gender or sex role men and women play and regardless of their sexual orientation. This notion of equality will be discussed further, with reference to Canadian constitutional law, later in the chapter.

Minority Gender Identities

In social theory and in Canadian society today, there is a growing appreciation that not all individuals fit neatly into the basic sex or gender categories of male and female. Some societies have historically recognized—and in some cases revered—three, four, or even five genders. Examples of these "extra" genders would be the *hijras* recognized in Pakistan (Nanda, 1998) or the "two spirit" people recognized traditionally by Aboriginal peoples of the Americas. Western society has not traditionally recognized more than two genders. But now, **transgendered** individuals—people whose understanding of their social gender does not coincide with their biological sex, or people who feel they do not fit within either traditional gender category—are emerging from their historical silence and shame to question our traditional categories. The term *transgender* is an inclusive word, meant to cover people who might refer to themselves more specifically as *crossdressers, drag kings* or *queens, transsexuals, androgynous, two-spirit, bi-gendered, multi-gendered,* or free from any gender labels.

The freedom of the transgendered to display their variance publicly has not come without struggle. Violation of accepted gender norms is too often met with reprisal; transgendered people, once classified as mentally ill, are now too often victims of hate-motivated violence (Goldberg & White, 2004). What the American Psychiatric Association (APA) called "gender dissonance" remained on the APA's list of mental disorders even into the 1990s. Increased understanding of transgendered people and their uniqueness has shed new light on old questions about biology, sex, and learned gender roles.

Sexual Orientation

A concept related to sex or gender identity is **sexual orientation**. It is important not to confuse sexual identity, which refers to a person's understanding of his or her own gender, with sexual orientation, which describes the gender to which a person is sexually attracted. Sexual identity and sexual orientation are of course deeply connected. Statistically speaking, the majority of Canadians are **heterosexual**: men attracted to women or vice versa. But a significant minority of Canadians, perhaps as high as 10 percent, are sexually attracted to individuals of the same gender or sex. These people, generally known as *homosexual, lesbian,* or *bisexual,* have reclaimed the term **queer** to describe all minority or variant sexual orientation.

There are many myths and misconceptions about sexual orientation that are based on a confusion of sexual identity with sexual orientation. For instance, there is often an expectation that queer men will act feminine or queer women masculine.

This is not necessarily the case, as recent films—such as the 2006 Oscar winner *Brokeback Mountain*, which depicted the struggles of two cowboys in their forbidden love for each other—have helped to publicize.

Definitions of gender identity have differed across cultures and time periods. So have attitudes toward non-heterosexual intimacy. For example, in ancient Greece it was quite acceptable, and even expected, for men to be bisexual. The works of the Greek lyric poet Sappho, a woman, have been taken as evidence that lesbian relationships, too, were acceptable in classical Greece. Canadian society, on the other hand, has historically been **heterosexist** or **homophobic**; that is to say, it has held up heterosexuality as the dominant or compulsory norm, and punished divergence from it. Although many great historical figures have been queer—writer Oscar Wilde, economist John Maynard Keynes, Renaissance painter Leonardo Da Vinci—sexual love between people of the same gender has until recently been "closeted," or hidden, known as "the love that dare not speak its name" (Douglas, 1894, l. 74). Irish playwright Oscar Wilde was twice charged with "sodomy and indecency" and sentenced to two years of hard labour by a British court for his homosexuality. Sexual activity between consenting persons of the same gender or sex was a criminal offence in Canada until 1969. As recently as 1967, Everett George Klippert was sentenced criminally in Canada to "indefinite detention" as a "dangerous sexual offender" for mutually consensual and private sex with other adult men (Supreme Court of Canada, 1967). During this period, homosexuality was listed as a psychiatric illness by the American Psychiatric Association, and men and women of minority sexual orientations were committed to asylums. The prevailing medical consensus was that homosexuality was dangerous and contagious (Hudspith, 2001).

Over the course of the 20th century, it became more widely understood and accepted that a significant minority of people are not heterosexual. As of 1973, the American Psychiatric Association removed homosexuality from its list of mental illnesses, and individuals were no longer committed to mental health facilities on the basis of their minority sexual orientation. The legal focus has shifted from prohibiting sexual relations between persons of the same sex or gender to protecting queer individuals from discrimination. Discrimination on the basis of sexual orientation has been progressively prohibited since 1977, when Quebec became the first Canadian province to prohibit such discrimination. Since then Canada has seen the equality protection provision set out in s. 15 of the 1982 *Canadian Charter of Rights and Freedoms* come into force through various legislative changes and precedent-setting cases (Hurley, 2005).

In the 21st century, homosexuality in Canadian society has become progressively more acceptable. Activists for gay rights, almost from the time same-sex relationships were decriminalized, have sought increased recognition of and protection for same-sex partnerships and families. Same-sex marriage became a major political issue in Canada around the turn of the century, when official refusals to grant same-sex couples marriage licences were challenged in various courts. As courts began to overturn such refusals as unconstitutional, Canada's federal Parliament started to debate the legalization same-sex of marriages. In 2005, the federal government voted in favour of allowing same-sex marriage. From then until December 7, 2006, over 12,000 couples of the same sex were legally married in Canada. In December 2006, a new government again brought the question of the legality of same-sex marriages before the House of Commons, this time for a free vote. The vote was settled in favour of same-sex marriage, and the matter appears now to be closed. Intimate partners of the same gender or sex are free in Canada not only to carry on their relationships without fear of criminal sanction or institutionalization, but to formalize them through marriage.

Inequality

If gender simply meant a dimension of human diversity that was celebrated, then we would be talking not about a social problem but a social phenomenon. Problems arise when different values are placed upon the different sexes or genders. When this occurs, people with minority sexual orientation or sexual identity are *marginalized* or *oppressed* while another gender or sex is *privileged*. In these circumstances, the marginalized group is disproportionately the victim of violence at the hands of the privileged group.

In 1980, the United Nations issued reports stating that women (who of course make up roughly half of the world's population) do two-thirds of the world's work, earn one-tenth of all the income, and own just one-hundredth of the world's property (Trinity University, n.d.). Throughout history, women have not been as highly educated as men, and have not been granted parallel rights.

The unequal treatment of gender worldwide has an important impact on children as well as on women. In its *State of the World's Children 2007* report, UNICEF indicated that women worldwide continue to have lower incomes than men and to have less say in household decisions than men do. Women's relative lack of power in this regard has meant that fewer of the world's resources are allocated to children's education, nutrition, and health care (CBC News, 2006).

Image and Identity Issues

Gender roles, as we have mentioned, pervade many areas of a person's life. The gender role assigned to a person affects the way he or she feels obliged to act, to appear, and to interact with others. Such roles can prevent people with minority gender identities from expressing their authentic individuality. Even men and women who do not view themselves as transgendered may feel confined by conventional gender roles.

Much of the writing about gender issues focuses on how women differ from men and how gender inequality hurts women. We should keep in mind that gender inequalities and gender stereotypes also hurt men. Generally speaking, gender stereotypes force people to adopt certain roles and prevent them from expressing their individual human potential. For example, a society's expectation that all women be nurturing and caring could disconnect a particular woman from her leadership abilities. The expectation that all men be strong and tough could disconnect a man from his emotional resources. Put more colloquially, gender stereotypes cause women to lose their voices and men to lose their hearts.

One gender issue concerns the social construction of beauty and body image in the media. Naomi Wolf, in *The Beauty Myth* (1991), has noted a relationship between women's advances toward social equality and the ever-increasing manipulation and sexualization of women by popular culture. Wolf writes as follows:

> The more legal and material hindrances women have broken through, the more strictly and heavily and cruelly images of female beauty have come to weigh upon us. ... During the past decade, women breached the power structure; meanwhile, eating disorders rose exponentially and cosmetic surgery became the fastest-growing specialty. ... [P]ornography became the main media category, ahead of legitimate films and records combined, and thirty-three thousand American women told researchers that they would rather lose ten to fifteen pounds than achieve any other goal. ... More women have more money and power and scope and legal recognition than we have ever had before; but in terms of how we feel about ourselves physically, we may actually be worse off than our unliberated grandmothers.

Wolf sees the media-driven myth of female beauty as a cultural backlash against feminism, a kind of "iron maiden" that uses images of female beauty to keep women subordinated to men.

Not everyone agrees that beauty is a cultural construct or that it is an oppressive tool used to subordinate women. Biological and medical research has found that "beauty" corresponds to certain mathematical proportions of the human face that are consistently recognized as beautiful in many human cultures. This implies that at least some of what we understand to be human beauty is objective, perhaps related to our evolutionary biology, not a social creation. Scientists have suggested that these universally acknowledged proportions may be "cues" revealing developmental and reproductive health, reflecting "the role of health assessment in mate choice" (Grammer, 2003).

Nonetheless, whether beauty—like gender—is a product of nature, nurture, or some combination of both, sufferers of eating disorders such as anorexia nervosa and bulimia cite gendered beauty standards as reasons for their pathological efforts to be thin. Plastic surgery for cosmetic purposes is a growth industry, as are cosmetics and diet pills. While women have historically been the gender group hardest hit by expectations about beauty and appearance, men are increasingly affected as well.

One aspect of human biology that is clearly not socially constructed is women's capacity to bear children. This unique capability is related to a wide range of gender issues, the most notorious being the question about where a woman's sovereignty over her body begins and ends. Our legal and cultural systems understand individuals as autonomous and singular, but the issue of two lives intersecting in a woman's body during pregnancy has produced much debate about a woman's right to control her own body during this process. Abortion aside, *birth control* was illegal in Canada from 1892 to 1969. During this time it was a criminal offence to sell or advertise for sale any birth-control device or medicine.

Inducing abortions was also illegal and remained so until 1988, when the Supreme Court of Canada struck down Canada's criminal prohibition against abortion, finding it to violate a woman's Charter right to "life, liberty and security of the person." This decision transformed abortion from a legal issue into a medical question. Although none of Canada's mainstream political parties is currently seeking to reopen this issue and a new abortion law is unlikely, a vocal minority of Canadians still opposes legal abortions, and there continue to be death threats against licensed abortion providers, bomb threats against abortion clinics, and formal protests outside clinics and hospitals where abortions are performed. Dr. Henry Morgentaler, a physician who defied Canada's abortion law and whose case gave rise to the Supreme Court's decision, has more than once been the victim of murder attempts (Supreme Court of Canada, 1988).

Economic and Financial Issues

LOWER WAGES

In Leviticus, God told Moses that a man is worth 50 shekels and a woman worth 30. Oddly enough, this biblical ratio roughly reflects contemporary wage gaps between men and women in both the United States and Canada. Although Canadian women have been entering the paid workforce in large numbers since the 1950s, they have not generally been working in the same occupations as men. Women are disproportionately involved in part-time work, which does not afford them many of the benefits—such as health and dental coverage, and access to employment insurance—that full-time workers receive. In their part-time capacity, women are also less likely to receive maternity or parental benefits. Women tend to be overrepresented in jobs that involve the use of skills traditionally characterized as feminine, such as the nurturing and education of children; and in jobs wherein they are subordinate to men, such as secretarial or administrative assistant roles.

As women entered the paid workforce in the 1950s and '60s, they moved into deeply sex-segregated work environments. Jobs were often advertised as openings for women or men specifically, and unions and employers frequently had separate pay scales for men and women who did the same work. By the 1960s, as provinces introduced human rights legislation, such explicit differentiation began to disappear.

It is abundantly evident, however, that gender-based discrimination did not end with its legal prohibition; it merely went underground. Because of their different roles within the workforce, men and women tend to be part of different bargaining units even when both work full time. Part-time workers, usually women, are still disadvantaged with respect to their pay. A "Current Population Survey" prepared by the US Census Bureau noted that American women in 1999 earned approximately 77 percent of what men did. In 2000, according to the Department of Labor, women's median weekly earnings were 76 percent of the male median (US Department of Labor, 2000). Recent Canadian figures are similar. As of 2001, women were still underrepresented among top income earners and represented only small minorities among skilled tradespeople (5 percent), police officers (10 percent), and senior managers (21 percent). Some estimates of women's incomes in 2001 as compared with men's have affirmed that Canadian women made 61 percent of what men did (Hadley, 2001).

It is not only in the United States and Canada that women are paid less than men. Wage disparities based on gender are common throughout the world. Internationally, according to the International Labour Organization, women earn 60 to 70 percent of what men do per month (Iyer, 2002).

Gender inequality in the workforce has many negative impacts. Studies by the World Bank have shown that societies with significant levels of gender inequality have greater problems with poverty, ill health, and malnutrition, and tend to have lower economic productivity and slower technological and social progress (World Bank, 2001). Partly as a result of these pervasive wage gaps, women are disproportionately poor worldwide, and countries are poorer as a result.

In addition to problems with unequal pay for women, gender is related to other problems in the workplace. **Sexual harassment** involves unwelcome attention of a sexual nature in the workplace. It can range from inappropriate jokes and posters to forced sexual activity. It continues to be a serious problem in Canada's workplaces, even though the *Canada Labour Code* makes it clear that employees have a legal right to work in an environment free of any comment, gesture, or contact of a sexual nature that is likely to cause offence or humiliation to any employee, or that might be perceived by that employee as placing a sexual condition on their employment or on any opportunity within that employment (Human Resources and Social Development Canada, 2005). It is predominantly women who are the victims of such harassment, although it is not unheard of for men to be victims. Complaints by men about sexual harassment are increasing. But it has been difficult for victimized men to come forward, since gender stereotypes concerning male *strength* make it shameful for them to acknowledge that such harassment is occurring.

UNPAID LABOUR

While many Canadian women have been in the paid workforce since at least the 1970s, they still bear disproportionately the burden of unpaid work, especially in the context of their work as mothers caring for minor children. Not all people see this issue the same way. Some think the solution is to increase women's participation in the paid labour force and to encourage men to do more unpaid labour in the home. Others celebrate women's unpaid roles of mother, cook, and cleaner as expressions of women's natural tendencies. Still others are dissatisfied with polarized arguments and don't think that these unpaid roles are necessarily tasks from which women want to be liberated, but that the labour itself should be counted and valued.

Feminists, most prominent among them New Zealand politician Marilyn Waring (Nash, 1996), have questioned our understanding of what constitutes "work." If, for example, a man is able to pursue his career for 80–90 hours a week because his wife or partner is at home cooking, cleaning, caring for his children, doing his banking, and managing all of the activities for which his paid work gives him no time, is it appropriate to say—as our tax system and economic calculations say—that the partner is not an active contributor to the acquisition of that income?

Economic theory that incorporates an appreciation of women's unpaid labour has often been termed "feminist economics." How to measure unpaid work was one major challenge for governments at the United Nations' Third and Fourth World Conferences on Women, in 1985 and 1995, respectively. Government commitments to value such unpaid labour have produced much talk and some research, but very little has changed with respect to how countries and economic institutions understand "work."

POVERTY

Compared with men, women are disproportionately poor. Single mothers, especially, are overrepresented among Canada's poor according to any measure, including Statistics Canada's low income cut-off (LICO). This means that a great deal of Canadian children are growing up in poverty. Research has shown that children who grow up in poverty are more likely to experience adversities as adolescents; drop out of school and not obtain a higher education; have early, unplanned pregnancies; and become single parents themselves in an intergenerational cycle. Women who are young, who have less education, who have multiple children, and who are single parents are at the highest risk of living in poverty in Canada (Status of Women in Canada, 2006). Even where women are financially well off, their situation is not secure; it is usually dependent not only on their own employment but on what they possess through marriage.

Poverty also has a significant impact upon people's health. The degree of poverty in which a person lives is a key predictor of their likelihood of falling ill and requiring medical care (Raphael, 2002). (And as in Canada, where health care is socialized, all people bear the financial cost of the ill health of the poor.) Poverty is also a factor in women's vulnerability to victimization by violence.

Violence

It has already been mentioned that people with unconventional gender identities and sexual orientations are at risk of violent reprisal for their variance from established gender norms. Women, too, are particularly vulnerable to, and suffer disproportionately from, violence in Canadian society. This is not to say that men are never the victims of violence perpetrated by women, but rather that most acts of violence recorded in Canada have male perpetrators and are committed against women and children. As same-sex relationships have become more socially visible, it has become apparent that abuse mars these relationships as well. Abused partners in same-sex relationships face unique challenges. One challenge is that a substantial number of Canadians still see same-sex relationships as morally abhorrent, which makes it difficult for an abused partner to come forward and seek or obtain help. Victims of abuse in gay male relationships have particular problems, and they are related to how social constructions of male gender affect the services available; shelters for female victims of violence often do not allow male residents access to their services.

Popular wisdom would lead one to believe that, where violent attack is concerned, strangers would pose the greatest risk to women. However, women are actually at far greater risk of being attacked by a spouse or partner. The Ontario Women's Directorate states that 7 percent of Ontario women living in common-law or marital relationships experienced physical or sexual assault by a spousal partner at least once during the period of 1999–2004 (Johnson, 2006). The Violence Against Women Survey, conducted as a one-time project by Statistics Canada in 1993, indicated that 51 percent (that is, the majority) of women in Canada had experienced at least one incident of physical or sexual violence since they turned 16 (Statistics Canada, 1993). Too often, intimate-partner violence can be severe, resulting in health-care costs and other expenses for the community. Tragically, there have been approximately 25 female victims of spousal homicide each year in Ontario from 1975 to 2004.

It is not just women but children, too, who are affected by intimate-partner violence. According to 2006 Statistics Canada figures, roughly 40 percent of women assaulted by their intimate partners reported that their children witnessed this violence (Johnson, 2006). A growing body of research shows that children exposed to domestic violence, even if they do not suffer directly, are at greater risk of developmental, behavioural, and emotional difficulties later in life. Further, children whose mothers are victims of violence are likely to experience disruptions in their lives and schooling. In 2003–2004, most (53 percent) women escaping abusive situations and fleeing to shelters were admitted with their children, and 65 percent of those children were under the age of 10 (Canadian Centre for Justice Statistics, 2005).

Violence affects women of all age groups, cultures, and ethnic and socio-economic backgrounds. No one is safe by virtue of their economic or demographic status. But the impacts of violence and gender inequality are not the same for all groups, and some groups are more likely to be affected than others. Aboriginal women are three times more likely to suffer spousal violence than other Canadian women (Johnson, 2006). Many factors contribute to the disproportionate vulnerability and victimization of Aboriginal women, including the childhood abuse suffered by many Aboriginal men (as well as women) who later may become victimizers. The formal and informal resources to which most women can turn for protection are not always available to Aboriginal women.

The impacts of violence against women are measurable, and they are major. Official statistics from 1995, for example, record that the health-related costs of violence against women—including the costs of medical and dental treatment for injuries, psychological care, lost work time, and the provision of shelters, transition homes, and crisis centres—exceeded $1.5 billion (Day, 1995). Statistics from 2006 indicate that the prevalence of domestic violence has not decreased, and neither has its social cost (Johnson, 2006).

In 1991, the Parliament of Canada established December 6 as the National Day of Remembrance and Action on Violence Against Women. The date is the anniversary of the 1989 mass murder of 14 female engineering students at École Polytechnique, in Montreal. The women were killed by a lone gunman who separated men from women and shot the latter only, leaving a note that said he had killed them for being "feminists." The incident was a dramatic marker of the broader social problem of violence against women. It is not only the victims of that shooting who are remembered on December 6th, but also women across Canada who have suffered from and survived—or not survived—gendered abuse. Women and men come together on that day to mourn these victims and to work for change.

ANALYSIS

IDENTIFYING A SOCIAL ISSUE

What Groups Are Calling for Attention and What Is Their Concern?

Feminists have long promoted the rights of women to live free of the threat of violence and to achieve economic equality. The Canadian government has implemented policies that suggest a commitment to the goals of feminism. What is troubling is that gender violence and gender-based economic inequality in Canada have not disappeared (Ogrodnik, 2006).

What Is the Vision or Goal of the Voices of Concern?

The vision or goal defines the feminist voice. Feminists speak against **sexism**, against **heterosexism**, and against gender-based oppression. They advocate for gender equality and are striving to change the social structures that have normalized gender violence and gender inequality in modern Western society. Many Canadians reject feminism while endorsing the egalitarian aims of the women's movement. For many Canadians, there is a stigma attached to the term *feminism.* Such people do not realize that, contrary to many popular beliefs and stereotypes, feminists are *not* antifeminine, they are *not* anti-male, and they do *not* advocate bizarre social behaviour. Feminism, as espoused by the women's movement, has the goal of freeing women from gender violence and from other consequences of gender inequality. The negative image of feminism has come from the media, which tends to reinforce stereotypes of feminists.

What Are the Means of Achieving the Goals?

Gender equality is broadly supported by the public, even though actions associated with the label *feminism* are not. In Canada, the women's movement has established itself as a political force. There are numerous public agencies and government initiatives that address gender inequalities, and inequalities have also been contested in the courts. Until the goal of equality is achieved, political action will continue.

EVOLUTION OF THE SOCIAL ISSUE OF GENDER INEQUALITY

What Groups and Organizations Are Advocating Change?

Within government, there are established agencies such as the Canadian Research Institute for the Advancement of Women, Status of Women Canada, and The Women's Directorate of Ontario. The mandate of each of these agencies is gender equality. Because these groups are based in government, they are vulnerable to the ebb and flow of public funding streams.

What Has Prompted Public Awareness and Concern?

Gender inequality is often challenged in Canada's courts, and the media attention on such cases reminds the public that the issue of gender inequality is not yet resolved. Stories of serious violence suffered by women and by homosexuals periodically reignite the public's indignation in this regard. And the withdrawal of government funding support from groups that advocate for gender equality tends to politicize the issue and to refresh the debates about it.

How Is the Public Aligned?

Feminism as an ideology is usually either ignored or resisted by the public. At the same time, the public tends to support actions it identifies as promoting gender equality and the reduction of violence. Nevertheless, statistics demonstrate that equality has not been achieved or violence eliminated. This suggests that a significant element of the public does not support changes in law and public policy designed to curb inequality and violence. Evidently, some perceive that changes in law and policy have unfairly degraded men, reduced men's privileges, and diminished men's worth. A number of organizations that promote men's rights and that advocate a return to "traditional family values" can be found on the Internet. One such organization is Fathers for Life.

What Initiatives Have Been Taken and What Policies Have Been Put in Place?

There have been many, many government initiatives focused on eradicating gender inequality. One example is the Domestic Violence Action Plan, launched by the Ontario Government in December 2004 and updated in January 2007. This is a multi-faceted plan that integrates the departments of health, education, justice, and immigration. The plan focuses on the complexity of factors that produce family violence. Other agencies, such as the Canadian Research Institute for the Advancement of Women (CRIAW), serve as public critics of government action or inaction to advance gender equality.

What Is the Public Reaction?

The public debate over the validity of feminist policy is ongoing. Some criticize feminist goals and accomplishments as clearly anti-male and anti-family. Until feminism is viewed as a legitimate challenge to unfair social structures and not as an anti-male supremacist movement for women alone, debate and issues will continue.

ANALYTICAL APPROACHES TO UNDERSTANDING GENDER INEQUALITY

Gender inequality is the subject of current political debates and social frictions, but as the following analyses will show, gender inequality is rooted in the cultural history and fundamental organization of society. The first analysis will adopt a micro feminist orientation—namely, a social constructionist analysis of the patterns of gender inequality evident in our society's language, values, and norms, especially as revealed in relation to spousal and gendered violence. This perspective will help explain the origins and persistence of social patterns that underlie gender inequality. Following this will be a structural functionalist analysis of the intersection of work and the family. The macro perspective of structural functionalism expands our understanding of gender inequality by showing that it did once have a function in society. But now that the political climate and the primary social institutions of work and the family have changed, gender inequality is no longer functional. Our final analysis, from the macro perspective of the social conflict paradigm, will reveal the meaning and mechanisms of social inequality. By examining how a heterosexist and patriarchal majority exploits those of bisexual and homosexual orientation, the social conflict analysis will explain the process of marginalization and inequality.

Feminist Analysis of Intimate-Partner Abuse and Domestic Violence

BRIEF REVIEW OF THE FEMINIST PERSPECTIVE

Feminist analysis is not unified. It consists of a loose grouping of social theories, philosophies, and political movements, all concerned with advancing women toward social equality. Philosophically, feminists seek to determine how gender and sex affect our understandings of the world, and they seek to determine, in the ethical sphere, what is appropriate or inappropriate conduct in the context of gender. Feminist activists have mobilized around reproductive rights: rights to birth control; to safe, legal abortions; and to prenatal care as well as daycare. Feminists variously look at gender and **stereotyping**, sexual objectification, social systems of patriarchy and oppression, and the privileging of men over women in the hierarchies of organizations.

PARTNER ABUSE AND DOMESTIC VIOLENCE

Statistics indicate that spousal abuse victimizes more women than men and is more likely perpetrated by men than by women. Many organizations, including government agencies, have been created to reduce domestic violence.

In *Gendered Lives* (2005), Julia Wood, speaking with a feminist voice, affirms that gendered violence is not just the result of individual attitudes and deviance. She writes that "widespread violence exists only if a society allows or endorses it. In other words, the epidemic of gendered violence reflects cultural values and social definitions of femininity, masculinity, and relationships between men and women" (p. 259).

Social Constructionist Analysis of Gendered Violence

BRIEF REVIEW OF THE SOCIAL CONSTRUCTIONIST PERSPECTIVE

Social constructionism is one perspective within the broader paradigm of symbolic interactionism. Its theories are based on the premise that what is popularly defined as "normal," or "natural," is actually a social construction. In other words, it is behaviour that cannot be explained as biologically determined or "hard-wired." A social constructionist would adopt a cross-cultural or historical perspective in demonstrating the great variety of "normal" gender behaviours. Given this variety, it follows that behaviours and beliefs have a social and cultural context. In other words, they are defined into existence rather than existing innately. Gender, gender roles, and gender inequalities, rather than being "natural," are socially constructed beliefs, behaviours, and values that can be altered through changing socialization practices. Changing what is socialized and challenging stereotypes and misinformation will result in a *reconstruction* of beliefs and norms in a society. Feminist activism aims to reconstruct **patriarchal** and heterosexist social structures so that gender equality can be achieved.

FORMS OF GENDERED VIOLENCE

Spousal or Intimate-Partner Violence

According to a Canadian Department of Justice fact sheet (2006), **spousal abuse** can assume many forms: physical, sexual, emotional, economic, and spiritual. This report defines such abuse as the

> violence or mistreatment that a woman or man may experience at the hands of a marital, common-law or same-sex partner. Spousal abuse may happen at any time during a relationship, including while it is breaking down or after it has ended.

Spousal or intimate-partner abuse is a misuse of power and a violation of trust. There are a number of *social* factors that put a person at risk of abuse. These include dislocation, colonization, racism, **homophobia**, disability, poverty, and isolation (Department of Justice, 2006).

Criminal Harassment

Criminal harassment is also known as *stalking*. Being stalked may involve being followed or repeatedly contacted, receiving threatening voice messages or unwanted gifts. Only 10 percent of stalking victims are strangers to the perpetrators. Most victims (approximately 80 percent) are harassed by ex-spouses (Brzozowski, 2004). Criminal harassment was entered as a *Criminal Code* offence in 1993, but we may assume that it existed long before it was *socially* acknowledged as problematic.

Sexual Assault and Rape

Sexual assault and rape can be part of intimate-partner and spousal abuse, and they deserve special mention in this connection. Sexual assault arises from a need to exercise or increase control over another. It is not simply an act of out-of-control lust, as was once popularly believed (Department of Justice, 2006). That it is now legally forbidden within the context of marriage and intimate relationships is a matter of some significance. Until recently, women in Western culture were defined as men's property (that is, the property of their husbands or fathers) and, by the rules of private property, men were free to treat their wives or daughters any way they wished. Women lacked any recourse in this regard (Packota, 2000). The fact that it is now a criminal offence for a man to physically mistreat his wife means that the relationship between a man and a woman or between intimate partners has been redefined as, *ideally*, one of equality and partnership rather than one of inequality and ownership. The reality is that the abuse of women and girls has prevailed throughout history because women and girls have almost always had less power—physical, economic, social, religious, and governmental—than men (Metropolitan Action Committee [METRAC], 2001).

SOCIAL STRUCTURES THAT SUPPORT GENDERED VIOLENCE

Language

The mid-1970s saw an academic focus on language as a reflection of social place. Feminists pointed to the language definitions of each gender as unconscious expressions of the normalized exploitation of women. By the 1990s, a refinement of this theory, one that is consistent with social constructionism, proposed that language "performs" gender. In other words, language is integral to an individual's creation of a gender identity and to the creation of gender relationships.

According to Wood (2005), feminists decry current language patterns that qualify the perception of violence against women and thus normalize its use. They argue, for example, that the term *domestic violence* implies that violence within a family is less severe or significant than the kind that occurs among strangers. To use the passive voice in saying that "many women are beaten" seems to obscure the brutality of the act and to render less visible the partners responsible. Sometimes the language of love is woven into these references to male violence, thus diminishing our sense of its brutality; for example, one might describe a beaten woman as a "victim of love" (Wood, p. 280). In short, language is the expression of cultural ideologies, and the continuing linguistic tolerance of violence reflects its entrenchment in the social institutions of Canadian society.

Violence in the Media

The media is a powerful **agent of socialization**. The entertainment media has many branches: TV, movies, music and music videos, and the Internet. All of these expose people to sexism and violence, and the rate of exposure is growing exponentially. The Media Awareness Network, citing a Laval University study of TV programming over seven years between 1993 and 2001, reports a 378 percent increase in the amount of physical violence shown. The same source reveals that, in 2001, TV shows averaged 40 acts of violence per hour. The amount of psychological violence portrayed was stable until 1999, but increased 325 percent from 1999 to 2001. The Media Awareness Network has said the following: "The presence of violence, degradation and cruelty in a range of media means that children are exposed to a continuum of violence, which ranges from the in-your-face attitude of shows like South Park to extreme depictions of misogyny and sadism" (Media Awareness Network, 2007).

According to the University of Michigan's Institute for Social Research, people who watch violence on TV behave more aggressively later in life. For example, the study showed that men in the top 20 percent with respect to exposure to violence were twice as likely to have pushed, grabbed, or shoved their wives during an argument. Women in the top 20 percent were twice as likely to have thrown something at their husbands in the previous 12 months (CBC News, 2003).

Critics of such studies argue that media violence does not encourage social violence. But the majority of theorists accept that media violence does influence people to accept violence as a normal part of interpersonal behaviour, and that the media play a powerful role in shaping attitudes that entail the denigration of women and the normalization of violence.

SOCIAL INSTITUTIONS AND CULTURAL TRADITIONS

Within social institutions such as the family, **gender scripts** are developed and enforced through **socialization**. A gender script is a set of social beliefs, values, and perspectives that define the role of woman or man in society. Studies suggest that intimate-partner violence is greater in cultures that emphasize family cohesiveness and masculine superiority in families. In other words, sex is less important than gender in explaining intimate-partner violence. The use of violence to control others is a gender script of masculinity (Wood, 2005). The feminine gender script includes nurturance, romantic love, self-sacrifice, maternalism, and a need for masculine protection and financial support. The masculine gender script, which emphasizes dominance and control, is founded in patriarchal traditions (Packota, 2000).

Patriarchy is a long-established form of social organization that delivers power to men at the expense of women. It is a social system that has endured through millennia and that exists across cultures. Patriarchy as a social organization is reflected in every social interaction that conforms to its structure and in socialization patterns that are accepted worldwide. Feminism forms an ideological challenge to patriarchy. From the feminist perspective, patriarchy is a "concept that explains the systematic gendered organization of all areas of social life—economic, political, and ideological—such that more social resources, power, and value accrue to men as a group at the expense of women as a group" (Against Patriarchy, 2007). Here is another feminist account of patriarchy:

> Patriarchy is a form of domination, which extends to and is manifested in all forms of oppression. This includes, but is not limited to, racism, classism, colonialism and neo-colonialism, the destruction and exploitation of the Earth, the murder of indigenous peoples, the commodification of daily life experience, and all forms of personal and societal oppression (Against Patriarchy, 2007).

There is evidence that patriarchal social structures are slowly being dismantled and that new social scripts are being created. Social surveys show, for example, that marriages today that are established on equality and, relative to the past, **androgynous gender roles**, are happier and much more likely to resolve conflict through effective communication (Ward, 2006).

However, the fact that women are still much more likely to be victims of spousal abuse than are men—85 percent of women as compared with 15 percent of men—suggests that violence remains embedded in the social institutions of society. Such statistics also suggest that abuse is a consequence of power imbalances in gendered social relationships (Brzozowski, 2004).

A Structural Functionalist Analysis of Work and Family Intersection

BRIEF REVIEW OF THE STRUCTURAL FUNCTIONALIST PERSPECTIVE

The structural functionalist view of society is a macro perspective that focuses on the integrated functioning of social institutions. Dysfunctions occur when an institution fails to serve society as expected, or when the integration of social institutions is disrupted. The economy and the family are major social institutions; they rely on each other extensively. But the demands of the modern workplace are placing a significant burden on the family. The lack of integration between the modern economy and the family emerges in the disadvantages experienced by women.

MANIFEST FUNCTIONS

The social institution of the economy is central to the functioning of society as a whole and to the family. The manifest functions of the economy are the production and distribution of goods and services and the employment of workers. A strong economy is considered to be one that creates ever more goods and ever more product choices. A strong economy also generates full employment, which in turn encourages education, health, and family well-being.

Among the manifest functions of the family are the procreation and socialization of children. The family is usually identified as the primary social institution because it generates competent workers to support the society's economy. The family is also primarily responsible for **cultural transmission**—the instilling and preservation of a society's moral values and traditions.

DYSFUNCTIONS

Dysfunctions are the negative consequences of social trends within and among a society's institutions. In today's society, the intersection of work and family is often dysfunctional. **Spillover** effects occur from family to work and vice versa. Typically, women permit family responsibilities to interfere with their work ones, and men allow work responsibilities to interfere with their family ones.

Spillover effects can be significant. Women experience **burnout** and stress over care issues. Women bear more responsibility than men for home care, child care, and elder care. Single parents are predominantly women, and female single parents constitute the majority of individuals who are poor. Women, in an effort to meet their familial obligations, also choose part-time rather than full-time work. This creates economic and independence issues for women. Lack of safe and affordable housing also forces many women and their children to stay in abusive relationships.

In the workplace, there are barriers that prevent women from earning what men earn. For example, women's occupations are typically paid less than men's, and the vast majority of part-time workers are women, not men. Women, because of family obligations, are ineligible for promotions and for jobs that require travel. The lack of gender equality in the workplace is perhaps most glaringly reflected in the lack of a national daycare system in Canada.

WHAT CAUSES SYSTEM DYSFUNCTION?

The structural functionalist perspective is a conservative one insofar as it takes the status quo or traditional practice as a standard, and deems any change or deviation from that standard dysfunctional. From this point of view, the entire social system is integrated around a core of common values. Take, for example, respect for authority. This value is cultivated and practised in the family in the form of the respect and obedience paid to adults, especially men. This same value is evident in the context of education, where respect is paid to adults and to those seen as intelligent. In the economy, the same value underlies the conventional deference paid to supervisors and bosses. Patriarchy is the key factor in the dysfunctional intersection of the economy and the family. In other words, changes that reflect feminist ideals conflict with traditional patriarchal social structures and with the assumption of male superiority. However, given that feminist goals for equality are popularly accepted, the dysfunction is *not* the feminist values themselves but the mismatch between feminist values and patriarchal social structures.

RECENT SOCIAL TRENDS

Feminist Drive for Equality

Feminism as embodied in the women's movement has advanced in waves of social activism for the past century and a half. Its primary goal has been to dismantle patriarchal social structures and replace them with social structures that support gender equality. One of the first steps was to give women a political voice. More recently, affirmative action initiatives have enabled women to become educated, to participate as equals in the workplace, and to live as independents. Women have gained a say in their reproductive choices, and now have equal rights before the law.

Dual-Income Families

Families where the man is the sole breadwinner, supporting a homemaker wife, are now a minority. Women first entered the workforce en masse during World War II, and since then the consumerist lifestyle adopted by most Canadians makes a full-time homemaker an impossible economic burden for the majority of families.

Rise in Divorce and Single Parenting

Many women, through choice or misfortune, are raising children independent of a spouse. This trend has necessitated a reordering of familial roles. It has also motivated women to become more educated and to advocate for social welfare supports to fill in for the old family supports.

Lifelong Learning and Serial Careers

One or two generations ago, a person could look forward to having one career throughout his or her work life. Today, it is not unusual for workers to have two or three careers in their lifetime. The availability of educational opportunities has contributed to this trend of "lifelong learning." Workers nowadays have to adapt to workplace changes much more quickly than their grandparent's generation could ever have conceived of doing.

EVIDENCE OF DYSFUNCTIONS

Burnout

Burnout is physical and emotional exhaustion brought on by the prolonged stress of trying to live up to impossible goals. It occurs because of excessive demands on an individual. A person suffering from burnout is unable to meet both the emotional needs of his or her family and the demands of work. Candidates at most risk of burnout are those who set high expectations for themselves and who have an excessive number of demands placed on them. For example, a woman who is

Figure 5.1 Average Income of Women and Men: 1993, 1997, and 2003

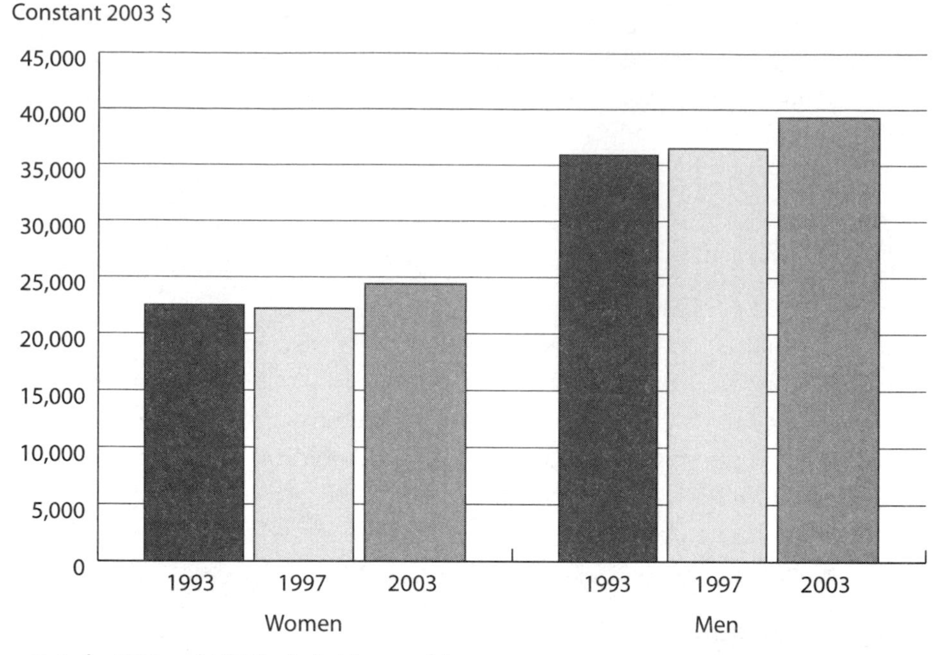

Data for 1993 and 1997 include 15-year-olds.

Average income is defined as the average annual pre-tax income of workers aged 16 and over from all sources, including employment earnings, government transfer payments, investment income, and other money income. In 2003, the average income of women was $24,400, which was just 62 percent of the average income of men.

It should be noted that in analyzing income data for individuals, payments for some government transfer programs, including social assistance, child tax benefits, and seniors benefits, are not taxable and are allocated to only one family member depending on variables such as age, income, and gender. As such, readers should be aware that these transfers are not equally divided among family members.

Source: Statistics Canada, Survey of Labour and Income Dynamics.

employed full time, who tries to keep a spotless house, and who is responsible for keeping her children actively involved in recreational pursuits is a candidate for burnout. Certain occupations, such as policing, place excessive stress on employees and their families (Ward, 2005). In short, burnout is an instance of the detrimental spillover effects of work to family and family to work.

Occupations that demand shift work and very long shifts, and occupations prone to sudden unscheduled demands, such as medicine, may make it hard for a person at risk of burnout to engage in restorative activities, such as physical exercise, and to have uninterrupted leisure time.

Inequitable Sharing of Domestic Responsibilities

It is almost a cliché to say that although women have assumed an equal share in the workplace, they are still responsible at home for the greater part of child and elder care, and for housekeeping. The many hours that women spend on domestic chores often equal their full-time work hours and have been called the "**second shift**." Traditional gender roles prescribe that women, not men, are responsible for domestic chores. Such norms create two dysfunctions: a busy woman becomes a candidate for burnout, and women are disproportionately employed in caregiving occupa-

Figure 5.2 Percentage of Employed Mothers Working Full Time, by Age of Youngest Child, 2004

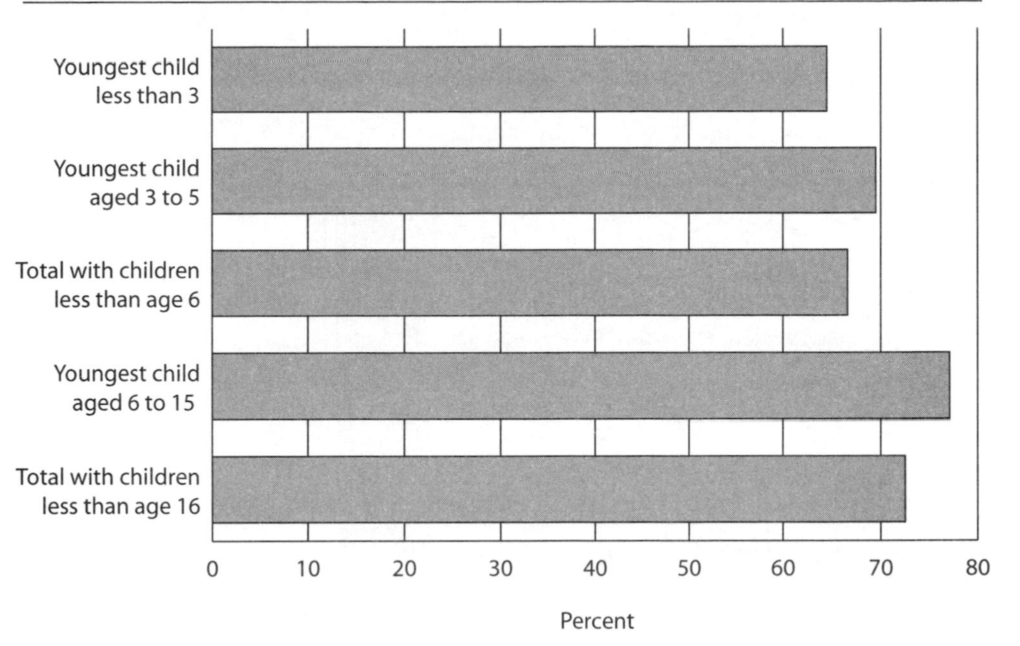

Source: Statistics Canada, Labour Force Survey, 2006.

tions that are typically underpaid compared to traditionally male occupations (Marshall, 2006).

According to the Vanier Institute of the Family, the typical division of labour within a Canadian family today is not equitable. In families with children, wives do more "total work"—that is, hours of paid and unpaid work combined—than their husbands do. Wives aged 25 to 44 who have children and full-time jobs work, on average, 12 minutes a day more than their husbands do; wives aged 45 to 64, 30 minutes more each day. Wives with full-time jobs but no children also do more total work than their husbands do. Wives aged 25 to 44 do 12 minutes more work than their husbands do each day; wives aged 45 to 64, an extra 6 minutes each day (Sauvé, 2002).

Inequalities in the Workplace

Pay inequities are the most glaring evidence of gender inequalities in the workplace. Recently released statistics reveal that family income is rising in Canada, but that the increase is due to a greater number of family members having jobs and working more hours (Sauvé, 2002). Figure 5.1 is from a 2006 Statistics Canada publication. As can be seen in figure 5.1, the statistics reveal that both genders have made income gains but that women still lag behind men.

Lack of Daycare Options

Recent statistics, shown in figure 5.2, indicate that the number of working women with children under 16 at home is growing.

The executive vice-president of the Canadian Labour Congress, Barbara Byers, in response to the federal government's choice to rescind national child-care initiatives has outlined that organization's official stand on a national child-care policy; she has stated that "child care is all about equality" (Canadian Labour Congress,

2006). Despite the fact that child-care spaces grew twice as fast from 2001 to 2003 as they did from 1990 to 1998 (Statistics Canada, 2006), there is still insufficient daycare available to parents.

University of Guelph (2006) research has shown that although men's satisfaction with work and family equals women's for the most part, women are more likely than men to have family responsibilities interfere with their work responsibilities. The Guelph researchers conclude that Canadian workplaces should offer flexibility to working parents.

ORIGINS OF DYSFUNCTIONS

As we have suggested, the intersection of work and family is problematic and disproportionately burdensome for women. A structural functionalist analysis can help determine how to resolve dysfunctions and thus restore equilibrium.

Questions That Guide a Structural Functionalist Analysis

WHAT SOCIAL INSTITUTIONS ARE CENTRALLY INVOLVED?

In this case the social institutions involved are the family and the economy. As our society's values have evolved, eroding the old gender-role distinctions and bringing greater equality between men and women, the social institutions of the family and the economy are no longer integrated.

What Are the Manifest Functions? What Are the Dysfunctions That Result in Gender Inequality?

Ideally, the family is a primary social institution responsible for the procreation and socialization of children. It is also the source of material and emotional support for its members, and the primary means of social organization. The economy is the social institution responsible for the production and distribution of goods and services and it is the means by which individuals provide for their families. As we have suggested, the family supports the economy by providing a stable and contented workforce. In turn, the economy supports the family by providing material wealth. Any faltering on either side results in dysfunctions that are felt both within the family and within the workplace. Dysfunctions in the family and the economy also have negative effects on society as a whole.

SOCIAL TRENDS RESULTING IN DYSFUNCTIONS

The social trends that have led to the specific dysfunctions outlined above have been detailed in this chapter. The main change is the shift from a gender-distinct division of labour to one founded on gender equality. The shift in values is not dysfunctional. It is the mismatch between patriarchal social structures and the new value of gender equality that is causing dysfunction.

Complete the structural functionalist analysis chart (found on the followng page), which provides a summary of the current dysfunctions occurring within the family and the economy. In the social actions column, include any additional social

Structural Functionalist Analysis of Work and Family Intersection			
Social Action	**Social Institution**	**Manifest Function of Social Institution**	**Dysfunction**
Affirmative action in the workplace	Economy	Provision of employment	More women engaging in full-time, career-track work
Dual-income trend to meet current materialist lifestyle demands	Economy	Production and distribution of resources Provision of employment	Increased expectations and demands placed on women
Pay inequities persist	Economy	Provision of employment	Rate of poverty among women increases
Child care, elder care, and domestic responsibilities remain predominantly with women	Family	Material and emotional support of members	Women experience burnout
Women balance work and family by working part-time	Economy	Provision of employment	High rate of poverty even among employed women
Decision not to institute national daycare Daycare spaces inadequate for demand	Government	Provision of social services	Increased burden on women

and political initiatives that have been implemented. Then assess how the social actions affect the continued dysfunction of gender inequality. After performing such an assessment, you can suggest the future social actions that would bring Canadian society closer to functional gender equality.

ACTIONS THAT WOULD RESTORE SYSTEM EQUILIBRIUM

Fundamentally, actions in support of economic equality for women would improve family life for women and their families. Second, measures to enhance women's status in the family (through education, for example) would improve women's employment opportunities and ease the work–family tension. Details of such initiatives are outlined in the article "New Federal Policies Affecting Women's Equality: Reality Check" (Canadian Research Institute for the Advancement of Women [CRIAW], 2006).

A Social Conflict Analysis of Sex Orientation

BRIEF REVIEW OF THE SOCIAL CONFLICT PERSPECTIVE

A social conflict perspective assumes that social issues stem from competition and conflict among social groups. In the case of the homosexual issues, gay and lesbian minority groups are in conflict with the heterosexist majority in modern society. Despite the gains that gays and lesbians have made in recent decades, heterosexist attitudes continue to predominate, and inequities remain.

ANALYSIS OF SEX ORIENTATION

Evidence of the Powerlessness and Victimization of Gays and Lesbians

The frequent discrimination against and victimization of homosexuals, as well as their elevated death and illness rates, are evidence that homosexuality is subject to **stigma** and **marginalization**.

The following terms are key ones. **Homosexuality** describes the sexual orientation of those who are attracted to members of their same sex. *Homophobia* refers to the fear or dislike of homosexuality. It can be expressed in a broad range of behaviours, from slander to outright violence. Homophobia is often accompanied by racist or *xenophobic* (that is, the intense fear of what is foreign or of a foreign culture) attitudes (Interagency Coalition on AIDS and Development, 2004). Homophobia involves subscribing to negative beliefs or myths or stereotypes about homosexuals and homosexuality (Banks, 2003).

Heterosexism is a more subtle negation of homosexuality. It refers to the dominant value system according to which any deviance from the heterosexual norm is seen as abnormal and undesirable. Cultural homophobia or cultural heterosexism refers to our culture's embedded prejudice against homosexuality. Everyday social patterns of language, entertainment, social institutions, laws, and stereotypes reinforce this prejudice (Banks, 2003).

Demographic statistics concerning illness, death, and life expectancy also reflect the marginalization of homosexuals. The book *Transgender Crossroads* (2003) includes an article claiming that homophobia shortens the lives of gays and lesbians. The article also affirms that homophobia costs Canadians $8 billion per year in increased health costs and loss of productivity.

Perhaps most symbolic of the prejudice against homosexuality has been the refusal to allow same-sex couples to marry. Not until December 2006 was the political threat of rescinding same-sex couples' right to marry laid to rest (Canadians for Equal Marriage, n.d.).

Prevailing Power Relationships

The gay rights movement in North America began with the Stonewall riots in New York City in 1969 (Wright, 1999). Since then, gay and lesbian activism has made steady progress worldwide in confronting and reducing the stigma attached to homosexuality. In Canada, the right of same-sex couples to marry has been established. Even ten years ago, this possibility was unthinkable. Gay and lesbian equality has not yet been accomplished, however. So long as discrimination and stigmatizing continue, activists have much to do.

Predicting the Future of the Issue

Gay and lesbian activism has made overt discrimination on the basis of sexual orientation socially unacceptable and illegal in Canada. However, the prejudice and discrimination against homosexuality is entrenched in the social structures of Canadian culture, enabling the right-wing, anti-gay faction to remain dominant despite its significantly eroded power.

Sociologist Robert Merton's classification of the relationship between discrimination and prejudice is cited in most introductory sociology texts. According to Merton, there are four combinations of prejudice and discrimination. *Blatant discrimination*, or *prejudiced discrimination*, is discrimination that is supported by prejudice. At the personal level, discriminatory behaviours of this kind may include violence and are justified, in the perpetrators' minds, by belief in prevailing stereotypes and ideologies. For example, in the case of blatant racist discrimination, violence against a minority person is justified by a belief that that person is inferior, even subhuman. Discrimination that is based on prejudice and that is incited at the institutional level is a kind of prejudiced discrimination known as *institutional discrimination*. Extreme violence against gays is a form of *prejudiced discrimination*, and the legal "cleansing actions" of gay bars by police was an instance of *institutional discrimination*. It could be argued that refusing same-sex couples the right to marry was another act of institutional discrimination.

With the category of *prejudiced non-discriminator*, Merton recognizes that prejudice and discrimination are not always present together. The *prejudiced non-discriminator* lacks the social power and initiative to act in a discriminatory manner. Very often this hidden prejudice is a consequence of changes in social laws and ideologies; that is, it is hidden because political correctness no longer allows overt discrimination. For example, a gay man can no longer be denied a job because of his sexual orientation; such discrimination is against the law. However, a prejudiced non-discriminator might claim that the position is already filled, thus obtaining the same results as overt discrimination would. The existence of prejudiced non-discrimination, though a negative thing in itself, is a sign of positive movement toward equality.

A penultimate step toward equality would be the removal of discriminatory customs and traditions. The third of Merton's categories is *unprejudiced discrimination*:

a person, though harbouring no prejudice, effectively discriminates against a minority by upholding traditions and policies. Heterosexist social patterns evident in language, entertainment, and jokes—all reflecting the dominant conception of what is "normal"—are examples of *unprejudiced discrimination.* These vestiges of prejudice can be dismantled through education and confrontation (Kismet, 2007).

The goal of equality will have been realized with the fourth category of social being: the *unprejudiced non-discriminator.*

QUESTIONS THAT GUIDE A SOCIAL CONFLICT ANALYSIS

Who Are the Major Stakeholders in the Issue?

There are many organizations actively fighting for equal rights for all Canadians. Egale is one such organization, and it has many affiliates, including the Equality Coalition and Canadians for Equal Marriage. Egale Canada is a national organization with representatives from all provinces and territories. It has acted in court interventions, as an advisory agent to Statistics Canada research, and in national education campaigns; it is an organization that is well known. Its mission statement is as follows: "Egale Canada is a national organization that advances equality and justice for lesbian, gay, bisexual, and trans-identified people and their families across Canada." One product of its activism is the annual National Day Against Homophobia. Its theme for 2007 was Zero Tolerance of Homophobic Bullying in our Schools; for 2005, it was eliminating homophobic practices in the workplace.

What Are the Resources of Each Stakeholder Group?

Gay rights activism has existed for many years and has expanded worldwide. Chronicling the events that led to same-sex couples gaining the right to marry will help us evaluate the gay activist lobby's effectiveness in gaining equality with heterosexuals. Some examples of resources on the gay activist side appear in the following list, whose items have been selected from a list compiled by Canadians for Equal Marriage (n.d.):

- Endorsements from respected institutions
- Support from popular culture (for example, the Canadian band "Habit" has created a song about the fight for marriage equality)
- Parliamentary action and debates devoted to equality ideals and compliance with the *Canadian Charter of Rights and Freedoms*

Banks (2003) produced a report that documents the reasons for the continuing existence of homophobia in Canada. These facts were drawn from studies that date from the early to the mid-1990s. (There are signs that the current media has become more progressive in its treatment of gay issues.) Banks cites the following factors:

- Absence of accurate and positive portrayals of GLBs (gays, lesbians, and bisexuals) in the media
- Absence of accurate information regarding same-sex orientation
- Homosexuality regarded as a psychopathology until 1973 and included after that date in the International Classification of Diseases (WHO, 1997)
- Established religious groups portraying homosexuality as immoral

- Education system not teaching school-age children about homosexuality
- Minimal sanctions against those who harass and discriminate against GLBs
- Popular tolerance for heterosexist attitudes
- Most GLBs hiding their true identity

The resources listed above may be organized in a power resources chart, to illustrate the competition between the two sides. Conclusions can help structure predictions about the likelihood of equality being achieved by homosexuals.

Which Side Is Dominant, and What Is the Future of the Issue?

According to the scoring in the power resources chart, the power gains on the side of the homosexual minority are significant. Discrimination on the basis of sexual

Power Resources Chart for the Sex Orientation Issue

Dominant Side: Heterosexist Majority			Minority Side: Gay Rights Activists		
WIN	LOSE	RESOURCE	WIN	LOSE	RESOURCE
♠♠♠♠♠♠♠		Heterosexist traditions, especially those rooted in religion, attack homosexuality as sin	♠	♦♦♦	National organizations like Egale Canada advocate on behalf of gays, lesbians, and bisexuals
♠♠♠♠	♦♦♦	Popular tolerance and promotion of heterosexist attitudes	♠♠♠	♦	*Charter of Rights and Freedoms* makes discrimination on the basis of sexual orientation illegal
	♦♦♦♦♦♦♦	Many homosexuals reluctant to reveal their orientation	♠	♦♦♦	Increased media coverage of homosexuality
♠♠♠	♦♦♦♦	Minimal sanctions against homophobic behaviours	♠	♦♦♦	Gay Pride parades and national celebrations of homosexuality
			♠♠	♦♦	Popular culture, music, and entertainment normalize homosexuality
			♠♠♠	♦	Homosexual marriage permitted by law in Canada
			♠♠♠	♦	Homosexual marriage a profitable source of tourism
14	14		14	14	

orientation continues to exist, but its power appears nearly extinguished. Tremendous gains in the fight for equality have been made. Discrimination is illegal, same-sex marriage is legal, and popular ideologies are more accepting of diversity. Work is continuing through popular education campaigns to erase what is left of systemic discrimination (non-prejudiced discrimination).

RESPONSES

GOVERNMENT AND POLICY

Unlike the constitution of the United States, a country where an Equal Rights Amendment for women failed to pass in the 1970s, Canada's constitution does ensure gender equality. Section 15 of the *Canadian Charter of Rights and Freedoms*, which came into force in 1985, requires that the government treat people equally regardless of gender or sexual preference. Sexual orientation has been "read in" to the Charter provision, thus affording protection for persons of minority sexual orientation. Officially, the Government of Canada has been committed to gender equality for decades; its official policies set out that women and men should benefit equally from the same rights under the law.

Status of Women Canada is the federal department that enables the government to assess whether programs and policies affect people differently according to gender. This department also provides expertise on policy initiatives. In October 2006, Federal Status of Women Minister Bev Oda announced that women had achieved equality in Canada, and over $5 million was cut from the budget of the Status of Women Canada department. When campaigning in the last election, Stephen Harper promised he would, if elected, "take concrete and immediate measures ... to ensure that Canada fully upholds its commitments to women" (CTV News, 2006). By October 2006, the government had ceased funding advocacy and general research for women's groups. Women's organizations now face financial and systemic barriers to participating in the public policy process. Women's voices are no longer contributing to public policy, at a time when the makeup of parliamentarians is only around 20 percent women.

The Canadian Feminist Alliance for International Action (FAFIA), a pan-Canadian alliance of women's and human rights organizations, has issued a press release protesting the cuts. So has the Canadian Federation for University Women (10,000 women university graduates in 121 clubs in Canada). It is troubling, given the difficult situations of diverse women across Canada, that the federal minister responsible for the status of women, Bev Oda, has stated publicly on behalf of her government that "the new government of Canada fundamentally believes that women are equal" (House of Commons, 2006). Feminist organizations have seized on this statement as evidence of official unconcern over continuing problems with gender inequality in Canada.

LAW AND POLICING

A person's gender is a significant factor in how he or she is treated by the law. Historically, there have been many laws that limited the freedom of women in such a way as to privilege men. For example, until 1917 women could not vote in Canada. The right to vote, also known as *suffrage*, was not fully attained by women in Canada until 1916, when the four western provinces of British Columbia, Alberta, Manitoba, and Saskatchewan allowed women to vote. As we have mentioned, women were not legally allowed to use birth control or procure abortions until relatively recently. In the 1930s, 26 of the 48 American states then in existence had laws prohibiting the employment of married women (Trinity, n.d.). Even today, government documents, beginning with birth certificates, indicate a person's gender. This becomes a particular problem for transgendered individuals when they travel after undergoing gender reassignment surgery; such individuals have sometimes had significant difficulty crossing international borders. Although no longer the case in Canada, in many countries same-sex sexual relationships are still criminalized and marriage is available only to heterosexual couples. Historically, violence in the home was treated as a private matter. Now it is treated as a public problem, and police will lay charges against perpetrators of domestic violence.

The history of the 20th century and the first years of the 21st century shows that the laws police are called upon to enforce change significantly and often quite rapidly. Students who undertake police work need to keep themselves acquainted with laws as they change.

Police forces themselves reflect the changing gender patterns in society. In the past, police officers were virtually all men. Now, the numbers of female police officers are growing. In 2004, Canada's police forces included about 9,900 female officers. Female police officers have been increasing since the 1970s, although women remain in the minority, making up (as of 2004) 5 percent of senior officers, 9 percent of non-commissioned officers, and 20 percent of constables (Statistics Canada, 2005). The RCMP and local police agencies are actively recruiting women. The problems facing female officers in the workplace are the same problems facing other Canadian women in the workplace. Female police officers must contend disproportionately with sexual harassment, wage gaps, and glass ceilings. But the problems in policing are often compounded by the traditionally "macho" culture of police forces, where there is continued resistance to the idea that women are a useful addition to the force.

Gender issues, especially violence against women, play a significant role in the work of police officers. Students who become police officers can expect to spend a good deal of their working lives dealing with domestic disputes, where, overwhelmingly, men are still the physical aggressors. Future police officers can also expect to have to deal with issues relating to gender identity and sexual orientation; they will be required to address hate-motivated incidents of violence against transgendered individuals or homosexuals. Still other calls and investigations will be concerned with the sex trade, where gender inequality helps sustain black-market structures. Students moving toward a career in policing need to understand the issues surrounding sex and gender in our society, and the inequalities too often related to them.

COMMUNITY

UNICEF's 2007 Status of Children report recommends the following seven measures for the benefit of women and children worldwide:

- *Education*: abolish school fees and encourage investment in girls' education by parents and communities.
- *Financing*: encourage investment and planning by governments toward the goal of gender equality.
- *Legislation*: national legislation in property law and inheritance rights should ensure a level playing field for women, and there should be measures to prevent and respond to domestic violence.
- *Legislative quotas*: ensure women's participation in politics.
- *Women empowering women*: grassroots women's movements should be involved in the early stages of policy formation so that programs are designed with the needs of women and children in mind.
- *Engaging men and boys*: educating males on the benefits of gender equality can help nurture more cooperative relationships.
- *Research and data*: more research into maternal mortality and violence against women, as well as into women's education, employment, wages, unpaid work and time use, and participation in politics (CBC News, 2006).

INDIVIDUAL INVOLVEMENT

It is important to note that, while government must play a crucial role in implementing these initiatives, individuals like you also have a very significant role to play in changing our society. It is in your power to help change gender from a social problem into a recognized and celebrated dimension of social equality in diversity.

CONCLUSION

The social constructionist analysis of gendered violence has revealed that gendered violence persists because of cultural definitions of masculinity and femininity and their relative social worth. We may conclude from this analysis that reducing gendered violence will require a change in gender roles and an embracing of equality within difference. The answers provided by a social constructionist analysis are an in-depth version of the answers that a symbolic interactionist analysis would have produced.

The structural functionalist analysis of the work–family intersection has provided a macro framework enabling us to see the social damage caused by gender inequality. Although less shocking than gender violence, gender inequality has immense social costs (dysfunctions). Finally, the social conflict analysis of gender minorities, particularly gays and lesbians, has given us insight into the resources of domination, thereby enabling us to predict whether gender equality is likely to be achieved.

It is clear that gender inequality persists and that it costs its victims and all society a great deal. This chapter has revealed the social forces behind the traditions of gender inequality and the costs associated with it, and has demonstrated that gender equality can be achieved—but only if each of us is willing to take issue with established norms and social structures.

KEY TERMS

agent of socialization any organization or social institution that has an important role in socializing individuals (for example, the family is a principal agent of socialization)

androgynous gender role a gender role that blends the positive attributes of both the masculine and feminine gender roles

burnout the physical and emotional exhaustion caused by the prolonged stress of trying to live up to impossible goals

criminal harassment the formal legal term for stalking; repeated unwanted contact or attention from a stranger or acquaintance

cultural transmission the passing of cultural knowledge and traditions from one generation to the next

gender the role a person learns to play as a member of the social category *man* or *woman*; the socialized or learned patterns of masculinity or femininity

gender scripts socialized sets of expectations or prescriptions concerning the appropriate behaviours and aspirations of each gender in specific contexts: traditionally the role of *wife*, for example, is subject to a gender script

heterosexism an ideology that promotes heterosexuality as the only true kind of intimacy and considers divergence from it to be abnormal

heterosexual attracted to the opposite sex

homophobia extreme fear or abhorrence of homosexuality, sometimes expressed in violent attacks on homosexuals

homosexual attracted to the same sex

marginalization the creation and enforcement of social barriers that keep specific groups from full participation in society

patriarchal the term applied to social organizations, social structures, and ideologies that preserve male dominance over women

queer a formerly pejorative term reclaimed by advocates to describe minority or variant sexual orientation in general, including homosexual, bisexual, and any other minority sexual orientations

second shift the domestic and care duties women perform at home after a full day at work

sex a person's biological characteristics in relation to the reproductive process: male, female, or, in some cases, a hybrid of the two

sexism an ideology based on inequality between the sexes

sexual harassment unwelcome attention of a sexual nature, from inappropriate jokes and posters displayed in the victim's workplace to forced sexual activity

sexual orientation a person's sexual tendency, whether toward the opposite sex (heterosexual), toward one's own sex (homosexual), or elsewhere

social constructionism a theoretical perspective, within the symbolic interactionist paradigm, that emphasizes that what is popularly taken to be *normal* and *natural* (gender, for example) is actually a product of social structures; that is, the assumption that much of human reality is a social creation

socialization the lifelong process of acculturation; the teaching and learning of a society's beliefs, values, and norms that occurs during social interaction; the process by which personalities, identities, and gender identities are formed

spillover the stresses and events at work that affect family life, and vice versa

spousal abuse violence—whether emotional, physical, or sexual—that occurs between spouses

stereotyping holding standardized perceptions, based on simplified notions, about a group of people or a person

stigma a social marker that identifies a person as a member of a negatively valued group, race, or ethnicity; a stigma makes a person a target for prejudice and discrimination

transgendered people whose understanding of their own social gender does not coincide with their given biological sex, or people who feel they do not fit within either traditional gender category

FOR FURTHER RESEARCH

Canadian Charter of Rights and Freedoms
http://laws.justice.gc.ca/en/Charter/index.html.

Canadian Federation for University Women
http://www.aztec-net.com/~cfuw.

REAL Women of Canada
http://www.realwomenca.com.

Status of Women Canada
http://www.swc-cfc.gc.ca.

Canadian Feminist Alliance for International Action (FAFIA)
http://www.fafia-afai.org.

REFERENCES

Against patriarchy. (2007). Vision statement. http://againstpatriarchy07.wordpress.com/about.

Banks, C. (2003, May). The cost of homophobia: Literature review on the human impact of homophobia in Canada. National Coalition for LGBT Health. http://www.lgbthealth.net/downloads/research/Human_Impact_of_Homophobia.pdf.

The Body Politic. (1971, November/December). We demand: The August 28th gay day committee. Reprinted in *Flaunting It!* (1982). http://www.clga.ca/Material/Records/docs/wedemand.htm.

Brzozowski, J. (2004). Family violence in Canada: A statistical profile 2004. Canadian Centre for Justice Statistics. http://www.statcan.ca/english/freepub/85-224-XIE/85-224-XIE2004000.pdf.

Canada Labour Code. RSC 1985, c. L-2.

CBC News. (2006, December 11). Gender inequality deals blow to mothers and children: UNICEF. http://www.cbc.ca/world/story/2006/12/11/unicef-report.html.

CBC News. (2003, March 10). Early exposure to TV violence bad for kids: study. http://www.cbc.ca/news/story/2003/03/10/violentTV_030310.html.

Canadian Centre for Justice Statistics. (2005). Transition homes in Canada: Ontario fact sheet, 2003/2004; Transition home survey 2003/2004. http://www.statcan.ca/english/freepub/85-404-XIE/85-404-XIE2005000.pdf.

Canadian Labour Congress. (2006). Why a child care program is important. http://canadianlabour.ca/index.php/Child_Care.

Canadian Research Institute for the Advancement of Women [CRIAW]. (2006, November). New federal policies affecting women's equality: Reality check. http://www.criaw-icref.ca/indexFrame_e.htm.

Canadians for Equal Marriage. (n.d.). Harper's motion to reopen equal marriage defeated! Prime Minister says the issue is settled. http://www.equal-marriage.ca.

Chidley, J. (1996, June 17). Toxic TV: Is TV violence contributing to aggression in kids? *Maclean's*, in *Media Awareness Canada*. http://www.media-awareness.ca/english/resources/articles/violence/toxic_tv.cfm.

Chudler, E. (n.d.). She-brains—he-brains. *Neuroscience for Kids*. http://faculty.washington.edu/chudler/heshe.html.

CTV News. (2006, March 8). Harper urged to stick to child care agreements. http://www.ctv.ca/servlet/ArticleNews/story/CTVNews/20060308/harper_women_060308/20060308.

Day, T. (1995). The health-related costs of violence against women in Canada: The tip of the iceberg. Centre for Research on Violence against Women and Children. http://www.crvawc.ca/docs/pub_day1995.pdf.

Department of Justice Canada. (2006, December 19). Spousal abuse: A fact sheet from the Department of Justice Canada. http://www.justice.gc.ca/en/ps/fm/spouseafs.html.

Douglas, Lord A. (1894). Two loves. *The Chameleon*. http://www.law.umkc.edu/faculty/projects/ftrials/wilde/poemsofdouglas.htm.

Egale Canada. (2007, May 17). National day against homophobia: Egale Canada calls for zero tolerance of homophobic bullying in our schools. http://www.egale.ca/index.asp?lang=E&menu=1&item=1364.

Fathers for Life. (2000, May 7). Canadian family violence statistics—Section 2. http://fathersforlife.org/Sodhi/fvcan2.htm.

Gayatri, R. (2005). With respect to sex : Negotiating hijra identity in south India. *Worlds of desire: The Chicago series on sexuality, gender, and culture.* Chicago: University of Chicago Press.

Goldberg, J., & White, C. (2004, Summer). Expanding our understanding of gendered violence: Violence against trans people and loved ones. *B.C. Institute Against Family Violence newsletter.* http://www.bcifv.org/resources/newsletter/2004/summer/trans.shtml.

Grammer, K., et al. (2003, August). Darwinian aesthetics and the biology of beauty. *Biol Rev Camb Philos Soc, 78*(3), 385-407.

Hadley, K. (2001). And we still ain't satisfied: Gender inequality in Canada. A status report for 2001. Toronto: Centre for Social Justice.

Henderson, S. (2006, Spring). HIV/AIDS and aboriginal communities in Canada—Rights and responses. Ministry matters, Anglican Church of Canada. http://ministrymatters.ca/2006/spring/mm10.html.

Hotz, R. (2005, March). Galaxy of differences between men and women. *The Scotsman—UK.* http://www.rense.com/general63/galaxyofgeneticdifferences.htm.

House of Commons. (2006). Standing Committee on the Status of Women.

Hudspith, M. (2001). Caring for lesbian health: A resource for Canadian health care providers, policy makers and planners. (Rev. ed.). Health Canada. http://www.hc-sc.gc.ca/english/women/facts_issues/lesbian_health.htm.

Human Resources and Social Development Canada. (2005). http://www.hrsdc.gc.ca/en/labour/publications/employment_standards/harassment.shtml.

Hurley, M. (2005). Sexual orientation and legal rights. Parliamentary Information and Research Service; Library of Parliament. http://www.parl.gc.ca/information/library/PRBpubs/921-e.htm#chronologytxt.

Interagency Coalition on AIDS and Development. (2004, June). HIV/AIDS and homophobia. http://www.icad-cisd.com/content/pub_details.cfm?id=113&CAT=9&lang=e.

International day against homophobia. (2006). Hiding its face: Homophobia becoming more subtle; National Day against homophobia, May 17th, 2006. http://www.homophobiaday.org/default.aspx?scheme=3181.

Iyer, N. (2002). Working through the wage gap. *Report of the task force on pay equity*. http://www.ag.gov.bc.ca/public/working_through_the_wage_gap.pdf.

Johnson, H. (2006). Measuring violence against women: Statistical trends 2006. Statistics Canada. http://www.statcan.ca/english/research/85-570-XIE/85-570-XIE2006001.htm.

Kismet Eler, A. (2007). Homophobia in the workplace: One story of what to do and how to deal. http://nathanr.ca/queer-related/homophobia-in-the-workplace-one-story-of-what-to-do-and-how-to-deal.

Lerner, G. (1986). *The creation of patriarchy*. New York: Oxford University Press.

Marshall, K. (2006, July). Converging gender roles. *Perspectives*. Statistics Canada catalogue no. 75-001-XIE. http://www.statcan.ca/english/freepub/75-001-XIE/10706/art-1.pdf.

Mead, M. (1935). *Sex and temperament in three primitive societies*. New York: William Morrow. (See also Mead, M. (1949). *Male and female: A study of the sexes in a changing world*. New York: Morrow Quill Paperbacks.)

Media Awareness Network. (2007). Violence in media entertainment. http://www.media-awareness.ca/english/issues/violence/violence_entertainment.cfm?Render.

Metropolitan Action Committee [METRAC]. (2001). Frequently asked questions on violence, girls and young women. Toronto, ON. http://www.metrac.org/new/faq_vio.htm.

Nanda, S. (1998). *Neither man nor woman: The hijras of India*. Belmont, CA: Wadsworth Publishing.

Nash, T. (Director), & Martin, K. (Producer). (1996). *Who's counting: Marilyn Waring on sex, lies and global economics*. Toronto: National Film Board of Canada [NFB].

Ogrodnik, L. (ed.). (2006). Family violence in Canada: A statistical profile 2006. Canadian Centre for Justice Statistics. http://www.statcan.ca/english/freepub/85-224-XIE/85-224-XIE2006000.pdf.

Ontario Government. (2007). Domestic violence action plan update—January 2007. http://www.citizenship.gov.on.ca/owd/english/resources/publications/docs/dvap.update.pdf.

Packota, V. (2000). Emotional abuse of women by their intimate partners: A literature review. Canadian Health Network: Education Wife Assault. http://www.womanabuseprevention.com/html/emotional_abuse_literature_rev.html.

The Phrase Finder. "The love that dare not speak its name." http://www.phrases.org.uk/meanings/364900.html.

Raphael, D. (2002, June). Poverty, income inequality and health in Canada. Centre for Social Justice: Foundation for Research and Education. http://www.socialjustice.org/uploads/pubs/PovertyIncomeInequalityandHealthinCanada.pdf.

Sauvé, R. (2002). CONNECTIONS—Tracking the links between jobs and family: Job, family and stress among husbands, wives and lone-parents 15-64 from 1990 to 2000. Vanier Institute of the Family. http://www.vifamily.ca/library/cft/connections.html#TRENDS41_42.

Schlafly, P. (1977). *The power of the positive woman.* New Rochelle, NY: Arlington House.

Starr, B. (2006). Ask a geneticist. *Understanding genetics.* http://www.thetech.org/genetics/ask.php?id=38.

Statistics Canada. (2006, March). Women in Canada: A gender-based statistical report. (5th ed.). http://www.statcan.ca/english/freepub/89-503-XIE/0010589-503-XIE.pdf.

Statistics Canada. (2005, January). Spotlight: Police officers—More women in uniform. http://www42.statcan.ca/smr04/2005/01/smr04_02505_04_e.htm.

Statistics Canada. (1998). General social survey cycle 12: Time use survey.

Statistics Canada. (1993). Violence against women survey (VAWS); Reported in *Assessing violence against women: A statistical profile (Federal/Provincial/Territorial Ministers Responsible for the Status of Women, 2002).* http://www.statcan.ca/cgi-bin/imdb/p2SV.pl?Function=getSurvey&SDDS=3896&lang=en&db=IMDB&dbg=f&adm=8&dis=2.

Status of Women Canada. (2006). Social policy, gender inequality, and poverty. http://www.swc-cfc.gc.ca/pubs/pubspr/0662653327/200102_0662653327_7_e.html.

Supreme Court of Canada. (1988). *Morgentaler, R v.* (1988), 44 DLR (4th) 385 (SCC).

Supreme Court of Canada. (1967, November 7). *Klippert, R v.*

Transgender Crossroads. (2003, May). Thousands die each year as a result of homophobia. http://www.tgcrossroads.org/news/archive.asp?aid=734.

Trinity University. (n.d.). *Gender and society.* http://www.trinity.edu/~mkearl/gender.html.

Trivia-Library.com. (n.d.). A list of famous gays and lesbians in history. http://www.trivia-library.com/a/a-list-of-famous-gays-and-lesbians-in-history.htm.

UNICEF. (2007). *State of the world's children 2007.* http://www.unicef.org.

University of Guelph. (2006, May 31). Working women more influenced by family pressures, says prof. *Campus News.* http://www.uoguelph.ca/mediarel/2006/05/working_women_m.html.

US Department of Labor. (2000). Highlights of women's earnings in 2000. Bureau of Labor Statistics. http://www.bls.gov/cps/cpswom2000.pdf.

Ward, M. (2006). *The family dynamic: A Canadian perspective.* (4th ed.). Toronto: Thomson Nelson.

Wolf, Naomi. (1991). *The beauty myth.* New York: Anchor Books.

Wood, J. (2005). *Gendered lives: Communication, gender and culture.* (6th ed.). Toronto: Thomson Wadsworth.

World Bank. (2001, January). *Engendering development through gender equality in rights, resources, and voice.* Policy research report. New York: World Bank and Oxford University.

Wright, L. (1999, July). Stonewall riots in New York City in 1969. *Socialism Today, 40.* http://socialistalternative.org/literature/stonewall.html.

CHAPTER 6

Family Problems

CHAPTER OBJECTIVES

After completing this chapter, you will be able to:

Understand significant dimensions of family problems

- Understand diverse family patterns and changing family forms.
- Understand problems such as divorce, family dysfunction, and abuse (domestic, child, and sexual).

Understand and apply different sociological perspectives to family problems

- Structural functionalist
- Feminist

Identify and critique various responses to family-related social problems, including the responses of

- Government and policy
- Law and policing
- Community
- Individuals

DIMENSIONS

Changing Family Forms

The family used to be something that Canadians defined quite easily and similarly. The definitions of marriage and family were predominantly religious in origin. Marriage was understood to be the lifelong union of one man and one woman, who consented to join their lives for the purposes of procreation and mutual companionship. In the 1950s, televised situation comedies like *Leave it to Beaver* and *Father Knows Best* epitomized how Canadian society then understood and defined the family. From the beginnings of the Industrial Revolution in the 17th century until the middle of the 20th century, the key family unit in European and Euro-Canadian culture was the *immediate*, *nuclear*, or *conjugal* family. These families were understood to be units lasting for the whole of the spouses' lives and to include one husband, one wife, and children who were their biological offspring, whose care was their responsibility and over whom the father exercised authority. The man was the head of the family, and all other members of it were subject to his authority. They would all bear his last name. This traditional conception of family implied certain relationships of authority and certain economic roles for each spouse, with the father acting as breadwinner in the *public sphere* of paid employment and the mother acting in the *private sphere* as unpaid caregiver for the couple's home and children. *Extended* family members—people closely related by blood to either spouse—traditionally figured in the spouses' lives on a regular basis (for example, at holiday gatherings), but were not people with whom the married couple resided or to whose authority they were subject.

Families have long been the fundamental, crucial organizing unit of our society. Relationships of birth or marriage have determined questions of property ownership and are very important to the organizing of communities. Anthropologists and other social researchers generally understand the family in a traditional society to be the primary economic unit of production.

However, this traditional definition of family has been called into question in recent years. In the past few decades a number of factors have caused the traditional form of the Canadian family to fragment into a diverse patchwork of alternative family patterns.

It is no longer safe to assume that the children in a family unit are the biological offspring of two married people living together with their children. Family relationships are a set of normative structures. Social scientists have long understood that these relationships, though commonly thought to be "blood" connections, are essentially social relationships. In other words, actual biological relationships between people are not necessary for family relationships to be formed. Most societies recognize some form of adoption, and, as DNA blood testing has begun to show, people's understanding of who their fathers are does not always coincide with the biological reality.

The economic and authoritarian roles for men and women implied by the normative structure of the traditional family form in Canada no longer apply in most cases. As we discussed in chapter 5 with reference to sex and gender more generally, the expected and accepted "place" for both men and women has been challenged since the middle of the 20th century. Women have entered the paid labour force in large numbers, and child-care and domestic work have often been consigned to professional daycare workers and housekeepers. Women no longer invariably take their husbands' last names. This practice is still the norm in Anglo-Canada; in Quebec, however, a woman cannot change her name unless she makes a formal application to do so. Many academics now consider the traditional family described above to be the *patriarchal family*, a unit that promotes in each new generation an authoritarian society of rigid hierarchy and male dominance and property ownership. Social researchers, philosophers, and psychiatrists—including Deleuze, Guattari, Reich, and Lang (Reich, 1975)—have critiqued the traditional family in this manner.

Canadian society has grown increasingly pluralistic as our cultural and ethnic demographics have shifted. Increased cultural diversity in Canada has affected Canada's family forms. We have always been a nation of immigrants, but the origins of new Canadians have become more diverse, as is discussed in more detail in chapter 9, in connection with globalization. People entering Canada in large numbers now come from all over the world, and they bring with them rich and diverse cultural heritages. These people sometimes bring understandings of family that are traditional for them but alternative to Euro-Canadian mainstream society. In many cultures, for instance, extended family relationships play a far more important role than they traditionally have in Canada. In many parts of China, Africa, and India, for example, newly married spouses, rather than form a new household of their own, will move in with the parents of one spouse and become subsumed into the authority structure, economic functioning, and other relationships of an existing, multi-generational household.

While monogamy has long been the mainstream family form in most of western Europe and North America, it is not the norm worldwide. Far from it. Anthropologists and other social researchers have observed that the most remarkable thing about human family forms is that every organizational possibility has been practised at some time.

Not all human societies have understood marriage to be a lifelong union. Most cultures have allowed some form of divorce. The Inuit, for example, have always freely divorced and remarried, with people expected to have more than one partner over the course of their lives.

There are two varieties of *polygamy*—that is, a spouse of one gender marrying several spouses of the other gender. The majority of known human societies have been *polygynous*, meaning that one man is married to several wives. Probably the example of polygamy most familiar to Canadians is that practised by the Mormons (members of the Church of Jesus Christ of Latter-day Saints) in North America up until the 19th century. The Mormon Church has officially abandoned the practice of polygamy, and that church has become sufficiently assimilated by the American mainstream that in 2007, one of its members (Mitt Romney) was a serious Republican candidate for US president. But there are breakaway Mormon sects, particularly in British Columbia and Utah, where polygamous marriages remain the norm. It is difficult to assess the number of polygamous Mormon marriages in Canada today because such marriages are illegal according to s. 293 of the *Criminal Code*. But it is reasonable to assume that there are hundreds (and probably thousands) of people living in such polygamous unions.

Others, such as the people of Tibet and Sri Lanka, have been *polyandrous*. This means that one woman would have several husbands. People from all around the world have entered Canada and brought with them their norms and cultural expectations even as they have adapted to mainstream Canadian values. Under Islamic law, for example, a man can have several wives, and this is the practice in many countries of the Middle East. There are reportedly more than 253,260 Muslims in Canada from over 60 countries, most of whom were born in those nations, and many of whom have immigrated with families in which the marriages are polygamous (Haddad, 1999–2007). While these polygamous marriages are not formally recognized under Canadian law, spouses whose marriages are not recognized can still obtain certain benefits to which common-law spouses are entitled, such as spousal support. Further, since the legalization of same-sex marriage, there has been a rising tide of calls for the legalization of polygamy, or at least for the official recognition, in Canada, of polygamous marriages entered into abroad. Professor Martha Bailey (2005), among others, has warned the courts to be prepared for a constitutional challenge to the illegality of polygamy—probably from a breakaway Mormon polygamist—in the near future.

Beginning in the 1960s, a change in sexual behavior and commonly accepted morality about sexual relationships took place in North America. This *sexual revolution* was related to a number of factors: the development of safe, reliable birth control in the form of oral contraceptives; the coming-of-age of the "baby boom" generation; and a growing secularization of society and liberalization of laws concerning the family. Where sexual relationships outside of marriage had been condemned as sinful or otherwise undesirable by traditional Euro-Canadian morality, premarital sex became normalized after the 1960s. It is now quite usual for people to live together, or *cohabit*, in **common-law relationships** outside of marriage. These are relationships that are not formalized by a marriage ceremony, but nonetheless involve the cohabitation and routine intimacies of marriage. Young people in Canada today quite often live together in conjugal relationships without marrying. Some refer to these as "trial marriages," which give the parties a chance to see what marriage would be like.

As people, beginning in the 1960s, began to talk more openly about sex, they took an interest in the works of some intellectuals who documented human sexual practices and questioned the appropriateness of the monogamous family as a unit of organization. They cited biological reasons as well as philosophical principles about free will in questioning our society's convention of monogamous relationships. Anthropologist Margaret Mead drew controversy when she published *Coming of Age in Samoa* in 1928, a book that documented a way of expressing adolescent sexuality more liberal than that accepted at the time in North America. Alfred Kinsey's studies of modern sexual behavior (*Sexual Behavior in the Human Male* and *Sexual Behaviour in the Human Female*) documented in great detail the sexual practices of American society. A biologist by training, Kinsey drew controversy when he stressed the biological nature of human sexuality and the fundamental drive, especially of men, to engage in sexual relationships with multiple partners.

While academic discourse and popular culture in the middle of the 20th century saw some questioning of the appropriateness or necessity of the family as an organizing unit for Canadian society, our society has returned to a greater acceptance of monogamy and, some would argue, a more conservative treatment of sexuality. Few now would argue that families are not important. More recently, as the importance of family has been questioned less, academic and legal debate has focused on who should be allowed to form families with whom and what protections they should be accorded.

The family is now defined much more broadly in Canadian society than it was in the past. The *Merriam-Webster Dictionary* (2007) now defines "family" as "the basic unit in society traditionally consisting of two parents rearing their children; also: any of various social units differing from but regarded as equivalent to the traditional family." Similarly, the US Census Bureau now defines a family as "two or more persons related by birth, marriage, or adoption, who reside together" (US Census Bureau, 2004). This definition of family is broad enough to extend to two or more adult siblings living together, to just one parent and a child or children, to two adults who are related by marriage or who cohabit but have no children, or to adults living together who adopt a child.

For the purposes of the Canadian census, Statistics Canada now defines the **family** gender-neutrally, as

> a now-married couple (with or without never-married sons and/or daughters of either or both spouses), a couple living common-law (with or without never-married sons and/or daughters of either or both partners), or a lone parent of any marital status, with at least one never-married son or daughter living in the same dwelling.

Many Canadians view the growing diversity in our family forms not as a problem but as a shifting reality that demonstrates cultural change. Nonetheless, same-sex families and single parents, while their legal status in Canada has improved, face discrimination and other challenges when they travel internationally. Canadian same-sex families often have trouble adopting children in the United States, because of the discrimination against them in that country.

Some *social conservatives*, particularly those with *fundamentalist* religious views, are opposed to this growing diversity. They see the diversifying of Canada's family forms as evidence of social decay. Their critique is based on the assumption that the normative, traditional family format provides a better, happier foundation for our social and economic order. Whether there was ever in fact a golden age of the family will be discussed below, with reference to contemporary and historical problems in Canadian families.

Problems in Canadian Families

In Canada, as in other Western democracies, the family is understood to be a refuge or haven from the world, a place where people can find personal fulfillment, nurturing, and protection. In the capitalist conception of human relationships, on which Canadian economics are largely based, the family is a safe harbour from the storm of dehumanizing competitive forces that dominate contemporary society (Zinn & Stanley Eitzen, 1987). This idealized view of families is inconsistent with some unfortunate realities prevalent in Canadian families.

The traditional family is the normative form of family unit, long viewed as the ideal. But there has always been deviance from this norm, and there is some debate among historians and other social scientists as to whether the changes in the family unit now being observed reflect actual change or just increased visibility, as people practise now more openly what was hidden in the past.

DIVORCE

Until the end of World War II, divorce in Canada was extremely uncommon, almost unheard of. Powerful religious leaders, and a government closely linked to them, condemned divorce as sinful and as a threat to the orderly functioning of the country. Because divorce was very difficult to obtain, spouses would separate and not divorce. It is very difficult to assess how many marriages effectively ended with separation.

The idea that marriage is divinely ordained and should be lifelong is alive and flourishing. Some people refer to this as the ideology of romantic love. Others call it compulsory heterosexuality or heteronormativity. The popular genre of Hollywood films known as "romantic comedies," which includes such movies as *When*

Harry Met Sally, *Sleepless in Seattle*, and *The Holiday*, is predicated on the idea that there is one perfect or ideal partner for each person and that the two of them are meant to spend their lives together and produce children. But despite North Americans' continuing belief in romantic love, many of their marriages do not last. Ironically, it is the country that produces these films that has the highest divorce rate of any Western nation. The divorce rate in the United States is about 44 percent. The Canadian divorce rate varies from year to year, but is around 35 percent. This Canadian statistic is lower than many would expect, but, in light of the normative ideal, it nonetheless reflects a high rate of marital failure.

Divorce is not necessarily a problem for those who choose it. In fact, it can be quite liberating. It is a way for people to leave abusive or otherwise intolerable situations, or to find happiness in other relationships or in new-found independence. Canada's family law has changed over the past few decades to make divorce easier to obtain.

However, there are several negative consequences to divorce. Divorce is expensive. Partners who choose this route have to pay money in legal fees that would otherwise go toward the support of their families. Divorce and relationship breakdown are also difficult emotionally and psychologically for the separating spouses, who may become depressed or suffer other mental health issues. This emotional pain is usually temporary, especially for men; they are particularly likely to recuperate emotionally and financially after divorce. Over 75 percent of divorced men remarry, compared with 65 percent of women (Ambert, 1998). Men tend to remarry regardless of their age at divorce, while women are less likely to find a new partner the older they are. In any case, those second and subsequent marriages are even more likely to end in divorce than the first ones were.

Many people who get divorced have had children together, and divorce can affect these children adversely. The most common duration of a marriage that ends in divorce is three to five years (CBC News Online, 2005). In 1998, divorcing spouses were most likely to be in their late twenties, with divorce rates diminishing consistently from that age upward (Ambert, 1998). With the increase in the average marrying age to 31 for women and 34 for men, people going through their first divorce are usually in their early thirties. The children of those getting divorced tend to be quite young at the time of the marital breakdown. They spend a large proportion of their formative years in single-parent households or, if and when their parents find new partners, in *blended* families. Divorce and remarriage are particularly hard on children. Many of them suffer negative emotional and psychological consequences that may affect them into adulthood. These can include the following: an inability to maintain their own relationships; depression; low self-esteem; and even violent behaviour, especially in the case of young men. What is more, the stress brought on parents by their relationship's breakdown and the pressures of single parenting may lead to child neglect or abuse.

It is not just on an emotional or psychological level that divorce can hurt children. Women tend to be left poorer by divorce than men are. As is discussed with reference to gender in chapter 5 and economic inequality in chapter 7, women tend to be poorer than men in general in Canada, and single mothers poorer still. Children raised by single mothers can have their economic circumstances and life chances impaired, especially as post-secondary education grows ever more expensive. While parents are legally required to financially support their children even if they do not live with them, thousands of "deadbeat" fathers—and, in some cases, mothers—do not meet their child support obligations. And child support amounts, though helpful, tend not to put households headed by single mothers on a financial par with the households of absented fathers. Most children reside with their mothers as sole custodians after their parents divorce, though statistical data from 2002 indicates that this may be changing. While over 75 percent of children in 1988 were in the sole custody of their mothers after their parents divorced, about 42 percent were in joint custody arrangements by 2002. This may reflect a growing involvement on the part of fathers in the lives of their children after divorce.

DYSFUNCTION AND ABUSE

The family is an institution in which people are vulnerable. Women have obtained a measure of independence through feminist activism and legal change, but the stereotype of women's dependence has a biological basis. Women are still reliant upon families during their childbearing years for support, financially and otherwise. Children rely upon families for virtually all of their needs. Men rely upon their families for emotional and, increasingly, economic support. The traditional family is ideally supposed to shelter, protect, and nurture family members. Unfortunately, the reality is that many families fall short of this ideal. Many families are the site of conflict and abuse. These families are sometimes described as *dysfunctional*. Children who grow up in these families may assume abuse and conflict to be normal family behaviours. These family dysfunctions may be caused by parents' substance addictions. Or they may be related to parents' mental illnesses or personality disorders. In other cases, the parents may simply be emulating behaviours they learned from their own parents. Some feminists and social scientists see these dysfunctional families as the norm in Canadian society—a consequence of power imbalances endemic to the traditional patriarchal family.

Very few families are perfect or ideal, and family dysfunctions vary widely. For example, family dysfunction may manifest itself in role reversals, with parents ascribing inappropriately high levels of maturity to children while they themselves act in an immature manner. Or the dysfunction may take the form of social isolation, with the family discouraged from establishing contacts with broader social units, such as friendships with non-relatives in the community. Some parenting styles have been described as dysfunctional. A child's not being permitted to develop his or her own identity or value system, or to express his or her own opinions, for example, is seen by some as dysfunctional. Dysfunction can obviously also involve abuse, neglect, violence, and sexual abuse in the family (see Farmer, 1990). The source of such dysfunction may be a member of the victim's immediate or extended family, and it may involve the complicity or sufferance of other family members, which can be as damaging as the actual abuse.

Domestic Abuse

Domestic abuse, also referred to as *domestic violence*, *partner abuse*, or *spousal abuse*, takes place when a family member, intimate partner, or former partner seeks to psychologically or physically dominate or harm another family member. Other terms for this are *wife battering* and *spousal abuse*. As was mentioned in chapter 5, most domestic violence involves a male perpetrator and a female victim. But there are cases of same-sex partner abuse and cases where women are the abusers and men the abused.

At one time, when a man's family was essentially seen as his private property over which he had authority, domestic abuse was not generally discussed in Canada. It is only in the past few decades that domestic violence has become publicly acknowledged and documented in this country.

There are many forms of domestic abuse. It can be psychological or physical, and is often both. Domestic violence can also be sexual. We now recognize that it can include spiritual abuse, with one partner using the other's religious or spiritual beliefs to manipulate and control him or her; stalking; and economic abuse, in which case the abusive partner has complete control over the victim's economic resources and uses that control to manipulate and humiliate him or her. The damage wrought by domestic violence obviously varies. Physical injuries may be minor or may result in a death. For example, according to police data, more than 500 women and 100 men were either seriously injured or killed at the hands of their spouses or intimate partners in 1999 (Canadian Centre for Justice Statistics, 2000).

Statistics about homicide are generally agreed upon, but there is debate about the prevalence of non-fatal domestic abuse in Canada. Like child abuse, spousal abuse takes place largely behind closed doors, in the *private sphere*; it is cloaked in shame and is therefore often hidden, sometimes not reported for years—if ever. Victims of abuse may remain emotionally attached or financially dependent upon their abuser, which may deter them from reporting incidents of abuse. The most thorough study of domestic abuse in Canada was the 1999 General Social Survey on Victimization (Canadian Centre for Justice Statistics, 1999). Somewhat surprisingly, this survey found that women and men suffer similar amounts of abuse in their intimate relationships. The key difference is that female victims are much more likely than male victims to be seriously injured or killed, and that the abuse of a female victim is more likely to be part of a repetitive and/or escalating pattern. It is also clear from this survey that young people are at greatest risk of being seriously injured or killed as a result of domestic abuse. This means that people in their twenties—college students, for example—are at serious risk of receiving serious injuries in their intimate relationships.

It is not only the direct victims of domestic abuse who suffer harm. Children who witness the violence or whose lives are disrupted by their parents' relationship trauma are also harmed. What is more, the social costs of domestic abuse affect all Canadians. Domestic abuse requires a costly social and health response. The federal Department of Justice estimates that $4.2 billion is spent annually in responses to abuse. These funds go to social services, criminal justice, employment disruptions, education, and health and medical costs (Greaves & Hankivsky, 1995).

Child Abuse

Child abuse is similar in many ways to domestic abuse, and may be a consequence of it. Victims of spousal abuse, traumatized and depressed, may neglect or abuse their children. Certainly domestic abuse interferes with the development of a secure parent–child relationship. But domestic abuse is not the only possible factor in child abuse. Others include parental substance addictions, poverty, illness, mental illness, and other family stresses.

Child abuse is the emotional maltreatment or neglect of children, and the physical or sexual mistreatment of children, by persons responsible for their care, whether these latter be parents, guardians, or others. Abuse threatens the safety, development and, too often, the lives of children.

It is difficult to estimate accurately the number of children abused in Canada or elsewhere. Like spousal abuse, such abuse takes place in secret, behind closed doors. Victims of child abuse are often absolutely dependent upon their abusers, which can deter them from disclosing the abuse. However, statistical information about child abuse is growing more reliable as child protection agencies and police document the cases. There are no official federal statistics about abuse, but the provinces do keep information about child protection within their jurisdictions. In 1992, about 40,000 Canadian children were living in foster care, largely as a result of having suffered serious abuse or neglect. In Ontario in 1993, the Children's Aid Society investigated over 13,000 new allegations of physical child abuse alone, in addition to allegations of neglect, emotional abuse, and sexual abuse involving children (Public Health Agency of Canada, 1997). The numbers of children who are abused and end up in foster care have not decreased in the past decade. In fact, the problem appears to be getting significantly worse. As of 2003, there were 8,864 children living as Crown wards in Ontario, up from 7,935 in 2002. In 2003, 18,126 children were in the care of Children's Aid Societies (Adoption Council of Canada, 2004).

Emotional abuse of children is difficult to measure and has not always been recognized as a problem. But emerging research is showing that it is particularly harmful to children. Generally speaking, emotional abuse is understood to be an attack on a child's self-worth or self-esteem. Unreasonable criticism, unfair expectations, rejection, or parental behaviour calculated to terrorize or emotionally torture children—for example, threatening to kill a family member or pet, or letting a child witness domestic abuse of a parent—are all examples of emotional abuse.

Neglect is a failure by caregivers or parents to provide for a child's needs. Rejection of children can result in emotional neglect. Neglect can also be physical, as when a child is not properly fed or supplied with appropriate medical attention. Failure to adequately supervise children or to ensure they attend school regularly are also forms of neglect. Some contend that social services' policing of neglect interferes with parental autonomy and religious freedoms. For example, in 2007, when sextuplets were born to Jehovah's Witness parents in Vancouver, two of the newborns were apprehended by child protection authorities to ensure they received blood transfusions which their parents refused to allow. The parents are now challenging the apprehensions as violating their right to freedom of religion—specifically, their right to raise their children in accordance with their religious beliefs, which proscribe blood transfusions as undermining a person's spiritual integrity. The case is before the courts at time of writing, and its outcome is yet to be determined (CTV News Online, 2007). However it is resolved, it is a good example of the tension between parental autonomy and individual freedom on the one hand, and our collective interest in the well-being of children on the other.

Physical abuse includes the use of undue or excessive force on a child: hitting, choking, kicking, burning, or any other action that puts the child's physical health at risk. There is sometimes debate over whether all physical discipline of children is abuse, and the extent to which *corporal punishment* is ever appropriate. There has been a general shift away from the physical disciplining of children in our society. Even a generation ago, teachers and school administrators were permitted to use the strap or ruler on children who misbehaved. This is no longer condoned in Canada. In 2004, a case before the Supreme Court of Canada was brought by an organization (Canadian Foundation for Children, Youth, and the Law) that challenged Canada's legal acceptance of "spanking," or mild corporal punishment not done in anger. The Supreme Court (2004) upheld the right of parents to use corporal punishment on their children in limited circumstances, where no marks were caused, and where the punishment was part of a disciplinary strategy. While this case settled the legal question, some people continue to advocate the abolition of spanking and other forms of corporal punishment against children.

Children who are abused or neglected will often manifest warning signs. Such children may not bring appropriate meals to school or daycare, and may be frequently hungry. They may look unkempt, unwashed, and not be dressed appropriately for the weather conditions. They may have strange recurrent injuries, such as burns, bite marks, layers of bruising, or other physical afflictions. They may not want to go home or may repeatedly run away from home. Children who are suffering abuse may display a wide range of problem behaviours; they may be extremely aggressive or unusually withdrawn.

In addition to the physical damage, children who are abused or neglected often suffer in their interpersonal relationships outside the family and even in their adult careers. While they have, theoretically, control over their own conduct, children raised in abusive homes have trouble being parents themselves; they have not seen appropriate role models, and they may ultimately abuse their own children. People abused as children often experience mental health disorders and may need psychiatric treatment for problems such as reactive attachment disorder, anxiety, and depression (Lyons-Ruth, Alpern, & Repacholi, 1993). They may fear intimacy, be preoccupied with fire, and have poor impulse control. Attachment disorder prevents a person from trusting others and from forming mutually rewarding relationships with other individuals. People abused as children also have difficulty experiencing empathy toward others and may not possess a "conscience."

Incest is sexual activity between close family members who are not permitted legally or by custom to marry. Anthropologists and other social researchers have noted that all cultures have an *incest taboo*, whereby people understood to be close blood relatives are prohibited from engaging in sexual relations or initiating romantic relationships with one another. There have been notable exceptions to this, as in the royal families of ancient Egypt and the Inca empire, but they are few and far between. Also, different societies have defined incest differently. In some societies, for example, first-cousin marriage is prohibited, while in others it is allowed and even encouraged. In 19 American states, cousin marriage is legal. Laws about cousin marriage also vary between Canadian provinces. But marriage between first cousins, even when it is legal, is apt to give people pause. Twentieth-century American rock singer Jerry Lee Lewis became the centre of a scandal when, at age 23, he married his 13-year-old cousin. First-cousin marriages aside, virtually all societies recognize that sexual relations between close family members are not appropriate.

But sexual relationships between family members do sometimes occur. It is not clear how prevalent they are. Estimates for the number of male children sexually abused range from 3 percent to 37 percent. For female children, the estimated range is even broader, from 8 percent to 71 percent (Terry & Tallon, n.d.). In Canada, as in other countries, incest is a crime even where the relations are consensual. The rationale here is that it is difficult for genuine consent to exist where partners are close relatives; there tends to be a power imbalance between the participants, with an authority figure on one hand (usually a man), and a child or younger person on the other.

Incest has come to be understood as a kind of sexual abuse. **Sexual abuse** is sexual contact in which a dominant partner uses his or her position of authority or physical strength to coerce or exploit a less powerful partner. Sexual abuse can also include the commercial sexual exploitation of people, including children, by means of pornography and the sex trade, which are discussed in more detail in chapter 4. It is important to note also that both male and female children and adults can be victims of sexual abuse, and that both males and females can be perpetrators. However, most reported perpetrators of sexual abuse (94 to 99 percent) are male, and the incidence of female perpetrators reported is extremely low by comparison (Committee on Sexual Offences Against Children and Youth, 1984). These numbers seem to indicate that women don't abuse as frequently as men. But some researchers and social advocates, especially male victims of past sexual abuse by women, have contended that these statistics regarding female abusers may be misleadingly low. They suggest that men are reluctant to report abuse due to gender stereotypes about male strength and virility; men are expected to desire sexual relations with virtually any woman who is willing.

Sexual abuse can take place in institutional settings. Recent lawsuits have shown that such abuse took place in residential schools run by Canadian churches for Aboriginal people. This kind of abuse was covered up in several separate instances by the Catholic Church both in the United States and in Canada. Sexual abuse also takes place in families. Child sexual abuse is illegal in all countries, including Canada.

There are several warning signs that a child is being sexually abused, including a precocious knowledge in the child of sexual behaviour or an interest in sexuality. Such a child may be promiscuous or unusually withdrawn, and may have issues with bladder and bowel control and bedwetting.

It is clear that a wide range of harms can result from sexual abuse. Children who are sexually abused often later experience anxiety, grief, flashbacks, emotional numbing, sexual dysfunction, and social dysfunction, as well as other emotional and social issues: dissociative identity disorder, borderline personality disorder, and eating disorders (Fergusson, Lynskey, & Horwood, 1996).

Young children are at the greatest risk of suffering serious harm from child abuse. Infants and preschoolers are at greater risk than older children are of serious injury or death as a result of abuse (Hegar, Zuravin, & Orme, 1994). However, even older children are at risk of emotional harm and long-term ill effects. The consequences of child abuse can be far-reaching and can affect public safety in general. A study of men incarcerated in Canadian prisons showed that those abused as children were three times more likely than non-abused men to be violent as adults (Dutton & Hart, 1992). Because victims of childhood abuse are at greater risk than others of becoming violent criminals, it is for all of our sakes that child abuse must be addressed.

ANALYSIS

SOCIAL ISSUES OF FAMILY LIFE: INFLUENCE OF MEDIA

As you have learned, the family is the fundamental organizing structure of society. In sociological terms, it is a **cultural universal**. A cultural universal is a social pattern or practice or institution that occurs in every society. In each culture, family is uniquely structured according to that culture's norms, values, and beliefs.

The family, in structural functionalist terms, is a primary social institution, *primary* denoting the essential and fundamental role of family to society. The institution of the family is responsible for the procreation and socialization of children, which ensures the very survival of a society. The family also has the primary function of providing material and emotional support for its members, so they can be healthy and useful members of society. Additionally, the family serves to define members of a society by naming them and by assigning them a social position or rank. Dysfunctions in families can result in societal disorganization and in lasting psychological scars on the family members. We noted earlier in this chapter the serious dysfunctions caused by an escalating divorce rate and by family violence. The Canadian institutions of government, law, education, and health care are continually needing to address family dysfunctions and thereby restore social stability.

Throughout this text, we have identified forces of change as the root cause of many social issues. This is true of the many challenges facing modern Canadian families. Globalization is one such precipitating change. Technological change is another. For the purposes of this chapter, we will focus on the effects on children of changes in the media. The advent of television during the 1950s irreversibly changed family life. Today there are also video, the Internet, and the reality games that many believe are a serious threat to the well-being of children and families. Many think that these media threaten children's mental, emotional, social, and physical well-being through their powerful and uncontrolled socializing influence. Children's social interactions are increasingly mediated by technology, and many believe that this is having a damaging impact on the cohesiveness of families.

Identifying a Social Issue

WHAT GROUPS ARE CALLING FOR ATTENTION, AND WHAT IS THEIR CONCERN?

Though lacking conclusive evidence of the malign influence of media on children, a number of groups in Canada have dedicated themselves to alerting the public about this dangerous influence. They cite children's uncontrolled access to media programming as a cause of impaired mental and physical health and as a root of social discord. Such groups are particularly passionate because they perceive children to be the members of society most vulnerable to negative media influences.

A primary concern is that the entertainment media is becoming ever more graphically violent, sexual, and sadistic. This constitutes a kind of **psychological violence** for the young viewer—feelings of intimidation, threat, and harassment. One study found that from 1999 to 2001, the psychological violence inflicted by entertainment media increased 325 percent over the levels between 1993 and 1999. In 2001 alone, TV shows averaged 40 acts of violence per hour (Media Awareness Network, 2007). Psychological violence, though it involves no physical component for the viewer, can leave lasting mental and emotional damage. The Canadian Paediatric Society (CPS) (Pyschosocial Paediatrics Committee, 2003) has taken the position that the influence of the media on the psychosocial development of children is profound. Child psychologist J. Santa Barbara (2001) attributes the readiness of Canadians to resolve differences through conflict to the omnipresent violence in our entertainment media. In short, we have been thoroughly socialized to solve problems through conflict.

WHAT IS THE VISION OR GOAL OF THE VOICES OF CONCERN?

There is much debate over whether, how, and to what extent media negatively influence children and families, so the visions of how to resolve the problem in question—in particular, the antisocial behaviour and deteriorating health of Canadians—are diverse. Most groups and organizations are calling for education to help children and parents understand the deceptions and dangers in the media so that they will be less vulnerable to its negative influences. Another proposal is to restrict the quantity of exploitive and negative content in the media. Such control, with its taint of censorship, is not very palatable to Canadians. A third proposal is to help parents monitor their children's access to negative media through technological options like the V-chip and through policy options like program rating systems. Another option is self-policing on the part of the industry. What most people desire are entertainment media and information technologies that do not put children at risk or strain family cohesion.

WHAT ARE THE MEANS OF ACHIEVING THE GOALS?

Information technologies and entertainment media are integral to a globalized world, so they are not only desirable, they are necessary. The goal is to minimize their detrimental impacts. Programming content can be controlled through legislation and access to it through technological mechanisms. Control can also be put in the hands of media consumers through education and choice.

Evolution of the Social Issue of Media's Negative Influences

WHAT GROUPS AND ORGANIZATIONS ARE ADVOCATING CHANGE?

Agencies concerned about mental health, especially children's mental health, are actively working to address the negative consequences of exposure to media (Psychosocial Paediatrics Committee, 2003; Nevins, 2004). Child and Family Canada, a partnership of non-profit organizations devoted to child and family welfare, has devoted a portion of its website to rallying citizens to the cause of combatting media violence. Religious organizations, too, have weighed in on the negative effects of graphic (violent and sexually explicit) media (Dueck, 2007).

Other agencies, such as the Media Awareness Network and Canadians Concerned About Violence In Entertainment, are advocating for an improvement in media content. Educators, too, with the help of government, are taking a leadership role in confronting the negative consequences of media; they are especially concerned about children's exposure to violence, diminished opportunities to practise social skills, and curtailed activity levels (Jaffe, 2007).

WHAT HAS PROMPTED PUBLIC AWARENESS AND CONCERN?

Public awareness is aroused when something tragic occurs: random shootings, school shootings, murders, child abductions, schoolyard bullying, or a perceived escalation of youth violence. The heightened fear precipitates a search for explanations and causes. When organizations can establish a link between their concerns and a tragic event of some magnitude, the public is compelled to act. The trial of the youngest Canadian (12 years old) ever to commit multiple murders (of her family) recently ended in a guilty verdict. Prior to the murders, the child and her 23-year-old boyfriend (now awaiting trial) watched *Natural Born Killers*, a movie about a young couple who plot to and then kill the young woman's parents. This very public case has generated an outcry for renewed examination of how violence in the media is affecting our society (Zickefoose, 2007).

HOW IS THE PUBLIC ALIGNED?

Concern about the media's effect on children, families, and social trends has existed for decades, but only recently have policies been introduced to confront the issue: entertainment ratings, education programs, and regulatory bodies. The public, however, is split over the issue: that there is a causal link between what is portrayed on the screen and what occurs in society is still hotly debated. The introductory section of the Media Awareness Network's "Media Violence" (2007) describes this tension as follows:

> The debate over media violence has eluded definitive answers for more than three decades. At first blush, the debate is dominated by one question—whether or not media violence actually causes real-life violence. But closer examination reveals a political battle. On the one hand, there are those who blame media violence for societal violence and want to censor violent content to protect children. On the other hand are those who see regulation as the slippery slope to censorship or a smokescreen hiding the root causes of violence in society.
>
> One thing is certain: the issue of media violence is not going away. Increasingly the debate is focusing on the "culture of violence," and on the normalization of aggression and lack of empathy in our society. (n.p.)

WHAT INITIATIVES HAVE BEEN TAKEN AND WHAT POLICIES HAVE BEEN PUT IN PLACE?

A chronology of Canada's initiatives concerning media content and programming—primarily in response to the perceived effects of violence in the media—can be found on the Media Awareness Network website. Here you can learn about the organizations, government acts, and public actions behind the policies now focused on creating responsible media in Canada. You will note that most action occurred in the 1990s. The analysis on the Media Awareness Network site also documents the loopholes in legislation. For example, sale of age-restricted materials to underage consumers is ongoing; ratings are governed more by box-office receipts than by children's health concerns; and music videos are mostly unregulated (Media Awareness Network, *Media and Canadian Cultural Policies Chronology*, 2007). In 2000, approval for a cross-Canada survey of young Canadians from grades 4 to 12 was approved. The results from the 2003 to 2005 phase of the survey are positive. In general, Canadian children rank among the most grounded in the world; their use of the Internet tends to complement and enhance their real-world activities and social relationships. According to the survey,

> The majority of young Canadians have integrated the Net into mainstream activities which strengthen their connections to their real world communities and enrich their social interactions with peers. At the same time, however, offensive content and risky situations on sites young people favour and their own concerns about privacy invasions and authenticating online information raise serious questions about how to provide them with the tools they need to wisely navigate the Net. (Media Awareness Network, *Young Canadians in a Wired World*, 2007, n.p.)

The study also notes that parental involvement in children's online activities has increased—a positive trend. The issue of media influence on children and families appears to be evolving in a positive direction. However, the most recent study also concludes that continued parental involvement is necessary and that responsibility for supplying the tools to improve media experiences lies with the government and media industries.

Education, rather than censorship, is the preferred approach. For example, the Centre for Media Literacy, an American site, has identified in bold lettering that "media literacy must be a necessary component of any effective effort at violence prevention for both individuals and society as a whole" (Thoman, 1993). Canada's preference for education initiatives and consumer awareness rather than censorship is discussed on the Media Awareness Network's site: "It seems clear that in a globalized, increasingly unregulated world, the protection of children is going to rely increasingly on the vigilance of media-aware parents, public pressure from consumers and professional groups, and the responsiveness of a responsible media sector" (*Government and Industry Responses to Media Violence*, 2007).

WHAT IS THE PUBLIC REACTION?

A positive public reaction to the issue would be consumers exercising choice. However, analysis has shown that consumer passivity in this regard has left the industry vulnerable to unconstrained profit motives. Consumers are passive in the sense that scheduling is more important than content in determining what they watch; they turn to the TV at certain times, regardless of what is on. Furthermore, popular media is distributed by satellite, and time restrictions are less and less an impediment to young viewers watching mature subject matter.

ANALYTICAL APPROACHES TO UNDERSTANDING NEGATIVE MEDIA INFLUENCES

We begin our theoretical analyses of family issues with a structural functionalist analysis of media and family. Family is a primary social institution. Media, government, and the economy are significant social institutions, and all are deeply integrated with one another. In fact, media influence is becoming so powerful that it is reducing the influence of family, education, and religion as agents of socialization. Furthermore, the media, being shaped by advertising interests, is a significant factor in the dysfunctional trend of consumerism. An analysis of the dysfunctions of media proliferation also reveals how enmeshed technology is in our everyday lives. In short, media is an element of every modern social structure. A structural functionalist analysis will show the difficulties of turning media influence into something positive.

After the structural functionalist analysis, this chapter moves on to a feminist analysis of the socializing influence of the media, especially with regard to the mental health and body image of children. Implicit in the feminist analysis of media trends and influences is the notion that powerful, usually corporate, stakeholders control the media. If you were to adopt a social conflict analysis of the competing interests within the media, you would be able to predict the direction of social change—to come closer to answering the question: How successful can government and concerned citizens be in their efforts to contain the negative media influences?

A Structural Functionalist Analysis of Media and Family

BRIEF REVIEW OF THE STRUCTURAL FUNCTIONALIST PERSPECTIVE

The structural functionalist paradigm provides a "systems" view of society; a fault or snag in the social system produces social instability and failure, and the result is a social issue. This perspective will help explain how the proliferation of media and its widespread integration into social behaviours and activities have caused dysfunctions in the family and in society.

FUNCTIONALIST ANALYSIS OF MEDIA INFLUENCE: SOCIAL TRENDS THAT FOSTER DYSFUNCTIONS

Before assessing the dysfunctions caused by media influence, let us use the structural functionalist perspective to assess how media influence became so powerful.

Children Are Spending More Time with Media

Statistics from the Canadian Paediatric Society show that the average Canadian child watches nearly 14 hours of television each week (Psychosocial Paediatrics Committee, 2003). By the time of high school graduation, a child's hours in front of the TV will exceed the hours spent in a classroom. Clearly, TV has become a powerful socializing influence. The Canadian Paediatric Society has also acknowledged that TV watching cuts into children's time for vital activities like playing, reading, learning to talk, spending time with peers and family, storytelling, and participating in regular exercise (Psychosocial Paediatrics Committee, 2003).

Young Canadians in a Wired World (Steeves, 2005) reports that 94 percent of young Canadians go online from home. This is up from 79 percent in 2001. Most said that their Internet experiences were positive. The report also revealed that many of the favourite sites had content intended for mature audiences and that most were commercial.

In short, integration of the media into everyday social behaviour is extensive. Sociologists note that as a **socialization** influence, the media may be replacing parents. This is especially true among certain "at risk" populations, according to the Psychosocial Paediatrics Committee (2003):

- Children from minority and immigrant groups
- Emotionally disturbed children
- Children with learning disabilities
- Children who are abused by their parents
- Children in families in distress

The question to ask is the following: How did the media become so entrenched in the lives of young Canadians?

Parents Are at Work

Since the 1970s, most families have had two parents working. The Vanier Institute of the Family reports that more and more women, even those with young children, have entered the workforce. The Vanier Institute has reported that employment among women with children has climbed steadily over the past few decades. In fact, mothers who work outnumber working women without children (Sauvé, 2002).

Workplace Spillover to Family

Increasingly, work needs and stresses spill into the family, and this has had a profound influence on parenting and family life. As a study by Daly (2004) notes, even the multi-tasking and efficiency methods used in the workplace are being applied to family life, as parents attempt to cope with the many demands on their time and attention at home.

Increasing Independence of Children

Children are spending more time away from their families, in daycare, school, or with peers in organized activities. This is encouraging a distinct youth and peer culture independent of family influence.

According to Ambert (2007), nowadays we find:

- Less parental or adult presence at home to anchor children's lives
- Fewer family rituals that attach youth to a regulating calendar of events
- Schools and neighbourhoods that no longer are effective communities, hence inadequate collective supervision
- Reduced importance of religion as a life-structuring element and agency of social control
- Young people with uncontrolled access to media products and programming of a materialistic, individualistic, and violent nature

In short, modern consumerist lifestyles, compared with those of the past, receive less influence from social institutions such as the family and religion. This has encouraged children's independence from family life.

Media Technologies Are Part of Every Aspect of Society

Canadian society has fully entered the information age. One can enter any workplace, school, library, or business and see evidence of a total integration of information technologies. As noted above, 94 percent of Canadian youth are connected to the Internet.

Children are significant consumers and users of information technologies. Their independence has encouraged a reliance on media technologies in a self-enclosed "youth culture." This may enhance their vulnerability to negative media effects.

CONCLUSIONS DRAWN FROM A STRUCTURAL FUNCTIONALIST PERSPECTIVE

The structural functionalist paradigm is inherently conservative; its main limitation is its tendency to view change as bad. But viewing media influence as all bad would be mistaken on two counts. First, we should not assume that children are empty vessels being filled by information from socializing agents. Modern psychology and sociology have taught us that learning is an interactive and interpretive process. As regards the media, some of the technologies adopted by children enhance their daily living and social patterns (Daly, 2004). Second, developing social patterns is an ongoing process; changing established patterns of interaction can be beneficial. Those who take this side of the debate and decline to demonize the media point to the adaptability of children and to their use of media to enhance their social relationships and their educational resources (Steeves, 2005). In other words, children's adaptation to media has functional qualities.

Questions That Guide a Structural Functionalist Analysis

WHAT SOCIAL INSTITUTIONS ARE CENTRALLY INVOLVED?

The issue being examined is the negative effects of media, especially with respect to children. The social institution of the family is at the centre of the issue. The socialization of children is one of the family's most important manifest functions. Obviously the media, too, as an important social institution in our modern culture and as the apparent root of the dysfunction, is at the centre of the issue. The social institutions of government and of law and justice, responsible for maintaining social order and protecting citizens from harm, are also involved in the issue. So is the social institution of health and medicine; much of the literature about the negative effects of media cites concerns raised by social workers and physicians. And with so many initiatives directed at educating the consuming public—parents and children—the social institution of education is also involved.

WHAT ARE THE MANIFEST FUNCTIONS OF MEDIA? WHAT ARE THE DYSFUNCTIONS OF MEDIA INFLUENCE?

Those concerned about a growing "culture of violence" and insensitivity in Canada's youth point to dysfunction in the family. Sociologists have termed the family the primary institution of society—the source of actual members of society and of their fundamental cultural values, beliefs, and norms. If many young Canadians seem to lack these values, beliefs, and norms, it follows that families are not functioning as they should—that they are dysfunctional. How has this happened? Research has shown that the media is a key factor in the proliferation of hate and violence in today's youth culture.

The manifest function of the media is to keep all members of society informed and to maintain the currency of cultural symbols. But it is also a lucrative part of the economy, and may be more concerned with seeking profit than with fulfilling its traditional functions. The manifest functions of government are to maintain social order and to provide social services. Escalation of violence and hate in a society suggests dysfunction in the government as well.

As we have mentioned, there is some debate about whether media influence is more negative than positive. The Media Awareness Network (2007) has summarized this debate, and this summary will be adapted as a functionalist analysis.

Dysfunctions in the Media

The issue being considered here—one aspect of the larger issue of negative media influence—is that the graphic, often sexualized violence found today in music, music videos, TV, and cinema is creating a society that is insensitive to real violence and that is increasingly inclined to use aggressive behaviours and means to resolve conflict (Santa Barbara, 2001).

What is more, news coverage of so-called real events tends to promote what sells at the expense of realistic coverage. The industry adage is, "if it bleeds, it leads." According to the Media Awareness Network (2007), "Violence and death, they say, keep the viewer numbers up. Good news doesn't" (*Violence in Media Entertainment*). Such skewed news coverage creates a **moral panic** in society—the mistaken public perception of a profound threat from crime or social disorder. Persuading the public that violence in society is out of control and lurks in every shadow will help maintain the status quo, and it will encourage conservatism and escalated militarism (Santa Barbara, 2001).

If the government were to use censorship as a means of containing the media's dissemination of violent images and concepts, then an important avenue of artistic expression and emotional release would be lost to young people. As psychologist Melanie Moore has said,

> Fear, greed, power-hunger, rage: these are aspects of our selves that we try not to experience in our lives but often want, even need, to experience vicariously through stories of others. Children need violent entertainment in order to explore the inescapable feelings that they've been taught to deny, and to reintegrate those feelings into a more whole, more complex, more resilient selfhood. (Media Awareness Network, *Media Violence Debates*, 2007)

Dysfunction in Government

It is the government's obligation to protect its citizens from violence and dangerous products. Where a government is stable and functioning, there should be adequate control over the production, sale, and consumption of offensive, anti-social media materials. The Canadian government has encouraged parental guidance systems by ranking the content of movies and discouraging juvenile access to "mature" subject matter, and by regulating imagery—that is, deeming it permissible or not. The dysfunction has arisen from the fact that much of current entertainment media is imported from the United States. The government's stringent controls curtail the domestic industry without controlling the imported US one. Globalized entertainment networks and broadcasts enter Canada regardless of official government acceptance (Media Awareness Network, *Government and Industry Responses to Media Violence*, 2007).

Dysfunction in the Economy

Globalization has altered the entire consumer market, including the content and distribution of entertainment media. The World Wide Web has made unsavoury material universally accessible. Time restrictions on program viewing are meaningless when programs are distributed via satellite from all time zones. The market forces that govern content in entertainment are now global rather than domestic. Global distribution is outside the jurisdiction of any one government; international audiences determine what is produced and available in our domestic markets. Action films, which tend to be violent and graphic, sell best because they rely on simple plots and simple dialogue; mass audiences appreciate action and special effects. Media production corporations, faced with tight competition, make content choices that will guarantee profits. In many cases, the items they choose are the ones with high levels of gratuitous violence (Media Awareness Network, *Government and Industry Responses to Media Violence*, 2007). In short, what sells is what gets produced and distributed, regardless of the social and health damages.

The above discussion, calling on the structural functionalist perspective, should demonstrate how society is an integrated system of social institutions in which dysfunction in one institution generates dysfunction in another. The spread and interdependence of dysfunctions in a social issue is analogous to a stone bruise on a windshield: the stone is the change that triggers a social issue. Its immediate impact is felt as a dysfunction in a certain social institution. The cracks that spread from the original site of impact are the spinoff effects—the dysfunctions that occur in response to the original dysfunction. To make this analogy work for you, try making a flow chart of the dysfunctions involved in the media content issue. Incidentally, such diagrams are a convenient way to plan an essay or report that uses a structural functionalist analysis of a social issue. They can also help you organize your structural functionalist analysis chart. See if you can summarize in the following chart the dysfunctions involved in the media issue.

ACTIONS THAT WOULD RESTORE SYSTEM EQUILIBRIUM

Restoration of equilibrium does not come by dismantling changes and trying to return to "yesterday." What is needed are social actions that will correct the dysfunctions while retaining the positive changes. In the case of negative media, most of the researched literature recommends equipping the consuming public with the knowledge they need to repel the negative influences of media. A public thus equipped can exercise prudent choice in the marketplace; advocate for safe and appropriate entertainment; and guide children away from consumerist, **misogynous**, and violent imagery. The researched literature also shows that the social institution of education is leading the way in providing such education to the public. For example,

Structural Functionalist Analysis of Negative Media Influence

Social Action	Social Institution	Manifest Function of Social Institution	Dysfunction
Distortion of news events	Media	To inform To encourage cultural cohesion through reinforcement of cultural symbols	
Censorship of programming	Media	To inform To encourage cultural cohesion through reinforcement of cultural symbols	
Inclusion of graphic and sexualized violence in entertainment	Media	To inform To encourage cultural cohesion through reinforcement of cultural symbols	
Globalized sale of entertainment media	Economy	Production and distribution of goods and services	
Regulation of entertainment imports	Government	Creation and implementation of laws and policies that promote social order and security	
Increasing independence of children	Family	Socialization of children	

the Ontario Public School Board has just released a report that pledges educational initiatives:

> There is no quick fix to this enormous problem. The issues have to be faced in individual homes and schools and in the broader community through public awareness campaigns, enhanced media literacy programs and new legislation and standards for the industry. Schools are an ideal venue for change because many educators and parents are concerned about this issue. Most parents struggle to understand what their children are exposed to and try to find ways to control the

> harmful impact. ... The Ontario Public School Boards' Association has made media violence a priority. (Jaffe, 2007, p. 26)

See the Ontario Education Association (Media Violence Coalition) website for guidelines about educating the public in media safety.

Other social institutions, such as health and medicine, are also trying to educate the public. For example, physicians, as part of their routines of diagnosis and treatment, are including assessments of children's media use. They are also using physician–patient interactions as an opportunity to educate their clients about the hazards of the media (Santa Barbara, 2001). For more information on activities promoted by Physicians for Global Survival (Canada), visit their website. Specific recommendations regarding measures physicians can take against the negative impacts of media can be found on the Canadian Paediatric Society website.

Young Canadians in a Wired World (Steeves, 2005) describes in a positive way how children have altered their patterns of interaction and social connection to include information technologies. The report also emphasizes that education can provide any further information children might need concerning safety and the media's shaping of consumerist attitudes. The Media Awareness Network summarizes as follows the value of education in resolving the negative impacts of media violence:

> If kids are growing up in a media-saturated culture—and they are—media education can help them articulate their attitudes and feelings towards violence, in real life as well as on the screen. It can also teach young people that they have a voice and a role to play as active media consumers who can talk to the entertainment industry and present their opinions in public forums. The Internet has opened up important avenues for reaching producers and sharing views. (*Media Education and Media Violence*, 2007, n.p.)

Notice the last line of this quotation. A structural functionalist would point out that the social institution in which the dysfunction originated is also, paradoxically, proving to be the source of the issue's resolution. The Internet offers unprecedented means for citizens to exercise their political voice. Consider the popularity of blogs, of YouTube, of personal websites. Look at websites associated with the CBC or with any newsmagazine. Everywhere you will find invitations for commentary and feedback on issues and events that have been broadcast. Further evidence that the social system is righting itself is the formation of organizations like Honest Reporting Canada.

A Feminist Analysis of Media: Issues of Access and of Content

The media presents a distorted view of reality, and the media is also a powerful agent of socialization. The Canadian Paediatric Society has published research indicating that teens rank the media as their primary source of information about sex, second only to school sex education; that the average child sees over 20,000 commercials each year, many of which promote poor nutrition; and that music videos may distort teen expectations about conflict resolution, race, and male–female relationships (Psychosocial Paediatrics Committee, 2003). Concern is that distortions figure large in the media's socialization of children. Of particular concern to feminists is the relationship of gender and media.

BRIEF REVIEW OF THE FEMINIST PERSPECTIVE

As you now know, feminist perspectives on society can be macro or micro. All feminism has the goal of gender equality. As a theoretical tool of analysis, feminism frames the assessment of social issues in terms of gender equality. A feminist analysis of the influence of mass media reveals two major issues. One is the male domination of the technology both in the language used and in access to information technologies. The second issue is that the content, especially in the entertainment media, is sexist. If the media are a powerful agent of socialization, it follows that their distorted gender images are adversely influencing the self-image of women and girls and, generally speaking, the treatment of women in society.

A FEMINIST ANALYSIS OF MEDIA'S TREATMENT OF WOMEN

> Mission: at MediaWatch people believe that change in the media is fundamental to altering individual thinking and behaviour that has allowed gender inequality, sexual harassment and violence against girls and women to exist and normalized their presence in today's society. (n.p.)

This is the mission statement from a website titled Youth Xchange: Toward Sustainable Lifestyles. It is the website of UNESCO and partners and is devoted to the empowerment of youth around the world. Its focus is on altering consumerist social trends. Such a mission statement, from an organization called Media Watch, reflects the concern many people have about the media's negative socialization influences with respect to gender identity and the lives of women around the world.

The Media Awareness Network has compiled an extensive review of the relationship trends between gender and media in Canada (Media Awareness Network, *Media Portrayals of Girls and Women: Introduction*, 2007). It provides an outline and reference list of research into current trends.

WHAT ARE THE CULTURAL MESSAGES SUPPLIED BY THE MEDIA?

Gender Images

Sociologists distinguish **gender** from **sex**. *Sex* refers to one's biological makeup. *Gender* refers to one's learned social role, one's construction of masculinity or femininity. The media tends to shape the gender expectations in our culture. Feminists challenge gender stereotypes because these stereotypes limit how men and women participate in society. Let us review the income statistics, for example. For every dollar a man earns, a woman earns 71 cents (Statistics Canada, 2006). The media—from magazines and the Internet to TV, movies, and music—define femininity in a particular way: to be feminine is to be young-looking, thin, beautiful, beautifully made-up and coiffed, and sexy. The ideals are excessive and for the most part unattainable, but girls and women are pressured to *attempt* these unattainable beauty goals. Failure diminishes their self-esteem and confidence. The same media shapes male expectations about female body image. Women's desperation about body image is reflected in the rates of plastic surgery and body alteration procedures in North America today. The "mommy makeover" procedures—breast augmentation, tummy tuck, and breast lift—ranked first, fourth, and fifth respectively, among all procedures performed on women ages 20 to 39 in 2006. Women are generally bearing children later in life because they are pursuing active careers. These "mommy makeovers" are a means for women, pressured by media-driven ideals, to return their bodies to a pre-pregnancy shape and size.

Women in their twenties had 95,500 breast augmentations (a 15 percent increase from the previous year), 14,500 breast lifts (an 11 percent increase), and 13,800 tummy tucks (a 9 percent increase). The number of procedures increases for women in their thirties, with 118,500 breast augmentations (up 9 percent), 34,000 breast lifts (up 11 percent), and 49,600 tummy tucks (up 12 percent) (American Society of Plastic Surgeons, 2007).

There has been progress with regard to the stereotyping of women, but female body image continues to be promoted in the media as the most prized aspect of femininity. The Media Awareness Network reports that women's magazines have 10 1/2 times more ads and articles that promote weight loss than magazines for men do (*Beauty and Body Image in the Media*, 2007).

Men are also subjected to unrealistic images. The media's portrayal of men as self-controlled, controlling, aggressive, violent, financially independent, and possessed of a physically desirable body promotes men's social dominance. According to studies by Children Now, the media's portrayal of men links masculinity with power, dominance, and control (Media Awareness Network, *How the Media Define Masculinity*, 2007).

Leadership, Competence, and Intelligence

The media's stereotypical gender images imply that men are more intelligent and more reliable as leaders than women are. The media coverage of women and women's issues is far less thorough than the coverage of men. Women in politics and sports are neglected. When women are in the spotlight, it is usually as part of a "human-interest" story or a story of criminal violence. Canada is not unique in its discrimination against women and femininity itself, as the following quotation suggests:

> Inadequate women's coverage seems to be a worldwide phenomenon. In 2000, the Association of Women Journalists (Association des femmes journalistes—AFJ) studied news coverage of women and women's issues in 70 countries. It reported that only 18 percent of stories quote women, and that the number of women-related stories came to barely 10 percent of total news coverage. (Media Awareness Network, *Media Coverage of Women and Women's Images*, 2007)

Gender stereotyping in the media underlines an enduring inequality between men and women. Because mass media is big business, its images are shaped less by social consciousness than by profit motives. As long as male-centred programming earns more than women-sensitive programming, change will be slow. Movies that sell internationally—action films riddled with sexual stereotypes—will be the movies that dominate the market both at home and abroad. Action and sex sell because they "do not rely on clever, intricate, culture-based scripts or convincing acting. Sex and action films therefore 'translate' easily across cultures" (Media Awareness Network, *The Economics of Gender Stereotyping*, 2007).

Feminist Response

There are indications that advertising is now promoting damaging physical stereotypes of men as it has long done for women. We are seeing the **objectification** of men's bodies and the use of them to sell products. In fact, the objectification of men is more extreme than that of women, because of past feminist efforts to curb sexism in the media (Preston, 2000).

Gender stereotyping in the media has been persistent, but positive changes are beginning to occur. We are seeing more programming that positively portrays strong female characters. But there may be a new problem on the horizon. Anthropologist David Murray has warned that our culture "is to a large extent experimenting with eroticizing the child" (Media Awareness Network, *The Economics of Gender Stereotyping*, 2007). Murray cites the media frenzy surrounding pop star Britney Spears and murdered six-year-old JonBenet Ramsey as examples of how eroticized children are becoming a saleable commodity. A brief glance at the current media confirms that younger girls are now being bombarded with images of sexuality—in many cases, stereotypical portrayals of women and girls as powerless, passive victims.

SOCIAL RESPONSE THROUGH USE OF MEDIA

There is growing opposition in our society to the destructive influence of media. Feminist voices among the young are calling for resistance to consumerist culture and to gender stereotypes. The alternative magazine *Teen Voices* is a forum for these voices, while the Youth Xchange website encourages youth activism against consumerism and against sexism in the media. Perhaps more important than what these groups actually do is what they stand for in general—a **sustainable future** that can be reached through youth empowerment—especially the empowerment of young women who have raised their voices worldwide in rejection of unsustainable consumerist lifestyles and the related unhealthy body image expectations.

RESPONSES

GOVERNMENT AND POLICY

The law, both domestic and international, has played an important role in recognizing, regulating, and protecting families. The United Nations' *Universal Declaration of Human Rights* states, at article 16(3), that the family "is the natural and fundamental group unit of society and is entitled to protection by society and the State."

While the right to form a family has long been understood as an entitlement of all Canadians, the form of the family has not always been a matter of choice. For most of Canada's history, the law coercively maintained the normative order of the idealized traditional family. Judges and the Canadian government saw themselves as maintaining order and ethical conduct through their regulation of family forms. Courts protected the institution of the traditional family—and the traditional authority of fathers within it. Divorce was rarely granted, and only after considerable litigation or if a bill in Parliament allowed for a statutory divorce. One party was required to prove grounds such as cruelty or adultery, and adultery was narrowly defined as activity that could lead to procreation. Violation of conventional gender roles could lead to penalties, especially for women. Women who committed adultery and then got divorced would almost invariably lose custody of their children and their entitlement to spousal support. Children resulting from sexual relationships outside of legal marriage were not protected under the law. Nor were their mothers. Such children did not have the same rights as *legitimate* children to inherit property. Domestic violence was considered to be a private matter, and police and courts would not intervene in a man's treatment of his wife or children unless his conduct was particularly egregious; they were essentially viewed as his property or *chattels*.

But as family forms have changed in the past decades, so has family law. It is beyond the scope of this book to look in detail at the dramatic transformations that have taken place in family law. The following summary will have to suffice.

Common-law relationships, once proscribed and frowned upon in Canada, are now legally recognized and protected, though not to the same extent as legal marriages. The treatment of common-law partnerships under the law is largely a matter of provincial jurisdiction. In Ontario, for example, common-law partners can be entitled to spousal support upon the breakdown of their relationship, so long as they have been in a common-law relationship for at least three years or have lived together in a relationship of "some permanence" and have children together.

Just as conjugal relationships outside of legal marriage are now given some legal recognition, children are no longer treated differently under the law if born outside the context of a legal marriage. Under the *Child Support Guidelines* first published by the federal government in 1997, all children are entitled to financial support from both their parents and from step-parents who have "stood in the place of a parent" to them, regardless of the form of relationship between their parents and regardless of whether those parents were in a long-term relationship or simply had a casual liaison that produced a child.

Child custody is now no longer determined by matrimonial fault. Decisions regarding custody and access are based on what is in the child's "best interests," a nuanced and multi-factorial question which takes into account the individual needs of the child, what he or she is accustomed to, and what the child's own views and preferences are, among other factors. Child custody is no longer awarded or denied on the basis of the court's moral judgments of parents' actions.

Where children were once regarded as their father's property, there is now acknowledgment that they are society's responsibility more broadly and that they are autonomous individuals with rights of their own, belonging to no one. A complex and comprehensive legal regime now ensures that children are protected from harm. Child protection laws are the primary response in Canada to child abuse. Different provincial jurisdictions in Canada have developed their own legal definitions of what constitutes child abuse, but all take a similar approach to the problem. In all provinces, allegations of child abuse can lead both to child protection proceedings—which may result in foster care for the child, and ultimately Crown wardship and adoption—and to criminal charges against the perpetrator.

In 2005 and 2007, Canada's Parliament twice debated and twice voted on the question of whether parties to a marriage must be of opposite genders in order for the marriage to be legal in Canada. As a result of these votes, same-sex marriage is now legal in Canada. As is discussed in more detail in chapter 5, the rights of homosexuals and other "queer" individuals have progressed a great deal in the past few decades. Where their relationships were once criminal, they are now protected under Canadian family law. While the question of whether same-sex partners should be accorded the same legal status as heterosexual spouses remains a controversial one, the law is now clear.

In sum, family law and public policy have shifted over the past few decades from being a means of upholding an idealized patriarchal family form to being a means of protecting those who are vulnerable in their personal relationships. Changes to family law are not complete. As our society continues to change, so will our family forms and the legal regulation of them.

LAW AND POLICING

Domestic abuse and other family problems were once thought of as private matters. Less than a generation ago, police were reluctant to attend at domestic disputes and would not lay charges unless a complainant laid a private charge against an alleged abuser. This situation has changed dramatically. Where physical abuse is alleged, police will attend and, as a matter of policy, will lay criminal charges under the *Criminal Code* of Canada provisions prohibiting assault, sexual assault, and criminal harassment. The laying of such charges is now *mandatory* in domestic abuse situations. *Criminal Code* provisions relating to child abuse, neglect, and sexual exploitation of minors will also lead to abusers being charged by police. In recent years, the federal Department of Justice has engineered several changes to the *Criminal Code*, increasing the maximum penalties for crimes related to domestic abuse. Police officers can now expect to spend a good deal of their time dealing with family problems by formal legal means.

Canadian police are dealing with family problems not just with harsher punitive measures but with closer connections to community agencies and an increased focus on prevention. The RCMP and other police services across Canada are actively engaged in education work to help prevent child abuse and encourage the reporting of it. Protocols are being developed in various communities to help strengthen links between such social service agencies as child welfare organizations and women's shelters, so that victims of abuse may promptly receive the protection they need.

COMMUNITY

Community groups have mobilized in ways that reflect changing family forms in Canada. For example, the past few decades have seen the development of coordinated community responses to domestic violence. These responsive organizations take different forms across the country, from counselling centres to women's shelters and advocacy groups. Their common goal is to reduce cultural and societal supports for domestic violence and to protect victims of violence from further abuse while holding abusers accountable for their actions. Among these community initiatives are the following:

- *Community intervention projects*—non-profit organizations that advocate reforming and coordinating institutional responses to domestic violence
- *Coordinating councils*—also called "domestic violence councils/task forces," these are set up in many communities as venues for inter-agency communication and collaboration in the matter of domestic violence (Shepard, 1999).

INDIVIDUAL INVOLVEMENT

The vast majority of us come from a family of origin (family into which one is born) and most students will ultimately form families of their own, if they have not yet done so. Police are not immune to having problems in their own families, and neither are college students. In our family lives we have the potential to actively address family problems in Canada. Students should be vigilant and assertive in their own personal relationships to ensure they neither perpetrate nor become victims of abuse. Again, it is normal for families to be imperfect; what defines us is not the imperfection but rather how we address it. Seeking counselling and making use of community and other resources is an appropriate way for students to address their own family problems.

We can all help protect children from abuse, and we have a duty to do so. Where a student becomes aware of child abuse, either in their professional or personal capacities, they are under a positive legal duty to report it to the appropriate authority. In Ontario, the *Child and Family Services Act* states that a person is guilty of a regulatory offence (and probably also of negligence) if he or she fails to report suspected child abuse. Students should be aware that they are under both an ethical and a legal duty to report their suspicions of child abuse to child welfare authorities, such as the Children's Aid Societies in Ontario. These reports can be made anonymously.

While the law does provide criminal and social welfare responses to child abuse and domestic violence, prevention is obviously the best option. Providing children, women, and families with resources at the community level may help in this regard. Besides taking a responsible and wary approach to their own family life, students can address family problems and family dysfunction in Canada by participating in community programs and helping agencies focused on prevention.

CONCLUSION

Two theoretical analyses were completed in this chapter, both directed at the impact of media on the modern Canadian family. The more common family issues, such as violence and divorce, could be addressed through other theoretical perspectives. For example, a social conflict assessment of domestic abuse would clarify the nature of domination and the strength of the opposing forces in the fight to eliminate family violence. The micro paradigms of symbolic interactionism and social constructionism would shed light on the influences of current and emerging patterns of socialization. The templates for these analyses can be found elsewhere in this text.

The lessons of sociology seem nowhere more relevant than in the matter of family issues. Sociology teaches us that problems will not be resolved as long as they are perceived as individuals' problems. Once they are deemed a social responsibility and not a private matter, problems are subjected to a public voice or discourse. Public attention drives social change. Spousal abuse, in the not too distant past, was considered a private matter. Women who were abused suffered behind closed doors, and were commonly seen as responsible for their situations by being in some way deficient. It was only after feminists took up the cause of exposing and eliminating family violence that laws protecting victims came to pass.

You too can add your voice and passion to a social cause and encourage positive change. As a consumer of media, for example, you have the freedom—and now the knowledge—to make informed choices. You need not passively succumb to media influence. Consumer choice drives markets and, ultimately, corporate decisions.

KEY TERMS

child abuse the emotional maltreatment, neglect, or physical or sexual mistreatment of children by persons responsible for their care, whether these latter be parents, guardians, or others

common-law relationship a relationship not formalized by a marriage ceremony but involving nonetheless the cohabitation and routine intimacies of marriage

cultural universal a practice or social pattern or institution that occurs in every society

domestic abuse also referred to as *domestic violence*, *partner abuse*, or *spousal abuse*, it occurs when a family member, intimate partner, or former partner seeks to psychologically or physically dominate or harm another family member

family a now-married couple (with or without never-married sons and/or daughters of either or both spouses), a couple living common law (with or without never-married sons and/or daughters of either or both partners), or a lone parent of any marital status, with at least one never-married son or daughter living in the same dwelling

gender the role a person learns to play as a member of the social category *man* or *woman*; the socialized or learned patterns of masculinity or femininity

globalization trends in telecommunications, trade, and migration that have resulted in an increasingly interconnected world

misogynous hating women

moral panic the public perception of a profound threat from crime or social disorder, usually a result of inflated, exaggerated media coverage; perceived threats are to fundamental values and morals

objectification a media-driven emphasis on sexiness and on physical body parts that can result in the understating or denial of an individual's personality or emotions

psychological violence psychological damage caused by an experience of intimidation, threat, or harassment; it leaves lasting mental and emotional scars

sex a person's biological characteristics in relation to the reproductive process: male, female, or, in some cases, a hybrid of the two

sexual abuse sexual contact in which a dominant partner uses his or her position of authority or physical strength to coerce or exploit the less powerful partner

socialization the lifelong process of acculturation; the teaching and learning of a society's beliefs, values, and norms that occurs during social interaction; the process by which personalities, identities, and gender identities are formed

sustainable future from the concept of sustainable development, defined by the UN as being built on three fundamental principles: economic development, social development, and environmental protection

FOR FURTHER RESEARCH

Big Brothers/Big Sisters of Canada
http://www.bbbsc.ca/defaultlanguage.asp.

Community Legal Education Ontario (family law publications)
http://www.cleo.on.ca/english/pub/onpub/subject/family.htm.

Kids' Help Phone
http://www.kidshelpphone.ca/en.

Ontario Women's Justice Network
http://www.owjn.org.

UNICEF Canada
http://www.unicef.ca.

The following article, published by the Vanier Institute of the Family, discusses changes in the "culture" of parenting (Daly, 2004). http://www.vifamily.ca/library/cft/parenting.html#Parenting_media.

For a further example of the Ontario Education Association's efforts to educate the public about media violence, see the following website: http://www.opsba.org/pubs/publications/media-violence.pdf.

For more information on activities promoted by Physicians for Global Survival (Canada), follow this link: http://www.pgs.ca. Specific recommendations regarding physician intervention in cases of negative media influence are available at the following site: http://www.cps.ca/english/statements/PP/pp03-01.htm.

For additional information on initiatives that address gender stereotypes, see the following website: http://www.media-awareness.ca/english/issues/stereotyping/women_and_girls/women_reform.cfm.

Further ideas about how to combat consumerism can be found at http://www.youthxchange.net/main/mediawatchcanada.asp.

REFERENCES

Adoption Council of Canada. (2004). Ontario to change domestic adoption law. http://www.adoption.ca/news/040407onlaw.htm.

Ambert, A. (1998). Divorce: Facts, figures and consequences. Child & Family Canada: The Vanier Institute of the Family. http://www.cfc-efc.ca/docs/vanif/00005_en.htm.

Ambert, A. (2007). The rise in the number of children and adolescents who exhibit problematic behaviours: Multiple causes. The Vanier Institute of the Family. http://www.vifamily.ca/library/cft/behavior.html.

American Society of Plastic Surgeons. (2007, March). Cosmetic plastic surgery: "Mommy makeovers" on the rise. *American Society of Plastic Surgeons New Procedurals Statistics Report.* http://www.plasticsurgery.org/media/press_releases/2006-Stats-Mommy-Makeover.cfm.

Bailey, M. (2005, November). Polygamy in Canada: Legal and social implications for women and children—A collection of policy research reports. Status of Women Canada. http://www.swc-cfc.gc.ca/pubs/pubspr/0662420683/index_e.html.

Canadian Centre for Justice Statistics. (1999). A profile of victimization: Results of the 1999 general social survey. http://www.statcan.ca/english/freepub/85-553-XIE/0019985-553-XIE.pdf.

Canadian Centre for Justice Statistics. (2000). Family violence in Canada: A statistical profile. http://www.statcan.ca/english/freepub/85-224-XIE/0000085-224-XIE.pdf.

Canadians Concerned About Violence In Entertainment [CAVE]. Addressing media violence and its harmful effects. Index of references. http://www.c-cave.com.

CBC News Online. (2005, March 9). Indepth: Marriage: Marriage by the numbers. http://www.cbc.ca/news/background/marriage.

Child and Family Canada. http://www.cfc-efc.ca/index.shtml.

Child and Family Services Act. (1990). RSO 1990, c. C.11.

Committee on Sexual Offences Against Children and Youth. (1984). Sexual offences against children in Canada. *Report of the committee on sexual offences against children and youth* [the *Badgley Report*]. Ottawa: Supply and Services Canada.

Criminal Code. (1985). RSC 1985, c. C-46, as amended.

CTV News Online. (2007, January 31). BC sextuplets' transfusion to spark legal row. http://www.ctv.ca/servlet/ArticleNews/story/CTVNews/20070131/sextups_seized_070131/20070131?hub=TopStories.

Daly, K. (2004). The changing culture of parenting. The Vanier Institute of the Family. http://www.vifamily.ca/library/cft/parenting.html#Parenting_performance.

Day, T. (1995). *The health-related costs of violence against women in Canada: The tip of the iceberg.* London, Ontario: Centre for Research on Violence Against Women and Children, 29-34.

Dueck, L. (2007, July 11). Challenging the hunger for violence. *Canada's Christian Community Online.* http://www.christianity.ca/NetCommunity/Page.aspx?pid=4701&srcid=5267.

Dutton, D.G., & Hart, S.D. (1992). Evidence of long-term, specific effects of childhood abuse on criminal behaviour in men. *International Journal of Offender Therapy and Comparative Criminology, 36*(2), 129-137.

Farmer, S. (1990). *Adult children of abusive parents: A healing program for those who have been physically, sexually, or emotionally abused.* New York: Ballantine Books.

Fergusson, D.M., Lynskey, M.T., & Horwood L.J. (1996). Childhood sexual abuse and psychiatric disorder in young adulthood: I. Prevalence of sexual abuse and factors associated with sexual abuse. *Journal of the American Academy of Child and Adolescent Psychiatry, 35*(10), 1355-1364.

Greaves, L., & Hankivsky, O. (1995). *Selected estimates of the costs of violence against women.* London, Ontario: Centre for Research on Violence Against Women and Children.

Haddad, Y., & Editors of The Canadian Encyclopedia Online. (1999–2007). Islam in Canada. *The Canadian Encyclopedia.* http://www.thecanadianencyclopedia.com/index.cfm?PgNm=TCE&Params=A1SEC822574.

Hegar, R.L., Zuravin, S.J., & Orme, J.G. (1994). Factors predicting severity of physical child abuse injury. *Journal of Interpersonal Violence, 9*(2), 170-183.

Honest Reporting Canada: http://www.honestreporting.ca/scripts/index_.asp.

Jaffe, P. (2007, Spring). Bridging the parent school gap. *Education Today* [Ontario Public School Board Association], *19*(1), 24-27. http://www.c-cave.com/files/ETPJ.pdf.

Lyons-Ruth, K., Alpern, L., & Repacholi, B. (1993). Disorganized infant attachment classification and maternal psychosocial problems as predictors of hostile-aggressive behavior in the preschool classroom. *Child Development, 64,* 572-585.

Media Awareness Network (2007). Media stereotyping:

Body and body image in the media. http://www.media-awareness.ca/english/issues/stereotyping/women_and_girls/women_beauty.cfm.

Children now in How the media define masculinity. http://www.media-awareness.ca/english/issues/stereotyping/men_and_masculinity/masculinity_defining.cfm.

The economics of gender stereotyping. http://www.media-awareness.ca/english/issues/stereotyping/women_and_girls/women_economics.cfm.

Introduction. http://www.media-awareness.ca/english/issues/stereotyping/index.cfm.

Media and girls. http://www.media-awareness.ca/english/issues/stereotyping/women_and_girls/women_girls.cfm.

Media coverage of women and women's issues. http://www.media-awareness.ca/english/issues/stereotyping/women_and_girls/women_coverage.cfm.

Media portrayals of girls and women: Introduction. http://www.media-awareness.ca/english/issues/stereotyping/women_and_girls/index.cfm.

Teen Voices in Resisting stereotyping and working for change. http://www.media-awareness.ca/english/issues/stereotyping/women_and_girls/women_reform.cfm.

Media Awareness Network. (2007). Media violence:

The business of media violence. http://www.media-awareness.ca/english/issues/violence/business_media_violence.cfm.

Government and industry responses to media violence. http://www.media-awareness.ca/english/issues/violence/govt_industry_responses.cfm.

Introduction. http://www.media-awareness.ca/english/issues/violence/index.cfm.

Media and Canadian Cultural Policies Chronology. http://www.media-awareness.ca/english/issues/cultural_policies/cultural_policy_chronology.cfm.

Media education and media violence. http://www.media-awareness.ca/english/issues/violence/role_media_education.cfm.

Media education in Canada. http://www.media-awareness.ca/english/index.cfm.

Media violence chronology, 1989–2000. http://www.media-awareness.ca/english/resources/issues_resources/violence/violence_cronology.cfm.

Media violence debates. http://www.media-awareness.ca/english/issues/violence/violence_debates.cfm.

Violence in media entertainment. http://www.media-awareness.ca/english/issues/violence/violence_entertainment.cfm.

Media Awareness Network. (2007). Young Canadians in a wired world: Key findings. http://www.media-awareness.ca/english/research/YCWW/phaseII/key_findings.cfm.

Media Violence Coalition. (n.d.). Media violence—Not a pretty picture: Putting children in harm's way. Ontario Public School Board's Association. http://www.opsba.org/pubs/publications/media-violence.pdf.

Merriam-Webster Dictionary Online (2007). s.v. "family." http://www.m-w.com/dictionary/family.

Nevins, T. (2004). The effects of media violence on adolescent health. Research report written for Physicians for Global Survival (Canada). http://pgs.wemanageyour.com/wp-content/uploads/2008/03/effectsofmediaviolence_final.pdf.

Preston, L. (2000, January). Sexual hunk or rocket scientist? Are men treated as badly in advertising as women? *Ireland's Marketing Monthly*. http://www.marketing.ie/old_site/january_00/article_b.htm.

Psychosocial Paediatrics Committee. (2003). Impact of media use on children and youth. Canadian Paediatric Society (CPS). *Paediatric Child Health*, *8*(5), 265, 301-306. http://www.cps.ca/english/statements/PP/pp03-01.htm.

Public Health Agency of Canada. (1997, February). Child abuse and neglect overview paper. http://www.phac-aspc.gc.ca/ncfv-cnivf/familyviolence/html/nfntsnegl_e.html.

Reich, W. (1975) *The sexual revolution.* New York: Pocket Books.

Santa Barbara, J. (2001). Media violence, real life aggression and militarism/PGS briefing paper. *Physicians for Global Survival (Canada).* http://www.pgs.ca/index.php/Health/9.

Sauvé, R. (2002). CONNECTIONS—Tracking the links between jobs and family: Job, family and stress among husbands, wives and lone-parents 15-64 from 1990 to 2000. The Vanier Institute of the Family. http://www.vifamily.ca/library/cft/connections.html.

Shepard, M. (1999). Evaluating co-ordinated community responses to domestic violence. Applied Research Forum, National Electronic Network on Violence Against Women. http://new.vawnet.org/category/Main_Doc.php?docid=379.

Statistics Canada. (2006). *Women in Canada: A gender-based statistical report* (5th Ed.). Industry Canada. http://www.statcan.ca/english/freepub/89-503-XIE/0010589-503-XIE.pdf.

Steeves, V. (2005, November). Young Canadians in a wired world phase II: Trends and recommendations. Media Awareness Network. Industry Canada. http://www.media-awareness.ca/english/research/YCWW/phaseII/upload/YCWWII_trends_recomm.pdf.

Supreme Court of Canada. (2004). *Canadian Foundation for Children, Youth and the Law, R v.* [2004] 1 SCR 76, 2004 SCC 4. http://csc.lexum.umontreal.ca/en/2004/2004scc4/2004scc4.html.

Supreme Court of Canada. (2004). *Reference re Same-Sex Marriage.* [2004] 3 SCR 698, 2004 SCC 79. http://scc.lexum.umontreal.ca/en/2004/2004scc79/2004scc79.html.

Terry, K., & Tallon, J. (n.d.). Child sexual abuse: A review of the literature. The John Jay College Research Team. http://www.usccb.org/nrb/johnjaystudy/litreview.pdf.

Thoman, E. (1993). Beyond blame: Media literacy as violence prevention. Centre for Media Literacy. http://www.medialit.org/reading_room/article93.html.

United Nations Office of the High Commissioner for Human Rights. (1996–2005). Universal declaration of human rights, article 16(3). http://www.unhchr.ch/udhr/lang/eng.htm.

US Census Bureau. (2004). Current population survey—Definitions and explanations. http://www.census.gov/population/www/cps/cpsdef.html.

Youth Xchange. (n.d.). Media watch mission statement. UNESCO. http://www.youthxchange.net/main/mediawatchcanada.asp.

Zickefoose, S. (2007, June). Girl's boyfriend watched movie on night of murders, court hears. CanWest News Service. http://www.canada.com/components/print.aspx?id=7c29a3ec-8a0f-45da-aa5c-a2e7f9ce9f83&k=25912.

Zinn, M., and Stanley Eitzen, D. (1987). *Diversity in American families.* New York: Harper and Row.

CHAPTER 7
Economic Inequality

CHAPTER OBJECTIVES

After completing this chapter, you will be able to:

Understand significant dimensions of economic inequality

- Disparities in wealth and income
- Measures of poverty
- Poverty and other measures of inequality: Who are the poor?
- Child poverty
- Social problems related to poverty
- Homelessness

Understand and apply different sociological perspectives to economic inequality

- Structural functionalist
- Social conflict
- Symbolic interactionist

Identify and critique various responses to social problems related to economic inequality, including responses from

- Government and policy
- Law and policing
- Community
- Individuals

DIMENSIONS

DISPARITIES IN WEALTH AND INCOME

The wealthiest Canadians constitute a small percentage of the population but dominate the country's economic, and to some extent its political, resources. Most politically prominent Canadians are wealthy. Great wealth tends to be celebrated and held in awe. *Canadian Business* magazine keeps an annual tally of the richest 100 Canadians, and has done so every year since 1999. The richest family in Canada in 2005 was that of the late Kenneth Thomson, whose posthumous fortune exceeded $22.16 billion. To put their wealth in global perspective, the Thomson family ranked 15th overall on the *Forbes* list of the world's richest people. The original source of the family's wealth was publishing. Rounding out the Canadian top five were Galen Weston of Weston Bakeries, whose fortune was estimated at $9.28 billion; James Arthur and Jack Irving, with $5.36 billion each in oil money; and Jeff Skoll, who amassed most of his $5.07 billion fortune in the movie business. Over the past few years, the richest Canadians have fared very well financially; in 2005 their collective net worth, at $141.6 billion, was the highest it had ever been (Mlynek, Olijnyk, Leung, Gagné, & Magnan, 2005), even allowing for inflation. The rich, in Canada and the rest of the world, are getting richer.

Few Canadians realistically expect to be among the richest people in the world or to amass billions of dollars. Nevertheless, many people strive to acquire great wealth, whether through financial planning or lottery tickets. A person who is able to amass a net worth of at least $1 million is referred to as a **millionaire**. The term *millionaire* has less meaning than it used to because inflation has diminished the value of the dollar; there are now more millionaires than ever before. According to the *World Wealth Report* (Rosenberg, 2006), 8.7 million people in the world each possessed more than $1 million (US) in wealth, an increase of 6.5 percent over 2004.

Not everyone would agree that the growing disparity in wealth and income between Canadians is a social issue. Some social researchers argue that income disparities are bound to exist in any complex society because not all occupations are equal. People naturally occupy different positions in the social hierarchy depending on their monetary wealth and on the social capital they may possess through membership in a highly regarded or powerful social group. These measures collectively define a person's **socio-economic status**. Historically, many cultures and societies have been structured according to **social class**, a set of hierarchical distinctions drawn between groups and individuals based upon, and often determining, an individual's socio-economic status. In a class system, socio-economic status is often perceived to be linked with other attributes, such as intelligence or "nobility."

In medieval Europe and in classical India under the Hindu *caste* system, social class membership was fixed and ordained; one was born a member of a certain social class and remained so until death, passing membership along to one's children. Nowadays, social class can be determined by occupation, qualifications, education, birth (including one's gender and race), and wealth. Most understandings of class recognize three levels: a small *upper class* of people who possess hereditary wealth and considerable power over the economic and, quite often, the political resources in a society; a *middle class* of people who have a certain degree of autonomy and control over their own lives but do not generally control substantial resources or have power over the lives of others; and a *lower class* of people who have little freedom and rely upon wages from the other classes for their livelihood. Canada, like most Western democracies, has been shaped for the past century or so by the existence of a large and powerful *middle class*.

Many human societies have embraced the notion of class as an organizing principle. In recent history, however, societies have emerged, based on egalitarian ideologies, that condemn differences in wealth or standards of living between people in the same country. The ideology of communism, for example, prescribes absolute financial equality between people and advocates a *classless* society.

Our democratic society, based on a modified *free market* or *capitalist* system, does not presuppose that all people will live at the same standard or have access to the same resources. It does, however, rely upon the classical liberal notion that all people should have an opportunity to be socially mobile, and that, even if differences in status and class exist, they should be dictated by a person's achievements or *merit*, not their rank at birth. It is arguable that, in our society, once wealth surpasses a certain level it becomes a social problem. Those who possess it become entrenched as a social class, passing on their socio-economic status to their children, and the ideal of social mobility is undermined.

Most Canadians accept that disparities in wealth will exist, but are uncomfortable with the notion of social class—that is, with the notion that a person can *inherit* a particular social status in an official and formalized way. The "Nickle Resolution" was adopted by Canada's government in 1919, officially forbidding the English king or queen to grant hereditary titles (such as knighthoods, baronetcies, and peerages) to Canadians. In 1967, Canada created the Order of Canada to acknowledge the particular achievements of individual Canadians without bestowing titles upon their heirs.

In 2001, Prime Minister Jean Chrétien upheld the Nickle Resolution in refusing to allow Canadian publishing magnate Conrad Black to accept a title from the English Queen while retaining his Canadian citizenship. Chrétien stated publicly that "conferring titles on Canadians is not compatible with the ideals of democracy as they have developed in Canada" (Sossin, 2002). Black renounced his Canadian status to become a British peer, "Baron Black of Crossharbour." More recently, Black's case has again brought to public attention issues relating to social class and hereditary title. He sought to regain Canadian citizenship in 2006, around the time that he was indicted for serious criminal offences relating to theft from shareholders in his companies; these offences included obstruction of justice, racketeering, money laundering, and wire fraud. Conrad Black was convicted in 2007 of three counts of mail fraud and one count of obstruction of justice. He was imprisoned in Florida in March 2008 and is not expected to be released until 2013. Black's situation has proved embarrassing for many in the upper classes of the United Kingdom and the United States, with whom he and his wife Barbara Amiel socialized. That Black acquired a peerage while perpetrating massive frauds undermines the assumption, inherent in formal social class systems, that the upper classes are somehow better, and more entitled to wealth, than everybody else.

Canada is one of the countries in which the gap between rich and poor has increased since the early 1980s. While the richest group of Canadians has continued to grow richer, the rest of the population has not. Statistics Canada found in 2005 that levels of income inequality are higher in Canada than in Europe, but lower in this country than in the United States (Picot & Myles, 2005). Similarly, a study released in March 2007 showed that average or middle-class Canadians have not participated in the economic prosperity they are helping to create; on average, Canadian families worked 200 more hours per year in 2004 than they did in 1996, while 80 percent of Canadian families are financially worse off than they were "a generation ago" (CBC News Online, 2007, n.p.). Although the richest 20 percent of families have seen their wealth and income grow over the past few decades, the remainder have not. Cutbacks in social programs and government spending in the 1990s, together with increased tax breaks for the wealthy, likely contributed to this trend. The result has been a "structural" increase in the number of poor Canadians and a shrinking of the middle class. Our social order has changed. With the rise in **poverty** and the growing disparity between rich and poor, we have regressed to where we were before the mid-1950s. Until that time, many Canadians (some estimate as many as 40 percent) struggled financially to meet their basic needs, such as food, clothing, shelter, and medical care. It is well worth noting that the relative economic equality that we now appear to be losing was short lived (Sarlo, 2001).

Canadians continue to have a relatively high degree of social and economic mobility. Many families who experience periods of low income later move to higher income levels. But this is not the case for everyone. For some, poverty is a pervasive life experience.

As the gap between Canada's rich and poor has widened, the barriers between social classes have grown stronger. Social segregation according to income level—what researchers term "social space"—has increased (Canadian Council on Social Development, 2002). This has negative implications for children's education, for crime rates, and for policing, among other things. When the children of the wealthy and poor are educated together, for example, the children will receive public education of parallel quality. If poor children predominate in certain public schools, as happens when neighbourhoods become more socially segregated, issues arise over public school funding. In a segregated society, policing resources may be allocated disproportionately to protect the homes of wealthy families, whose taxes pay the bulk of law enforcement costs. The residential segregation of the very poor makes it more difficult for them and their children to move out of poverty.

MEASURES OF POVERTY

Poverty is not easy to define. Most measures of poverty are relative to the general living conditions in a particular country or region. In developed nations, such as Canada, poverty means something quite different from what it means in sub-Saharan Africa, for example. In countries such as Nigeria, Mali, Burundi, Zambia, Niger, and Madagascar, over 85 percent of the population has access to no more than $1 (US) per day.

The majority of individuals in these African countries are living in *absolute poverty*. Absolute poverty is a universal global measure of a particular individual's ability to access consumer resources. People living in absolute poverty struggle to meet their basic survival needs: sufficient food, water, clothing, and shelter.

Very few Canadians live in *absolute poverty*. Canada's *social safety net* is a system of services provided by both the federal and provincial governments; it is intended to ensure that no one in Canada falls below a certain level of poverty. This *net* includes services such as welfare (known in Ontario as "Ontario Works"), unemployment benefits, short-term shelters, and universal health care. Poverty in Canada is classified as *relative poverty*; it is a measure of a person's access to consumer resources as compared with other people in his or her region or country. As such, relative poverty is a measure of social inequality. According to 2003 statistics, about 15.9 percent of Canadians live in relative poverty (United Nations Development Program, 2005). Such people can usually meet their basic survival needs, but their prospects and material resources are poor compared with those of others in their communities.

Disparities in **wealth** are not the same as disparities in **income**. Wealth and income are two very different measures of a person's economic situation. The former is a measure of net worth—the sum of a person's *assets* less their *liabilities. Assets* are what an individual owns or possesses, including (but not limited to) cash, equipment, property, vehicles, and personal items. *Liabilities* are debts, usually monetary, that an individual owes to other people or entities, such as mortgagees or other creditors. *Income* is the amount of new money a person receives in a particular time period, usually a year. There may be a high correlation between income and wealth, but an individual's wealth does not always come from income; people may inherit money or obtain it through gifts or other means.

The United States has an official poverty "line" to measure income: the minimum amount a person requires to meet his or her needs. This is not the case in Canada. Here, poverty is measured officially by a series of thresholds called **low income cut-offs (LICOs)**. These LICOs measure income, not net worth. These figures are published annually by Statistics Canada and are intended to show which people are "substantially worse off than the average" (Sarlo, 2001, p. 5). The LICO thresholds measure *relative*—not *absolute*—poverty, meaning that people whose income levels fall below the relevant LICO are not necessarily unable to meet their basic needs. It means, rather, that they have access to fewer resources than others in their country and community. Because these thresholds measure *income*, they may not reflect an individual's access to other resources. Many students involved in post-secondary education would fall below the LICO threshold applicable to their situation. But some of them have access to resources from informal sources, such as their parents, so it is inaccurate to classify them as "poor."

POVERTY AND OTHER MEASURES OF INEQUALITY: WHO ARE THE POOR?

Canadians are uncomfortable with the notion of inherited social rank. Statistics clearly show, however, that a person's socio-economic status at birth significantly affects his or her prospects with respect to income and wealth. A certain demographic tends to be—and to stay—poor, while others are perennially wealthy. A study conducted in 2000 by Status of Women Canada, looking at gender and poverty, confirmed this to be so:

> Gender, age and educational attainment are key variables in determining economic vulnerability ... [I]ndividuals with disabilities, recent immigrants and members of visible minorities also have a higher incidence of persistent poverty and are more likely to enter poverty than members of the general populace. (Lochhead & Scott, 2000, p. 42)

What poverty analysts from Statistics Canada describe as "persistent" low income, according to a 2005 study, tends to be concentrated in five identifiable groups of people: single parents (particularly mothers), recent immigrants to Canada, people with disabilities that interfere with their ability to work, unattached people in their later years, and Aboriginal people (Picot, 2005).

These particular groups of Canadians are more vulnerable than others to poverty, and their children will be, too. Single parents, especially lone female parents, are disproportionately poor, and their children grow up in poverty. Figures from 2006 indicate that approximately half of the children (52 percent) growing up poor in Canada live in families headed by lone female parents. Forty-nine percent of recent immigrants' children are poor; 34 percent of children in "racialized" or "visible minority" families; and 40 percent of Aboriginal children (Campaign 2000, 2006). What these statistics mean, in short, is that you are much more likely to be wealthy if you are born male and white to a married couple in Canada.

The poverty of women has been the subject of much discussion and debate in the past few decades. Several factors have been identified in the economic inequality of women. As we discussed in chapter 5, Canadian women still earn less than men in Canada, making about 70 cents to every dollar men make. Around the world, women on average earn about 50 cents for every dollar men earn. Globally, female children have less access to education than male children do.

Here in Canada, women are generally paid less than men for the same work. They also tend to be segregated into jobs such as clerical work, child care, and clothing production. Sometimes called "pink collar ghettos," these kinds of jobs provide lower status and lower pay than jobs traditionally held by men. More than men, women put in many hours of unpaid labour caring for children or adult family members, which often reduces the time they have for paid work. Frequently, women do paid work only part time, conserving their time and energy for unpaid labour in the domestic sphere—to the benefit of their husbands or male partners. Single mothers have custody of their children more often than single fathers do; as the number of single mothers has increased in Canada and globally, so too has the percentage of women and children living in poverty (United Nations Platform for Action Committee Manitoba [UNPAC], 2006). Elderly women, who tend to live longer than men, tend also to live in poverty, because they generally do not have pension entitlements of their own.

Income inequality is also a regional issue in this country. Certain provinces, regions, and territories are themselves wealthier than others, and contain wealthier people. The Arctic and Maritime provinces, as well as Quebec, are experiencing particular difficulties with economic disadvantage. For example, the Maritimes tend to be less wealthy overall than oil-rich Alberta.

Poverty has been increasing in Atlantic Canada since the fisheries there went into crisis at the end of the 20th century. Many generations of Maritimers had made their livelihoods by fishing, until environmental concerns and overfishing led to restrictions on their work. The federal government has recently introduced measures, such as changes to taxation of fishing and a substantial investment in fisheries (over $30 million), to ameliorate Maritime poverty. In a 2007 press release, Fisheries and Oceans Minister Heam stated the following:

> These changes allow those who want to invest in their enterprise an opportunity to grow and enable those who wish to leave the industry an opportunity to leave on their own terms. Today, we have given fishers greater flexibility than ever before in determining their future and the ability to make decisions that allow them to adjust to ever changing market conditions. (Government of Newfoundland and Labrador, 2007, n.p.)

Even when permitted to fish and to earn income by other means, such as peat harvesting, many people in Atlantic Canada worked only seasonally and became dependent upon the public purse. Populations in the Maritimes are decreasing as large numbers of young people leave the region to find work and prosperity elsewhere. This exodus of the young is further impoverishing the region.

There is a saying in Alberta that the city of Fort McMurray, in the northern part of the province, is the largest city in Newfoundland. All of Alberta has prospered from oil wealth in the past decade, but Fort McMurray is Canada's largest boom town. It is the headquarters of the oil sands, an area that yields—at great cost and with significant labour investment—enough oil to deliver North America from its current dependence upon oil from the Middle East. The town is reminiscent of gold-rush boom towns of the 19th century. As of 2006, Fort McMurray was growing too fast for its infrastructure; there was a huge influx of people, many of them from Atlantic Canada. The town's population doubled between 1996 and 2006 (Cook, 2006). The movement of people to Alberta has contributed to a surge in property values, with homes now so expensive in Calgary that there are "tent cities" at the city's outskirts where recent migrants, unable to find housing, are living.

There are regional patterns with respect to wealth and poverty in Canada. But it is important not to confuse a region's overall wealth with the individual lives of its inhabitants. For example, the Thomsons, Canada's wealthiest family, are from the Maritimes, and poverty persists in Alberta despite the oil wealth gained in the past few years (PovNet, 2004).

Child Poverty

Children who grow up in poverty have less chance of fulfilling their potential than wealthier children do. They are at greater risk of being neglected or abused by their parents due to a wide range of factors, including parental depression. They are less likely than the wealthy to receive a quality education. Poverty can impede children's learning in a variety of ways, direct and indirect. Physical hunger makes it hard for poor children to focus on their schoolwork. Poor students may be less effective at school because, unable to afford the name-brand clothing of their wealthier peers, they are socially stigmatized. Poor childhood nutrition has been linked to poverty. Sadly, it can be cheaper to buy fast food than to purchase fresh vegetables, meat, and other nutritious foods. Lacking time to prepare nutritious meals is also linked to poverty: single working mothers, working two or more jobs, may not have the time or energy to cook. There are some school breakfast and lunch programs in Canada, set up by charitable organizations or in individual schools, but schools are in the business of providing education, not food. There is no national system in place to ensure that a child sent to school hungry will be fed.

The liberal philosophical concern about child poverty is the massive waste of human potential it represents; we can't know which child has the capacity to discover a cure for AIDS or cancer, for example. If we fail a child who has the potential to advance human society, we fail ourselves.

Politicians have paid a great deal of attention, at least in their rhetoric, to the problem of children living in poverty. In 1989, the House of Commons voted unanimously in favour of a resolution seeking "to achieve the goal of eliminating poverty among Canadian children by the year 2000" (Campaign 2000, 2006, n.p.). The issue of child poverty received international attention at this time, at the 1990 UNICEF World Summit for Children, and with the UN Convention on the Rights of the Child ratified by Canada's Parliament the same year. However, despite the politicians' expressed commitment to this goal, about 1.2 million Canadian children lived in poverty as of 2006 (Campaign 2000, 2007). In fact, rates of child poverty are actually worse now than they were when the commitment was made to end child poverty, in 1989.

SOCIAL PROBLEMS RELATED TO POVERTY

People who are healthy and well educated are generally the most productive individuals in any economy, and contribute greatly to the country's overall economic health. Individuals who grow up in poverty—with poor access to educational, nutritional, and other resources—contribute less to workforce productivity. Individual poverty has negative consequences for the broader community and, ultimately, for all Canadians.

Poverty, as we have seen, makes it difficult for people to meet their basic needs, puts children at risk, and impairs its victims' self-esteem and overall sense of well-being. Poverty is also linked to poor health outcomes more generally. Smoking is strongly correlated with low socio-economic status, and smoking, as discussed in chapter 3, is also correlated with serious illness, disability, and early death. Excess alcohol consumption and abuse of other substances also coincide with poverty in complex ways that are discussed in more detail in chapter 3. The Public Health Agency of Canada has found low socio-economic status to be correlated more generally with lower life expectancies, higher rates of adolescent pregnancy, and higher rates of avoidable hospitalization and mortality rates (Public Health Agency of Canada, 2002). The ill health suffered by the poor is a problem not just for them but for other Canadians as well, who must bear the financial costs of our socialized health-care system.

Poverty is also linked to crime. Many individuals who live in poverty are law-abiding, and many wealthy individuals commit white-collar crime. But there are clear connections between poverty and crime. Very poor individuals are more likely to commit breaking-and-entering crimes to obtain money and food. Individuals living in poverty may "panhandle," which is a crime in this country. It is also a crime to sleep in public areas in buildings or parks, which is something to which poor individuals without homes or other shelter may have to resort. Individuals growing up in poverty are more susceptible to recruitment into criminal organizations, particularly ones related to the international drug trade. Such people turn to crime because they lack legitimate avenues to social advancement and prosperity.

Particular social problems arise when a nation's youth faces economic inequality. This has been the case in Canada for the past decade or so. The phenomenon sometimes called "failure to launch"—when a young person's adulthood is postponed due to slacking or lack of opportunity—has become a growing social issue in Canada. Low income is disproportionately widespread among the young. Burdened by student debt, they often cannot afford to purchase homes of their own, and this is causing them to postpone other adult commitments, such as marriage and children.

As our population ages, the economic disadvantage of the elderly, especially elderly women, will become more obvious as a social problem; they will place an increasing burden on our social welfare system.

HOMELESSNESS

There are relatively few people living in absolute poverty in Canada, but there is a significant minority living close to that level. Human Resources and Social Development Canada currently estimates that about 0.5 percent of the population in any Canadian community is in this position. This translates into about 15,000 people nationwide. These people are often **homeless**. To be homeless is to lack permanent or even temporary housing owing to poverty. The term *homeless* has replaced older terms for transient individuals, words such as *vagrant*, *hobo*, *bag man/lady*, or *tramp*. Homeless people have to seek some sort of makeshift or temporary shelter, and may live in tents, public places (for example, in parks or under bridges), or vehicles.

A homeless person encounters significant barriers to finding permanent shelter and re-integrating with mainstream society, and will find it hard to escape a life full of risk and hardship. The social safety net is difficult to access without an address. Homeless people are particularly vulnerable to assaults, thefts, and other crimes. Health issues for the homeless are significant: they have difficulty accessing medical care, though physically undermined by exposure to severe weather, crowded conditions in shelters, and poor hygiene. These conditions put them at higher-than-normal risk of infections, communicable diseases, injury, and death. Moreover, people often become homeless as a direct result of mental illness, substance abuse problems, or domestic violence. In other words, becoming homeless often coincides with an acute need for medical care.

Homeless people are a minority in Canada, but their condition is still too common. Among developed nations, we have a high per capita rate of homelessness, second only to the United States (City of Toronto, 2000). And this rate has recently been increasing. The following are often cited as causes for this increase: a lack of safe or affordable low-income housing, especially in urban areas and especially in Toronto; a movement, beginning in the 1960s and 1970s, to "deinstitutionalize" the mentally ill; and increases in income inequality rendering the poorest of the poor unable to access basic resources.

ANALYSIS

SOCIAL ISSUES OF ECONOMIC EQUALITY

The notion of **poverty** encompasses a complexity of issues, contexts, and consequences. It is variously defined. Poverty is sometimes understood as economic insecurity, economic inequality, and relative disadvantage. In the United States, poverty is identified as income below a certain "line." In Canada, the LICO, often described as the poverty line, is a Statistics Canada measure of inequality, not of poverty itself (Sarlo, 2001). Poverty is also sometimes viewed as absolute or as relative—in other words, income poverty versus consumption poverty. In each case, the interpretations differ. People also differ in their views on whether poverty is growing or stable in Canada, or whether the standard of living is equal or progressing toward that point.

CANADA'S STATUS ON POVERTY

The United Nations' Index of Human Development places Canada in the top five of all developed countries. However, recent UN criticism of Canada's track record with respect to income distribution and child welfare indicates that we are lagging behind other developed nations in this regard (UNICEF, 2007). Anti-poverty activist groups have been advocating increased support for the poor since the mid-1900s. In 1989 and again in 2000, resolutions to end domestic and global poverty were made. But poverty continues to grow in Canada (Campaign 2000, 2006).

Campaign 2000 is a particularly active coalition of over 120 national, provincial, and community organizations in Canada that has clear goals for combating child and family poverty. We will adopt Canada 2000's agenda in defining economic inequality as a social issue in Canada.

Identifying a Social Issue

WHAT GROUPS ARE CALLING FOR ATTENTION, AND WHAT IS THEIR CONCERN?

Campaign 2000, other non-governmental organizations (NGOs), and government agencies have long been mobilized to combat or reduce poverty. That some people in this country live in uncomfortable and unhealthy circumstances is unacceptable to Canadians who believe in democracy, in a high standard of living, and in equality of opportunity. The gap between the rich and the poor in Canada is a national outrage. The failure of actions undertaken both nationally and internationally to remedy this problem is particularly troubling to Canadians.

WHAT IS THE VISION OR GOAL OF THE VOICES OF CONCERN?

In 1989, the Canadian House of Commons unanimously resolved to "seek to achieve the goal of eliminating poverty among Canadian children by the year 2000" (Campaign 2000, 2006, n.p.). More recently, the UN (2006) has identified the Millennium Goals: "The eight Millennium Development Goals (MDGs)—which range from halving extreme poverty to halting the spread of HIV/AIDS and providing universal primary education, all by the target date of 2015—form a blueprint agreed to by all the world's countries and all the world's leading development institutions" (United Nations Millennium Development Goals, 2006). These goals envision of a world without poverty. This vision is shared and promoted by Canada.

WHAT ARE THE MEANS OF ACHIEVING THE GOALS?

Critics of Canada's fight against poverty point to dismal statistics: one in six children in Canada is poor; Canada's child **poverty rate** is three times as high as in Nordic Europe; and every month, 770,000 people in Canada use food banks. This is a full 15 years after the 1989 resolution, and 5 years after the deadline for ending poverty cited in the resolution (Howlett, 2005).

In the face of such failure, many suggestions are being made. The leading suggestion is that a political will to make change is needed. Other measures proposed include expanding affordable housing, raising the minimum wage, and increasing the child tax benefit and child-care options. Strong voices advocating on behalf of the poor have come from Campaign 2000. Their most recent initiative has been the "Make Poverty History" campaign.

Evolution of the Social Issue of Economic Inequality

WHAT GROUPS AND ORGANIZATIONS ARE ADVOCATING CHANGE?

The number of groups and organizations in Canada working on behalf of the poor indicates that there is a crisis of poverty in Canada. Among the NGOs are Campaign 2000, the National Anti-poverty Organization (NAPO), the Make Poverty History group, and Raising the Roof. Among government agencies are international organizations such as UNICEF. There are national government agencies such as the Canadian Council on Social Development, the Canadian Policy Research Network, and political parties such as the NDP. Municipal organizations include such organizations as the Youth Shelter Interagency Network (YSIN) in Toronto. A number of these organizations have documented, through statistics, the extent and character of poverty in Canada. Other organizations and agencies are advocating on behalf of the poor and homeless and trying to implement anti-poverty measures.

WHAT HAS PROMPTED PUBLIC AWARENESS AND CONCERN?

Public awareness of poverty as an issue has existed for nearly 50 years. The sense of urgency about the issue has fluctuated. Events such as the death of a homeless person or outbreaks of violence in disadvantaged neighbourhoods tend to refocus public attention. The recent shooting deaths of Toronto school students have brought renewed attention to the hardships of Canada's immigrant populations and visible minorities, and to the issue of children being raised in poverty. An account of the public's awareness and demands for action is a CBC *Fifth Estate* program called "Lost in the Struggle" (2006).

HOW IS THE PUBLIC ALIGNED?

The NDP's website claims the following: "Poverty denies us freedom and hope, and it's the biggest single factor in ill health. Confronting poverty means recognizing the human dignity in everyone—and our responsibility to help those neighbours who fall through the cracks" (NDP, 2007). The fact that poverty is on the public agenda in Canada suggests that a majority of citizens favour remedial action, as does the overwhelming public support of soup kitchens and other charities. At the same time, the stigma still attached to poverty and homelessness reflects a national tendency to blame the victims. The widening gap between the rich and the poor attests to a lack of **political will** for change (Campaign 2000, 2006). Political will is usually achieved by public pressure.

WHAT INITIATIVES HAVE BEEN TAKEN AND WHAT POLICIES HAVE BEEN PUT IN PLACE?

Since the Canadian House of Commons' declaration that child poverty would be eliminated by the year 2000, many public and private initiatives to reduce poverty have been implemented. However, the problem of poverty in Canada, by most accounts, stubbornly persists and has even increased. Every document concerning the current poverty trends concludes with a list of recommendations. These documents also review the success of already implemented programs. In its 2006 Report Card on Child and Family Poverty in Canada, Campaign 2000 lists a number of the policies undertaken by Canada. It also identifies where Canada has failed in its commitment to end poverty.

WHAT IS THE PUBLIC REACTION?

Public opinion supports government spending to reduce poverty (Campaign 2000, 2006).

ANALYTICAL APPROACHES TO UNDERSTANDING ECONOMIC INEQUALITY

The different terms for poverty (*economic insecurity* or *economic inequality*, for example) reflect different theoretical perspectives. The term *economic insecurity* encourages a focus on the vulnerability of certain social groups, such as single parents and their children or Aboriginal Canadians. Poverty understood in this way, in terms of circumstances to which some are vulnerable, connotes failure on the part of society to effectively support all Canadians. Societal failure is a focus of the structural functionalist paradigm. In this chapter, the *feminization of poverty* will be analyzed from that perspective.

The notion of poverty implied by the term *economic inequality* lends itself to a social conflict analysis. From this perspective, poverty is the exploitation of the have-nots by the haves. A social conflict analysis of the plight of Canada's Aboriginal peoples will take this approach to poverty.

The term *economic inequality* also implies the shame or **stigma** associated with poverty. Poverty viewed this way is best addressed through a symbolic interactionist perspective. A symbolic interactionist analysis of homeless youth is included in this chapter.

A Structural Functionalist Analysis of the Feminization of Poverty

BRIEF REVIEW OF THE STRUCTURAL FUNCTIONALIST PERSPECTIVE

The structural functionalist views society as a stable and integrated system of social institutions. According to this perspective, any social issue is the consequence of a disruption in this system. The term **feminization of poverty** seeks to register that the poor are increasingly women and their children. From the structural functionalist perspective, this represents a system failure. In other words, what are the **dysfunctions** contributing to the feminization of poverty?

MANIFEST FUNCTIONS

The issue of poverty makes it very clear that the interaction of social institutions influences social outcomes. Poverty in a developed country like Canada is seen by many as inexcusable. Critics point to the ineffectiveness of *government* in managing social welfare initiatives. They emphasize the necessity of government intervention in the *economy* to provide a decent standard of living for all Canadians (Hay, 2007; Jenson, 2003). The fact that many *families* with full-time earners still live under the LICO is unacceptable to these critics, and it reflects a significant *dysfunction* in the economy. There are many factors besides income that determine children's well-being; **social institutions** such as *family*, *health*, and *education* are also important. Theoretically, a stable and functioning social system would have the following: a government that effectively regulates the economy; an economy that provides sufficient employment and benefits for the well-being of all employed; an education system that prepares young adults and new Canadians for gainful employment; and stable families that support their members. Where poverty prevails (and grows), none of these **manifest functions** is being fulfilled.

WHAT CAUSES SYSTEM DYSFUNCTION?

Within the structural functionalist paradigm, social change causes dysfunction. In the case of the feminization of poverty, structural changes in the family have made women and their children more vulnerable than in the past. Changes in the prevailing social values—from **patriarchy** to gender equality—have resulted in strains owing to **cultural lag**. Pressures from **globalization** and from the computerization of the workforce have changed the nature of employment. Government intervention in the economy has also changed. In short, disparities between men and women with respect to poverty are increasing.

EVIDENCE OF DYSFUNCTIONS

Statistical measures are the clearest evidence of the feminization of poverty. The following statistics were cited in Campaign 2000's 2006 Report Card on Child and Family Poverty in Canada:

- Fifty-two percent of low-income children live in female lone-parent families.
- Forty-nine percent of children in recent immigrant families and 34 percent of racialized families are poor (2001 census).
- Forty percent of off-reserve Aboriginal children live in poverty.
- Twenty-eight percent of children with disabilities are poor.
- The average low-income female-led single-parent family is living $9,400 below the LICO.

Recall that *LICO* is an acronym for *low income cut-off*, a Statistics Canada measure of relative poverty in terms of income that has been popularly defined as the "poverty line." A LICO income for a family of four in urban centres with more than 500,000 people was $25,574 in 1992 and $31,865 in 2004. See the Statistics Canada article "Low Income Cut-offs for 2005 and Low Income Measures for 2004" (Statistics Canada, 2006). For more complete information on how low income is measured, see the following articles: "Understanding the 2000 Low Income Statistics Based on the Market Basket Measure" (Canadian Council on Social Development, n.d., 22-26) and "Canada's Global Cities: Socio-economic Conditions in Montreal, Toronto and Vancouver" (Heisz, 2006).

The above statistics are from Campaign 2000, an anti-poverty activist group. Obviously, it is in their interest to cite high poverty rates. And yet their statistics are supported by statistics from a paper written for Women and Urban Environments, a Health Canada initiative (Khosla, 2005), whose findings are as follows:

- In the period 1990–2000, the number of poor Canadians increased from 4.39 million to 4.72 million.
- In 2000, the total number of children living in poverty in Canada had increased to 1,245,700, an increase of 40,000 from 1990.
- Thirty-eight percent of immigrants who have lived in Canada less than five years are poor.
- Sixty percent of high-poverty neighbourhoods in Canada were located in Montreal and Toronto.
- The average income of poor families with working-age members was $14,500; this is one quarter of the average income in Canada.
- One in five (2.8 million) Canadian women live in poverty.
- The poverty rate for lone-parent women was 45.4 percent; for lone-parent men it was 24 percent.
- Of women over 65, 45.6 percent were poor.
- Among women with disabilities, 25 percent lived in poverty.

If the above statistics reflected an improvement in the relative well-being of Canadian women, the term "feminization of poverty" would be misleading. But they do not demonstrate such improvement. Nor does a study published in March 2001 by Federal/Provincial/Territorial Ministers Responsible for the Status of Women. This report succinctly identifies a number of contributing factors in the feminization of poverty:

> Discrimination in education and training, hiring and remuneration, promotion and horizontal mobility practices, as well as inflexible working conditions, lack of access to productive resources and inadequate sharing of family responsibilities, combined with a lack of or insufficient services such as child care, continue to restrict employment, economic, professional and other opportunities and mobility for women and make their involvement stressful. Moreover, attitudinal obstacles inhibit women's participation in developing economic policy and in some regions restrict the access of women and girls to education and training for economic management. (Status of Women Canada, 2001, p. 13)

ORIGINS OF DYSFUNCTIONS

The above excerpt clearly identifies that social problems have complex origins. Adoption of a structural functionalist analysis can help clarify the nature of the dysfunctions.

Questions That Guide a Structural Functionalist Analysis

WHAT SOCIAL INSTITUTIONS ARE CENTRALLY INVOLVED?

The feminization of poverty is primarily a consequence of dysfunctions in the social institutions of the government and the economy. The social institutions of education and the family clearly play a large role as well, given the inevitable significance of **gender socialization**: "Gender socialization is a pervasive and integral component of all of the key factors influencing women's economic independence and security" (Status of Women Canada, 2001).

WHAT ARE THE MANIFEST FUNCTIONS? WHAT ARE THE DYSFUNCTIONS RESULTING IN THE FEMINIZATION OF POVERTY?

Poverty discourages and debilitates its victims; it also signals a society's failure to enrich its members' lives. Considering that Canada is supposedly a democratic nation, the unequal distribution of resources in this country seems very significant. Competition for variable rewards encourages productivity, excellence, and talent. But barriers to **social mobility** that are based on discrimination by gender, race, age, culture, or ethnicity—these are unacceptable.

The Canadian *government* is primarily responsible for intervening in the market economy so that the country's resources are distributed fairly and the economy remains viable and competitive. Without exception, reports on poverty in Canada call for such intervention. For example, there have been calls for increased minimum wage, housing subsidies, and a national daycare program.

The *economy* is the engine of society. When functioning effectively, it generates economic growth and well-being among the people. However, many of the former "laws" of economics no longer apply, given the modern influences of globalization and of the transition from a manufacturing economy to a service-information economy. For example, economic growth may now occur without a corresponding increase in employment and job stability (Canadian Labour Congress, 2006).

The socializing influences of *family* and of *education* have brought about a value shift from gender inequality and male dominance to gender equality. But as long as women continue to be viewed as primary caregivers, they will be responsible for the greater share of child and elder care in their own homes, and they will be channelled into occupations that rely on their caregiving traits. Both trends place women at an economic disadvantage. The social institution of education is predominantly responsible for preparing the workforce for employment. Ideally, education translates into employability, and this benefits each individual worker and ensures that the economy has the best in skills and knowledge. There is clearly dysfunction in this relationship when, as statistics suggest, women have more education than men but lag behind them in both remuneration and employment. In 1997, 58 percent of university graduates were women and yet, in the same year, "women at all levels of education had fewer earnings from full-time, full-year employment than their male counterparts. The full-time female to male earnings ratio is 74% for university graduates and only 65% for those who did not finish high school" (Status of Women Canada, 2001, pp. 11, 14).

SOCIAL TRENDS RESULTING IN DYSFUNCTIONS

According to a report by Canadian Policy Research Networks, there are four sources of social welfare: market income (earnings in paid employment); benefits and services provided by the family; government (social welfare programs); and community (volunteers and charity supports). The challenge for governments is to establish policies that encourage the right welfare mix. The task is challenging because of the changes that societies continually face: aging society, changing family patterns, and economic marginalization and social exclusion (Jenson, 2003).

Government Policy Changes/Inaction

Their successful use in northern European countries has proven that government social welfare programs assist low-income families in escaping from poverty. Increased income is insufficient to resolve issues of poverty (Campaign 2000, 2006). Some key government failures are the following:

- A universal system of early learning and child-care is essential for the development and health of children across the socio-economic spectrum. Canada, when on the brink of establishing such a system, stalled the implementation.
- A full decade has elapsed since completion of the Royal Commission on Aboriginal Peoples and "the landmark commitment" of the government to address the systemic impediments to Aboriginal advancement in Canadian society. No action on the commitment has been made.
- Canada is one of the few countries in the world without a comprehensive strategy for ensuring affordable housing. One of the greatest barriers to the poor improving their socio-economic status is lack of low-income housing.
- An adult worker who works full time at minimum wage does not earn enough to rise above the poverty line. It follows that the government should legislate a higher minimum wage. This was done in the spring of 2007, but the increase was very small and did little, critics allege, to improve the lives of the poor.
- Finally, women are a distinct minority in government. According to the Status of Women Report of 2001, only 20 percent of the members of the House of Commons were women. This was up from 5 percent in 1980, but at 20 percent, women's voices remain weak.

Trends in the Economy

Across Canada, the unemployment rate has never been lower and there has been a marginal growth in wage rates. And yet there has been no improvement in the number of workers uncertainly employed or earning poverty wages. In short, as the Canadian Labour Congress has said (2006), "getting a job is becoming increasingly disconnected with getting ahead for too many Canadians." There are a number of reasons for this negative trend:

- Market globalization and international trade agreements are particularly important to Canada. While globalization presents distinct opportunities for Canadians in some sectors, such as self-employed women in the trade sector, it disadvantages those in the service sector (fast food and health care, for example) and in manufacturing.

- Emerging labour market trends are as follows: decline in salaried work; growth in self-employment in the 1980s and 1990s; increased part-time work and a growing number of workers with multiple jobs; and the emergence of telecommuting. These trends exert disproportionate hardships on women, who hold the majority of part-time positions, and on youth, whose unemployment rate greatly exceeds that of the general population (Canadian Labour Congress, 2006).
- In female-dominated occupations, wages tend to be lower.
- Women at all levels of education earn less than men.
- Most part-time work is done by women (Status of Women Canada, 2001; Canadian Labour Congress, 2006).
- Divorce and separation exert a greater financial burden on women than on men (men's incomes tend to rise after divorce).
- Women are responsible for the greater share of unpaid domestic and caregiving work, and more women than men cite family obligations as their reason for working part time (Status of Women Canada, 2001).

Demographic changes

The overall composition of a society's population with respect to such variables as average age, income, and marital status—the **demographic** structure—also influences the economy. Canada's birth rate is below replacement rate, and immigration can be expected to play an increasingly important role in the country's economy. Canada will also grow increasingly culturally diverse, a factor which also shapes the kinds of work available. The following is a list of changes projected to occur in Canada's economy as the population ages, the **birth rate** remains low, and immigration remains high:

- A shrinking labour force
- A higher proportion of women and immigrants within the labour force
- Increased use of technology
- Growth of the services sector and shrinking of the durable goods sector (mainly the construction industry)
- Conversion of unpaid household work to paid services (for the elderly)
- A higher personal savings rate
- A higher proportion of the adult population providing care to elderly parents or friends
- Greater social expenditures by government
- A lower unemployment rate, especially for young workers (O'Reilly, 2001; Statistics Canada, 2007).

Note that the last change projected is a positive one: that there will be more work available for youth once the "boomers" retire.

As in previous chapters, a structural functionalist analysis chart can be used to summarize the events contributing to system dysfunction and thus help to determine the social actions that would restore social equilibrium.

Structural Functionalist Analysis of the Feminization of Poverty

Social Action	Social Institution	Manifest Function of Social Institution	Dysfunction
A universal system of early learning and child care stalled	Government	Maintain social welfare	Poverty perpetuated through generations; rise in other social problems such as crime
Royal Commission on Aboriginal Peoples shelved: no action	Government	Maintain social welfare	Aboriginal people remain majority among poor
Slow progress on low-income housing strategy	Government	Maintain social welfare	Poor people lack the means to get ahead and to resolve their poverty: the number of poor children grows
A small rise in the minimum wage	Government	Maintain social welfare	Insufficient to enable full-time workers to rise above the LICO
Women are a distinct minority in government	Government	Maintain social welfare	No women's voice advocating for family-centred policies; social welfare cuts continue
Globalization restructures domestic economy	Economy	Production and employment	Manufacturing sector in decline: predominance of "McJobs" in service industry
Wages in female-dominated occupations tend to be lower	Economy	Production and employment	Feminization of poverty increases
Women at all levels of education have lower earnings than men	Economy	Production and employment	Feminization of poverty increases; number of children living in poverty grows
Divorce and separation places an inequitable financial burden on women	Family	Material and emotional support	Feminization of poverty increases; children experience greatest losses in well-being
Women are responsible for the greater share of unpaid domestic and caregiving work	Family	Care and nurturing of family members	Devaluing of care work continues, so women continue to be disadvantaged in economy

ACTIONS THAT WOULD RESTORE SYSTEM EQUILIBRIUM

Social stratification is perceived differently depending on the theoretical paradigm adopted. Social stratification, according to the structural functionalist model of society, is functional, or useful, because different reward levels encourage the development of talent and create incentives to work. This benefits each individual and society as a whole because the best individual talents are drawn out and utilized, thus contributing to the general good. However, if stratification barriers are founded on discriminatory factors such as sexism or racism, then society is not benefiting from whole segments of its capable citizenry—people with significant contributions to make. The existence of such barriers, which are contrary to prevailing social values, means that the relationships among such social institutions as education, the economy, and government cannot function as expected. Changes proposed by anti-poverty and feminist groups are most likely to restore system equilibrium. Most anti-poverty organizations emphasize that the government's initiatives must respond to Canada's changing demographics, families, and economy.

Actions Recommended to Government

The Canadian government has been urged to do the following:

- Redesign the welfare mix: provide child benefits; create housing allowances and other housing programs; implement early childhood education programs (Jenson, 2003; Khosla, n.d.; Howlett, 2005)
- Raise the minimum wage (Canadian Labour Congress, 2006; Khosla, n.d.; Howlett, 2005)
- Improve access to collective bargaining and raise employment standards (Canadian Labour Congress, 2006)
- Institute employment and pay-equity legislation (Khosla, n.d.; Howlett, 2005)
- Provide guaranteed adequate income (Khosla, n.d.; Howlett, 2005)

If the government initiated such changes, the poor would benefit from participating in the economy, and it is likely that their improved well-being would have a positive effect on their families, especially the children. Such changes would be realized in improved health overall and a lighter burden for health-care agencies.

A Social Conflict Analysis of Aboriginal Poverty

BRIEF REVIEW OF THE SOCIAL CONFLICT PERSPECTIVE

If one adopts a social conflict perspective, one sees a social issue as the product or outcome of inequality. Viewed from this perspective, poverty occurs when the powerful in society put the less powerful at a disadvantage—that is, they create social barriers that keep certain marginalized groups in society from gainful employment and other social amenities. The social conflict perspective also helps an analyst predict, on the basis of the various stakeholders' actions and interests, the future developments of a social issue. With regard to poverty in Canada, a social conflict analysis should make it possible to predict whether current trends are likely to resolve poverty or make it worse. According to a social conflict analysis, social stratification produces exploitation of the disadvantaged by the advantaged, and for this reason tends to diminish the well-being of society. When great segments of the population are denied a significant role in the economy or government, then society loses the potential of their expertise.

ANALYSIS OF POVERTY AMONG CANADA'S ABORIGINAL PEOPLES

Canada's Aboriginal peoples predominate in the lower socio-economic ranks. Their concentration there, along with Canada's **visible minorities** and immigrants, suggests that racism and discrimination are responsible for the widening gap between wealthy, mainstream Canadians and visible minority Canadians. The dynamics of inequality, prejudice, and discrimination are best assessed from a social conflict perspective, which will show the poverty of visible minorities to be an outcome of their exploitation.

Evidence of the Victimization of Aboriginal Peoples

The following statistics are drawn from a 2001 report by the Ontario Federation of Indian Friendship Centres. These statistics reflect the situation of Aboriginal Canadians who live outside reservations.

- Aboriginal people are at least four times more likely to report experiencing hunger than any other ethnic group in Canada.
- They lack affordable and appropriate clothing.
- The elimination of rent controls has resulted in a lack of affordable subsidized housing.
- They lack access to over-the-counter medications and basic supplies for infants.
- They lack transportation to support programs and services.
- Many suffer the psychological effects of poverty, from low self-esteem to shame and hopelessness.
- The participation of Aboriginal children and youth in the sex trade is disproportionately high—90 percent of all sex trade workers in some communities where the Aboriginal population is less than 10 percent—and it is growing.

This report also cites a number of actions and inactions on the part of the Ontario government that have created particular hardship for Ontario's Aboriginal people.

From 1995 to 2001, child poverty rates increased in Ontario even though across the rest of Canada they decreased. This discrepancy suggests that actions by the Ontario government had damaging effects. The Indian Friendship Centres (2001) report has identified government cuts to social assistance, elimination of child-care subsidies, and reductions in both welfare funding and the funding of children's mental health services as contributing to a serious increase in Aboriginal child and family poverty levels.

The report also lists new programs that have been implemented, but asserts that they have been inadequate in reducing Aboriginal child poverty: nearly 52.1 percent of Aboriginal children at the time of the report were poor. Aboriginal poverty is complicated by the fact that off-reserve families are not covered by programs that specifically target Aboriginal issues.

Reports like the one above point to government faults (in keeping with a structural functionalist view) as the main cause of Aboriginal poverty. But most reports on this topic cite **systemic** or **blatant discrimination** as the root of the problem. Some point to the lack of political will to effectively address Aboriginal poverty as evidence of underlying racism. The UN seemed to support this conclusion with its observation, in 1999, that the "situation of Aboriginal peoples in Canada is the most pressing human rights issue facing Canadians" (Ontario Federation of Indian Friendship Centres, 2001).

Prevailing Power Relationships

Clearly, the poverty among Aboriginal peoples of Canada is a product of discrimination. Matthew Coon Come, former national chief of the Assembly of First Nations, has charged that racism against First Nations people is structural or systemic (Farrar, 2001). Systemic racism stems from the colonial past that has dispossessed and displaced First Nations, Métis, and Inuit communities. The situation is evident in the rates of poverty suffered by Canada's Aboriginal peoples, and it is preserved by the social, economic, and political dominance of mainstream Canada. Matthew Coon Come, in an address to Canada about his statements at a conference on racism held in South Africa, said: "I stated that there was structural racism against Aboriginal peoples in Canada. I read from the 1998 and 1999 rulings of the United Nations Committee on Economic, Social and Cultural Rights and Human Rights Committee. I read from the 1996 Final Report of the Royal Commission on Aboriginal Peoples, including the passages regarding Canadian state policies, which could push Aboriginal peoples to economic, cultural and political extinction" (Canadian Bar Association, 2001).

Unemployment, shockingly poor living conditions, and hopelessness contribute to continued poverty and to the very high rate of suicide among Aboriginals. These factors also contribute to the stigmas that support continued discrimination against Aboriginals. Aboriginal peoples, visible minorities, and immigrants to Canada have more trouble than white Canadians finding employment everywhere in Canada. Those with a university education are less likely than their white or mainstream peers to hold managerial and professional jobs (Heisz, 2006). The Ontario Network for Human Rights (2001) has reported the following:

> Higher education yields fewer payoffs for minorities and Aboriginal peoples in terms of employment and income. Given the same level of education, white Canadians (both foreign-born and Canadian-born) are three times as likely as Aboriginal peoples and about twice as likely as foreign-born visible minorities to be in the top 20 per cent of income earners." (Ontario Network for Human Rights, 2001, n.p.)

Predicting the Future of the Issue

The greatest asset of those seeking to reduce Aboriginal poverty is public discourse about the Canadian government's inexcusable foot-dragging on this issue. The public is concerned that a majority of First Nations communities do not have a source of clean water and that land claim settlements are not being conducted in a timely manner. The recent militancy of First Nations people has attracted public attention. But because Canada's relationship with First Nations people is rooted in the entrenched inequality of a colonial past, the favourable resolution of the issue is not near at hand.

QUESTIONS THAT GUIDE A SOCIAL CONFLICT ANALYSIS

Who Are the Major Stakeholders in the Issue?

The major stakeholders are the First Nations people and the Canadian government on all levels. Within the Aboriginal population are activist groups such as the Ontario Association of Friendship Centres. In addition, organizations such as Campaign 2000 and the Canadian Policy Research Networks have joined forces to reduce or eliminate child poverty in Canada.

What Are the Resources of Each Stakeholder Group?

The resources held by each side in this controversy are quite distinct. The Canadian governments and public derive power from their entrenched assets, built from colonial exploitations of Aboriginal peoples. First Nations people are relying on the public outcry over the appalling poverty in which they live, and their own emerging pride in their Aboriginal heritage. Aboriginal self-awareness is fuelling land claim actions and self-government initiatives.

Which Side Is Dominant, and What Is the Future of the Issue?

Despite the growing awareness of inequality and the escalating public outcry, there is much work to be done. The elimination of child poverty and of poverty among First Nations seems to be no closer than it was in 1989, when poverty was targeted for eradication by 2000. A more detailed evaluation of the relative power on each side of this issue is summarized in the chart on the following page.

This power resources chart succinctly summarizes the impact of various social events, both the intentional social actions and the unexpected events and trends. Though fundamentally a *subjective* evaluation, it is more or less reliable depending on how extensively the background events are researched. Here it reveals systemic discrimination in the Canadian world view. Only continued activism on the part of the minorities and their supporters will loosen the hold of these prejudices. As the chart's list of minority assets shows, some gains have been made.

A Symbolic Interactionist Analysis of Youth Homelessness

BRIEF REVIEW OF THE SYMBOLIC INTERACTIONIST PERSPECTIVE

Symbolic interactionism is a micro perspective that reveals a social issue as the outcome of interpersonal behaviour among major stakeholders. Youth homelessness is the particular aspect of economic inequality we are examining from this perspective. It is interesting to note that even though homeless youth constitute about 30 percent of all homeless, there is no specific social agency or outreach group designed for

Power Resources Chart for Poverty of Aboriginals and Visible Minorities					
Dominant Side: Status Quo			**Minority Side: Visible Minorities/Aboriginals**		
WIN	LOSE	RESOURCE	WIN	LOSE	RESOURCE
♠♠♠♠		Prejudices preserved from colonial past	♠	♦♦	Activism born of growing pride in Aboriginal cultural traditions
♠♠	♦♦	Health issues of Aboriginal people (especially addictions) reinforce prejudices	♠	♦♦	Some land claim successes
♠♠♠♠		Growth of urban visible-minority populations means competition for political and economic positions		♦♦♦	Some official restitution for past crimes (for example, abuse in residential schools)
				♦♦♦	Community poverty crises and issues, such as water quality, bring public attention to discriminatory practices
10	2		2	10	

youth alone (Raising the Roof, n.d.). Does this not send the message that youth are not important?

ANALYSIS OF YOUTH HOMELESSNESS

The most significant factor in youth homelessness is abuse and neglect. It is estimated that 70 percent of all homeless youth have experienced some form of sexual, physical, or emotional abuse. Once homeless, these young people suffer more physical abuse, sickness, injury, and mental health problems than their non-homeless peers do. A Quebec study found that the death rate among homeless youth was 11 times higher than in the general youth population.

Defining Homelessness

A *home* is simply a *shelter*, considered to be a basic human right. But even the most rudimentary homes can be unaffordable for people on the low end of the socio-economic scale. Such individuals may be on fixed pensions, as the elderly and disabled often are, or they may lack, as young people often do, the education or experience to gain the required income. However, there are *social* factors apart from poverty that force homelessness on certain marginalized groups. In the case of youth homelessness, as we have said, up to 75 percent of homeless youth have been abused or neglected.

The CBC News *Fifth Estate* program "No Way Home" (2004) cites a number of other factors in youth homelessness. Close to 60 percent of homeless young people identified a poor relationship with one or both of their parents as their reason for leaving home. A disproportionate number of homeless youths come from single-parent homes. They are more likely to be lesbian, gay, or bisexual than young people in the general population. Close to half of homeless youth have come from foster care or youth shelters.

A structural functionalist analysis would emphasize the role of society-wide social changes in the escalation of youth homelessness. A social conflict perspective would emphasize how certain powerful groups in society have the resources to marginalize the poor. A symbolic interactionist perspective, however, emphasizes how socio-cultural patterns of poor treatment and neglect have produced growing numbers of young people who are poor, homeless, and undermined by mental illness and addiction.

QUESTIONS THAT GUIDE A SYMBOLIC INTERACTIONIST ANALYSIS

1. What does the issue mean to the individuals involved in the issue? How is this meaning expressed? What labels, myths, stereotypes, and language do individuals use to refer to the issue and to the other individuals involved in it?

   The CBC *Fifth Estate* rebroadcast a program called "Lost in the Struggle" (CBC News, 2006) after the 2007 shooting death of Toronto teen Jordan Manners at his high school. Jordan's killers were two teens from his neighbourhood. The program explores the question of why youth are drawn to a culture of violence. The transcript of this program (available at the link in the "References" section) is a vivid account of life in the "hood." It poignantly describes the reasons for violence and the challenges of avoiding a criminal life. It tells of the struggles born of deprivation and marginalization. As you read through the transcripts, identify the **stereotypes** that encourage segregation and reinforce deprivation. Pick out any **myths** about youth and crime. Contrast these myths and stereotypes with the reality experienced by the Jane-and-Finch residents of Toronto.

2. What is the source of these meanings? What is the social context in which these meanings are expressed? How are these meanings enforced or resisted?

   The United Way report "Poverty by Postal Code" (United Way of Greater Toronto, 2004) describes a social context—impoverished neighbourhoods—that is at once a threat to its residents' well-being and their best resource. Poor neighbourhoods are inhabited by poor people. Poor people who are clustered together invite prejudice and stereotype from the general public. When poor neighbourhoods decline, as they tend to do, these stereotypes are reinforced, and residents are less likely to escape their situation through job opportunities elsewhere. The consequences are felt by the poor people themselves and by the community at large, which must bear increased burdens of danger and the financial costs of supporting the poor. The beginning of "Poverty by Postal Code" refers to the lessons

> to be learned from successful neighbourhood revitalization efforts in the United States and Britain. Both countries experienced the bitter consequences of neighbourhood-based social and economic exclusion; they learned these lessons the hard way—after many of their urban neighbourhoods had become areas of intense, racialized poverty and urban desolation. And both countries have seen these neighbourhoods transformed—through reinvestment and collaboration—into strong, vibrant foundations of healthy cities offering their citizens an improved quality of life and economic opportunities. (n.p.)

There is an interrelationship between social context and social behaviour. The context shapes perception and action, and in turn these shape the lives of the marginalized persons.

3. What are the consequences of this activity? How does it affect the individuals involved? How does it affect society's perception of an issue, and how does this affect, in turn, individual participation in the issue?

   Each of the previous documents acknowledges that interpersonal beliefs, perceptions, and behaviour influence social issues. The action plans proposed by government and community reflect the same acknowledgment. In other words, poverty is not simply a matter of numbers, solved by raising the minimum wage to *x* dollars or providing housing subsidies of so many million dollars. Especially with regard to youth poverty and homelessness, financial want is a small element within a complexity of needs. See, for example, "System in Crisis: An Action Plan for the Future of Toronto's Homeless Youth" (Youth Shelter Interagency Network, 2007). The report continually acknowledges the need to address more than the basics of food, shelter, and safety. It recommends using the network of shelters to address the multifarious needs of marginalized, vulnerable, and homeless youth. The organization Raising the Roof has recognized that multi-faceted support is needed if homeless youth are to become financially independent and productive members of society. The same is true of Campaign 2000's Components of a Poverty Reduction Strategy for Canada. Among the recommended components are an early learning and child-care system, as well as affordable and accessible post-secondary education.

Despite lip service to the notion that our youth are Canada's future, Canada's indifference to the problems endured by our youth defines them as a marginalized and discounted minority. Only a serious commitment to enfranchising the young and accepting them as equals will resolve issues like poverty, homelessness, and violence.

RESPONSES

GOVERNMENT AND POLICY

The Canadian government's most significant policy response to poverty in the 20th century was the gradual development of our social safety net, in a process sometimes called *the growth of the welfare state.* This policy was based on an understanding that capitalist, or free-market, societies require state intervention to ensure stability. The construction of Canada's welfare state mostly took place in the years following World War II. Three key goals underlie the welfare state: provision of minimum income to Canadians; reduction of economic insecurity resulting from sickness, old age, and unemployment; and the provision of social services to all members of society (The Canadian Encyclopedia, 2007).

Our social safety net included the following: old-age pensions; governmental legislation of free and mandatory basic education for children; student loans and government grants to make post-secondary education accessible to people regardless of their socio-economic status; the institution of employment insurance to assist people through periods of unemployment; legislation of a minimum wage; basic welfare payments allowing the poor to survive; and universal health care.

Many politicians and advocates argue that Canada's state is not sufficiently developed and has in fact been eroded over the past few decades. Many identify a need for universal child care and publicly funded early childhood education. This would assist children in achieving their personal potential regardless of their socio-economic status while enabling women, and especially single mothers, to participate in the paid workforce. Others have proposed that minimum wages or selective welfare benefits be replaced by "a guaranteed annual income" or minimum income for all Canadians regardless of their circumstances, as a way of reducing economic inequality and poverty.

LAW AND POLICING

In general, poverty is seen by police and criminologists as a risk factor potentially leading to crime. Poor neighbourhoods are more likely to be perceived as unsafe than wealthy areas both by those who live there and those who do not, and there is often a more intensive police presence in impoverished areas. Self-fulfillingly, this heightened police presence increases the likelihood of a crime being reported to police or seen by them directly; there may be higher charge rates in poorer areas than in affluent ones for this reason. In recent years, police have begun to shift their focus from intensive policing of poorer areas to community policing and crime prevention through social development. Police have become involved in addressing directly some of the risk factors leading to crime: they participate in crime prevention programs in schools, and they advocate for programs and funding to alleviate poverty, to reduce political disenfranchisement of racialized minorities, and to address the problem of women's social isolation and vulnerability to violence. Police departments are also striving for better integration with the mental health agencies and other health organizations with a view to addressing the root causes of crime before offences are committed and damage done.

COMMUNITY

Community responses to poverty and economic inequality are an old feature of human society. In the ancient world and throughout the Middle Ages, *sectarian* (that is, composed of people subscribing to a religious doctrine) organizations such as synagogues, mosques, and churches have been involved in collecting goods and monies from their members to be redistributed to the poor. Religious organizations today continue to be involved in such community responses to poverty as soup kitchens for the homeless and food drives. The Salvation Army is one particularly well-known sectarian organization dedicated to alleviating the burdens of the poor.

As Canada's church and state have become separate and our society more secular, community organizations that are not overtly religious have come to play an important role in responding to economic inequality. Not-for-profit food banks, for example, have been developed to assist those facing economic adversity. More broadly, any community organization that promotes equal participation in Canadian society by all people—women's shelters, organizations assisting new Canadian immigrants, anti-racism advocacy groups, for example—is contributing to the cause of economic equality.

INDIVIDUAL INVOLVEMENT

Economic inequality is not a small or simple social problem. It is being addressed on many fronts by governments and community groups. Students can become involved in this work by, for example:

- Volunteering at a local food bank or other community agency dedicated to helping the poor
- Becoming politically involved, either with a political party or non-partisan advocacy group, to try to reduce levels of economic inequality
- Working or volunteering with a local church or other sectarian organization to help the poor
- Volunteering time with organizations such as Big Brothers or Big Sisters to help alleviate the social isolation and difficulties faced by single-parented children growing up in poverty

CONCLUSION

However poverty is defined, the fact that it affects 11 percent of Canadian children is a blight on our international reputation as a compassionate and peaceful nation. The statistics speak loudly about the indifference of most Canadians toward the poor. The numbers of the impoverished in Canada have grown, and minority

Canadians continue to be marginalized. A social constructionist analysis would illuminate the language, beliefs, and value structures underlying the apparent apathy of Canadians toward this issue.

There are a number of anti-poverty activists in Canada who are working to create public awareness and to lobby for meaningful changes in public policy. One of the best known of them is Campaign 2000. This association, which produces annual reports on the state of poverty in Canada, is a non-partisan league of national, provincial, and community organizations that has increased public awareness of the plight of the poor and continually pressured government to address the problem of poverty. In short, it has approached poverty as a serious issue, not easily solved by canned-food drives and toy donations over the holiday season.

KEY TERMS

birth rate the rate of population growth (or decline) expressed as a ratio of the number of births per year to the number in the population

blatant discrimination discrimination that often takes violent or offensive forms and that is prompted by prejudice

cultural lag W.F. Ogburn's theory that, because social change occurs unevenly among cultural components, it is disruptive until all components have changed and reintegrated

demographic having to do with the structure of populations or population statistics

dysfunctions in the structural functionalist paradigm, the negative consequences of change or of social actions; dysfunctions occur as breakdowns within social institutions or as the impaired integration of social institutions

feminization of poverty as a consequence of women's socio-economic disadvantages, the majority of the poor in our society are women

gender socialization the process of teaching cultural beliefs, values, and norms with respect to acceptable behaviours and expectations of masculinity and femininity

globalization trends in telecommunications, trade, and migration that have resulted in an increasingly interconnected world

homeless the condition of lacking permanent or even temporary housing owing to poverty

income the amount of new money a person receives in a particular time period, usually a year

low income cut-off (LICO) a Statistics Canada measure of relative poverty—in this case, a person's income in relation to the average income

manifest functions the structural functionalist term for the expected consequences of a social structure, which ensure the smooth functioning of society (for example, the economy's manifest function is the production and distribution of goods and services)

millionaire a person who is able to amass a net worth of at least $1 million

myths widely shared but usually incorrect beliefs about aspects of social reality

patriarchy an ideology, embedded in traditional history, that gives men privilege and dominance over women

political will a government's desire to pursue and effect change; usually a consequence of public pressure

poverty state of being poor; lacking resources to sustain an adequate standard of living. *Absolute poverty* is extreme deprivation that results in starvation or homelessness. *Relative poverty* is having insufficient resources relative to the average standard of living in a particular social context

poverty rate the number of poor persons in a society, sometimes expressed as a ratio of *x* per 1,000

social class a set of hierarchical distinctions drawn between groups and individuals based upon, and often determining, an individual's socio-economic status; in a class system, socio-economic status is often perceived to be linked with other attributes, such as intelligence or "nobility"

social institutions the structural functionalist term for social structures; the assemblages of norms, values, beliefs, statuses, roles, and organizations that collectively answer a society's basic needs (for example, education and family are social institutions)

social mobility a person's movement (usually understood as ascendance) through social class levels

social stratification separation of a society into socio-economic levels; usually a reflection of inequality of opportunity

socio-economic status a person's position in the social hierarchy, determined by their monetary wealth and by the social capital they may possess through membership in a highly regarded or powerful social group

stereotypes generalizations and "stories," usually negative, about a person or group; often used to justify the marginalization of or discrimination against minorities

stigma a social marker that identifies a person as a member of a negatively valued group, race, or ethnicity; a stigma makes a person a target for prejudice and discrimination

systemic discrimination discriminatory practices that are entrenched in the social structures of society

visible minority a (usually marginalized) group in society that visibly differs from mainstream society

wealth a person's total net worth—the sum of his or her assets less his or her liabilities

FOR FURTHER RESEARCH

Big Brothers/Big Sisters of Canada
http://www.bbbsc.ca.

Campaign Against Child Poverty
http://www.childpoverty.com.

Canadian Association of Food Banks
http://www.cafb-acba.ca.

Canadian Business Magazine
http://www.canadianbusiness.com.

Forbes Magazine
http://www.forbes.com.

Salvation Army
http://www.salvationarmy.ca.

For a more complete understanding of the consequences and characteristics of systemic racism, a review of former National Chief of the Assembly of First Nations Matthew Coon Come's October 1, 2001, remarks to the Canadian Bar Association would be valuable. Matthew Coon Come's remarks also serve as a clear illustration of a social conflict perspective on the differences between two groups in society: http://www.ellisctaylor.com/firstnation.html.

For further information about the initiatives of anti-poverty activists, see the following website: http://www.makepovertyhistory.ca/e/aim4.html. See also the following: http://www.campaign2000.ca.

Raising the Roof is an organization devoted specifically to acting on behalf of homeless youth: http://www.raisingtheroof.org/lrn-youth-index.cfm.

REFERENCES

Campaign 2000. (2006). Oh Canada! Too many children in poverty for too long ... 2006 report card on child and family poverty in Canada. (2006). http://www.campaign2000.ca/rc/rc06/06_C2000NationalReportCard.pdf.

Campaign 2000. (2007). It takes a nation to raise a generation: Campaign 2000 report card on child and family poverty 2007. http://www.campaign2000.ca/rc.

Canadian Council on Social Development. (2002). A decade of decline: Poverty and income inequality in the city of Toronto in the 1990s. Retrieved November 26, 2007, from the United Way of Greater Toronto website: http://www.unitedwaytoronto.com/whoWeHelp/reports/Decade_in_Decline/Poverty_Report.htm#top.

Canadian Council on Social Development. (n.d.). Canadian fact book on poverty: Working definitions of poverty. http://www.ccsd.ca/facts.html.

Canadian Encyclopedia. (2007). Welfare state. Citing Briggs, A. (1967). *The welfare state.* http://www.canadianencyclopedia.ca/index.cfm?PgNm=TCE&Params=A1ARTA0008518.

Canadian Labour Congress. (2006). Is your work working for you? Report card 2006. http://www.working4you.ca.

CBC News. (2004, March). No way home. *The Fifth Estate.* http://www.cbc.ca/fifth/main_nowayhome_printer.html.

CBC News. (2006, October). Lost in the struggle. *The Fifth Estate.* http://www.cbc.ca/fifth/lostinthestruggle/hood.html.

CBC News Online. (2007, March). Wage gap widening despite boom: Study. http://www.cbc.ca/canada/story/2007/03/01/wage-gap-070301.html.

City of Toronto. (2000). Housing and homelessness report card. http://www.toronto.ca/homelessness/index.htm.

Cook, D. (2006, December). How transportation stress is being addressed in Ft. McMurray. *Oilsands Review.* http://www.oilsandsreview.com/articles.asp?ID=342.

Farrar, S. (2001, October). Structural racism pushing Canada's indigenous to the edge. *Indian Country Today.* http://www.indiancountry.com/content.cfm?id=2253&print=yes.

Fellegi, I. (2007, September). On poverty and low income. Statistics Canada. http://www.statcan.ca/english/research/13F0027XIE/13F0027XIE1999001.htm.

Government of Newfoundland and Labrador—Fisheries and Aquaculture. (2007, April). Renewing the Newfoundland and Labrador fishing industry. http://www.releases.gov.nl.ca/releases/2007/fishaq/0412n03.htm.

Hay, D. (2007, May). The Feds are widening, not closing the prosperity gap. Special to *The Globe and Mail.* Canadian Policy Research Networks. http://www.cprn.org/doc.cfm?doc=1712&l=en.

Heisz, A. (2006, July). Canada's global cities: Socioeconomic conditions in Montreal, Toronto and Vancouver. Statistics Canada, Ministry of Industry. http://www.statcan.ca/english/research/89-613-MIE/89-613-MIE2006010.pdf.

Howlett, D. (2005, February). We can make child poverty history in Canada. National Anti-Poverty Organization (NAPO). http://www.makepovertyhistory.ca/e/take-action/make-child-poverty-history.pdf.

Human Resources and Social Development Canada. (n.d.). Homelessness partnering strategy. http://homelessness.gc.ca/home/index_e.asp.

Jenson, J. (2003, February). Redesigning the "welfare mix" for families: Policy challenges; Discussion Paper F/30. Family Network. Canadian Policy Research Network. http://www.cprn.org/doc.cfm?doc=157&l=en and http://www.cprn.org.

Khosla, P. (2005). Women and urban environments: Women's poverty in cities. Women's Health and Gender Analysis, Health Canada. http://www.twca.ca/documents/povertyEN.pdf.

Kroll, L., & Fass, A. (Eds.). (2007). The world's billionaires. *Forbes* Magazine Online. http://www.forbes.com/2007/03/07/billionaires-worlds-richest_07billionaires_cz_lk_af_0308billie_land.html.

Lochhead, C., & Scott, K. (2000). The dynamics of women's poverty in Canada. The Canadian Council on Social Development. http://www.swc-cfc.gc.ca/pubs/pubspr/0662281594/200003_0662281594_e.pdf.

Mlynek, A., Olijnyk, Z., Leung, C., Gagné, C., & Magnan, M. (Eds.). (2005). The rich list 2005. *Canadian Business* Online. http://www.canadianbusiness.com/after_hours/lifestyle_activities/article.jsp?content=20051205_73206_73206.

NDP. (2007). Confronting poverty in Canada. http://www.ndp.ca/page/4824.

Ontario Federation of Indian Friendship Centres. (2001). Urban Aboriginal child poverty background. http://www.ofifc.org/page/notes.htm.

Ontario Network for Human Rights. (2001, January). Hidden discrimination and polite racism prevents Aboriginal peoples and visible minorities from gaining equal access to jobs, study finds. http://www.geocities.com/CapitolHill/6174/hidis.html.

O'Reilly, E. (2001). Making career sense of labour market information. (2nd ed.). Human Resources Development. http://makingcareersense.org.

Picot, G., & Myles, J. (2005, February). Income inequality and low income in Canada: An international perspective. Statistics Canada. http://www.statcan.ca/english/research/11F0019MIE/11F0019MIE2005240.pdf.

PovNet. (2004, October). Despite Alberta's oil wealth, poverty is persisting. http://www.povnet.org/node/1021.

Public Health Agency of Canada. (2002). Income inequality as a determinant of health. http://www.phac-aspc.gc.ca/ph-sp/phdd/pdf/overview_implications/02_income_e.pdf.

Raising the Roof. (n.d.). What is the Youthworks initiative? http://www.raisingtheroof.org/lrn-youth-index.cfm.

Rosenberg, I. (Ed.). (2006). World wealth report. Capgemini US. http://www.us.capgemini.com/DownloadLibrary/files/Capgemini_FSI_WWR06.pdf.

Sarlo, C. (2001, July). Measuring poverty in Canada. *Critical Issues Bulletin.* The Fraser Institute. http://www.fraserinstitute.org/Commerce.Web/product_files/Measuring%20Poverty%20in%20Canada%20-%20Part%201-Poverty-part1.pdf.

Shelter House, Thunder Bay. (n.d.). The Reality: Poverty and homelessness in Thunder Bay. http://www.shelterhouse.on.ca/article/the-reality-145.asp.

Sossin, L. (2002). The rule of law and the justiciability of prerogative powers: A comment on Black v. Chretien. *McGill Law Journal.* Retrieved November 26, 2007, from the World Wide Web: http://www.law.utoronto.ca/documents/Sossin/prerogative.pdf.

Statistics Canada. (2007, June). Labour force projections for Canada, 2006–2031. Canadian Economic Observer. http://www.statcan.ca/english/ads/11-010-XPB/pdf/jun07.pdf.

Statistics Canada, Income Statistics Division. (2006, April). Low income cut-offs for 2005 and low income measures for 2004. Income Research Paper Series. Ministry of Industry. http://www.statcan.ca/english/research/75F0002MIE/75F0002MIE2006004.pdf.

Status of Women Canada. (2001, March). Women's economic independence and security: A federal/provincial/territorial strategic framework. Federal/Provincial/Territorial Ministers Responsible for the Status of Women. http://www.swc-cfc.gc.ca/pubs/0662655427/200103_0662655427_e.pdf.

UNICEF Report card 7. (2007). Child poverty in perspective: An overview of child well-being in rich countries. UNICEF Innocenti Research Centre. http://www.unicef-icdc.org/publications/pdf/rc7_eng.pdf.

United Nations Development Program. (2005). Human development report 2005: International cooperation at a crossroads: Aid, trade and security in an unequal world. http://hdr.undp.org/en/media/hdr05_complete.pdf.

United Nations Millennium Development Goals. (2006). What are the millennium development goals? (MDGs). http://www.un.org/millenniumgoals.

United Nations Platform for Action Committee Manitoba [UNPAC]. (2006). Women and the economy: What causes women's inequality? http://www.unpac.ca/economy/whatcauses.html.

United Way of Greater Toronto. (2004, April). Poverty by Postal Code: The Geography of Neighourhood Poverty—City of Toronto 1981–2001. http://www.uwgt.org/whoWeHelp/reports/pdf/PovertybyPostalCodeFinal.pdf.

Youth Shelter Interagency Network. (2007, February). System in crisis: An action plan for the future of Toronto's homeless youth. http://www.toronto.ca/legdocs/mmis/2007/cd/bgrd/backgroundfile-2777.pdf.

CHAPTER 8

Rural and Urban Inequality

CHAPTER OBJECTIVES

After completing this chapter, you will be able to:

Understand significant dimensions of rural and urban inequality

- Urbanization
- Suburbanization and urban sprawl
- Social isolation
- Uneven access to social resources

Understand and apply different sociological perspectives to rural and urban inequality

- Structural functionalist
- Social conflict
- Symbolic interactionist

Identify and critique various responses to social problems related to rural and urban inequality, including responses from

- Government and policy
- Law and policing
- Community
- Individuals

DIMENSIONS

URBANIZATION

In chapter 7 we observed that economic conditions in Canada vary with its regions. Where one lives can strongly affect one's quality of life and social conditions. A key factor in this regard is whether one lives in a rural, urban, or suburban area. Such variables can translate into social issues, and such issues are the subject of this chapter.

Colonial settlement of Canada took place in waves of immigration westward, as new immigrants took over Aboriginal lands. Immigrants to Canada came predominantly from Europe, but also from Asia and—as of the 20th century—from other regions of the world as well. The first waves of settlement produced small, geographically dispersed rural communities based on a diverse range of primary production economies: fishing in the Atlantic regions, for example, and agriculture on the prairies. With time, these small rural communities have become less prominent in Canadian society and economics than our urban areas. Provincial and federal governments have undertaken to subsidize and assist rural communities and local industries, but government intervention can rarely offset broader social and market forces.

However, rural and remote areas remain an important part of Canada. Over 95 percent of our nation's territory is rural. Many people—almost 9 million Canadians—live in rural and remote areas (Public Health Agency of Canada, 2003).

Urban areas are places with a dense human population and an abundance of created structures, such as buildings. In Canada, an urban area is one with over 400 people per square kilometre and over 1,000 people in total (Statistics Canada Dictionary, 2007). All other areas in Canada are considered to be *rural.* Urban areas have existed since ancient times and **rural areas** much longer than that, but until the Industrial Revolution, rural areas predominated. Most people worldwide lived in small agricultural communities. With the Industrial Revolution, people moved into cities to find employment in the new factories and other manufacturing centres.

Urbanization is the movement of the world's population from rural to urban areas. In the 20th century, the human population worldwide rapidly urbanized. In 1900, about 13 percent of the world's population lived in cities; in 1950, the percentage of *urbanites* was 29 percent. By 2005, this percentage had increased to 49 percent. The World Bank projects that 60 percent of the world's population will live in cities by the year 2030 (World Bank, 2005).

In Canada, 20th-century urbanization was even more pronounced than it was worldwide. In 1871, about 20 percent of Canadians lived in cities. By 1961, 70 percent of Canadians did. In 2006, over 80 percent of Canadians lived in urban or suburban areas (Sustainability Report, 2004). It is important to recognize, however, that these statistics are based upon the peculiarly Canadian understanding of "rural" and "urban." As mentioned above, *urban*, by the official Canadian definition, is an area with more than 1,000 people living in relatively close proximity—400 people per square kilometre. It is arguable that Canadian urbanity is to some extent a myth: we choose to see ourselves as urban and sophisticated despite the fact that many of us live in an unsettled northern hinterland.

As the world has urbanized, the cities have grown larger. The world's largest city is Tokyo, Japan, with an estimated population of 31,729,844 in 2000 (Japan Statistics Bureau, 1996–2007). Canada's largest city is Toronto, with a population of 5,555,912 according to the 2006 census (Statistics Canada, 2007). In the 1990s, governmental action forced the *agglomeration* of several municipalities in Ontario and Quebec, which resulted in the creation of what were termed *megacities*—large urban areas made up of what had formerly been several small centres. These megacities made possible the streamlining of local government and the coordination of transportation. But many people were, and are, opposed to municipal agglomeration because they believe it decreases the accountability of politicians and school boards and reduces the reach of public transport and local health care.

Traditionally, urbanization followed the centralization of production and commerce; people gathered around a central *downtown* core in order to participate in economic activities. But in the 20th century, despite the fact that urbanization was increasing, many downtown cores in North America began to decay. **Urban decay** refers to a city's falling, in whole or in part, into disrepair. Among its symptoms are depopulation, abandonment of inner city property, a high unemployment rate in downtown areas, family fragmentation, high crime rates, and the political disenfranchisement of downtown residents. There are many reasons for urban decay. A combination of factors tends to cause it: planning decisions by municipal governments providing incentives for people and businesses to relocate; suburbanization in general; immigration restrictions; and racial discrimination.

Over 70 percent of Canada's poor live in our largest urban centres (Canadian Council on Social Development, 2007). At the same time, the costliest accommodation is in these urban areas. Both employed and unemployed struggle to find affordable housing and often spend a large proportion of their household income on accommodation. The high cost of accommodation makes it difficult for poor families to meet their basic needs. Urban poverty too often leads to homelessness, as is discussed in more detail in chapter 7. Today's urban poor sometimes have more trouble surviving than the rural poor once did. In rural areas, people could often grow or hunt food to meet their basic survival needs. City dwellers are completely dependent on employment and social assistance.

Urbanization can negatively affect rural areas in several ways. In Canada, it has placed heavy burdens on government and infrastructure funding for which all citizens—not just city dwellers—must pay. Many Canadians like to believe in the equality of all Canadian communities—large or small, urban or rural. But the unique and growing needs of big cities belie this belief. For example, the provincial government funnels considerable money into Toronto—subsidizing public transportation, for example—because it is a populous city and a primary driver of the province's economy. This causes citizens of smaller, less prosperous communities to grumble that Toronto gets "favoured."

One might well ask: are governments really trying to address rural needs equitably? Urban areas are increasingly short of physicians and other health-care workers, but so are rural areas—because of urbanization. Young people growing up in rural areas are often drawn to cities by the lure of money, education, and work, among other opportunities; hence, the average age of rural people is increasing. The elderly require more medical attention than the young, and the aging rural population is overwhelming the already meagre health-care services available to them. Another problem for rural Canadians is that technology in farming has increased farm sizes and reduced the personnel required to run them. Many small farmers and their families have been forced to leave the land. The amalgamation of farms and the exodus of people have hurt the economic viability of rural service communities. At the same time, Canada's birth rate continues to be low, and we maintain our population through immigration. Immigrants tend to settle in major urban centres where, as they see it, job opportunities are better and where there are other people like themselves, with similar ethnic backgrounds. These trends present problems for rural areas trying to retain their population levels and pursue economic development.

Urbanization continues in Canada. At the same time, economic opportunities have emerged in rural areas: tourism; organic farming; and recreational developments and retirement homes for Canada's aging baby boomers. Some have called it the "new rural economy."

SUBURBANIZATION AND URBAN SPRAWL

Both a cause and an effect of urban decay is the movement of affluent residential areas away from downtown cores. Urban sprawl and **suburbanization** are the consequence of this movement. *Suburbanization* is the movement of people away from city cores and small towns into fringe areas bordering the major urban centres. The trend toward suburbanization remains strong, although there has recently been a contrary movement back to inner city living by young and affluent professionals. In Toronto, for example, this trend has caused a boom in the construction of inner city condominiums. Suburbs tend to have relatively low population density. Suburbanites live in single-family homes and commute to work in the downtown core by automobile or public transit. Suburban communities tend to be founded on the notion that motor vehicles will be used for virtually all activities of life. It is impractical for suburban dwellers not to own a car.

Suburbanization creates social and environmental issues. The heavy reliance on motor vehicles contributes to the carbon emissions now linked to global warming, and leads to motor vehicle fatalities. It also contributes to the poor health of commuters, whose sedentary jobs, in combination with long hours in the car, may lead to poor fitness levels and obesity. Long commutes to work have been linked to headaches, chest pain, high blood pressure, increased absence from work, and lack of time for exercise (Weiss, 2007). Long commutes are also associated with *road rage*, or angry, violent behaviour by drivers. They can also affect a commuter's family life; the hours spent commuting cut into the time commuters could otherwise spend with their families.

Suburbanization is one of several causes of **urban sprawl**, which is the geographic spreading of urban development across formerly rural land. Urban sprawl poses environmental concerns because of its contribution to carbon emissions and because the land it consumes is no longer available to plant and animal species.

In small communities, wealthy and poor individuals often live in close proximity. With increased urbanization, there tends to be segregation on the basis of race or class. Since at least 1980 in North America, there has been a per capita income gap between central areas of cities and suburban regions. Lower-income people often live in urban areas or "poor" suburbs, while people of different income levels live in integrated communities (Casey, Dreier, Flack, & Swanstrom, 2004). Housing subdivisions—tracts of land containing many similar, similarly priced residences, built around the same time—are a central feature of suburbanization. This architectural *homogeneity* promotes segregation on the basis of social status. Suburbanites commonly interact only with those of a comparable social status—that is, with neighbours. Indeed, the desire for such segregation is one of the causes of suburbanization. Social researchers have linked the growth of suburban areas with racial segregation. As discussed in chapter 7, people of visible minority status in North America are disproportionately poorer than their white counterparts. Economic differentials between ethnic groups, "steering" by real estate agents, and home buyers' desire to live in their own ethnic communities (as in, for example, Chinatown)—these factors have contributed to the creation of racial and ethnic "enclaves" in suburbia (Thomas, 2003).

SOCIAL ISOLATION

There are many ways to be isolated. Rural, urban, and suburban communities all offer different forms of connectedness and isolation. The rural communities of Canada's North are obviously isolated in a geographic sense. This can present problems for inhabitants who need medical care or other resources. In our harsh northern climate, the weather can be a serious challenge for rural people. Many people in the Canadian Shield, across northern Ontario and Quebec, are snowed in for months every year, their communities accessible only by plane. In the Yukon and Northwest Territories, communities are sometimes accessible only by ice road. Blizzards still represent a very real danger for people across Canada.

But despite their geographic isolation, people in rural communities often have close-knit networks of relatives, friends, and religious institutions. For example, women victimized by domestic violence in rural areas can sometimes find shelter in informal settings with friends, relatives, or church leaders, whereas urban women may not have such resources. Of course, the very closeness of rural communities can sometimes be a problem. "Close-knit" can mean *closed*. For example, class divisions among families in small communities can be almost insurmountable. And rural communities can be uncomfortable places for people who experience gender dissonance, such as homosexual people and transsexuals. Such people tend to move from rural areas to cities, where they are more likely to find like-minded individuals and communities where they are accepted.

Where rural dwellers often compensate for their physical isolation by establishing close ties in their community, urbanites often experience *social isolation*. Canada's urban dwellers are highly mobile. They may live thousands of miles from family members, in a place where they only stay a year or two. Nineteenth-century pioneering sociologist Emile Durkheim noted how urbanization had contributed to impersonality in people's lives. He saw that urban people lack deep relationships with those around them and often find themselves "alone in a crowd," not attached to their neighbours by common histories or shared values. He called this state "*anomie*," and linked it to depression, deviant behaviour, crime, and suicide. Of course, urban life is not isolated in every sense. Vibrant cultural communities exist in urban centres; clubs, community organizations, restaurants, and theatres afford people social opportunities.

Suburbs, offering neither the vibrant culture of urban communities nor the close community ties of rural ones, have been linked by some writers to depression. The crushing homogeneity of suburban life can lead people to question their position and purpose in life. Historically, this has been especially true for suburban women, long relegated to lonely days of homemaking while their husbands went off to work in the city. Betty Friedan, in *The Feminine Mystique* (1963), documented the unease and depression of middle-class American women living in the suburbs. She found that these women, socially isolated and unfulfilled by housework, were experiencing serious psychological problems. Suburban conformity was satirized in the 1972 book by Ira Levin *The Stepford Wives*—a horror story in which a woman moves to a suburban community and discovers that the other women in the town have been murdered and replaced by life-like robots.

UNEVEN ACCESS TO SOCIAL RESOURCES

Access to Professional Services

Canada's socialized health-care system originated in 1946 in Saskatchewan and became a reality across the country with the passage of the *Medical Care Act* in 1966. Under this system, all of us have equal access to free medical care. The system has been held up as an example to the world, and particularly to the United States, where over 45 million people do not have medical insurance and have to pay for medical treatment themselves. Michael Moore's celebrated 2007 documentary *Sicko* held up Canada's health-care system as an example of how the American system could be improved.

However, there are growing problems with Canada's health-care system. Canada is currently facing a crisis in doctor shortages, especially in rural areas. A study released by the Canadian Institute of Health Information in 2006 indicated that the less than 9 percent of Canada's doctors working in rural areas are serving over 20 percent of the country's population (Global National, 2006). Doctor shortages are most acute in rural areas, but even some provincial capitals, such as Winnipeg, are now experiencing them (CBC News, 2000). According to Statistics Canada, more than 3.6 million Canadians—nearly 15 percent of the population—do not have a family doctor (Krauss, 2004). There are vacant positions for physicians across the country. Patients can wait years for diagnostic tests, cancer treatments, and surgeries. And, although the vast majority of Canadians profess to support our public health-care system quite passionately, every year thousands of Canadians travel to the United States and elsewhere to pay for faster treatment in private hospitals. The government is trying to remedy the doctor shortage, with initiatives we will discuss in the "Responses" section below. But recent reports predict that the number of doctors per capita in Canada will continue to decline until at least 2015 (CBC News, 2006).

There are several factors contributing to the physician shortage. The number of physicians in Canada has not grown in proportion to our population. The Canadian Medical Association estimated in 2004 that Canada needed to graduate 2,500 physicians from medical school each year. At the time, only 2,200 new doctors were graduating annually. More and more family physicians, especially women, are working shorter hours to accommodate their family and other needs. At the same time, the population is aging, which is increasing the general need for medical care.

The shortage of physicians has a wide range of consequences. Physicians in under-serviced areas can barely meet the demands of their communities. Distances are a problem for patients in rural areas. While people in urban areas have to travel, on average, only 3 kilometres to see a pediatrician, for example, people in rural areas can expect to travel an average of 149 kilometres. It is worse in Canada's northern territories; there, the average distance to a pediatrician is 846 kilometres (Global National, 2006). The long waits and long drives required of many sick Canadians do their medical problems no good.

The doctor shortage in Canada is well documented. It is less well known that other professional shortages are beginning to be felt, particularly in rural areas of Canada and especially in the North. Politicians and local officials have begun to document and are seeking to respond to a shortage of lawyers. In a process many call the "graying of the bar," few new lawyers are setting up practices in Canada's rural and, especially, northern towns. Members of these communities who have complained to media and government that they are unable to access lawyers are defining this problem as a social issue. Not just lawyers, but judges, too, are under-represented in rural communities.

Several factors are contributing to the shortage of lawyers in rural communities. One is the closure of some rural courthouses. Another is the increased mobility of the public. As urban sprawl continues, people are growing accustomed to driving long distances to access services. Some of the factors in the growing lawyer shortage are the same as those in the physician shortage: not enough lawyers graduating annually; female lawyers opting for part-time work. But the problem is different because legal services are privately run and not government funded. Law students are drawn by the prospect of high salaries to do corporate/commercial work in major urban centres, such as Toronto and Calgary. The most talented students are actively recruited by large urban firms who service multinational corporations and wealthy individuals. Given this trend, many question whether it is appropriate for the government to fund law schools and invest in students' legal educations while average Canadians face shortages, and whether there should be governmental regulation—as with health care—to ensure that all Canadians have access to justice.

As is discussed in the "Responses" section below, governments are taking measures to encourage doctors to set up practices in rural areas. They are also beginning to address rural shortages of lawyers and other professionals.

Access to Abortion

Unequal access to professional and other social services can impinge on people's human rights. One health service that remains especially controversial in Canada is therapeutic **abortion**, which is the procedure of expelling an embryo or fetus from a woman's uterus in order to terminate a pregnancy. In Canada, a woman's right to choose when and whether she will have children is considered part of her legal right to liberty and security of the person. Abortion has been performed throughout human history by many different methods. Internationally, about 46 million abortions are performed every year. Around the world, there are about 26 induced abortions for every 100 known pregnancies (Henshaw, Singh, & Haas, 1999). In Canada, about 110,000 abortions are performed annually, about 30 abortions for every 100 live births (Statistics Canada, 2004). In 1998, women from 27 countries were asked why they would seek abortions, and the most common reasons cited were the following: concern over the interruption of work or education; financial and relationship issues; and their own immaturity and unreadiness to have children (Bankole, Singh, & Haas, 1998).

In many countries, inducing abortion is illegal. In Canada, abortion was illegal for 100 years, from 1869 to 1969. It was punishable by life imprisonment for abortion providers; there were criminal penalties for women who underwent the procedures. These laws were actively enforced until 1969, when Pierre Trudeau amended the *Criminal Code* to allow for abortions in certain circumstances. Making abortions illegal did not prevent them from taking place—it simply drove them underground. Many women died or were permanently harmed from undergoing illegal abortions in unsanitary conditions.

Abortion remains a controversial issue among some Canadians, but the matter is legally settled. In the 1960s and 1970s, Dr. Henry Morgentaler began performing safe, sanitary, therapeutic abortions at clinics across Canada, openly flouting the criminal prohibition against doing so. He was jailed in 1974. Upon release, Dr. Morgentaler continued to perform therapeutic abortions. Since the Supreme Court of Canada (1988) issued its decision in *R v. Morgentaler*, abortion has been legal in Canada, considered a health-care issue and not a matter for the criminal law. Canada is unusual among countries worldwide in that the law imposes no restrictions upon the time during a pregnancy at which abortion is permitted. Although it is—strictly speaking—legal for a woman to have an abortion at any point during a pregnancy, most health-care practitioners will not perform late-term abortions. Over 90 percent of abortions in Canada take place before the fetus is 12 weeks in gestational age, while only about 2 to 3 percent of abortions are performed after the fetus is 16 weeks old (Statistics Canada, 2004).

Although all women in Canada are legally entitled to choose whether to carry a pregnancy to term, many women, for all practical purposes, still have no access to abortions. The right to exercise reproductive choice is always in jeopardy. Abortion clinics and practitioners face risks—attacks on clinics and abortion providers are not uncommon. There have been a number of fatal sniper attacks on abortion doctors in Canada and the United States (Brewer, 2001). In 1992, Dr. Morgentaler's Toronto clinic was bombed, one of many such incidents of violence perpetrated by those who oppose abortion.

There is another interesting statistic concerning abortion and crime. In the 1990s, US researchers proposed a link between the legalization of abortion 20 years before and a dramatic decline in the current crime rate. Economists Steven D. Levitt and John Donohue (2001), in their 1999 paper "The Impact of Legalized Abortion Upon Crime," suggested that legalized access to abortion reduced the birth rate of children at high risk of committing crime. Their suggestion that legal access to abortion ultimately protects the general public has been highly controversial. But as yet no statistical evidence has refuted it.

Both provincial governments and health-care providers have resisted the legalizing of abortion. It has been a struggle to get provincial governments to allow for, let alone ensure, access to abortion across Canada. Canadian federal law requires that all provinces fund abortion clinics fully. However, not all provinces comply with this mandate; Quebec and Nova Scotia provide only limited funding, while New Brunswick provides none at all. Until 2004, Manitoba did not fund abortion clinics, either. But that year a not-for-profit organization successfully sued the government over its failure to fund clinics. Not all Canadian medical schools provide or require training in how to perform abortions.

Even where government funding is not a central issue, women in rural areas may have trouble accessing abortion. In rural and northern areas, especially in the Atlantic provinces of New Brunswick, Nova Scotia, and Prince Edward Island, facilities that provide legal abortions are likely to be distant. There are currently no facilities in Prince Edward Island that perform abortions. Rural women often have to travel long distances at their own expense to obtain abortions. Some Canadian hospitals may refuse to provide abortions to patients from out of province. This poses a particular problem for women from PEI.

ANALYSIS

SOCIAL ISSUES OF URBAN–RURAL DIFFERENCES IN CANADA

Canada as a nation offers one of the best standards of living in the world. It is part of the world's economic core, and its territory is one of the largest in the world. Canada is also one of the least populated nations in the world. It is also a somewhat unusual country in that it has been shaped by its dualities: of indigenous and immigrant, of rural and urban, and of high tech and low tech. The urban–rural contrasts and competitions are the social issue focus of this chapter.

Public awareness of urban–rural tensions has emerged from environmental concerns about the degradation of Canada's rural communities, the waste of its farmlands, and the destruction of its wilderness. Public concerns about global warming and greenhouse gas emissions have brought attention to bear on the damaging consequences of urbanization. In this chapter, we will look at urban sprawl as a social issue.

Identifying a Social Issue

WHO OR WHAT GROUPS ARE CALLING FOR ATTENTION, AND WHAT IS THEIR CONCERN?

The Canadian Urban Institute's definition of *urban sprawl* is as follows: "new development consuming land at a faster rate than the rate at which the population is growing" (Pim & Ornoy, 2005, p. 8). The Green Door Alliance, a community environmental group in Toronto, provides another definition: "Urban sprawl is low-density development ... which separates where people live from where they shop, work and recreate—thus requiring cars to travel between zones" (p. 8).

The Sierra Club (2007) of Canada attributes traffic congestion, air pollution, waste-disposal problems, and the loss of some of the county's most productive farmland to the unregulated urban growth across much of Canada. This view is endorsed by the David Suzuki Foundation, in its recent publication *Understanding Sprawl* (Gurin, 2003). The Sierra Club has also suggested the following: that, since 1994, about 50,000 hectares of prime farmland around Montreal alone have been lost to urban sprawl; that the desire of urbanites to escape the expenses and crowding of cities has pushed the growth of suburban development; and that such growth trends have created an inevitable but unsustainable dependence on the automobile (Sierra Club of Canada, 2007). Automobile emissions make up a significant portion of the greenhouse gas emissions that create global warming. Urban sprawl has been cited as the cause of other problems currently facing Canadians: increased air pollution, which has been linked, in turn, to a rising incidence of cancer; sky-rocketing numbers of asthma sufferers; rising obesity rates; a growing number of traffic fatalities and injuries; and increased social isolation, which can result in mental health problems (Bray, Vakil, & Elliott, 2005).

WHAT IS THE VISION OR GOAL OF THE VOICES OF CONCERN?

Arresting the output of **greenhouse gases** is a number-one priority for Canadians committed to curbing **global warming**. Reducing dependence on auto travel will do a great deal to reduce these gases (Sierra Club of Canada, 2007). David Suzuki has affirmed that addressing sprawl is crucial to helping Canada meet its **Kyoto Accord** targets (David Suzuki Foundation, 2003). The Sierra Club (USA) has designed and recommended a path of change called "smart growth" (Sierra Club, 2001). **Smart growth** is defined as "intelligent, well-planned development that channels growth into existing areas, provides transportation choices and preserves farm land and open space" (Sierra Club, 2001). The benefits of smart growth would be many, but can be summed up as a reduction in our dependence on the automobile. This would lead to health-related improvements and to reduced pressures on the natural environment. The Sierra Club (USA) projects that, in 50 years, smart growth would reduce carbon emissions by 200 million metric tons per year. The Ontario College of Family Physicians, cited by the CNW Group (2005), has said that how we choose to build our communities has a direct impact on the health of our citizens. Only through deliberate planning to contain sprawl will we create safe, healthy, and integrated communities.

WHAT ARE THE MEANS OF ACHIEVING THE GOALS?

Urban sprawl has been defined as *unchecked* urban growth. Redirecting—that is, *checking*—urban growth is primarily a responsibility of government. Organizations working for an improved environment, for improved public health, and for reductions in greenhouse gases all recommend that strong government action is needed. The Ontario government may be beginning to respond. In 2004, Ontario put forth a plan called "Places to Grow: Better Choices, Better Future" that addresses urban planning, land use, economic development, and infrastructure. The plan proposed changes in such areas as laws, tax laws, and land use costs to make fringe development less viable (Adair, 2004).

The second necessity identified by the organizations for change is a strong voice from the citizenry. Only a strong public voice will encourage governments to oppose developers whose interests are contrary to the public's. The David Suzuki Foundation's report on the dangers of urban sprawl included a "tool kit" instructing citizens in how to pressure government to act against urban sprawl (David Suzuki Foundation, 2003).

Finally, the academic community has been publishing reports on the dangers of greenhouse gas emissions and their role in global warming, and these reports have been alerting the public about popular trends that contribute to global warming. Some academics are also calling for a restructuring of government—that is, for breaking new ground in intergovernmental relations. A policy brief published by the University of Saskatchewan has suggested that, although urban and rural interests have always tended to conflict, the dangers posed by urban sprawl to public health and the environment make it necessary that urban and rural communities, with their respective governments, make common cause. Doing so would open the door to partnerships that could resolve many sprawl-related problems (Olfert & Partridge, 2005). Furthermore, Canada's lack of a federal agricultural policy means that there are no incentives for farmers to continue farming and thereby slow the spread of urban development. This general lack of policy and planning has meant that development has been at once costly and amorphous. Clearly, the established approach is no longer suitable, and a restructuring of government responsibilities is needed (Pim & Ornoy, 2005).

More specific objectives have been identified in P.J. Wade's article "Urban Sprawl Threatens Canadian Lives" (2003). She cites Suzuki's demand that provincial governments

- Legislate urban growth boundaries
- Increase funding for public transit
- Intensify town centres by enhancing economic activity and promoting mixed-use development
- Create more compact cities with better bike paths and pedestrian-friendly walkways

Evolution of the Social Issue of Urban Sprawl

WHAT GROUPS AND ORGANIZATIONS ARE ADVOCATING CHANGE?

Because of the ties between urban sprawl and global warming, there are a number of environmental organizations interested in curbing the former. Some of these organizations are specifically advocates of **sustainable development**. The David Suzuki Foundation and the Sierra Club of Canada are prominent among the voices warning against urban sprawl. Others are the Ontario Smart Growth Network and the Federation of Ontario Naturalists. Other groups and organizations are connected to the issue by virtue of their concern for problems linked to urban sprawl, such as the loss of farmland to highways, health problems related to air pollution, and the rise in childhood obesity (children must be driven everywhere because distance and safety concerns preclude their walking). The Pembina Institute and the College of Family Physicians are two such organizations.

WHAT HAS PROMPTED PUBLIC AWARENESS AND CONCERN?

For most people, having an urban lifestyle and an automobile are markers of success. Most people do not question urban sprawl because they themselves aspire to a home in the "country" with all of the amenities of city living, a place from which they can commute to work and school. But the spectre of global warming has people reconsidering this standard lifestyle. People are beginning to reduce their carbon emissions and, evidently, to question their own behaviours. If the media continues to publicize the "green" voices, the public will start to link urban spread with rising greenhouse emissions and with problems related to health. Government policies limiting development will prompt public debate over urban sprawl. To date, however, public awareness of the relationship between greenhouse gas emissions and urban development is weak.

HOW IS THE PUBLIC ALIGNED?

The statistics reflect disregard in Canada for the problems being created by the spread of cities into the countryside. The current growth rate in peripheral municipalities—the areas surrounding the core cities of Canada's 33 census metropolitan areas—is 11.1 percent, more than double the national growth rate of 5.4 percent, according to figures recently released by Statistics Canada. The report identified Milton, Ontario, as the fastest growing municipality. Milton, just west of Toronto, showed a 71.4 percent increase in population. The average growth rate in the urban core of Canadian cities is 4.2 percent (Bonnell, 2007).

Canadians are beginning to talk about the need for change, but they have yet to walk their talk (Pim & Ornoy, 2005). According to a July 2002 Environics poll commissioned by the Sustainability Network for the Federation of Ontario Naturalists and other conservation groups, over one-third of Ontarians were *very concerned* that neighbourhoods and businesses in the downtown cores of cities and towns are being hurt by the suburban spread of commercial strips and big-box stores. Despite the poll results, little real action has been taken to reduce suburban spread.

WHAT INITIATIVES HAVE BEEN TAKEN AND WHAT POLICIES HAVE BEEN PUT IN PLACE?

The organizations opposed to urban sprawl are lobbying for government intervention. The Kyoto standards for greenhouse gas emissions have made containing urban development seem an urgent matter in Canada. Some small steps have been taken, but flaws persist in the way development is governed and in the interactions between urban and rural authorities. Nevertheless, the plan drafted for the Niagara region of Ontario represents a useful step toward sustainable urban development (Minister of Infrastructure Renewal, 2006). Another is a BC initiative called Smart Growth BC. Canadians in general are concerned that farmers across the country are being forced to till poorer land as cities gobble up the good soil (Paraskevas, 2005). One response has been the development of organizations devoted to creating sustainable communities. Smart Growth BC is one of these organizations.

WHAT IS THE PUBLIC REACTION?

Canadians appear concerned about global warming, but are less familiar with the hazards of urban sprawl. As a social issue, urban sprawl is in an emerging state.

ANALYTICAL APPROACHES TO UNDERSTANDING URBAN SPRAWL

Our theoretical analysis of the urban–rural relationship in Canada will begin with a structural functionalist analysis, which will show urban sprawl to be the result of legislative failures or dysfunctions. Then we will use a social conflict analysis to explain why Canada is slow to correct the dysfunctions that encourage sprawl. We will conclude with a brief symbolic interactionist assessment of the health consequences of urban sprawl.

A Structural Functionalist Analysis of Urban Sprawl

BRIEF REVIEW OF THE STRUCTURAL FUNCTIONALIST PERSPECTIVE

From the structural functionalist perspective, a social issue is a dysfunction in the system. The dysfunction to be examined here has to do with the automobile.

The development of Detroit clearly shows how the automobile has shaped the modern city. Detroit is representative in this respect (Sugrue, 2004). Modern cities have been built to accommodate the automobile. The architecture of our homes and of our shopping malls was devised with the car in mind. Less of our urban space than you might expect is actually used for people; a full 40 percent is devoted to the automobile (Gellner, 2006).

Designing cities around the automobile originally served the public interests of enabling people to live away from the grime of the industrial sectors of the city and to escape, more generally, the city core's bustle and noise. But the consequences of this arrangement—people driving into the city to work—are hugely dysfunctional: air pollution, degraded city cores, segregated neighbourhoods, and road hazards of unprecedented magnitude. In short, the functional success of the automobile has led to the demise of the city—a dysfunction.

MANIFEST FUNCTIONS AND DYSFUNCTIONS

In Canada as in most democratic nations, the government and the economy work hand in hand—a benefit to all. Sometimes, however, success in one can cause dysfunction in the other. The dysfunction of urban sprawl is one such example.

The economy is based on free enterprise—the provision of goods and services according to market demand and in order to generate profit. Land is a commodity that is traded in the free market system. As the demand for family-friendly living increased during the post-World War II economic boom, suburban development flourished. Land at the periphery of cities—unwanted by industry—was inexpensive and lightly taxed, and plentiful compared with land in the city centre. These factors, together with the tremendous success of the private automobile industry, brought about the boom in suburban development.

The government's role in general is to provide the public with goods and services. Municipal government services encompass water and waste disposal, public transit, and schools. Such services are more easily provided in high-density regions than in low-density ones, such as suburbs, but the government is obliged to provide them everywhere. Funding the services in low-density suburbs has become increasingly burdensome for municipalities. Their response has been to introduce cutbacks and to encourage commercial and secondary industry in the suburbs. Cutbacks have resulted in some tragedies, such as the 2001 Walkerton water scandal, and in the curtailing of services, such as public transit. To raise additional revenue, municipal governments have encouraged commercial and light industrial development (the manufacturing of consumer products in industrial parks at the periphery of most cities) in suburban areas, but in doing so have allocated money from certain services, such as public transit, to road and expressway development. In short, commercial and industrial development in suburban areas increases revenues for municipalities while fostering unsustainable dependence on the automobile. Implicit in the word "unsustainable" is *dysfunction*. For a good summary of these issues, see "Green Issues? Canadians Choose Urban Sprawl in Staggering Numbers: Census" (Bonnell, 2007).

EVIDENCE OF DYSFUNCTIONS

Increased Traffic Congestion

Up to half the land used in urban areas is used to accommodate vehicles, moving or standing. The number of automobiles in Canada has more than doubled in the last 20 years, but road capacity has increased by only 7 percent.

Increased Greenhouse Gas Emissions

Statistics Canada reports that vehicles consuming fossil fuels produce approximately 27 percent of all greenhouse gases emitted in Canada.

Decline of the Urban Core

As suburbs advance, the city core tends to deteriorate. The so-called doughnut effect is most marked in US cities, but Canadian cities are touched with it. In 2005, 91 percent of Ontarians lived in urban areas, but many urgent urban needs have been largely ignored by the government. Only in the last two years has there been any sign that these issues will be addressed at both provincial and federal levels.

Decline in Environmental Health

Loss of green space is not merely troubling to people; it means loss of habitat for wildlife and diminished air and water quality for all creatures (Pim & Ornoy, 2005).

Increased Obesity Rates

Recent studies have looked at obesity in suburbanites. Those living in suburban areas weigh, on average, six pounds more than those living in compact communities. Commuter lifestyles are not conducive to fitness routines or stress-relieving activities. The consequence is obesity and its related health problems.

Decline in Quality of Life

Toronto's former mayor John Sewell has observed that suburbs are designed to reduce social contact and interaction, and that the low population densities in suburbs preclude reliance on public transit (Wade, 2003).

Loss of Prime Agricultural Land

Loss of prime agricultural land is perhaps the most directly negative impact of urban sprawl. In 1971, urban areas occupied less than 6 percent of "Class 1" land in Ontario. By 2001, that had increased to 11 percent (Paraskevas, 2005).

Damage to Health

The Ontario Medical Association estimates that 1,900 Ontarians die prematurely each year from air pollution (Pim & Ornoy, 2005). Poor air quality caused by commuters' cars is being blamed for the astronomical increase in the incidence of asthma (David Suzuki Foundation, 2003).

Questions That Guide a Structural Functionalist Analysis

WHAT SOCIAL INSTITUTIONS ARE CENTRALLY INVOLVED?

The government and the economy are central to the issue of urban sprawl, but there are other social institutions critically involved. The family is involved insofar as the housing market, and especially suburban development, is driven by young families. Because of the health problems linked to urban sprawl, the institution of health care is also crucially involved. The media also plays an important role in promoting public awareness of problems generated by sprawl.

WHAT ARE THE MANIFEST FUNCTIONS? WHAT ARE THE DYSFUNCTIONS THAT RESULT IN URBAN SPRAWL? WHAT ARE THE DYSFUNCTIONS THAT RESULT FROM URBAN SPRAWL?

The manifest functions of the economy are to produce and distribute goods and services and to provide employment. Land and housing are significant commodities of the economy. In fact, one often measures the health of an economy by the number of housing purchases and the land values. In the case of urban sprawl, the trade of real estate and the development of residential housing are controlled by developers; they alone reap the rewards of suburban development. The compromising of citizen health, the loss of **green space**, the polluting of air and water—these are the deeper costs of development, and they are paid by taxpayers, not developers. Clearly, there is a dysfunction in this arrangement.

The manifest functions of government are to provide public services and to regulate the economy. Uncontrolled urban development that is eating up prime farmland and creating health hazards is glaring evidence of the inability of government to guide the real estate and development market.

The dysfunctional relationship between the government and the economy is producing physical and mental health burdens, losses in the agricultural sector of the economy, and environmental cleanup costs.

SOCIAL ACTIONS THAT HAVE LED TO DYSFUNCTIONS

Critics have charged the Ontario government with various faults in policy-making. Upper levels of government have shifted responsibility for social services onto the municipal level. With this new financial pressure, municipalities have encouraged urban development in an effort to boost municipal tax revenues. Such an arrangement is not sustainable.

In Ontario, the Ontario Municipal Board is supposed to oversee land-use planning. Currently, it tends to be developer-friendly, and the planning process is structured in an adversarial way that puts citizen groups and municipalities at a disadvantage. Land-use appeals from developers tend to be expensive for municipalities, so municipalities choose concessions rather than challenges.

There are no regional planning authorities. This means that planning is done haphazardly, on a community-by-community basis. As a result, no economies of scale can be realized and there is no consistency in planning objectives.

Property tax structures tend to penalize farmers and define green areas as waste land. The result is the growth of low-density residential areas and low-density light industry. Nowhere in the tax structures is the health and environmental value of green spaces recognized (Pim & Ornoy, 2005; Gurin, 2003).

There is a lack of existing legislation for curtailing the growth of urban areas and encouraging homeownership in urban centres. Ontario is not unique in this respect. Prospective homeowners, even those aware of global warming and of the problems posed by urban sprawl, cannot meet the high cost of living in an urban centre. Such people feel that they have no recourse but to locate outside the city centre and commute to work (Bonnell, 2007).

Following is a structural functionalist analysis chart. The social actions that have led to the dysfunctions associated with urban sprawl—dysfunctions we have now identified—have been included in the table. The completed table will constitute a summary analysis of this issue from a structural functionalist point of view.

ACTIONS THAT WOULD RESTORE SYSTEM EQUILIBRIUM

Curbing the four social actions described above would do a great deal to check urban sprawl. But to do so would require strong government leadership. According to the David Suzuki Foundation (2003), provincial governments need to

- Establish a legislated urban growth boundary to protect agricultural and rural areas
- Put more funding into public transit
- Invigorate town centres by encouraging economic activity and variegating development
- Make cities more compact, with better bike paths and walkways for pedestrians

In short, we need to make better use of our urban space before expanding into—and destroying—the countryside.

A Social Conflict Analysis of Urban Sprawl

BRIEF REVIEW OF THE SOCIAL CONFLICT PERSPECTIVE

A social conflict orientation enables the analyst to look at social change in terms of key parties involved and their interests in an issue. It also enables the analyst to predict the direction an issue will take. No one would suggest that any group or organ-

Structural Functionalist Analysis of Urban Sprawl			
Social Action	**Social Institution**	**Manifest Function of Social Institution**	**Dysfunction**
Responsibility for social services shifted to municipal governments			
Ontario Municipal Board is developer-friendly and adversarial for citizens' groups and municipalities			
Planning authorities act independently without regional considerations			
Tax structures define green spaces and farmland as "waste land"			
Cost of living in urban centres significantly higher than in suburbs			

ization actually wants urban sprawl. But a structural functionalist analysis has shown that powerful forces stand in the way of our controlling it. A social conflict analysis should help us understand why so little is being done to stop urban sprawl.

ANALYSIS OF URBAN SPRAWL

Urban sprawl is uncontrolled urban development. The term *uncontrolled* suggests a lack of power. The term *development* suggests that there are organizations driving and thus benefiting from this process. A social conflict analysis will help us see the major stakeholders in the issue and understand their power differences. How close we are to resolving the issue depends on which side is likely to be dominant in the days ahead.

Prevailing Power Relationships

Developers are the only group benefiting from urban spread. The citizen groups who oppose them—who wish to diminish our **ecological footprint** by preserving our agricultural and green spaces—do not appear to be making much headway. Statistics show that suburban growth still greatly exceeds urban growth (Bonnell, 2007). The costs of this, in terms of human health, are mounting (Wade, 2003).

Since 2003, lobby groups in Canada have been calling on federal and provincial governments to act. But little has been accomplished.

Predicting the Future of the Issue

As long as it is legally permissible to build low-density residential and industrial suburbs, and as long as tax structures and laws make suburban living more favourable than urban living for many people, little will change. Activists invariably appeal to the public to get involved. Evidently, the key to changing the course of events is a strong public voice. It is likely that, as the damaging effects of urban sprawl are increasingly felt by Canadians, the public will voice its discontent and the voice will be heard and responded to.

QUESTIONS THAT GUIDE A SOCIAL CONFLICT ANALYSIS

Who Are the Major Stakeholders in the Issue?

The developers and the public they serve dominate the issue. A strong oil and gas and auto manufacturing sector supports the developer side in the issue. The consuming public is by and large ignorant of the subsidies that steer them toward suburban living; they too support the developer side. On the other side are "green" organizations that are working to educate the public and lobbying the government to step in and act for the environment. These organizations include the David Suzuki Foundation, the Sierra Club of Canada, Ontario Naturalists Organization, and the Sustainable Communities Network.

What Are the Resources of Each Stakeholder Group?

The developer side is well entrenched. It is supported by the "car culture" and has a well-established and sophisticated marketing strategy (Gurin, 2003). Existing laws, tax structures, and government agencies all support the developer at the expense of competing interests such as agricultural development (Pim & Ornoy, 2005). Developers also have the support of a consumer culture that tends to prefer technological innovation to real change. For example, rather than reverse the migration to suburbs, consumers pressure the market for "green technologies" like the hybrid car (Bonnell, 2007).

Specific events and circumstances have benefited the pro-development side (Pim & Ornoy, 2005):

- The ground-breaking recommendations of the Commission on Planning and Development were abandoned in 1996.
- Downtown real estate prices make housing unaffordable for most prospective home buyers with families.
- Building on **greenfield**—that is, farmland untouched by industry or development—is highly convenient and profitable.
- Low commodity prices make sale of farm land to developers irresistible for farmers.
- Building on **brownfield**—that is, reclaiming former industrial sites within existing urban borders—is very expensive, so developers prefer to build on new land.

- "Not In My Back Yard" (NIMBY) is a typical and usually successful reaction of neighbourhood groups to any proposal for the development of affordable housing or land-use intensification in their existing neighbourhoods.
- The Ontario Municipal Board is pro-development, and the cost of appeals from developers is borne by municipalities, not developers.

Unfortunately, the anti-sprawl lobbies have comparatively few resources. In fact, it may take tragedy to elevate public awareness to the point where change seems imperative. As it stands, they possess the following resources:

- Public concern about global warming has given anti-sprawl activists an issue on whose coattails their own issue can ride.
- Green groups such as the David Suzuki Foundation and the Ontario Naturalists Association are vocal and well organized. They keep media attention on environmental issues, including that of urban sprawl, and thereby educate the public bit by bit.
- Green issues are now entering mainstream political platforms: both the Green Party and the New Democratic Party have promoted specific environmental policies.
- Rising gasoline prices may force consumers and would-be commuters to reconsider moving to the suburbs.
- **Gridlock** and road rage incidents may do something to discourage homebuyers from moving to the suburbs.

We have now identified the respective assets of the two sides in the urban sprawl issue. Create a power resources chart that lists these assets. Then, with reference to current events, analyze the power of each side. As time passes, the power relationship between the two sides may change. Your completed chart will help you see whether the balance of power is shifting or is likely to shift.

Which Side Is Dominant, and What Is the Future of the Issue?

Clearly the pro-development side is dominant, and there are few signs that this will change. The key to change appears to be a shift in public sentiment. Sustained media exposure of the green objectives together with increased recognition of the many evils caused by urban sprawl will encourage the public to demand government action.

A Symbolic Interactionist Analysis of Urban Sprawl

BRIEF REVIEW OF THE SYMBOLIC INTERACTIONIST PERSPECTIVE

Urban sprawl is a macro issue in its impacts, but it is also the result of individual decisions (micro). Analyzing it from the micro perspective of the symbolic interactionist paradigm will show us how public perception has created the issue and how this perception needs to change if the issue is to be resolved. Remember that, according to a symbolic interactionist perspective, a social issue is the product of beliefs and interpersonal behaviour that are rooted in socially shared perceptions and values.

Power Resources Chart for the Urban Sprawl Issue					
Dominant Side: Developers			**Minority Side: Green, Anti-Urban-Sprawl**		
WIN	LOSE	RESOURCE	WIN	LOSE	RESOURCE

ANALYSIS OF URBAN SPRAWL

We have used the expression "car culture." The symbolic interactionist perspective will help us understand this term. What is a car to North Americans? The simple answer is that it is a mode of transportation. But its cultural meaning is much more than that: North Americans do not just rely on cars for transportation; they have actually developed a strong sense of identity, both personal and national, with the car. A car symbolizes adulthood and independence and freedom. It is like a mobile family room; it serves as a status marker. David Shi (2000) has nicely summarized what the car means to North Americans:

> Americans have always cherished personal freedom and mobility, rugged individualism and masculine force. The advent of the horseless carriage combined all these qualities and more. The automobile traveled faster than the speed of reason; it promised to make everyone a pathfinder to a better life. It was the vehicle of personal democracy, acting as a social leveling force, granting more and more people a wide range of personal choices—where to travel, where to work and live, where to seek personal pleasure and social recreation. As a journalist explains, the automobile is the "handiest tool ever devised for the pursuit of that unholy, unwholesome, all-American trinity of sex, speed and status."

Public transit, by contrast, is thought of as inconvenient, disagreeable, and sometimes unsafe. It represents a lower socio-economic status. Car culture aside, there is a North American romanticism about country living and about living in a detached, single-family home. Given that these beliefs about cars and suburban living are widely held in our culture, it is easy to see why developers have a ready market for their suburban "products."

A symbolic interactionist perspective reminds us that beliefs and perceptions drive behaviours, choices, and decisions, and that policy decisions are ultimately based on how a situation is popularly defined. The role of advocacy groups is to educate the public and shape public perception to the point where government will be pressured to enact policy changes.

One of the ill effects of urban sprawl, as we have said, is the damage to human health through environmental damage and through the stress and physical idleness it forces on carbound commuters. Now we will explore these health consequences from a symbolic interactionist perspective. We have chosen to look at health issues because the general unwillingness to curb urban sprawl is partly based on widespread misconceptions about *healthy living.*

Urban Sprawl and Its Impact on Health

Urban sprawl involves the invasion of the wilderness and of green areas immediately adjacent to any city. In general, loss of wilderness negatively affects health. Recreational space—green space that is free of noise, noxious fumes, crowding, and pavement—is necessary for the physical and psychological development of children and for adult relaxation. Urban sprawl deprives great numbers of people of these benefits. The flight to the suburbs in search of peace and natural space is stimulating a process—urban sprawl—that diminishes both (Pim & Ornoy, 2005).

Suburban life is alienating. Suburbia is designed to accommodate the car, not pedestrians, and social interactions do not easily prosper in neighbourhoods built mainly with cars in mind (Pim & Ornoy, 2005; Wade, 2003). Human alienation is often at the root of violence and of mental and physical illnesses.

Suburbanites drive to work, to school, and to the grocery store. Cyclists who dare venture out have to compete for the road with fast-moving car traffic—a health and safety risk. Suburban life discourages walking, too. Not surprisingly, obesity has been linked to suburban living (CTV News, 2007; David Suzuki Foundation, 2003, p. 12).

Urban sprawl damages air and water quality. As a result, asthma and other respiratory problems are on the rise. According to Gurin's *Understanding Sprawl* (2003), up to 16,000 premature deaths per year can be attributed to air pollution, and respiratory illnesses linked to air pollution account for $1 billion annually in lost productivity and health-care costs. European studies cited in this article suggest that air pollution, even where it is within regulated limits, has a persistently negative impact on health. One statistic cited in the article is particularly eye-opening:

> Results of a study by the Centers for Disease Control and Prevention during the 1996 Olympic Games in Atlanta, at which time vehicular traffic was kept at artificially low levels by city authorities, showed that the peak daily ozone concentrations decreased 27.9 percent and the number of asthma emergency medical events dropped 41.6 percent. (Gurin, 2003, p. 13)

In short, numerous health problems in Canada are directly related to urban sprawl. However, the health-care system pays little if any attention to the social causes of illness; it views illness in isolation from its social and physical contexts. So long as this approach prevails, the relationship between health and environmental damage caused by urban sprawl will remain invisible to health practitioners and the public. Medical practice will continue to approach disease as a problem of individuals in isolation and to ignore the social, political, and environmental factors in their illnesses. It will continue to focus on curing technologies, rates of need versus capacity to serve, and the availability of pharmaceuticals. In short, there will be little attention paid to preventing health damage through environmental interventions. And yet reports such as *Understanding Sprawl*, along with critical reviews by organizations such as the Canadian Association of Physicians for the Environment, are encouraging a paradigm shift in the conception of medicine. A *paradigm shift* is an alteration in conceptual models—that is, a change in perceptions, beliefs, and consequent behaviours. A paradigm shift in medicine will be the focus of a symbolic interactionist analysis.

QUESTIONS THAT GUIDE A SYMBOLIC INTERACTIONIST ANALYSIS

1. What does the issue mean to the individuals involved in the issue? How is this meaning expressed? What labels, myths, stereotypes, and language do individuals use to refer to the issue and to the other individuals involved in it?

   In Canada today, what does the term *health* refer to, and how does one achieve good health? We can probably determine the popular notion of *health* by reviewing Canada's health and medicine websites. Two such cites are Statistics Canada, which annually compiles statistics on the health of Canadians, and the Canadian Diabetes Association, which urges lifestyle changes that would reduce the incidence and severity of diabetes. These two examples alone reveal that, at present, contextual factors in health are ignored in favour of a concentration on individual lifestyle factors. In other words, health care in Canada focuses on prevention and treatment at an individual level rather than any broader level. As long as disease is viewed this way, no questions will be raised about how societal trends may be causing ill health.

How Healthy Are Canadians? is an annual report published by Statistics Canada that focuses on the health of a specific demographic group within Canada. Each report relies on a set of standardized criteria for measuring health. These reports also measure the "health" of Canada's health-care system in terms of timeliness and appropriateness of service. The following excerpt reflects the prevailing assumptions about disease and ill health. Note how it emphasizes lifestyle practices that encourage or damage health. Note also how little attention it pays to the connection between health and the environment.

> "Healthy Living Among Seniors" explores good health in relation to health behaviours and psychosocial factors. While some seniors experience functional decline or more negative perceptions of their health, many others either remain healthy or regain their health after such a decline. This article reveals the importance of positive health behaviours, such as exercising regularly, drinking moderately, eating fruit and vegetables, and abstaining from smoking. The analysis also finds that seniors who feel connected to their communities and those without a lot of stress in their lives are more likely to be in good health. (Statistics Canada, 2006, p. 5)

In this passage, the terms "health behaviours" and "psychosocial factors" posit a straightforward choice between healthy and unhealthy behaviours. There is no consideration of what may prompt "bad" health behaviour. If, for example, suburbs do not provide safe walking paths, how probable is it that walking for health will be incorporated into a suburbanite's lifestyle? With health issues like obesity, too, there is a common tendency to blame individual ignorance or weakness rather than consider the underlying social trends that may be causing weight gain. For purposes of illustration, go to the HealthyOntario.com website at http://www.healthyontario.com/FeatureDetails.aspx?feature_id=1 and read through "Lowering your cholesterol through diet and lifestyle." For purposes of comparison, look up any popular website on weight loss. As you browse through the site, consider words, headings, and other features of the presentation that say something about the current view of *health.* Notice that the popular concept of health and fitness is tied to body image ideals and weight loss. These elements of the social meaning of health are even more remote from looking at health as a component of environmental trends that are of a far greater scope than is the context of personal lifestyle choices.

From your analysis of this website or others like it, you will see how perceptions and beliefs direct the choices and even the questions that are asked about an issue. The numerous weight loss clinics and diets being advertised indicates that Canadians have not expanded their definition of health beyond lifestyle and individual choice. Only when our notion of good health expands to include a society-wide, even global, context will we begin asking the kinds of questions that could lead to change. There are indications that new understanding is emerging from the front lines of health-care delivery.

2. What is the source of these meanings? What is the social context in which they are expressed? How are these meanings enforced or resisted?

   The fact that the Canadian Nurses Association (CNA) website refers to the *social determinants of health* suggests that the meaning of health has expanded to include context. In other words, genetics and traditional diagnostic considerations, such as the patient's lifestyle choices, are no longer being seen as the only reliable predictors of good health. The relevant passage at the CNA website is the following:

> Social determinants of health are the economic and social conditions that influence the health of individuals, communities and jurisdictions as a whole. Social determinants of health determine whether individuals stay healthy or become ill (a narrow definition of health). Social determinants of health also determine the extent to which a person possesses the physical, social and personal resources to identify and achieve personal aspirations, satisfy needs and cope with the environment (a broader definition of health). Social determinants of health are about the quantity and quality of a variety of resources that a society makes available to its members. (Canadian Nurses Association, 2005, pp. 1–2)

As long ago as the 1940s, the World Health Organization defined health as something more than the absence of disease (Üstün & Jakob, 2005). Health results from individuals' interaction with their social and physical environment. Conceptually, it can no longer be compartmentalized or separated from its context. The following quotation from Health Canada's "Determinants of Health" confirms this conclusion. The article emphasizes that health is affected by the physical environment—that is, by access to clean air and water and, in general, to an environment free of toxins:

> To take action on these direct effects requires cooperative action by all levels of society. In the longer term, if the economy grows by degrading the environment and depleting natural resources, human health will suffer. Improving population health requires both a sustained, thriving economy and a healthy, sustainable environment. The challenge is to maintain a thriving economy while preserving the integrity of the environment and the availability of resources. Factors in the human-built environment such as the type of housing, the safety of our communities, workplace safety, road design are also important. (Health Canada, 2003)

Sonia Anand (2006) has likewise made the point that the health of a population requires the cooperation of all levels of government, not just interventions from health-care institutions. Such cooperation will occur only if health is popularly understood in the broadest sense, not simply seen as the absence of disease or as the effect of individual lifestyle choices.

A final sign that health is at last being more broadly defined is the UN pronouncement about the link between health and poverty. Poverty and the health issues related to it cannot be remedied without development. This conclusion is implicit in the UN's Millennium Development Goals for Health. The UN's plan for achieving health in developing countries includes, as one might expect, the goal of reducing and eliminating diseases. More interesting is that it also includes goals of improving maternal health, relaxing debt obligations for poor nations, and giving all citizens of developing countries access to education (World Health Organization, 2001–2002).

The upshot of all this is that *health*, as a concept, is now being understood as the product of individual choices in connection with social, physical, and environmental contexts. Once such thinking becomes mainstream, issues such as urban sprawl will be aggressively addressed.

3. What are the consequences of this activity? How does it affect the individuals involved? How does it affect society's perception of an issue, and how does this affect, in turn, individuals' participation in the issue?

Obesity is one health issue that Canadians fully acknowledge and are trying to combat. But despite the myriad diets, the loud warnings about the dangers of obesity, and the social stigma attached to being fat, Canadians are getting fatter. Our inability to overcome obesity suggests that our approach to the problem needs to change. Perhaps we need to broaden our examination of this issue. Shouldn't our dependence on automobile travel be acknowledged as a contributing factor? The fact that Canadians spend more time at work than ever before in their history—might not that also be a factor? Such questions would follow from an expanded view of what health is and what health care comprises.

John Howard (2005/2006, p. 2) has identified the struggles faced by the health-care system and has described a paradigm shift occurring in the medical field. Traditional health care conformed to a doctor–patient model, with the doctor diagnosing and then treating a patient. The system has been moving toward a patient-centred model, whereby the doctor diagnoses and also considers the patient's context of family and community. The **ecosystem model of medical practice** must be the next model for the health-care system, according to Dr. Howard:

> Under the ecosystem model, a patient with asthma will not just be prescribed medication to ease symptoms, but the model will force the health care provider to consider: What caused the patient to suffer from asthma? What can the physician or society do to prevent the problem from developing in other people?
>
> Under the ecosystem model, less government spending would be allocated to health care, but more would go to clear determinants of health—things such as education and social programs. This model focuses on the health needs of an entire population and allows

decisions to be made on a regional level, since it is only on this level that leaders are able to understand the collective needs of people.

Howard proceeds to offer an assessment of where the health-care system in Canada is today: "We have a system that delivers health care in a traditional medical model to a population that wants the patient-centred model, but really needs an ecosystem health model. Fortunately, the implementation of the ecosystem model will allow us to best meet the needs of the population, which will best meet the needs of individuals" (p. 2).

Without a paradigm shift, we can expect continued deterioration of Canadians' health. The wider social focus of the ecological model of medicine would clarify incentives to reverse environmentally damaging trends, trends such as urban sprawl.

RESPONSES

GOVERNMENT AND POLICY

All levels of government, especially the municipal level, have tried to address urban decay with various initiatives. They have tried redeveloping downtown areas through *gentrification* and public housing complexes. They have funded community centres and park spaces in city centres, trying to reclaim the urban cores from decay.

To contend with social issues arising from contemporary suburbanization, governments must do more. Suburbs are a reality in most Canadian cities. Urban planners and other public officials are seeking to address the problem of suburbanization by planning cities more effectively. Municipal governments, by means of planning and zoning legislation, are trying to ensure that suburbs contain vibrant local communities and economies. For example, they are adding parks and community centres, as well as schools and bus routes, to existing suburbs in an effort to beautify and enliven them. Ideally, suburbs would be reshaped so as to offer residents the amenities and vibrancy of urban communities along with the rural benefits of space and close-knit community.

One environmental measure taken by Canada's policy-makers has been to offer people incentives to use public transit. Government funding of public transit has increased as well. Another measure has come from the current Conservative federal government, which recently introduced tax incentives for people to purchase more fuel-efficient vehicles.

There has also been a policy response to the shortages of professional services in rural areas. Governments have increased quotas for medical school enrolments and taken measures to facilitate recognition of foreign-trained doctors' professional credentials.

A factor contributing to the shortage of physicians in rural—and particularly in northern—communities is that Canada's medical schools are located in major urban centres in the southern part of the country. All medical students have to relocate to large cities, mostly in southern Ontario and Quebec, for several years to become trained as physicians. These tend to be crucial years in the students' personal lives (their late 20s and early 30s), when many of them meet partners and marry and have children, thus establishing links to the communities. One way of returning medical graduates to underserviced northern communities has been to ensure that they don't leave in the first place. The Northern Ontario School of Medicine opened in 2005—the first new medical school in Canada in over 30 years. The school is divided between two campuses in northern Ontario, one in Sudbury and one in Thunder Bay. The school's key goals are to train more new physicians and to enhance the chances of their practising in underserviced northern regions. When the school's first class graduates in 2009, we will see whether the second of those goals has been achieved.

Following the same rationale, academics, politicians, and lawyers in northern Canada are seeking to establish a law school in the region. In 2006, Lakehead University, located in Thunder Bay, Ontario, approved a law school in principal, and subsequently sent proposals to the Ministry of Training, Colleges, and Universities and to the Law Society of Upper Canada (LSUC). The proposal is for a small law school, with 30 students per year to start class in 2008.

Lakehead University's proposal is for a law school fundamentally different from the ones currently open in Canada. The proposed school is to focus on Aboriginal issues and on training law students to practise as sole practitioners or in small firms. It will be the first law school in Ontario to be located up north. Ontario's six existing law schools are significantly larger than the school proposed by Lakehead, and all compete for student recruiters and funding from large firms in Toronto, Ottawa, and New York. The Lakehead law school would offer a work/study program.

Lakehead's law school proposal clearly comes directly from a need to increase access to justice. However, not everyone is satisfied that the reasoning behind the school is sound. Some wonder how Lakehead and the bar of Ontario's North hope to keep law school graduates up north. Some graduates may stay. But the lure of articling salaries in the urban centres may draw many of them south. Another pessimistic prediction is that opportunistic students who can't get into law school elsewhere will apply to Lakehead as a last resort, then abandon the North once they have their degree.

One way of keeping law graduates in the North would be to use the methods of the Rural Ontario Medical Program (ROMP), which provides financial incentives—signing bonuses and tuition refunds—for medical graduates who agree to practise for several years in an *underserviced* area.

The Ontario government and the LSUC have yet to approve Lakehead's proposal. In February 2007, the LSUC voted to defer its decision on the proposal, primarily because Lakehead had not yet discussed the proposal's feasibility with the deans of Ontario's other law schools. In the meantime, two other Ontario universities have also expressed interest in opening law schools.

Political parties continue to take positions on abortion, even though the basic question of its legality is settled. The Bloc Québécois and the NDP are pro-choice, while the Liberal and Conservative parties do not have official political positions on the matter. The Green party is pro-choice but leader Elizabeth May made headlines in 2006 when she made comments about its not being appropriate to take abortion lightly, comments that seemed to imply her personal reservations about the practice.

LAW AND POLICING

Police face different challenges depending on whether they are addressing the needs of rural, suburban, or urban populations.

In rural areas, police are fewer and must cover large terrains. For obvious reasons, response times are slower. Police departments have been criticized for responding inadequately to the needs of remote communities, especially Aboriginal populations on reserves. Police in rural areas have to learn to capitalize on community connectedness; community policing programs have been implemented in many areas. In Alberta, for example, the RCMP's Rural Crime Watch involves cooperation between police officers and community members to enhance property security and public safety. More and more reserves are being authorized to create their own police forces; they recruit and train members of their own Aboriginal communities rather than rely solely on the RCMP.

Community policing is also useful in urban areas. Police in many urban areas are working with community groups and enlisting the help of community members to ensure public safety and law enforcement. Where ethnic or racial segregation has become an issue, police have successfully involved leaders of particular demographic communities in such programs. For example, the Community Crime Awareness Association (CCAA) Asian Community Policing Experience is a 2007 recruiting initiative in Toronto run jointly by the RCMP and various local police forces; the aim is to recruit Asian youths to become police officers (Community Crime Awareness Association, 2007).

COMMUNITY AND INDIVIDUAL INVOLVEMENT

There are many ways for students to address social issues related to urban and rural living in Canada.

Students concerned about the environmental issues arising from urban sprawl may lend their support to such environmental organizations as Greenpeace, Nature Canada, the Canadian Environmental Law Association, and the Canadian Council on Ecological Areas, to name only a few.

Students concerned about the inadequacies in Canada's health-care system can of course become politically active and work for change either through partisan advocacy, as members of political parties, or through non-partisan advocacy via non-governmental organizations (NGOs). There are many NGOs that work for equity and justice in the provision of health care, including the People's Health Movement and World Vision.

There are many advocacy and educational groups in Canada that are addressing the issues of abortion and access to it. Students, depending upon their ideological and personal views, may wish to become involved with either pro-choice or pro-life organizations. Dr. Henry Morgentaler is working to open private abortion clinics in Canada's Arctic region.

CONCLUSION

This chapter's analysis of urban–rural issues exemplifies the central tenet of the sociological perspective: that social patterns and events are cued and shaped by their social contexts. For example, the socially shared ideal of a home in the country has prompted the majority of Canadians to move to the city periphery and build. The impact of this pervasive ideal has been disastrous. Urban sprawl is arguably one of the most serious social and environmental issues yet to face Canada. The sociological perspective discloses social patterns and allows one to predict future trends. Such perceptions are the foundation of good decision-making.

Further analysis of suburbanization could be undertaken from a feminist perspective. (One could argue that feminism was to some extent a by-product of the suburban lifestyle, whose numbing isolation and tedium was mostly felt by women.) Certainly the changes in family structures and relationships that the suburban commuter lifestyle has wrought would be appropriate for a feminist analysis.

A social constructionist analysis would investigate further how the meaning of *lifestyle* has changed. Currently, individual achievement has the greatest social value, and this has diminished the sense of community and responsibility to community. By the current scale of values, detached homes and upscale vehicles symbolize individual achievement. North American consumerism has created a destructive path. Meanwhile, counter-consumerist groups strive to reshape the meaning of sustainability, so it does not connote drabness and deprivation.

Urban sprawl is a problem that stands at the intersection of the micro and macro contexts, and it can be usefully examined from both micro and macro theoretical perspectives.

KEY TERMS

abortion the procedure of expelling an embryo or fetus from a woman's uterus in order to terminate a pregnancy

brownfield former industrial site reclaimed for use by developers

ecological footprint a statistical measure of humans' impact on the natural environment

ecosystem model of medical practice health practice that includes consideration of the wider social and societal factors in health

global warming the increase of atmospheric or climate temperatures that is drastically altering ecosystems

green space undeveloped land that provides relief from the urban landscape

greenfield land that has been untouched by industry or development and that is therefore appealing to developers

greenhouse gases industrial, home, and automobile emissions of carbon-based gases into the atmosphere; considered to be the primary cause of accelerated global warming

gridlock traffic congestion that brings all intersecting traffic routes to a halt

Kyoto Accord an international treaty (drawn in 1997) that bound a number of nations, including Canada, to meeting targets of greenhouse gas reductions

rural areas places with a sparse human population that are largely dominated by the natural landscape

smart growth an initiative that aims to achieve sustainable growth in cities and to prevent urban sprawl by encouraging compact development and resource conservation

suburbanization the movement of people away from city cores and small towns into fringe areas bordering the major urban centres

sustainable development economic and social development that is harmonious with the natural environment and that relies on renewable energy sources so it does not deplete natural ones

urban areas places with a dense human population and an abundance of created structures

urban decay a city's falling, in whole or in part, into disrepair, characterized by depopulation, abandonment of inner city property, high unemployment rates in downtown areas, family fragmentation, high crime rates, and the political disenfranchisement of downtown residents

urban sprawl the uncontrolled geographic spreading of low-density urban development into the rural environments surrounding cities

urbanization the movement of the world's population from rural to urban areas

FOR FURTHER RESEARCH

Alberta Rural Crime Watch
http://www.ruralcrimewatch.ab.ca.

Canadian Association of Physicians for the Environment (CAPE)
http://cape.ca.

Canadian Council on Ecological Areas
http://www.ccea.org.

Canadian Environmental Law Association
http://www.cela.ca.

Canadian Institute for Health Information (CIHI). *Health Care in Canada.*
http://secure.cihi.ca/cihiweb/products/hcic2006_e.pdf.

Canadian Nurses Association (CNA). "Social Determinants of Health and Nursing." http://www.cna-nurses.ca/CNA/documents/pdf/publications/BG8_Social_Determinants_e.pdf.

Canadians for Choice (CARAL)
http://www.caral.ca/index.html.

David Suzuki Foundation. "Climate Change: Impacts and Solutions."
http://www.davidsuzuki.org/Climate_Change.

Life Canada
http://www.lifecanada.org.

Pembina Institute
http://www.pembina.org.

Public Health Agency of Canada
http://www.phac-aspc.gc.ca/about_apropos/index-eng.php.

World Vision Canada
http://www.worldvision.ca.

You can play a role in encouraging sustainable development. The following are some organizations that would welcome your contribution:

David Suzuki Foundation
http://www.davidsuzuki.org.

Green Door Alliance
http://www.thegreendooralliance.ca/index1.html.

Ontario Nature
http://www.ontarionature.org.

Sierra Club of Canada
http://www.sierraclub.ca.

REFERENCES

Adair, J. (2004, July 15). Ontario tackles urban sprawl. *Realty Times: Real Estate News and Advice.* http://realtytimes.com/rtpages/20040715_urbansprawl.htm.

Anand, S. (2006, October 24). Obesity: The emerging cost of economic prosperity. *Canadian Medical Association Journal* [CMAJ], *175*(9), 1081. http://www.cmaj.ca/cgi/content/full/175/9/1081.

Bankole, A., Singh, S., & Haas, T. (1998). Reasons why women have induced abortions: Evidence from 27 countries. *International Family Planning Perspectives, 24*(3), 117-127, 152. http://www.guttmacher.org/pubs/journals/2411798.html.

Bonnell, G. (2007, March 13). Green issues? Canadians choose urban sprawl in staggering numbers: Census. *2006 Census Report.* http://cponline.insinc.com/census_pop.php?id=304&pid=8&tid=12.

Bray, R., Vakil, C., & Elliott, D. (2005, January). Report on public health and urban sprawl in Ontario. Ontario College of Family Physicians. http://www.cfpc.ca/local/files/Communications/Current%20Issues/Urban%20Sprawl-Jan-05.pdf.

Brewer, A. (2001, November 8). The deadly risks of being pro-choice. *The Globe & Mail.*

Canadian Council on Social Development. (2007). Urban poverty project 2007: Community profiles. http://www.ccsd.ca/pubs/2007/upp/community_profiles/index.htm.

Canadian Diabetes Association. (2007, June 19). Canadian Diabetes Association fuels a healthy lifestyle with new resource. Toronto, Ontario. http://www.diabetes.ca/section_main/newsreleases.asp?ID=199.

Canadian Institute for Health Information (CIHI). (2006). Health care in Canada. Statistics Canada. http://secure.cihi.ca/cihiweb/products/hcic2006_e.pdf.

Canadian Nurses Association (CNA). (2005, October). Social determinants of health and nursing: A summary of the issues. *CNA Backgrounder*. http://www.cna-nurses.ca/CNA/documents/pdf/publications/BG8_Social_Determinants_e.pdf.

CAPE News. (2005-2006, Fall/Winter). From the president's corner. Canadian Association of Physicians for the Environment [CAPE]. http://cela.ca/uploads/8bec5e4c37224a6ed209166d0544fb7c/capenewsfall_winter_05_06.pdf.

CBC News. (2000, December 7). Clinic closing blamed on doctor shortage. http://www.cbc.ca/news/story/2000/12/07/mb_clinics120700.html.

CBC News. (2006, August 28). Canada's doctor shortage to worsen without changes: Fraser report. http://www.cbc.ca/health/story/2006/08/28/doctor-shortage.html.

CNW Group. (2005, January 19). Urban sprawl leads to poorer health outcomes. The Ontario College of Family Physicians. http://www.ocfp.on.ca/local/files/Communications/Current%20Issues/Urban%20Sprawl%20Media%20Release.pdf.

Community Crime Awareness Association. (2007). What is CCAA Asian community policing experience? http://www.ccaatoronto.ca/AsianExperienceCover.htm.

Criminal Code. (1985). RSC 1985, c. C-46, as amended.

David Suzuki Foundation. (2003, October 14). Stopping urban sprawl must be a priority for provincial governments. http://www.davidsuzuki.org/Campaigns_and_Programs/Climate_Change/News_Releases/newsclimatechange10140301.asp.

David Suzuki Foundation. (2007). Driven to action: Stopping sprawl in your community. http://www.davidsuzuki.org/Climate_Change/Sprawl.asp.

Gellner, A. (2006). Cities of tomorrow shaped by hybrid technology. Do it yourself.com. *Inman News*. http://www.doityourself.com/stry/hybrid-technology-future.

Global National. (2006, January 11). Study: Major doctor shortage in rural Canada. http://www.canada.com/national/globalnational/story.html?id=50304bc1-9c68-4cc8-8576-a57d41b508a9.

Gurin, David. (2003). Understanding sprawl. The David Suzuki Foundation. http://www.davidsuzuki.org/files/Climate/Ontario/Understanding_Sprawl.pdf.

Health Canada's determinants of health. (2002–2003). Visions, Centre for Innovation: A Directory of Online Aboriginal Health Resources. http://www.visions.ab.ca/content/healthdeter.asp.

Henshaw, S.K., Singh, S., & Haas, T. (1999, January). The incidence of abortion worldwide. *International Family Planning Perspectives, 25* (supplement). http://www.guttmacher.org/pubs/journals/25s3099.html.

Howard, J. (2005–2006, Fall–Winter). Ecosystem health: Prescribing a new vision for the future of medicine. Canadian Association of Physicians for the Environment. *Cape News, 31*(3).

Japan Statistics Bureau. (1996–2007). http://www.stat.go.jp/english/index.htm.

Krauss, C. (2004, September 18). Doctor shortage cripples Canada's free health care. *Minneapolis—St. Paul Star Tribune.* http://www.angelfire.com/pa/sergeman/issues/healthcare/docshortage2.html.

Levitt, S., & Donohue, J. (2001, May). The impact of legalized abortion upon crime. *Quarterly Journal of Economics, 116*(2).

Minister of Infrastructure Renewal. (2006, January 19). Places to grow—Better choices, brighter future: Proposed growth plan for the Greater Golden Horseshoe (GGH). http://escarpment.org/Publications/Proposed_Growth%20Plan.Jan.19.06.pdf.

Olfert, R., & Partridge, M. (2005, January 31). Urban sprawl shows rural–urban interdependence new governance needed to bridge rural–urban divide. Canada Rural Economy Research Lab, University of Saskatchewan. http://www.crerl.usask.ca/policy_briefs/C-RERL_on_SRAWL_and_rural-urban_cooperation_Feb1-05.pdf.

Paraskevas, J. (2005, February 1). Urban sprawl forcing farmers to cultivate poorer soil. CanWest News Service for Immigration Watch Canada Organization. http://www.immigrationwatchcanada.org/index.php?module=pagemaster&PAGE_user_op=view_page&PAGE_id=221&MMN_position=92:90.

Pim, L., & Ornoy J. (2005, February). A Smart Future for Ontario: How to create greenways and curb urban sprawl in your community. Ontario Nature Federation of Ontario Naturalists. http://www.ontarionature.org/enviroandcons/smart_growth/index.html.

Public Health Agency of Canada. (2003). Rural health. http://www.phac-aspc.gc.ca/about_apropos/index-eng.php.

Shi, D. (2000, July 9). Well, America: Is the car culture working? *Philadelphia Inquirer.* http://www.commondreams.org/views/070900-104.htm.

Sierra Club. (2001). Sprawl hurts us all—Global warming: Sprawling across the nation. http://www.sierraclub.org/sprawl/globalwarming.pdf.

Sierra Club of Canada. (2007, June 5). Act fast to halt urban sprawl. Reprinted from *Montreal Gazette.* http://www.sierraclub.ca/national/media/inthenews/item.shtml?x=1126.

Smart Growth BC. (n.d.). Creating more liveable communities. http://www.smartgrowth.bc.ca.

Statistics Canada. (2004). Induced abortion statistics. Table 3-1. http://www.statcan.ca/english/freepub/82-223-XIE/82-223-XIE2007000.htm.

Statistics Canada. (2006, February). Health reports: How healthy are Canadians? Annual report, Special issue supplement to Vol. 16. Ministry of Industry. http://www.statcan.ca/english/freepub/82-003-SIE/2005000/pdf/82-003-SIE2005000.pdf.

Statistics Canada. (2007). Population and dwelling counts, for Canada, provinces and territories, census divisions, and census subdivisions (municipalities), 2006 and 2001 censuses—100% data. Figure is the total population of the Census Divisions of Durham, Peel, Halton, Toronto, and York. http://www12.statcan.ca/english/census06/data/popdwell/Table.cfm?T=304&PR=35&S=1&O=A&RPP=10.

Statistics Canada Dictionary. (2007). Urban area. http://www12.statcan.ca/english/census01/Products/Reference/dict/geo049.htm.

Sugrue, T. (2004). From motor city to motor metropolis: How the automobile industry reshaped urban America. *Automobile in American Life and Society*. http://www.autolife.umd.umich.edu/Race/R_Overview/R_Overview3.htm.

Supreme Court of Canada. (1988). *Morgentaler, R v.* 1 SCR 30.

Sustainability Report. (2004) The urbanization of Canada. http://www.sustreport.org/signals/canpop_urb.html.

Casey, C., Dreier, P., Flack, R., & Swanstrom, T. (2004). Pulling apart: Economic segregation among suburbs and central cities in major metropolitan areas. The Brookings Institution. http://www.brook.edu/metro/pubs/20041018_econsegregation.htm.

Thomas, A. (2003, May 21). Suburbs' growth feeds segregation, race expert says. *The Columbus Dispatch*. http://www.kirwaninstitute.org/about-us/in-the-news/suburbs-growth-feeds-segregation.php.

Transport Canada and Health Canada. (2004, March). Road safety in Canada—An overview. http://www.tc.gc.ca/roadsafety/stats/overview/2004/menu.htm.

Üstün & Jakob. (2005). Re-defining 'health': Bulletin of World Health Organization. World Health Organization. http://www.who.int/bulletin/bulletin_board/83/ustun11051/en.

Wade, P.J. (2003, November 3). Urban sprawl threatens Canadian lives. *Realty Times: Real Estate News and Advice*. http://realtytimes.com/rtpages/20031104_sprawl.htm.

Weiss, E. (2007, April 22). Long commute takes toll on health. *Fort Wayne Journal Gazette*. http://www.fortwayne.com/mld/journalgazette/living/17119015.htm.

World Bank. (2005). 2005 world development indicators: Urbanization. http://siteresources.worldbank.org/DATASTATISTICS/Resources/table3_10.pdf.

World Health Organization. (2001–2002). Health in the millennium development goals. http://www.hlfhealthmdgs.org/MDGchart%20en.pdf.

CHAPTER 9

Globalization

CHAPTER OBJECTIVES

After completing this chapter, you will be able to:

Understand significant dimensions of globalization and the issues surrounding it

- Social and cultural
- Economic
- Technological
- Political and legal
- Environmental

Understand and apply different sociological perspectives to globalization

- Structural functionalist
- Social conflict
- Symbolic interactionist

Identify and critique various responses to social problems related to globalization, including responses from

- Government and policy
- Law and policing
- Community
- Individuals

DIMENSIONS

GLOBALIZATION

The term **globalization** has many definitions. Most people agree that it refers to the increasing *interconnectedness* of our world, an effect of technological progress, human innovation, and social change. Another term often used in this connection is the "global village." Nation-states, individuals, corporations, households, and other organizations are increasingly *interdependent*, no matter how geographically disparate they are. This increasing interdependence is being experienced in many spheres, social and cultural, environmental and ecological, political and legal, technological and economic.

People are divided over the benefits of globalization. But whether it is seen in a negative or positive light—whether it is understood as a relentless flow of goods and cultural influence from the industrialized West to the rest of the world or as a complex and beneficial exchange between cultures—there can be no doubt that it is taking place.

Globalization is the product of many factors. One is the centuries-old expansion of the world's human population and the spread of civilization. The first multinational corporations were born in Europe in the 17th century. **Colonialism** can be defined as the extension of a nation's authority over land or territory not its own. Such expansion has occurred throughout human history. When we use the term *colonialism* nowadays, we are usually referring to the European conquests of the 17th through the 19th centuries. The term *colonialism* also implies the *ethnocentric* beliefs of the *colonizing* nation—the assumption that its customs and values are superior to those of the people it is overrunning. From the 18th century and into the 20th, there was a heavy exportation of European values to Africa, Asia, and the Americas. European colonialism peaked in the 19th century. By the 1960s and 1970s, the process of *decolonization* was virtually complete. Most former colonies had gained their independence by that time.

There has long been a degree of interconnectedness and integration between the peoples of the globe. But globalization as currently understood was only introduced into popular thinking in the 1980s. The concept is associated with the dramatic increases in population growth, technological innovation, social change, and economic interdependency that have characterized the end of the 20th century and the beginning of the 21st. It is also associated with the consequences of the 1989 fall of the *Eastern bloc*, a group of nations—Poland, Czechoslovakia, East Germany, Bulgaria, Romania, and Hungary—that were under the influence of the Soviet Union and communist rule. This event radically changed the worldwide balance of power and signified a victory for global capitalism over communist control. The individual credited with coining the term *globalization* is the late Theodore Levitt, an influential 20th-century American economist and professor at Harvard Business School.

Most social scientists contend that globalization is responsible for the *homogenization* (increasing standardization or sameness) of contemporary societies. In other words, it is seen as eroding historical differences between local cultures. Western products now appear all over the world, in the most unlikely places. We see Coca-Cola transported by mule into the Andes, far beyond the reach of running water. Critics of globalization view it as a process of *recolonization*, by which Western nations, most of them formerly colonial powers, are reasserting their domination and influence over the *indigenous* or local people of the former colonies.

But some social scientists—particularly social anthropologists, whose work involves the study of small or remote social groups—argue that globalization is not so disempowering to the people of former colonies as it might initially appear. Researchers have noted that indigenous cultures have unique ways of incorporating Western products and media into their local realities. For example, in some Asian countries, soft drinks such as Coca-Cola are consumed hot, like coffee. Exported Western food—fast food, for example—takes on very different flavours depending upon the culture in which it is offered, because there is a need to suit the tastes of the local people. *Commodities* or products circulated via international trade do not necessarily have the same uses or meanings in the importing country as they do in the exporting one. On some tropical islands, refrigerators are not plugged in—electricity is scarce—but are kept as decorative cupboards. The 1980 film *The Gods Must Be Crazy* provides a humorous, satirical depiction of how a single commodity can be understood and used differently in different contexts. Local cultures, with their individual and sometimes surprising adaptations of Western commodities, may be able to hold on to their uniqueness in the face of globalization.

Multinational Western companies, in trying to establish markets in the developing world, often adapt their products to the local culture. McDonald's sells some of its items worldwide, but it also includes on its menus items that are inspired by the local cuisine. In other words, McDonald's restaurants accommodate regional and cultural differences to some extent. So do many other international companies. For example, Western companies sell individual-use portions of shampoo cheaply to customers in India, with the aim of easing local consumers into familiarity with Western conventions and brands.

Social or Cultural Issues

The level of cross-cultural contacts currently experienced by average citizens worldwide is a new phenomenon and an important aspect of globalization. The past few decades have seen increased tourism and other travel, increased immigration across national borders (both legal and illegal), and, in consequence, increased ethnic and cultural diversity within most nations of the world.

One source of cross-cultural contacts is international travel. **Tourism**—that is, travel for leisure or other personal purposes—was once a rare activity engaged in only by the wealthy or the adventurous. Now it is a popular activity accessible to travellers from all social classes in the industrialized First World. In 2004, over 763 million people travelled across international borders as tourists (World Tourism, 2005). Improvements in technology, such as the development of large jet airplanes, made it possible to transport many people in short periods of time for an affordable price. Another factor in the growth of tourism has been the enforcement of workers' rights in the West—for example, the legislation of paid vacations; this has provided a burgeoning market for tourist travel. Owing to economic globalization, business travel has also proliferated. Whether propelled by business or pleasure, travellers are encountering new worldviews and cultures and exposing the countries they visit to their own culture. Travel and tourism are now central to the economies of many countries.

Cultures now interact through recreational and business travel, which are temporary. Another key element in globalization is **immigration**—the movement of people from the country where they are citizens to another country, for the purposes of long-term or permanent residence. Human migration has always occurred, but its current scale is unprecedented.

Nationality law provides new immigrants with the means of regularizing their status in their new countries and, in many cases, of becoming citizens. Some countries have agreements that allow their respective citizens to travel freely across their borders. For example, the European Union allows citizens from any member state to live and work in any other. But such freedom is not the case everywhere. Not all immigration is legal. Many thousands of people cross international borders illegally each year.

Most immigration is from poorer countries to richer ones. Most immigrants come to the developed countries of the First World or to wealthy ones such as the oil-rich countries of the Middle East (for example, Kuwait and Saudi Arabia) seeking work or, more generally, a better life. The educated and wealthy individuals in poorer countries, many of them professionals, often end up leaving to seek better prospects elsewhere. This phenomenon is sometimes called the *brain drain.* In the context of Canada, this term is applied to the flow of educated Canadian professionals—scientists, academics, lawyers, and physicians—to the United States.

Populations in much of the First World, including Canada, are growing slowly, and they are aging. In terms of numbers, people are not replacing themselves. In many other nations, population growth is extremely high. For countries with slow-growing or shrinking populations, immigration makes possible a continuous labour supply. Canada's government is relying heavily upon immigration for the labour supply that ensures the long-term viability of our economy.

Large-scale global immigration in the second half of the 20th century has increased ethnic and cultural diversity in most nations of the world. This is especially true of Canada. Canada has an official policy of *multiculturalism.* As described by Jean Chrétien in 2000, Canada is

> a post-national, multicultural society. It contains the globe within its borders, and Canadians have learned that their two international languages and their diversity are a comparative advantage and a source of continuing creativity and innovation. Canadians are, by virtue of history and necessity, open to the world. (Canadian Heritage, n.d., n.p.)

Officially, Canada sees the global trend of increasing cross-cultural contact as greatly advantageous. Prime Minister Chrétien's 2000 speech includes some of the arguments often cited in favour of multiculturalism and, more generally, of contact between different cultures and societies. Creativity, innovation, prosperity, and open-mindedness—these are often cited as reasons for encouraging cultural diversity and international travel.

For all its many benefits, the cross-cultural contact brought about by contemporary globalization also offers challenges. Some people worry, for example, about uncontrolled homogenization. Many parents, in particular, are concerned about the development of a homogenous, worldwide pop culture shaping the minds of their children. Parents in Canada, coming as they do from many different ethnic groups, are particularly concerned about this. Teenagers are a key target market for globalized commodities. Younger children are heavy consumers of popular culture, and parents are concerned about these children becoming teenagers before their time by imitating the pop stars they see on music television. Sometimes, the values to which popular culture exposes children are problematic. The term "prosti-tot" was coined in the early years of this decade in reference to young children's dressing with unwitting provocativeness, in innocent imitation of hypersexualized pop music stars.

Parents have long expressed concerns not just about the celebrities' images but about their music and its possibly subversive influence on young people. This is admittedly an old concern. Fifty years ago parents took fright at "rock and roll" music, which they saw as inciting immoral, anti-police, and anti-government sentiments in their teenaged children. Today it is popular music stars like "shock rock" performer Marilyn Manson who have raised the ire of a new generation of parents and have been accused of inciting immoral behaviour in teens—violence, in this case, and even the extreme criminality of school shootings.

Parental concerns about the influence of popular culture are not a new phenomenon, but with globalization these concerns have taken on new dimensions. Parents originally from China, India, and other Eastern nations are often concerned about "abhorrent" Western values encroaching on their moral and cultural traditions. Moral outrage over Western decadence and the cultural imperialism of the West has fuelled terrorist attacks and other violent resistance to globalization.

The *brain drain* phenomenon mentioned above is a problem for many countries, including Canada. The concern is that, after investing taxpayers' money in the education and training of our youth, we lose them to more lucrative opportunities in the United States and Europe. Many consider this a waste of resources.

A concern that some people have about a multicultural society is the potential for conflict and inequality between ethnic groups. In Canada, there are concerns about racist attitudes in the general public and in the justice system. As a "nation of immigrants," we have a long history of coexistence between different ethnic and cultural groups. But insofar as some of these groups have been *racialized*, or conceived of as separate *races*, this history has not been very harmonious. As Canadian legal scholar Constance Backhouse has pointed out, our legal system has historically expressed systemic racism against non-white individuals by passing laws that mandate racial segregation—for example, it was once illegal for Chinese restaurant owners to hire white women—and by prescribing different taxes and minimum wages for non-white groups (Gao, 2001). Our country's cultural makeup is becoming ever more diverse, but statistics support allegations that Canadian society is still unfairly controlled by white people. As is discussed in chapter 7, visible minorities and Aboriginals in Canada are disproportionately poor.

There is some concern that tourism—a significant element in globalization—financially exploits people in the host country and leads them to abandon authentic cultural productions and creativity in favour of a theatre of stereotypes marketable to tourists. Parisians tend to leave their city in the summer to avoid the hordes of North American and Asian tourists who arrive then, all panting for checkered tablecloths and the Eiffel Tower. In Calgary, during the Stampede, citizens of that city—most of them born and raised in central or eastern Canada—dress in western costume, decorate their offices with cowboy bric-a-brac, and host western-themed parties. Whether this production is entirely for the sake of tourists is unclear. But the fact is that local people—in this case, native Calgarians—often resent and resist the stereotypes tourism can encourage. Critics of international tourism fear that it turns the developing world into a form of zoo where Western sightseers can turn their gaze and expensive cameras on an exotic "other" with no concern for their common humanity.

Economic Issues

The most obvious aspect of globalization, certainly the most widely discussed, is its economic dimension. Since the end of World War II, the legal and other barriers that hindered large-scale international trade—tariffs, for example (financial penalties imposed when goods cross borders)—have been reduced or eradicated. A system of free trade has developed through international agreements such as the General Agreement on Tariffs and Trade (GATT). As a result, *commodity*, or trade item, production frequently crosses national borders. It is not unusual for goods to be made in one country for a corporation based in another, then sold in a third nation or various other nations. Fifty years ago it was difficult to access imported goods in rural Canada; with **economic globalization**, however, markets in far corners of the world can distribute widely a broad range of goods and services. Coca-Cola and McDonald's french fries, for example, are available virtually everywhere in the world. Worldwide financial markets have emerged, so that corporations and other business organizations now have access to financing from beyond the borders of the nation in which they are based.

Proponents of economic globalization stress the benefits of international commerce and argue that globalization brings increased diversity in available products, increased corporate profits, lower rates of interest, lower prices, and, to some extent, higher workers' wages. They say that international markets promote product exchange and the availability of better commodities and services from which all consumers gain. In theory, this development should bring improvements worldwide in the following areas: standards of living, literacy levels, health conditions, child mortality rates, and general living conditions. The fact that the 20th century saw a strong increase in the global average per capita income has been linked by many to economic globalization.

Critics of economic globalization counter that it produces widespread inequality and slows social progress. They do not believe that it creates wealth worldwide; they believe that globalization enriches a select few people in First World nations. These critics cite the fact that Third World countries remain impoverished, and often become worse off, once they begin engaging in international trade. The report that noted a general global increase in income over the 20th century also found that the distribution of that income had become more unequal during this period. Poor countries became poorer relative to the rich (International Monetary Fund [IMF], 2007). For example, critics of economic globalization cite the existence of Third World **sweatshops**, a term used to describe manufacturing facilities where workers are physically or mentally ill-treated, typically by confinement in crowded conditions for long hours at a very low rate of pay. Child labour is common in sweatshops.

Multinational corporations often locate their factories in poor countries, where labour is cheap and safety standards are low, to cut the costs of commodity production. Many consider this trend damaging to First World nations, including Canada. Because of globalization, our country's role in manufacturing has greatly decreased worldwide. Because our workers are legally entitled to unionize, to be paid a minimum wage commensurate with their provincial cost of living, and to have a work week of no more than 40 hours, they cannot compete internationally except when it comes to highly skilled work. Over the past several decades, economic globalization has been linked to thousands of layoffs of factory employees in Canada, and to high rates of unemployment in the manufacturing sector.

Outsourcing is the name commonly given to the reorganization of labour within and between societies. It is a phenomenon that began in earnest in the 1980s and continues today. It is a strategy whereby corporations based in North America and Europe move non-core (that is, non-management) operations to external sites, often Third World locations where labour is comparatively cheap. While not all outsourcing involves *offshoring* (that is, using employees in another country), the two often go together. They enable companies to radically cut their production costs. Consumer advocates worry that outsourcing and offshoring compromise production quality and jeopardize employee job security in the Western world. The North American pet food recall of 2007 suggests that the first of these worries is well founded. Several varieties of canned pet food were recalled in the United States and Canada when a number of pets died from consuming tainted food (Demirjian, 2007). The food, sold under American brand names, had been imported from China, where production costs are cheaper and regulatory standards less stringent. The food had been contaminated by melamine, a chemical used in the production of fertilizer, which can be toxic to pets.

Opinions vary about whether the benefits of economic globalization justify Third World sweatshops and First World layoffs. Proponents of globalization often defend sweatshops as preferable to what Third World workers would otherwise experience. A 1997 UNICEF study showed that when child labour in carpet production sweatshops was legally banned in Nepal and Bangladesh for companies based in the United States, tens of thousands of unemployed children had to resort to crime and prostitution (UNICEF, 1997). Those in favour of economic globalization also say that factory closings in countries like Canada are simply a bump on the road to increased specialization. In other words, Canada's sophisticated and highly educated people are moving toward more highly skilled and interesting tasks: what we do best.

Technological Issues

It would be hard to overestimate the impact of new communications technology—satellites, fibre-optic cable under oceans, global telecommunications networks—and the Internet on contemporary globalization. These advances have brought together people divided by geography. Two political events of the past 20 years show how the world has changed in this respect: the 1989 Tiananmen Square crisis in Beijing, China; and the 1990 American deployment of troops against Iraq, known as Operation Desert Storm.

In the spring of 1989, thousands of civilians gathered in Tiananmen Square to protest China's communist regime and advocate for democracy. What was fundamentally new about the event was protesters' use of fax machines to inform the outside world about their treatment during the harsh government crackdown that followed. The Chinese government banned international media outlets from the area, but protesters, thanks to new technology, were able to send out accounts of events.

When Iraq invaded neighbouring Kuwait in August 1990, American and UN forces joined together to repel Saddam Hussein's Iraqi invasion forces. Television networks such as CNN (Cable News Network), which was founded in 1980, offered continuous 24-hour reportage on events. Three of the network's reporters were in a Baghdad hotel while the city was under American attack. They telephoned the network, making CNN the only media outlet able to communicate from inside Iraq during the early days of the invasion. CNN's 24-hour coverage of the 1990 Gulf War was a watershed event in global interconnectedness.

The September 11, 2001 terrorist attack on the United States was another occasion when global news coverage and telecommunications technologies served to connect people from all over the world. The attacks on the twin towers were televised live, in real time. Telephone calls made by the passengers on Flight 93, the plane diverted by Al-Qaeda terrorists, and by people trapped in the burning World Trade Center underscored how mobile telecommunications technology has revolutionized our ability to communicate.

Clearly, there are benefits to the increased global awareness technology has brought. Governments are more likely to be held accountable for oppressing their citizens, for example. But there is a negative side to all this increased public awareness. Violent events are often reported more widely and more intimately than in years past. Viewers may be upset or—as was the case with the September 11, 2001 attacks—traumatized by the images conveyed. This is especially a danger for children. The heightened public awareness of crime and violence can encourage harsh responses from police and lawmakers, responses that are out of proportion to the actual situations. Intense media coverage can damage the lives of people subjected to it. One example is the tragic death of Princess Diana, who was killed in a car crash while fleeing paparazzi photographers.

The Internet is made up of globally interconnected computer networks. It is unique among communications media for several reasons. First, its scale is tremendous. It is made up of millions of smaller networks which comprise, in turn, millions of homes, institutions, and offices worldwide. Canada is one of the highest per capita users of the Internet in the world. As of 2004, we were the second-best-connected country in the world, behind only the United States (CBC News, 2004). Statistics Canada estimates that 7.9 million (64 percent) of the 12.3 million households in Canada had at least one member who used the Internet regularly in 2003 (Statistics Canada, 2004).

The Internet was initially developed by the United States military for defence purposes, but its most significant feature now is its public accessibility. Anyone can post or access an unprecedented variety of information on the Internet. The public nature of the Internet distinguishes it fundamentally from other forms of mass media, where information is controlled by a few powerful individuals and corporations. For this reason, many see the Internet as responsible for the "democratization of knowledge" (Denning, n.d.). As well as disseminating information via the World Wide Web, the Internet is also used for services such as file transfer, electronic mail, and online chat.

At its best, the Internet is a powerful tool enabling global communities to form and discuss issues of common interest, such as medical problems and political matters. It enables students, researchers, and laypersons to access information and communicate with one another. In general, it enables people to establish and maintain relationships—professional or personal—to an unprecedented degree. However, the Internet is not free of problems. There is a growing technological generation gap between young people, who are adept at using computers, and their technologically challenged elders. This has contributed to anti-youth sentiment in Canada's aging population.

More seriously, global telecommunications technology has given rise to new forms of crime and misconduct. **Cybercrime** is the term for criminal activity that involves the Internet. There is no shortage of such activity. Common varieties of cybercrime include fraud (often by means of identity and credit card theft), mischief (by means of the creation and spreading of computer viruses and other malicious code), hate speech, pornography, and child pornography. It is easy for individuals with malicious or criminal purposes to misrepresent themselves in online communications. For example, heterosexuals may pose as homosexuals online in order to "out" people in cyberspace. There was a recent case of a straight man who posted on Craigslist the contact information of men he'd tricked into revealing their homosexuality. Worse still, sexual predators and pedophiles have posed as children in online chat rooms to gain access to underage children. People also use the Internet to breach intellectual property laws. There are documented cases of the Internet being used for industrial espionage and the theft of trade secrets. Internet use has been linked to school shootings. In some of these cases, students have boasted in online blogs about their plans to kill classmates and teachers. The Internet has also been linked to "instructional" crime, whereby people learn how to make bombs and toxic substances based on information found on the Web. Information stored on the Internet may be "hacked" into and used by terrorists or other criminals. A terrorist might, for example, access subway or water system plans online in planning attacks. In 2006, 17 young Canadians in Toronto were arrested on suspicion of terrorist activity, and investigations revealed that much of their planning and communications with one another had been done via the Internet; they had even ordered explosives online (Meserve & Ensor, 2006).

It is not only the Internet that has been linked to instructional crime. Global telecommunications via television are problematic in this regard. When the United States commenced its 2003 invasion of Iraq, it was careful to limit television reporters' access to information. Governments have accused televised news networks of abetting instructional crime by offering detailed accounts of attack plans and strategy discussions, accounts that could aid enemies during wartime.

Political and Legal Issues

With globalization, countries have become more interdependent, and the laws governing their relationships—economic and political—have become more important. The development of internationally recognized values and laws is a consequence of globalization.

Historically, a nation's political organization essentially concerned power and governance within its own borders. Now politics has gone transnational. Globalization has required nations far apart geographically to forge political and economic relationships. Multinational corporations need legal protection in countries where they operate. On the personal level, people travelling to new countries need to know that their family relationships—whether with spouses, children, or other relatives—will be formally recognized in the countries to which they emigrate. The international law governing these sorts of private relationships, business as well as personal, is known as *private international law*.

Public international law deals with relationships between countries. It consists primarily in international agreements or conventions, most of them signed in the second half of the 20th century. The Geneva Conventions, which aim to protect soldiers and civilians during times of war or other conflict, are among the most important of these—four treaties dealing with international law with respect to humanitarian matters such as refugees, non-combatants, and prisoners of war. Other international agreements are the United Nations Universal Declaration of Human Rights and the UN Convention on the Rights of the Child. These conventions are meant to enshrine a set of commitments and values that the signatory countries have agreed upon. Some international conventions are viewed as the basis of international norms, applicable even to countries that are not signatories. The development of public international law greatly accelerated when the United Nations was formed after World War II. The United Nations plays an important role in the global administration of international law.

But not all international agreements affecting Canada originate with the UN. Canada made its first free trade agreement in 1987, and, with the US and Mexico, launched the **North American Free Trade Agreement (NAFTA)** in 1994. This significantly increased Canada's economic ties with the United States and furthered the process of economic globalization. NAFTA is an agreement between Canada, the United States, and Mexico that eliminated tariffs and other trade barriers that had, until 1994, impeded free trade between the three countries. The agreement, unlike the treaties on which the European Union is founded, does not create a *supranational* level of government or law; it merely links the three signatory countries economically.

Most public international law does not apply as domestic law does; it cannot be directly enforced against individuals. However, this traditional truth is changing in the 21st century. The European Union, for example, provides a *supralegal* framework, including human rights and labour standards, on which member countries have agreed to collaborate; it is a system of courts and political institutions that are binding on both the member countries and their citizens. Similarly, the International Criminal Court (ICC), established in 2002 as a permanent venue for enforcing international norms concerning human rights and standards of conduct during wartime, enforces international law directly against individuals. People can be prosecuted in the ICC for crimes against humanity, war crimes, and genocide, among other offences.

Environmental Issues

Another significant dimension of globalization is the growing awareness of our worldwide dependence upon the natural environment. This consciousness is especially strong in North American, where Al Gore's 2007 Nobel Peace Prize has brought environmental activism into the cultural mainstream. But people around the world are concerned about environmental degradation. With all of our technological advances, we have put the future of our planet in jeopardy. One factor in the heightened global awareness of the ecosystem is the space travel of the last few decades, which has allowed us to visualize and apprehend our planet in a fundamentally new way.

In addition to the environmental activism of private citizens, the governments of the world have begun to concern themselves with environmental issues. The

United Nations Environment Programme (UNEP) addresses various environmental issues. There are many international treaties intended to address environmental concerns. Several other international bodies monitor environmental issues, among them the Intergovernmental Panel on Climate Change (IPCC). There are controversies surrounding these international environmental agencies. Countries just emerging from Third World status, such as India, have charged that environmental agencies like UNEP are hindering their efforts to industrialize. Their argument is that, since the current environmental problems were caused by First World polluters, the newly industrialized countries should be given environmental leeway as they seek to convert their economies.

Perhaps the most widely recognized and pressing environmental concern is global warming—the increase in the earth's average temperature owing to the greenhouse effect. Former American vice-president Al Gore brought this issue to the forefront of global consciousness in 2006 with his documentary film *An Inconvenient Truth*, which won an Academy Award and earned him a Nobel Peace Prize. Though the phenomenon is widely recognized, there has been some debate among scientists about whether global warming is actually taking place and to what extent it is caused by human activity. In February 2007, the IPCC concluded that "the evidence for human-caused global warming is now 'unequivocal'" (United Nations Environment Programme [UNEP], 2007). Some continue to disagree with this conclusion, but the vast majority of scientists agree that carbon emissions and other pollutants are causing world temperatures to rise. And the rising temperatures themselves are only part of the concern; the secondary effects of global warming are a rise in ocean levels and an increase in storm activity.

Global warming will have particularly significant consequences for Canada, because of its far northern latitude. Ice sheets in the north are melting, which is causing ocean levels to rise. Formerly iced-in waters will soon be opened up for navigation. This will cause increased tension over the disputed waters of the Northwest Passage, whose possession Canada contests with countries such as the United States. Global warming threatens fragile Arctic ecosystems; animals such as seals and polar bears, upon which the indigenous Inuit have long relied for survival, are in danger of becoming extinct.

CRITICISM AND CONCERNS ABOUT GLOBALIZATION

Globalization is less clearly a social issue than any other issue discussed in this book. There are numerous proponents of globalization and numerous benefits associated with it. Nonetheless, there are concerns about globalization. These concerns include:

- Loss of cultural, linguistic, ethnic, and creative uniqueness
- Recolonization, or, as some call it, "*Coca-colonization*"—the spread of Western influence and power to the rest of the world (Howes, 1996)
- Exploitation of the Third World and the persistence of poverty there
- Environmental degradation
- Terrorism made possible by the increased mobility involved in globalization

ANALYSIS

SOCIAL ISSUES OF GLOBALIZATION

Globalization actually began with international trade hundreds of years ago, but the term itself is relatively modern. It has been defined many ways, but most understand it to involve the increased mobility of people, goods, services, labour, technology, and capital throughout the world (CBC News, 2006). This has produced unprecedented interconnectedness between regions of the globe. The idea of globalization appeals to many people: the concept of the "global village"; the idea of being electronically transported to any corner of the world; the vision of the world as a smorgasbord of cultures. At the same time, there are a number of organizations—local, national and international—that identify themselves as *anti-globalization*. An anti-globalization group called Anti-Marketing has described globalization as "the process of exploiting economically weak countries by connecting the economies of the world, forcing dependence on (and ultimately subservience to) the western capitalist machine" (CBC News, 2006). Their contention is that global free markets benefit multinational corporations at the expense of smaller businesses, local culture, and average workers. In 2001, Maureen O'Neil, president of the International Development Research Centre, described globalization as a "phenomenon of paradoxes": it is a force of "integration and of division, it empowers and it disables, and it enriches as it impoverishes" (n.p.). Globalization has brought economic advantages, but the costs have also been great.

Identifying a Social Issue

WHO OR WHAT GROUPS ARE CALLING FOR ATTENTION, AND WHAT IS THEIR CONCERN?

The main concern of those opposed to globalization is that it is bringing more havoc than benefit, and that those reaping its huge benefits are insulated from its hardships. Opponents of globalization believe that it is exploiting those least able to repel its negative forces. In Canada, many believe that globalization is threatening the country's labour force and its **sovereignty**.

WHAT IS THE VISION OR GOAL OF THE VOICES OF CONCERN?

Anti-globalization advocates have diverse objectives. One objective is that Canada assert itself as a world leader in trying to create a world that is more safe, just, prosperous, and democratic.

The single greatest hazard of globalization, according to its opponents, is its sacrificing of national interests to the corporate needs of multinational organizations. Nations affected by globalization will experience

- Lower wages and fewer employee benefits
- Higher unemployment
- Lower health and safety standards

- Lower environmental protection standards
- Weaker, less effective government
- Fewer social programs, such as health care and education
- Less protection for developing industries and countries

But globalization is not a process that can be stopped. Trade is not only inevitable, it is desirable. Anti-globalization groups advocate harnessing it in a productive way. In other words, Canada risks losing its social democratic values if it embraces globalization without caution or control. The challenge is for Canada to find a balance between economic globalization and **humanitarian globalization** (Gray, 2001).

WHAT ARE THE MEANS OF ACHIEVING THE GOALS?

Opposition to globalization is a relatively recent development. Historically, Canada has prospered and grown through trade. Canada is also one of the most multicultural nations in the world—a global village in itself. In other words, certain features of globalization are quite agreeable to Canadians. Anti-globalization activists are using the media to challenge this accepting attitude, in the hope that widespread public awareness of the dangers of globalization will eventually lead to astute political action. Daily news coverage of environmental and terrorist threats is helping the activists' cause. Activists are making sure, in turn, that the public associates such threats with unchecked globalization. The anti-globalization message is being heard, evidently. Recent summit meetings of leading economic powers have been conducted against a backdrop of public demonstrations. The demonstrations at the 2007 G8 summit in Germany were a powerful expression of anti-globalization sentiment (BBC News, 2007).

Evolution of the Social Issue of Globalization

WHAT GROUPS AND ORGANIZATIONS ARE ADVOCATING CHANGE?

In a non-economic context, the term *globalization* tends to be used, approvingly, as a synonym for **cosmopolitanism**—that is, freedom from national limitations or prejudices. These positive associations are strong. For this reason, it tends to be not globalization itself but its negative consequences that are addressed as social issues. These negative consequences include the following: world economic inequalities; extreme poverty in developing nations; the outsourcing of work from developed countries; the terrorist activities coming from disadvantaged nations; the destruction of the natural environment; and the depletion of natural resources. Each of these social issues has a core of organizations addressing it. Globalization itself is not the issue that is named. As of 2007, climate change is the most prominent of the social issues spawned, recognizably or not, by globalization. It is being addressed by such organizations as the World Wildlife Fund (WWF), the David Suzuki Organization, and Greenpeace.

WHAT HAS PROMPTED PUBLIC AWARENESS AND CONCERN?

The need to understand certain unprecedented events, natural and man-made, has drawn public attention to issues of globalization. These events include disasters such as Hurricane Katrina, the hardships resulting from the North American Free Trade Agreement (NAFTA), and the post-9/11 threat of terrorism. It is now widely recognized that resolving such issues will require global action.

The media has transformed the general public's experience of global events. Desert Storm, in 1991, involved the first real-time broadcast of war events. Now, a decade and a half later, the US is having to deal with bloggers in the armed forces posting photos and comments directly from the trenches in Iraq. Such blogs are extremely popular.

Perhaps a more inspiring illustration of how the media has globalized public awareness is the Live 8 concert of 2005. This was a round-the-world rock concert—10 concerts were held simultaneously—staged on July 2, four days before the G8 Summit, the proceeds of which went to relieve the poverty of underdeveloped nations, Africa in particular. It was a spectacular success in every respect (Robertson, 2005). In short, it is thanks to the media—itself a key factor in globalization—that the benefits and ill effects of globalization are very much in the public eye.

HOW IS THE PUBLIC ALIGNED?

Public attitudes vary depending on the particular globalization-related issue being considered. Climate change has a high profile, and there are many initiatives underway to combat it. For example, hydro power suppliers, building suppliers, car dealers, and other organizations now offer to make "green donations" on behalf of purchasers who make green choices. David Suzuki is now seen on billboards with a message of energy conservation.

Issues such as world poverty and terrorism have smaller followings. In the case of the latter, there is great fear over the issue in general and great annoyance over border delays and passport problems. As regards terrorism, there is no organization trying to lead public opinion in any particular direction.

WHAT INITIATIVES HAVE BEEN TAKEN AND WHAT POLICIES HAVE BEEN PUT IN PLACE? WHAT IS THE PUBLIC REACTION?

Globalization today generates changes and questions of unprecedented magnitude. For example, the global movement of labour and capital has raised questions about whether the old idea of statehood is still relevant and whether sovereignty or cultural independence can be maintained. Globalization threatens old notions of nationhood. Gabrielle Gray (2001) has questioned Canada's status as a unique and independent nation in the face of globalization and of overwhelming American economic interests. Michael Dobbin (2007) cites ten signs that Canada is disappearing into American culture. (He writes from the standpoint that Canada is worth preserving.) Confronting this enormous issue is hampered by the tendency to address the particular consequences of globalization rather then globalization itself.

ANALYTICAL APPROACHES TO UNDERSTANDING GLOBALIZATION

The theoretical analyses of this chapter will begin with a structural functionalist analysis of cybercrime, then proceed to a social conflict analysis of terrorism. Finally, a symbolic interactionist perspective will be applied to global warming.

Structural Functionalist Analysis of Cybercrime

BRIEF REVIEW OF THE STRUCTURAL FUNCTIONALIST PERSPECTIVE

A structural functionalist analysis investigates how change has fractured a social system. Once the systemic faults or failures are known, structural functionalism can show how to return the system to stability.

Let us now analyze cybercrime from a structural functionalist point of view. Cybercrime, an issue within the larger context of globalization, is crime that occurs on the Internet. It can be anything from identity theft and fraud to pornography. What is glaringly clear is that the technology of the World Wide Web makes traditional methods of crime apprehension and containment ineffective. In other words, conventional systems of combatting crime are dysfunctional.

ANALYSIS OF CYBERCRIME

The Internet has rendered all activity, whether legal or illegal, global in scope, so controlling Internet content and access is impossible from fixed jurisdictions that are limited by physical borders. Technological innovation has changed the way commercial, political, and personal relationships are conducted, but the norms, laws, and values that govern relationships have not kept pace. The result is social turmoil. For example, crimes in the area of pornography have greatly increased. Identity theft has proliferated in the last decade. Data corruption caused by computer viruses has raised the costs of doing business to unprecedented levels.

EVIDENCE OF DYSFUNCTIONS

Pornography and Child Pornography

The following excerpt from an episode of the CBC's *Fifth Estate* (2003) indicates that the problem of **child pornography** on the Internet is enormous: "The Internet is a sordid playground for people who are interested in accessing, sharing and selling child pornography; it's estimated that there are more than 100,000 child porn web sites." Terri Moore, a Texas prosecutor of criminal pornography, has identified child pornography as an international problem. Her investigation of one child pornography portal revealed the names and credit card numbers of 300,000 subscribers from 37 American states and 60 countries (CBC News, 2003, n.p.). Research of RCMP publications provides further evidence that the sexual exploitation of children by means of the Internet is a significant issue.

Canada's laws against child pornography are among the harshest in the world, but they have done little to curb the problem, practically speaking. With the passage of Bill C 15-A in July 2002, which expressly forbids both depicting persons under the age of 18 engaged in sexual activity and depicting their sex organs, the laws have changed. But loopholes persist, and the drafting of further legislation is required (CBC News, 2003).

Identity Theft

In January 2006, *Business Edge* published an article reporting that in that year alone, 9,000 Canadians had reported **identity theft** losses totalling $7.1 million (Keenan, 2006). Internet-based fraud can no longer be ignored or dismissed as the frivolous work of pranksters. The problem is the scope. All of us, young and old, small business and multinational corporations, are relying daily on high-tech communication and thereby committing ourselves to a borderless, virtual, fast-paced world where identity thieves are lurking (Pang, 2006).

Data Corruption

Electronic computer technologies are integral to the operation of business today. Bill Gates has observed that the "digital nervous system" both improves the nature of work and opens the doors to enormous risks. As businesses grow they become more reliant on this system and less on its human accessories. This makes businesses vulnerable to computer crime. Cybercriminals can steal financial assets, disrupt communications among employees or business partners, make off with intellectual property, hurt an organization's reputation, and sabotage e-commerce (KPMG Investigation and Security Inc., 2000).

ORIGINS OF DYSFUNCTIONS

Dysfunction has arisen from the mismatch between current communication technology capabilities and the cultural components traditionally relied on to support and control the technologies. Until we learn to protect assets in a virtual world—until we fully understand that the mechanisms required for such protection are entirely different from those required for protecting assets in a physical world—businesses, governments, and individuals will be at risk. In other words, this dysfunction in the system will continue.

Questions That Guide a Structural Functionalist Analysis

WHAT SOCIAL INSTITUTIONS ARE CENTRALLY INVOLVED?

Ever since the alarm over **Y2K**, *government* has been actively responding to cyber issues. It has, for example, revised legislation to apprehend high-tech criminals more effectively, and it has promoted public education about computer crime. The global nature of cybercrime and Internet problems requires cooperation across the globe, and negotiating multinational agreements is a traditional function of government. Cybersystems and the products needed to secure them are very important to the business world, so the social institution of the *economy* is a major stakeholder in this issue. Law enforcement is the responsibility of *law and justice* systems, which represent, collectively, another social institution. Finally, because new norms and values are needed to ensure the well-being of the public, the social institution of *education* is centrally involved in the issue.

WHAT ARE THE MANIFEST FUNCTIONS? WHAT ARE THE DYSFUNCTIONS THAT HAVE RESULTED IN THE GROWTH OF CYBERCRIME?

The government is primarily responsible for coordinating all efforts to limit cybercrime. Cybercrime is global, so government interventions and initiatives must be international ones. In 2001, the Genoa Summit of the G8 countries met to draft cybercrime legislation: *Transnational Organized Crime and Terrorism* was the fruit of their efforts. Most economies are global as well: few corporations can afford to be bound by borders and nationality. Producing goods and services and creating trading partnerships are two main functions of the economy, now dependent on the Internet and on computer networks. But these essential systems increase the vulnerability of the economy, and reliable security is needed for them. Law enforcement has two dominant functions: to contain and minimize crime and thereby maintain social order, and to illuminate the boundaries between conformity and deviance. In other words, law enforcement's manifest function of maintaining social order occurs through the testing and enforcement of laws passed by government. The laws illuminate by their very existence the boundaries between acceptable practices and unacceptable or criminal practices. Cybercrime is new territory, so the laws addressing it have only just been created. One of the defining features of the Internet is that it operates without legal constraints.

Achieving social stability in the face of rapidly changing technologies calls for increased integration of all political levels, enhanced corporate security measures, and coordinated law enforcement measures. The need for networking and the integration of all social institutions, domestically and internationally, has never been greater (Pang, 2006; CBC News, 2007).

SOCIAL ACTIONS THAT HAVE LED TO DYSFUNCTIONS

A December 2000 report prepared by McConnell International outlined a number of social trends and patterns of communication and data management that threaten global information systems. This report conveniently lists corporate behaviours that are no longer viable:

- Reliance on "terrestrial" laws—that is, laws that predate the general reliance on cybercommunications structures and are therefore inadequate for prosecuting cybercrime.
- Weak penalties—cybercrimes can have serious economic and social effects, but the penalties for them are weak and therefore ineffective as deterrents.
- No consistent approach in law enforcement—most protection measures have been left to private sector development of technical solutions for improved management of data security.
- Lack of infrastructure in the developing world, and lack of technical and economic resources to make information systems secure. In China, for

example, there are many cybercriminals but very few have been brought to justice. China's partners in the World Trade Organization are encouraging it to improve in this regard (Keenan, 2006).

Fighting cybercrime effectively will require that the international borders that cybercriminals move across so easily do not impede the officials trying to apprehend them. The international cooperation of law enforcement officials is needed for this, as are common standards for defining cybercrime, and the free exchange of information about how best to fight it (Pang, 2006).

ACTIONS THAT WOULD RESTORE SYSTEM EQUILIBRIUM

We have identified the general direction in which the fight against cybercrime needs to go. The McConnell report provides some particular recommendations.

- Laws are effective only if "property" owners adopt measures to secure their properties: corporations as well as individuals need to develop and strictly follow information transmission protocols, and make data management systems secure.
- Governments must make concerted efforts to upgrade laws against cybercrime. There have been many initiatives on this front: the OPP/RCMP's PhoneBusters and the RCMP's Reporting Economic Crime On-Line (RECOL) are examples of protection and reporting programs specifically designed to apprehend cybercrime.
- Corporations, all levels of government in all nations, and the whole of civil society worldwide should work cooperatively to create strong defences against cybercrime. Advances are being made. (See T. Keenan (2006) for an account of the initiatives that emerged from the Society for the Policing of Cyberspace international summit.)

If existing methods of law enforcement can be adapted to deal with cybercrime, we should be able to reduce crime levels without sacrificing the many benefits of conducting business in a virtual world.

The analysis chart will give you an opportunity to complete a structural functionalist analysis of the factors that have contributed to cybercrime. The events, changes, and trends described above can be inserted in the "Social Action" column, their consequences in the "Dysfunction" column.

A Social Conflict Analysis of International Terrorism

BRIEF REVIEW OF THE SOCIAL CONFLICT PERSPECTIVE

A social conflict perspective is based on the assumption that social issues arise from inequality. In the case of globalization and of **terrorism** in particular, the social conflict analyst must focus on global disparities in wealth and power. The inequalities and deprivations being felt by developing nations are affecting the West directly in the form of terrorist activity. Comparing the relative power of the stakeholders in the issue should enable the analyst to predict whether terrorism will continue to threaten the peace and security of Canadians.

Structural Functionalist Analysis of Cybercrime

Social Action	Social Institution	Manifest Function of Social Institution	Dysfunction

ANALYSIS OF GLOBALIZATION

Global stratification, or inequality, is often identified as the root of terrorism. Hence the social conflict perspective is a natural choice for exploring this social issue. It could be argued that terrorism is the only recourse for disadvantaged nations in their fight against Western dominance. But such an argument is simplistic. It is more accurate to say that globalization, as well as bringing unprecedented benefits worldwide, has opened the door to increased terrorist activity. Terrorism may be viewed as a form of illegitimate globalization. The adversarial groups, as seen from a social conflict perspective, are not *globalization* versus *anti-globalization* but *legitimate* globalization versus *illegitimate* globalization.

Prevailing Power Relationships

Global stratification is increasing. The gap between the rich and the poor worldwide is widening, despite relief and development efforts. It was reported in 2005 that the gap between rich and poor nations was wider than it was ten years before (Price, 2005). The same source noted that development efforts that focus on economics alone serve merely to enrich wealthy nations. What developing nations need are initiatives that address their education and health needs (Price, 2005). The following quotation offers a useful account of global stratification:

> The greatest contributors to world income inequality are the large countries at either end of the spectrum, the "Twin Peaks," as defined by D. Quah, 1997. One pole represents the 2.4 billion people whose mean income is less than $1000 year and includes people living in India, Indonesia and rural China. With 42% of the world's population, this group received just 9% of the world PPP income [**purchasing power parity**]. The other pole is the group of 500 million people whose income exceeds $11,500. This group includes the US, Japan, Germany, France and the UK. Combined, they account for 13% of the world's population yet garner 45% of the world PPP income.
>
> The gap between these two poles is so large it comprises the major component of the world's income inequality. Populous countries with middle income, such as Brazil, Mexico and Russia, do contribute to world income inequality, but to a much smaller degree. (UC Atlas of Global Inequality, 2006)

Crime, terrorism, and corruption in the global environment are linked to economic imbalances between countries and to the lack of economic opportunity in many regions of the world (Shelley, 2006).

Predicting the Future of the Issue

Despite improved living standards for many in the world, the disparities between rich and poor appear to be increasing. As well, despite heightened efforts to curtail terrorist violence, its threat appears to be increasing. These issues are discussed on both the RCMP's and Canada's Foreign Affairs websites.

Globalization has been accelerated by telecommunication technologies. As a result, the means of furthering terror are inseparable from legitimate and beneficial global networks. At the same time, while crime detection and apprehension are physically anchored, criminal activity is both global and virtual. The power balance appears to favour continued terrorist activities and global violence.

Questions That Guide a Social Conflict Analysis

WHO ARE THE MAJOR STAKEHOLDERS IN THE ISSUE?

Trying to find Canadian roots for the social issue of terrorism would be pointless. Terrorist organizations exist all over the world, and each has distinct grievances and aims. The particular ideologies of terrorist groups tell us little about their connection to globalization. It is useful to keep in mind, as a general rule, that anti-globalization groups and terrorist groups are fundamentally aligned (Porter, 2004). Only tactics and targets differ. For the purposes of a social conflict analysis of terrorism, we will try to determine what characteristics of globalization contribute to the power and control of terrorist organizations. We will not try to identify the primary stakeholders of any specific terrorist action.

What Are the Resources for Terrorist Organizations?

How have political dissenters and international criminal organizations globalized? How has globalization enhanced the power of anti-social fringe organizations? Shelley (2006) has argued that the current prominence of terrorist organizations is not owing to any particular ideology. They have gained power through globalization, as have other transnational criminals. Shelley suggests that globalization has benefited these criminals more than anyone.

Terrorist organizations have gained from globalization in the following ways:

- It has enabled crime networks to intersect with terrorist networks more efficiently and more profitably. The distinction between crime networks and terrorist cells has been rendered obsolete by globalization, and state-based authorities only disadvantage their anti-terrorist efforts by observing this old distinction.
- The increased flow of money, people, and commodities caused by globalization provides an effective cover for criminal and terrorist flow of money, commodities, and people.
- Globalization enables terrorist and criminal organizations—just as it enables legitimate ones—to expand geographically and thereby for improve "markets," recruit personnel, and obtain raw materials.
- The increased mobility made possible by globalization has enabled terrorist organizations to gain access to politically unstable regions, which—with their damaged economies, social upheaval, and disenfranchised refugees—are fertile recruiting grounds.
- The ideology of free markets underlying globalization has reduced regulation and border controls and thereby provided greater freedoms to terrorist and criminal interactions and movement.
- Globalization enables crime and terror organizations to evade or find loopholes in state-based laws and regulations. They live in regions from which they cannot be extradited, operate in countries with inept or venal law enforcement, and launder their money in countries with policies of bank secrecy or minimal government supervision. Thanks to globalization,

these organizations are able to distribute their operations strategically around the globe (Shelley, 2006).

What Are the Resources for Anti-terrorist Organizations?

The main resource of anti-terrorism organizations—a resource they imperfectly possess as yet—is their ability to redefine crime and the relationship between crime and terrorism (Shelley, 2006). Terrorists have acquired power because they have been effective in seizing the technological and political opportunities offered by globalization. Opponents of terrorism, such as governments and military organizations, have been less effective in this regard. The ability to reimagine and restructure themselves as cooperative networks will increase the power of the anti-terrorist side. Shelley recommends the following initiatives:

- Greater international cooperation, harmonized legislation, and increased sharing of intelligence
- Adoption of the perception that fighting crime is essential to the fight against terrorism
- Recognition of the relationship of poverty, inequality, and terrorism

Carrying out these initiatives will require knowledge, political skills, financial resources, and improved technologies.

Which Side Is Dominant, and What Is the Future of the Issue?

Statistics show that terrorism is a growing threat and that the incidence of terrorist acts is increasing. It appears that terrorism has dominance. It appears, too, that the terrorist threat will endure as long as international crime and terror organizations continue to adapt more quickly to our increasingly globalized world than legitimate, state-sanctioned organizations do. There is some irony in the fact that global terrorism was made possible by globalization and now poses the most serious challenge to it (Khan, 1994). Parasitically, global terrorism at once feeds off and diminishes the strength of globalization.

The lists of opposing assets can be effectively summarized in the following power resource chart. Then, with reference to researched information, you can determine the relative and evolving power controlled by each side. Extend the table as required.

A Symbolic Interactionist Analysis of Global Warming

BRIEF REVIEW OF THE SYMBOLIC INTERACTIONIST PERSPECTIVE

Analysis from the symbolic interactionist perspective focuses on the micro level of human interaction. Adopting a micro focus for an issue such as *global* warming (an issue by definition global, not micro, in scope) may seem inappropriate to you. To the contrary, a symbolic interactionist analysis can tell us what brought the issue of global warming to the forefront of public attention. From the perspective of symbolic interactionism, a social issue is the product of interpersonal behaviour—that is, the product of how we treat one another and of what we believe about one another. Our definition of global warming and our understanding of its cause will determine the decisions and choices that the public is willing to make to effect a resolution.

Power Resources Chart for the Issue of Terrorism					
Dominant Side: Terrorist Organizations			Minority Side: Anti-terrorist Organizations		
WIN	LOSE	RESOURCE	WIN	LOSE	RESOURCE

Questions That Guide a Symbolic Interactionist Analysis

1. What does the issue mean to the individuals involved in it? How is this meaning expressed? What labels, myths, stereotypes, and language do individuals use to refer to the issue and to the other individuals involved in it?

   Social issues are controversial. The very definition of an issue, let alone how to resolve it, is likely to be disputed. In the case of climate change, we will adopt the position that environmental interests conflict with those of business and economic progress. Historically, business interests have stigmatized environmentalists to some extent and viewed their measures as unprogressive and in some cases economically damaging. The two sides—business and environmentalist—are divided over the meaning and cause of climate change. At present, however, there seems to be some consensus that the consequences of doing nothing about carbon emissions (the dominant cause of global warming) will be dire. And yet the two sides interpret the problem differently, and this has caused a stalemate. Shellenberger and Nordhaus (2004) have written about the role of perception and social values in the controversy over carbon emissions and how to reduce them. Their thesis is that global warming cannot be solved by means of the "old politics and perceptions" and that a profound change in perception must take place.

   Language of environmentalism: The word *environment* means *surrounding* or *background*. The connotation of this is that humans and their culture are not of the environment, but are separate and distinct from the world in which they live. This understanding of the world is the basis of some troubling perceptions, the foremost being that human actions may be separated from their consequences. It also encourages the belief that the problem can be fixed with more technological innovation. Shellenberger and Nordhaus describe the problem as follows:

   > Thinking of the environment as a "thing" has had enormous implications for how environmentalists conduct their politics. The three-part strategic framework for environmental policy-making hasn't changed in 40 years: first, define a problem (e.g. global warming) as "environmental." Second, craft a technical remedy (e.g., cap-and-trade). Third, sell the technical proposal to legislators through a variety of tactics, such as lobbying, third-party allies, research reports, advertising, and public relations. ... What each of these recommendations has in common is the shared assumption that a) the problem should be framed as "environmental" and b) our legislative proposals should be technical. (p. 9)

   The notion that humans are separate from their environment also invites debate about who is *responsible* for "cleanup." Should those who destroy the environment be charged with the task of cleanup or should someone be specially delegated to do this—a kind of global janitor? But such debates, given the urgency of the issue, seem almost laughably trivial. They amount to a kind of procrastination, and most experts agree that delay will only make this issue worse.

Conceiving human society and its doings as separate from the environment permits debate over what is "environmental" and what is not, and it encourages a misguided kind of prioritizing. What is more important, the environment or jobs? Such questions preclude solutions in which diverse interest groups cooperate. The result is competition among conflicting interests. If the environment were accepted as part of social life, then arguments about the importance of the environment relative to poverty would not occur. Shellenberger and Nordhaus (2004) make this point as follows:

> The tendency to put the environment into an airtight container away from the concerns of others is at the heart of the environmental movement's defensiveness on economic issues. Our defensiveness on the economy elevates the frame that action on global warming will kill jobs and raise electricity bills. The notion that environmentalists should answer industry charges instead of attacking those very industries for blocking investment into the good new jobs of the future is yet another symptom of literal-sclerosis. (p. 29)

One of the basic assumptions of sociology is that language shapes reality. It follows that language breeds myths and beliefs that collectively constitute world views. Again, the notion that the environment is separate from humankind opens the door to the ranking and negotiation of environmental responsibilities. The matter is not viewed with sufficient urgency. In the face of environmentalists' warnings that greenhouse gas emissions are accelerating global warming and that the situation is almost terminal, non-environmentalists argue that global warming is part of a natural cycle and that environmental crusades are economically irresponsible. The language in which we frame the environmental issue admits of disagreement. The political wrestling over the Kyoto Protocol is an example of how environmental debates typically play out. The Kyoto Protocol was an amendment to the United Nations Framework Convention on Climate Change, intended to reduce greenhouse gas emissions. Canada was party to this agreement. In 2005, this agreement was ratified. Since then, greenhouse emissions have actually risen in Canada, and the government is bending to domestic pressure to renege on the agreement. In the meantime, Canada has opted to buy "carbon credits" in order to buy time to meet the emission targets (Makarenko, 2007).

To better understand what carbon credits are, see the website Carbontrading.com. Carbon trading is essentially a point system that allows an industry that is a producer of greenhouse gases to trade with an industry that has negative greenhouse emissions. In an effort to reduce global warming by lowering carbon emissions, industry must meet carbon emission targets; that is, industry is charged by policy or law to reduce its carbon emissions. Where actual emissions cannot be lowered, buying carbon neutral emissions present in other industries can be used to decrease a high emitter's emission damage "score."

The stigma of environmentalism: Not long ago, environmentalists were stereotyped as fanatical alarmists—Luddite opponents of progress and technology—and derided with names like "tree-hugger." Lately this has changed. Not since the 1970s has being "green" been so socially valued. Recent political trends reflect this shift in public sentiment. More and more Canadians expect their leaders to take stands on the environment. At the same time, the Green Party has not yet been accepted as a major national political party in Canada.

2. What is the source of these meanings? What is the social context in which these meanings are expressed? How are these meaning enforced or resisted?

   The title of the article by Shellenberger and Nordhaus (2004), "The Death of Environmentalism: Global Warming in a Post-Environmental World," suggests that public sentiment is not entirely behind environmentalism. The fact that greenhouse gas emissions in Canada have risen 30 percent since the Kyoto agreement was struck suggests that Canadians are not fully committed to environmental goals. Canadian proponents of the Kyoto Protocol have suggested that recent government actions have positively damaged the cause of curbing greenhouse gas emissions.

   The social meaning of global warming is being shaped and contested in the political sphere, and also on the Internet. Environmental organizations invite bloggers to weigh in with comments and observations. The virtual context and the airing of opinion are shaping the issue as Canadians know it. Public discourse appears to be encouraging community-based environmental action. Such action is reflected in the growing number of citizens who are recycling.

   Shellenberger and Nordhaus have addressed why, to date, environmentalism has been politically crippled as an issue while the conservative political agenda has been enormously successful. Their explanation is that the conservative political organization has provided the public with a vision. Good leaders have vision and they motivate public action on the basis of it. Gloomy scientific prognostications, however well founded, do little to inspire the public, but this is all the environmentalist side seems to offer. Shellenberger and Nordhaus accuse the environmental movement of suffering from **groupthink** (p. 11). But David Suzuki now seems to be emerging as a visionary for the environmental movement in Canada, his passion for the cause evident in every one of his public addresses.

3. What are the consequences of this activity? How does it affect society's perception of an issue and thus the direction in which the issue is evolving?

   Shellenberger and Nordhaus (2004) criticize the environmental movement for being empty of vision and lacking in core values. Instead of working toward a real goal, environmentalists have entrenched themselves in an emptily adversarial role. Defining itself by what it is *not* rather than by what it *is*, the environmental movement invites contest rather than cooperation. Shellenberger and Nordhaus believe that cooperation among all stakeholders is essential for any resolution of environmental issues such as global warming. Environmental organizations need to think about the issue in new ways. Aggressive lobbying and statistics-citing can take their cause no further. Leaders of the movement need to step back, discover their core values, and craft a vision. Only then will progress on the global warming issue be possible.

Has environmentalism turned the corner? There are signs that it may have: the growth of wind-power generation; the solar suburb in Okotoks, Alberta, which has made headlines with its commitment to sustainable energy and is acknowledged as a world leader in this regard; and corporations like Bullfrog Power, which provides energy from entirely green sources. Across Canada, wind farms developed by the government are being built to supplement the power grid. In Ontario alone, the Ontario Sustainable Energy Association (OSEA) has set itself the short-term goal of helping Ontario establish 500 megawatts of power by 2012. Its long-term goal is that, by 2025, Ontario will be powered entirely by renewable energy.

RESPONSES

GOVERNMENT AND POLICY

Canada's governmental and policy responses to globalization have been receptive, on the whole. The government welcomes interconnectedness with other nations and assists international trade by multinational corporations. Canada has signed international treaties, such as NAFTA, the Geneva Conventions, the UN Convention on the Rights of the Child, and endeavours to be a leader in international peacekeeping and in other UN initiatives. Canada signed the 1997 Kyoto Protocol. The main problem for Canada with respect to globalization has been balancing a desire to maintain its sovereignty, or autonomy, with a desire to collaborate with the international community. Canada's proximity and close trade ties to the United States make this a significant issue. We do protect ourselves with certain policies, such as mandates for Canadian content in media regulated by the Canadian Radio-television and Telecommunications Commission (CRTC), and funding for Canadian arts production. These policies are meant to protect local culture in the face of globalization. In other areas—environmental policy, for example, mainly notable for our ongoing failure to comply with the Kyoto Protocol—many feel we could be doing more to create globalized economic and governmental links between countries.

Institutionalized racism continues to be a problem in our society and has long been an issue in Canadian law. But changes to immigration legislation, along with increased public awareness of our economic dependence on immigration, are helping to resolve this issue. So are official policies of equality and multiculturalism.

LAW AND POLICING

Social change always alters the nature of crime to some degree. Globalization is no exception in this regard. Where there is crime, there must be a police response. Police have had to change the way they do business in order to respond to changes brought about by globalization.

Because business dealings and human travel are now so often international, local police forces have had to think beyond their traditional areas of authority, or *jurisdictions*, in pursuing transnational criminals. The proliferation of global telecommunications technology has brought cybercrime, which includes the following: fraud; the creating and spreading of computer viruses; hate speech; and certain kinds of pornography, especially child pornography. Police forces around the world have had to collaborate to apprehend cybercriminals. Police and intelligence agencies have had to do likewise in responding to other sorts of globalized crime, including international terrorism and the smuggling of narcotics. The international drug trade, discussed in chapter 3, is a tremendously lucrative and truly globalized industry. Other international crime problems that police have had to deal with include the smuggling of humans across borders, the international sex trade, and sex tourism.

Resistance to globalization by citizens' groups can also require a policing response. Protests against economic globalization, in particular, do not always remain peaceful. At the recent G8 summits in Quebec City and Alberta's Kananaskis regions, Canadian riot police were called in to quell protests and protect the safety of the political leaders.

COMMUNITY

Communities have offered different kinds of responses to globalization. As we have seen, some people see globalization as by and large a benefit to humanity, and seek to support initiatives—such as international free trade agreements—that promote it. Others see globalization negatively and work together to resist what they see as its negative impacts.

Some of these anti-globalization groups feel that coordinated resistance from citizens across the world is the best form of opposition. Ironically enough, it is owing to globalization that people are increasingly aware of themselves as "citizens of the world" rather than citizens of one region or nation. As this awareness grows, so does the potential for a *global citizens' movement.* In the past few decades there have been a number of such groups raising concerns about or opposing globalization. These organizations are diverse and varied in their structure. A good summary of them can be found in Orion Kriegman's (2006) *Dawn of the Cosmopolitan: The Hope of a Global Citizens' Movement.*

Other groups feel that such a unified, coordinated resistance to globalization would amount to complicity with the enemy: globalized resistance would erode the very cultural diversity they are trying to preserve. They advocate a *grassroots*, or local, resistance strategy.

INDIVIDUAL INVOLVEMENT

As we have mentioned, private citizens have organized globally and locally in various ways both to support globalization and to resist it. Students can certainly become involved in such advocacy. Global environmental organizations, such as Greenpeace, and NGOs, such as Amnesty International, always welcome involvement by students. The international aid and human rights protection work of Bono, George Clooney, Audrey Hepburn, and Angelina Jolie, among other celebrities, provide high-profile examples of individual involvement in international development and human rights. Students interested in policing a globalized world can look for opportunities in peacekeeping missions with the Canadian forces.

CONCLUSION

Evidently, globalization as a social issue can be conceived only in terms of its various impacts, not as a monolithic entity. One of globalization's dysfunctions is discussed in this chapter's structural functionalist analysis of cybercrime. The social conflict analysis of global terrorism has demonstrated that globalization in itself is a neutral process that can be effectively adopted by destructive or beneficial interest groups. The micro perspective offered by the symbolic interactionist analysis of global warming has shown that even though social issues span the globe, they are the product of everyday social patterns and individual choices. This theme of the micro basis of macro issues could be extended with a social constructionist exploration of the meaning of race, nationality, and ethnicity in the face of globalization. One common fear about globalization, not extensively addressed in this chapter, is that all cultures of the world will be homogenized into one, a culture driven by American, consumerist social patterns.

What would a feminist perspective show us? Globalization tends to illuminate contrasts among cultures. For example, global media coverage has exposed the systemic gender inequities in many cultures of the world and brought us stories of women having to suffer as a result of their gender alone. Feminism, as a social movement, has globalized much as the human rights movement has globalized, through organizations like Amnesty International.

How are you going to participate in globalization? A sociological perspective will help you make informed choices in this regard.

KEY TERMS

child pornography the depiction of children under the age of 18 in sexually explicit material

colonialism a nation's extension of its authority over land or territory not its own

cosmopolitanism the belief that everyone belongs to a world community; freedom from national limitations or prejudices

cybercrime criminal activity that involves the Internet

economic globalization the seamless movement of goods, services, and capital around the world, unhindered by national borders

global stratification inequality among the nations of the globe with respect to economic and social well-being; nations are defined as *core* (developed), *semi-peripheral* (semi-developed), and *peripheral* (undeveloped)

globalization trends in telecommunications, trade, and migration that have resulted in an increasingly interconnected world

groupthink the tendency for members of a like-minded group to think rigidly and make decisions without weighing all the facts

humanitarian globalization globalization underpinned by the cherished Canadian values of social democracy and humanitarianism

identity theft fraudulent acquisition of a person's personal identification documents, such as social insurance numbers, bank account numbers, and credit card information, which are then used to defraud victims of money and other valuable assets

immigration the movement of people from the country where they are citizens to another country for the purposes of long-term or permanent residence

North American Free Trade Agreement (NAFTA) a 1994 agreement between Canada, the United States, and Mexico that eliminated tariffs and other trade barriers between the three countries

outsourcing the reorganization of labour within and between societies; a strategy, common since the 1980s, whereby corporations in First World nations move non-core (that is, non-management) operations to external sites, often Third World locations where labour is comparatively cheap

purchasing power parity an economic theory according to which the price of goods in one country will be the same in another country once the exchange rate is factored in

sovereignty the absolute and independent authority of a nation; its right to autonomy or self-government

sweatshops manufacturing facilities where workers are physically or mentally ill-treated, typically confined in crowded conditions for long hours at a very low rate of pay

terrorism politically motivated acts of violence against civilian (non-combatant) targets

tourism temporary travel for leisure or other personal purposes

Y2K the nickname given to the fear, as the year 2000 approached, that computers would not recognize the dates of the new millennium and that all computers would fail and global chaos would ensue

FOR FURTHER RESEARCH

Amnesty International
http://www.amnesty.org.

Canadian Forces
http://www.forces.gc.ca.

Geneva Conventions
http://www.icrc.org/Web/Eng/siteeng0.nsf/htmlall/genevaconventions.

Greenpeace
http://www.greenpeace.org/canada.

Intergovernmental Panel on Climate Change (IPCC)
http://www.ipcc.ch.

Kyoto Protocol
http://unfccc.int/resource/docs/convkp/kpeng.html.

NAFTA Secretariat
http://www.nafta-sec-alena.org/DefaultSite/index.html.

United Nations Environment Programme (UNEP)
http://www.unep.org.

United Nations
http://www.un.org.

The following organizations are well known for their environmental activism. Their websites provide updates on the successes and challenges facing the environmental movement. There are also clearly defined opportunities for interested supporters to participate.

David Suzuki Foundation
http://www.davidsuzuki.org.

Greenpeace
http://www.greenpeace.org/canada.

World Wildlife Fund (WWF)
http://www.worldwildlife.org.

There are a number of websites that provide information about how to protect one's identity.

Phone Busters
http://www.phonebusters.com.

Reporting Economic Crime Online
http://www.recol.ca.

For an interesting glimpse of the diversity and number of terrorist organizations in the world, go to the following site: http://www.fas.org/irp/world/para.

Listen to the CBC interview with David Suzuki on *The Hour*, with George Stroumboulopoulos: http://www.cbc.ca/thehour/video.php?id=951.

See the Green Pages website for articles on "green" actions being undertaken by Canadians: http://www.thegreenpages.ca/portal/ca/index.html.

The following are links to websites of organizations and government sites that are providing leadership and action toward making Canada green and thereby helping it reduce its greenhouse gas emissions.

Bullfrog Power
http://www.bullfrogpower.com.

Okotoks, Alberta
http://www.okotoks.ca.

Ontario Sustainable Energy Association
http://www.ontario-sea.org.

REFERENCES

BBC News. (2007, June 2). Riots break out at German rally. http://news.bbc.co.uk/1/hi/world/europe/6714429.stm.

Canadian Heritage. (n.d.). Multiculturalism—Canadian diversity: Respecting our differences. http://www.pch.gc.ca/progs/multi/respect_e.cfm.

CBC News. (2003, November 5). Child porn on the internet: What is child porn? *The Fifth Estate.* http://www.cbc.ca/fifth/landslide/porn.html.

CBC News. (2004, April 27). Canada logs second place in Internet use. http://www.cbc.ca/canada/story/2004/04/27/www040427.html.

CBC News. (2006, March 30). Summit of the Americas: What is globalization? http://www.cbc.ca/news/background/summitofamericas/globalization.html.

CBC News. (2007, May 15). Is Canada losing the fight against online thieves? http://www.cbc.ca/news/background/tech/online-crime-war.html.

CBC Television. (2006, May). Climate change of plans. *The Hour.* http://www.cbc.ca/thehour/video.php?id=951.

Demirjian, K. (2007, April 13). Pet food recall has lawmakers examining flaws. *Chicago Tribune.*

Denning, S. (n.d.). Knowledge management—The democratization of knowledge: Anyone can know anything. http://www.stevedenning.com/democratization_knowledge.html.

Dobbin, M. (2007, June 30). The plan to disappear Canada: Deep integration comes out of shadows. Centre for Research on Globalization: Global Research.ca. http://www.globalresearch.ca/index.php?context=va&aid=6194.

Federation of American Scientists: Intelligence Resource Program. (2006). Liberation movements, terrorist organizations, substance cartels, and other para-state entities. http://www.fas.org/irp/world/para.

Foreign Affairs and International Trade Canada. (2007). Terrorism. http://www.dfait-maeci.gc.ca/internationalcrime/terrorism-en.asp.

Gao, Y. (2001, February). Author challenges systemic racism. *The Peak, 107*(6). http://www.peak.sfu.ca/the-peak/2001-1/issue6/ar-colour.html.

Gray, G. (2001). Does Canada have a future? Globalization. http://globalization.icaap.org/content/v1.1/gabriellegray.html.

Howes, D. (1996). *Cross-Cultural Consumption.* London: Routledge.

International Monetary Fund [IMF]. (2007). Globalization: Threat or opportunity? International Monetary Fund Publications. http://www.imf.org/external/np/exr/ib/2000/041200.htm#II.

Keenan, T. (2006, January). Cybercrime gives experts virtual headache: Investigators find that national boundaries can prove brick wall. *Business Edge, 6*(1). http://www.businessedge.ca/article.cfm/newsID/11625.cfm.

Khan, M.A.M. (2004, February 2). Teaching globalization in the era of terrorism. *GlocalEye.* http://www.ijtihad.org/globalterror.htm.

KPMG Investigation and Security Inc. (2000). E-commerce and cyber crime in Canada: New strategies for managing risks of exploitation. http://www.kpmg.ca/en/services/advisory/forensic/documents/eCommerceCyberCrime.pdf.

Kriegman, O., Amalric, F., & Wood, J. (2006). Dawn of the cosmopolitan: The hope of a global citizens' movement. Boston, MA: The Tellus Institute. http://www.gtinitiative.org/documents/PDFFINALS/15Movements.pdf.

Makarenko, J. (2007, February 1). The Kyoto Protocol on climate change: History & highlights. Maple Leaf Web. http://www.mapleleafweb.com/features/environment/kyoto.

McConnell International. (2000, December). Cyber crime and … punishment: Archaic laws threaten global information. http://www.iwar.org.uk/law/resources/cybercrime/mcconnell/CyberCrime.pdf.

Meserve, J., & Ensor, D. (2006, June 7). Lawyer: Government says terror plans included beheading. CNN.com. http://www.cnn.com/2006/WORLD/americas/06/06/canada.terror/index.html.

O'Neil, M. (2001). Globalization—Is Canada ready? The International Development Research Centre [IDRC]. http://www.idrc.ca/en/ev-2593-201-1-DO_TOPIC.html.

Pang, B. (2006). Fighting cyber-crime through global partnerships. *Royal Canadian Mounted Police Gazette, 68*(3). http://www.rcmp-grc.gc.ca/gazette.

Porter, K. (2004, December 31). Globalization and terrorism: Coming to grips with the new shape of the world. Global Envision. www.globalenvision.org/library/8/703.

Price, S. (2005, August 25). UN finds global inequality rising. BBC News. http://news.bbc.co.uk/2/hi/americas/4185458.stm.

Robertson, C. (2005, June 1). World's rock superstars line up for show to end all shows. Mirror.co.uk. http://www.mirror.co.uk/news/tm_objectid=15577861&method=full&siteid=94762&headline=live-gr-8-name_page.html.

Royal Canadian Mounted Police [RCMP]. (2006). Strategic priority: Terrorism. http://www.rcmp-grc.gc.ca/terrorism/index_e.htm.

Shellenberger, M., & Nordhaus, T. (2004). The death of environmentalism: Global warming politics in a post-environmental world. *The Breakthrough Institute.* http://www.thebreakthrough.org/images/Death_of_Environmentalism.pdf.

Shelley, L. (2006, February). Globalization of crime and terrorism. *E-Journal USA.* http://usinfo.state.gov/journals/itgic/0206/ijge/shelley.htm.

Statistics Canada. (2004, July 8). Household internet use survey. *The Daily.* http://www.statcan.ca/Daily/English/040708/d040708a.htm.

UC Atlas of Global Inequality. (2006). Income inequality. http://ucatlas.ucsc.edu/income.php.

UNICEF. (1997). The state of the world's children 1997. http://www.unicef.org/sowc97.

United Nations Environment Programme [UNEP]. (2007, February 2). The evidence for human-caused global warming is now "unequivocal," says IPCCC. Press Release. http://www.grida.no/Newsroom.aspx?m=54&pressReleaseItemID=1050.

World Tourism. (2005). World's top 25 tourist destinations. http://www.world-tourism.org/facts/eng/pdf/indicators/Top25_ita.pdf.

CHAPTER 10

Final Thoughts

Thinking about social issues could be viewed as a depressing, negative activity likely to produce a sense of futility. The authors hope this course has shown otherwise. We hope it has shown that, despite the trauma and frustration and conflict that attend social issues, understanding their origins and seeking their solutions can be inspiring and empowering. The real benefits of sociological thinking are to be found in the analytical method, with its basis of theoretical paradigms.

C.W. MILLS AND THE SOCIOLOGICAL PERSPECTIVE

C.W. Mills was a well-known modern sociologist who first spoke of the *sociological imagination.* With this term, he drew attention to the nature and benefits of a sociological perspective. Mills was among the first to recognize that understanding personal problems requires understanding their social context. If, for example, unemployment is viewed as a matter of individual failing or misfortune, there can be no real social response to it. But if it is viewed as, say, the product of an economy in transition, solutions will present themselves. The converse is also true. The sociological perspective reveals that social trends are the collective consequence of individual decisions and choices. To understand social trends requires an understanding of individual perspectives; to understand individual issues requires an understanding of social trends.

BENEFITS OF A SOCIOLOGICAL ASSESSMENT OF SOCIAL ISSUES

John J. Macionis (1995) has outlined four benefits of sociological thinking:

1. *Sociological thinking helps us assess the truth of commonly held assumptions.*

   In other words, sociology directs a person to go beyond the immediately apparent—to investigate the social trends and contexts that have shaped a social event. Doing so will reveal the origins and dynamics of a social event, and these revelations go beyond gut reactions and preformulated or biased opinions.

   The analytical method provides the discipline that enables researchers to view social trends and their dysfunctions as social issues. It enables the student researcher to apprehend the exaggerations and misleading impressions created by the media, by hearsay, and by stereotypes, stigmas, and biases. In this way, the student researcher learns the pitfalls of approaching social issues with too little knowledge or with knowledge that is biased.

2. *Sociological thinking prompts us to assess our lives' opportunities and constraints.*

    The second benefit reflects Mills's insight that the social world affects individual life experiences. It also reinforces the notion that social life is patterned, not random. Once one recognizes that patterns exist, one begins to see *how* problems emerge and *how* they might be resolved. Patterns are by definition somewhat predictable, and by carefully changing them one can *map* a path *through* the difficulties of social existence.

    Researching the facts about a social issue can help students see solutions. It can also get them fully engaged with an issue and put them in touch with groups and organizations that are similarly engaged.

3. *Sociological thinking empowers us to participate actively in our society.*

    Sociological analysis will help students become citizens who are aware of social issues and prepared to contribute to their resolution. This should produce a sense of agency, not futility.

4. *Sociological thinking helps us recognize human variety and meet the challenges of living in a diverse world.*

    Throughout this book, you have been introduced to many diverse issues facing Canada. At the outset, you learned that social issues result from such trends as globalization, environmental degradation, technological innovation, and increasing social diversity. Resolving social issues requires that we abandon prejudices and unfounded opinions and commit ourselves to disciplined analysis. Addressing the fears and concerns that social issues create will require openness to change and to innovation. There are key features of a healthy sociological perspective.

The primary intention of this text has been not to advocate particular solutions for specific social issues, but rather to stimulate critical thinking and an urgency to act.

FOR FURTHER RESEARCH

For links to essays about C.W. Mills and the sociological imagination, the following is a helpful link: http://www.camden.rutgers.edu/~wood/207socimagination.htm.

REFERENCE

Macionis, J. (1995). *Sociology*. New Jersey: Prentice Hall. http://cwx.prenhall.com/bookbind/pubbooks/macionis7/chapter1/objectives/deluxe-content.html.

Glossary

abortion
the procedure of expelling an embryo or fetus from a woman's uterus in order to terminate a pregnancy

agent of socialization
any organization or social institution that has an important role in socializing individuals (for example, the family is a principal agent of socialization)

analytical method
a method or system of steps that provides a structure for the investigation and analysis of contemporary social issues

androcentricity
the condition of being male-centred or male-dominated in research and perspective; for example, adopting topics or perspectives that have relevance only to men and that underrepresent women

androgynous gender role
a gender role that blends the positive attributes of both the masculine and feminine gender roles

APA citation style
American Psychological Association style; a method of documenting research resources in social science papers

birth rate
the rate of population growth (or decline) expressed as a ratio of the number of births per year to the number in the population

blatant discrimination
discrimination that often takes violent or offensive forms and that is prompted by prejudice

brownfield
former industrial site reclaimed for use by developers

burnout
the physical and emotional exhaustion caused by the prolonged stress of trying to live up to impossible goals

child abuse
the emotional maltreatment, neglect, or physical or sexual mistreatment of children by persons responsible for their care, whether these latter be parents, guardians, or others

child pornography
the depiction of children under the age of 18 in sexually explicit material

child pornography
the production, trade, and sale of materials in which children under the age of 18 are sexually exploited

colonialism
a nation's extension of its authority over land or territory not its own

common-law relationship
a relationship not formalized by a marriage ceremony but involving nonetheless the cohabitation and routine intimacies of marriage

context
the circumstances or background within which social actions occur; the context not only shapes social events (macro) and behaviour patterns (micro), it cues them as well

cosmopolitanism
the belief that everyone belongs to a world community; freedom from national limitations or prejudices

criminal harassment
the formal legal term for stalking; repeated unwanted contact or attention from a stranger or acquaintance

cultural lag
W.F. Ogburn's theory that, because social change occurs unevenly among cultural components, it is disruptive until all components have changed and reintegrated

cultural transmission
the passing of cultural knowledge and traditions from one generation to the next

cultural universal
a practice or social pattern or institution that occurs in every society

cybercrime
criminal activity that involves the Internet

demographic
having to do with the structure of populations or population statistics

domestic abuse
also referred to as *domestic violence*, *partner abuse*, or *spousal abuse*, it occurs when a family member, intimate partner, or former partner seeks to psychologically or physically dominate or harm another family member

double standard
adoption of expectations or benchmarks that differ for men and women; amounts to bias or unfairness

drug
materials, either naturally occurring or synthetic that, when ingested by various means, are psychoactive

drug abuse
use of psychotropic substances that is out of the user's control and may constitute a physical or psychological dependency

drug addiction
the situation or condition in which a person takes a drug by compulsion, despite the potential harm to him- or herself and to others, and despite, in many cases, a desire to stop doing so

dysfunctions
in the structural functionalist paradigm, the negative consequences of change or of social actions; dysfunctions occur as breakdowns within social institutions or as the impaired integration of social institutions

ecological footprint
a statistical measure of humans' impact on the natural environment

economic globalization
the seamless movement of goods, services, and capital around the world, unhindered by national borders

economy
in the structural functionalist paradigm, the economy is a social institution; its manifest functions are the production and distribution of goods and services and the employment of a workforce

ecosystem model of medical practice
health practice that includes consideration of the wider social and societal factors in health

education
in the structural functionalist paradigm, education is a social institution; its manifest functions are the teaching and training of society's members (so they can move into the economy and become productive members of society), developing knowledge, and reinforcing fundamental social values

entheogen
psychoactive substance used in the context of religious ritual

equilibrium
in the structural functionalist paradigm, the state achieved when all social institutions are functioning as expected and society is stable

family
(1) a now-married couple (with or without never-married sons and/or daughters of either or both spouses), a couple living common law (with or without never-married sons and/or daughters of either or both partners), or a lone parent of any marital status, with at least one never-married son or daughter living in the same dwelling; **(2)** in the structural functionalist paradigm, family is a primary social institution; its manifest functions are procreation (generating members of society), socialization, and the instilling of fundamental cultural values

feminist
a paradigm and a social movement aimed at achieving equality for women; in sociology, feminism has brought forth research topics of pertinence to women, and it has corrected male-centred research assumptions and conclusions

feminization of poverty
as a consequence of women's socio-economic disadvantages, the majority of the poor in our society are women

gender
the role a person learns to play as a member of the social category *man* or *woman*; the socialized or learned patterns of masculinity or femininity

gender blindness
having the assumption that gender differences do not exist

gender scripts
socialized sets of expectations or prescriptions concerning the appropriate behaviours and aspirations of each gender in specific contexts: traditionally the role of *wife*, for example, is subject to a gender script

gender socialization
the process of teaching cultural beliefs, values, and norms with respect to acceptable behaviours and expectations of masculinity and femininity

global stratification
inequality among the nations of the globe with respect to economic and social well-being; nations are defined as *core* (developed), *semi-peripheral* (semi-developed), and *peripheral* (undeveloped)

global warming
the increase of atmospheric or climate temperatures that is drastically altering ecosystems

globalization
trends in telecommunications, trade, and migration that have resulted in an increasingly interconnected world

green space
undeveloped land that provides relief from the urban landscape

greenfield
land that has been untouched by industry or development and that is therefore appealing to developers

greenhouse gases
industrial, home, and automobile emissions of carbon-based gases into the atmosphere; considered to be the primary cause of accelerated global warming

gridlock
traffic congestion that brings all intersecting traffic routes to a halt

groupthink
the tendency for members of a like-minded group to think rigidly and make decisions without weighing all the facts

heterosexism
an ideology that promotes heterosexuality as the only true kind of intimacy and considers divergence from it to be abnormal

heterosexual
attracted to the opposite sex

homeless
the condition of lacking permanent or even temporary housing owing to poverty

homophobia
extreme fear or abhorrence of homosexuality, sometimes expressed in violent attacks on homosexuals

homosexual
attracted to the same sex

humanitarian globalization
globalization underpinned by the cherished Canadian values of social democracy and humanitarianism

identity theft
fraudulent acquisition of a person's personal identification documents, such as social insurance numbers, bank account numbers, and credit card information, which are then used to defraud victims of money and other valuable assets

ideology
an overarching belief system that guides perspectives and social behaviours and trends (for example, feminism or patriarchy)

illegal drug trade
the international black market in illegal psychotropic substances

immigration
the movement of people from the country where they are citizens to another country for the purposes of long-term or permanent residence

income
the amount of new money a person receives in a particular time period, usually a year

Kyoto Accord
an international treaty (drawn in 1997) that bound a number of nations, including Canada, to meeting targets of greenhouse gas reductions

labelling
the process of applying a label or stigma to a person or group; stigmas, or negative labels, can marginalize persons and groups

labels
a word or phrase that is used to identify a person or group of persons; usually used by the powerful in society to marginalize or stigmatize less powerful or less valued social groups

(latent) dysfunctions
within the paradigm of structural functionalism, this is another term for *dysfunctions*; see above

latent functions
the structural functionalist term for the unexpected benefits of social actions; they enhance the functioning of society

low income cut-off (LICO)
a Statistics Canada measure of relative poverty—in this case, a person's income in relation to the average income

macro perspective
a theoretical perspective (for example, structural functionalist or social conflict) that ignores the everyday details of social interaction and instead focuses on the social forces outside the sphere of individual influence

manifest functions
in the structural functionalist paradigm, the positive consequences expected of a social institution

marginalization
the creation and enforcement of social barriers that keep specific groups from full participation in society

marginalize
create social barriers that prevent persons and groups from full participation in society (for example, racial minorities may be marginalized by mainstream society)

micro perspective
a theoretical perspective (for example, the symbolic interactionist paradigm) that focuses on everyday social interactions as the processes that produce society, culture, gender identity, and identity of self

millionaire
a person who is able to amass a net worth of at least $1 million

misogynous
hating women

moral crusade
activism based on an ideology that is promoted as a reality; the implications are that there can be no reasoned dissent; often driven by fanaticism and extremism

moral panic
the public perception of a profound threat from crime or social disorder, usually a result of inflated, exaggerated media coverage; perceived threats are to fundamental values and morals

myths
widely shared but usually incorrect beliefs about aspects of social reality; stereotypes and false beliefs that enable some members of society to marginalize or stigmatize others

North American Free Trade Agreement (NAFTA)
a 1994 agreement between Canada, the United States, and Mexico that eliminated tariffs and other trade barriers between the three countries

obesity
great excess of body weight

objectification
a media-driven emphasis on sexiness and on physical body parts that can result in the understating or denial of an individual's personality or emotions

outsourcing
the reorganization of labour within and between societies; a strategy, common since the 1980s, whereby corporations in First World nations move non-core (that is, non-management) operations to external sites, often Third World locations where labour is comparatively cheap

paradigm
a model that is based on theory and that guides thinking and research; in sociology, models are of society, and can be macro or micro in focus

patriarchal
the term applied to social organizations, social structures, and ideologies that preserve male dominance over women

patriarchy
an ideology, embedded in traditional history, that gives men privilege and dominance over women

pimp
an individual, usually a man, who lives off the proceeds of sex work by prostitutes

plagiarism
using information (intellectual property) without acknowledging its source or author

political will
a government's desire to pursue and effect change; usually a consequence of public pressure

pornography
depictions or images of sexual activity, usually visual, that are produced not for their artistic merit but for the sexual stimulation of the -consumer

poverty
state of being poor; lacking resources to sustain an adequate standard of living. *Absolute poverty* is extreme deprivation that results in starvation or homelessness. *Relative poverty* is having insufficient resources relative to the average standard of living in a particular social context

poverty rate
the number of poor persons in a society, sometimes expressed as a ratio of x per 1,000

prohibition
a system of legal regulation that made alcohol and drugs illegal and made it a criminal offence to produce, import, possess, or distribute an illegal substance

psychoactive
affecting the user's central nervous system and changing brain function in ways that change the user's mood, consciousness, perceptions, and behaviour

psychological violence
psychological damage caused by an experience of intimidation, threat, or harassment; it leaves lasting mental and emotional scars

purchasing power parity
an economic theory according to which the price of goods in one country will be the same in another country once the exchange rate is factored in

queer
a formerly pejorative term reclaimed by advocates to describe minority or variant sexual orientation in general, including homosexual, bisexual, and any other minority sexual orientations

real and ideal society
culture and social structure as it actually exists (real society) as opposed to culture and social structure as they are believed to exist according to theoretical paradigms or models of reality (ideal society)

resources of power
in the social conflict paradigm, resources of power are assets that give one side in an issue advantage over another side

rural areas
places with a sparse human population that are largely dominated by the natural landscape

second shift
the domestic and care duties women perform at home after a full day at work

sex
a person's biological characteristics in relation to the reproductive process: male, female, or, in some cases, a hybrid of the two

sex trade
prostitution, or the exchange of sexual services for money or other material gain, with no emotional involvement

sexism
an ideology based on inequality between the sexes

sexual abuse
sexual contact in which a dominant partner uses his or her position of authority or physical strength to coerce or exploit the less powerful partner

sexual harassment
unwelcome attention of a sexual nature, from inappropriate jokes and posters displayed in the victim's workplace to forced sexual activity

sexual orientation
a person's sexual tendency, whether toward the opposite sex (heterosexual), toward one's own sex (homosexual), or elsewhere

smart growth
an initiative that aims to achieve sustainable growth in cities and to prevent urban sprawl by encouraging compact development and resource conservation

social change
alteration to established patterns at both the micro and macro levels; at micro levels, social change would entail alteration to norms and values; at a macro level, social change would entail changes to prevailing ideologies

social class
a set of hierarchical distinctions drawn between groups and individuals based upon, and often determining, an individual's socio-economic status; in a class system, socio-economic status is often perceived to be linked with other attributes, such as intelligence or "nobility"

social conflict
a macro theoretical paradigm with origins in Karl Marx's theories; a view of society as comprised of competing groups, the more powerful of which exploit those with fewer assets

social constructionism
a theoretical perspective, within the symbolic interactionist paradigm, that emphasizes that what is popularly taken to be *normal* and *natural* (gender, for example) is actually a product of social structures; that is, the assumption that much of human reality is a social creation

social constructionist
a micro theoretical paradigm within the symbolic interactionist perspective; outlines that reality is a creation of society, and that it has no universal or inherent properties

social institutions
the structural functionalist term for social structures; the assemblages of norms, values, beliefs, statuses, roles, and organizations that collectively answer a society's basic needs (for example, education and family are social institutions)

social mobility
a person's movement (usually understood as ascendance) through social class levels

social power
the ability to impose one's will or interests on another; the ability to dominate

social stigma
a negatively valued marker or characteristic that makes a stigmatized person or group a target for prejudice and discrimination

social stratification
separation of a society into socio-economic levels; usually a reflection of inequality of opportunity

socialization
the lifelong process of acculturation; the teaching and learning of a society's beliefs, values, and norms that occurs during social interaction; the process by which personalities, identities, and gender identities are formed

socio-economic status
a person's position in the social hierarchy, determined by their monetary wealth and by the social capital they may possess through membership in a highly regarded or powerful social group

solicit
overtly offer or procure sexual services

sovereignty
the absolute and independent authority of a nation; its right to autonomy or self-government

spillover
the stresses and events at work that affect family life, and vice versa

spousal abuse
violence—whether emotional, physical, or sexual—that occurs between spouses

stakeholders
in the social conflict paradigm, stakeholders are groups and organizations that have a critical interest or investment in an issue (and are in competition with each other)

status quo
established norms and perspectives of a society's dominant majority

stereotypes
generalizations and "stories," usually negative, about a person or group; often used to justify the marginalization of or discrimination against minorities

stereotyping
holding standardized perceptions, based on simplified notions, about a group of people or a person

stigma
a social marker that identifies a person as a member of a negatively valued group, race, or ethnicity; a stigma makes a person a target for prejudice and discrimination

structural functionalist
a macro theoretical paradigm that views society as an organic system of integrated social structures; each structure has specialized functions that maintain the whole society

structures
in the structural functionalist paradigm, this term is used interchangeably with "social institution"

substance use
ingesting by various means certain materials known as drugs

suburbanization
the movement of people away from city cores and small towns into fringe areas bordering the major urban centres

sustainable development
economic and social development that is harmonious with the natural environment and that relies on renewable energy sources so it does not deplete natural ones

sustainable future
from the concept of sustainable development, defined by the UN as being built on three fundamental principles: economic development, social development, and environmental protection

sweatshops
manufacturing facilities where workers are physically or mentally ill-treated, typically confined in crowded conditions for long hours at a very low rate of pay

symbolic interactionist
a micro paradigm that describes society as an ongoing product of everyday social interactions, which employ language (that is, symbols)

systemic discrimination
discriminatory practices that are entrenched in the social structures of society

terrorism
politically motivated acts of violence against civilian (non—combatant) targets

theoretical paradigm
a model of society that has been constructed from sociological theories; used to guide thinking and research about society and social issues

theoretical perspective
a term used interchangeably with *theoretical paradigm*

tourism
temporary travel for leisure or other personal purposes

transgendered
people whose understanding of their own social gender does not coincide with their given biological sex, or people who feel they do not fit within either traditional gender category

urban areas
places with a dense human population and an abundance of created structures

urban decay
a city's falling, in whole or in part, into disrepair, characterized by depopulation, abandonment of inner city property, high unemployment rates in downtown areas, family fragmentation, high crime rates, and the political disenfranchisement of downtown residents

urban sprawl
the uncontrolled geographic spreading of low-density urban development into the rural environments surrounding cities

urbanization
the movement of the world's population from rural to urban areas

virtual communities
groups and organizations, established through the Internet, of people with shared interests and ideals; members interact electronically and not face to face

visible minority
a (usually marginalized) group in society that visibly differs from mainstream society

wealth
a person's total net worth—the sum of his or her assets less his or her liabilities

Y2K
the nickname given to the fear, as the year 2000 approached, that computers would not recognize the dates of the new millennium and that all computers would fail and global chaos would ensue

Index